NEW YORK LEGAL RESEARCH GUIDE

By
ELLEN M. GIBSON

Professor of Law and Law Library Director
State University of New York at Buffalo

William S. Hein & Co., Inc.
Buffalo, New York
1988

Library of Congress Cataloging-in-Publication Data

Gibson, Ellen M.
New York legal research guide.

Includes index.
1. Legal research—New York (State) I. Title.
KFN5074.G53 1988 349.747'072 88-80721
ISBN 0-89941-622-5 347.470072

Printed in the United States of America

Dedication

This book is dedicated to the memory of my parents,
Niles and Margaret Thompson,
and to Jim, Sarah, and Eric

PREFACE

This book is written chiefly for attorneys, librarians, and law students who need a guide to the most important current and historical sources for performing New York legal research. It should also be a useful resource for anyone interested in the development and use of New York legal publications.

The scope of this guide includes legal materials of statewide interest. The subject of research in the City of New York's legal materials deserves its own book-length treatment and is not attempted here.

The guide is designed to acquaint the reader not only with the standard New York print, microform, and online database sources but also with media sources such as radio and television programs, cable networks, and audiotape and videotape productions that provide significant legal and law-related information.

Throughout this work I have assumed that the reader is familiar with basic legal bibliography and research techniques. For readers without this background, reference to one or more of the several comprehensive guides to legal research available today will be helpful. Among these are: Cohen and Berring's ***How To Find the Law*** (8th ed. 1983) and its abridgment, ***Finding the Law;*** Jacobstein and Mersky's ***Fundamentals of Legal Research*** (1987 edition) and its abridgment, ***Legal Research Illustrated;*** Wren and Wren's ***Legal Research Manual*** (2nd ed. 1986); and Statsky's ***Legal Research and Writing: Some Starting Points*** (3rd ed. 1986).

The ***New York Legal Research Guide*** complements these comprehensive legal research guides by providing detailed information on New York legal materials.

Milton Kaplan, Professor Emeritus, State University of New York at Buffalo Law School made useful suggestions on Chapter Eleven (Local Legislation) and Jacob D. Hyman, Professor Emeritus, State University of New York at Buffalo Law School, offered helpful comments on several chapters, particularly Chapter One (New York's Constitutions).

The following librarians offered helpful comments on earlier versions of this work: Susan Dow, Nina Cascio, and Marcia Zubrow of the Charles B. Sears Law Library, State University of New York at Buffalo; Robert Allan Carter of the New York State Library; and Sue Wood and Mary Beth Dunn of the Supreme Court Library in Syracuse. Renee Chapman, also of the Charles B. Sears Law Library, provided invaluable bibliographic assistance.

Amy Loucks-DiMatteo provided microcomputing advice and Iris

Reese performed essential typing services. I am very grateful to all of them for helping to bring New York's first legal research guide into being.

Buffalo, New York
February, 1988

E.M.G.

NEW YORK LEGAL RESEARCH GUIDE

Summary of Contents

NEW YORK LEGAL RESEARCH GUIDE

Table of Contents

Chapter One
NEW YORK'S CONSTITUTIONS

1. THE PRESENT CONSTITUTION

New York's present constitution is the Constitution of 1894 as amended over 200 times.[1] The New York Constitution is arranged in twenty articles which are numbered in Roman numerals as follows:

I.	Bill of Rights
II.	Suffrage
III.	Legislature
IV.	Executive
V.	Officers and Civil Departments
VI.	Judiciary
VII.	State Finances
VIII.	Local Finances
IX.	Local Governments
X.	Corporations
XI.	Education
XII.	Defense
XIII.	Public Officers
XIV.	Conservation
XV.	Canals

[1] NEW YORK (STATE). MANUAL FOR THE USE OF THE LEGISLATURE OF THE STATE OF NEW YORK 196-218 (1984/85).

XVI.	Taxation
XVII.	Social Welfare
XVIII.	Housing
XIX.	Amendments to Constitution
XX.	When [Amendments] to Take Effect

a) Methods of Amending the Constitution. Amendment of the New York Constitution is governed by article XIX. Article XIX provides for two methods of amending the Constitution: proposal by the legislature or proposal by a constitutional convention. Under either method, the amendments must be approved by the voters.

(1) Legislative Method. Under the legislative method of amending the constitution, the proposed amendment originates in the legislature. The proposed amendment is introduced as a bill.[2] Passage in both the Senate and the Assembly by a majority of the membership must be repeated by a majority of the membership in each house in the "next regular legislative session convening after the succeeding general election of members of the assembly ...."[3] Whether the first passage of the amendment occurs in the first or second session of the previous legislature, the next consideration of the amendment by the legislature must be in the *first* regular session of the next succeeding legislature.[4]

Following the second passage in the legislature, the proposed amendment must be submitted to the people at a general election. If the majority of the voters approve the amendment, it becomes law on the "first day of January next after such approval."[5]

The legislative method of amendment, for all the difficulties attendant in achieving passage in two sessions and at a general election, is still easier to accomplish than amendment through a constitutional convention. Consequently, most amendments enter the constitution via this method. However, the legislative method has resulted in piecemeal change[6] that has burdened the Constitution with an amount of detail inappropriate for the organic law of a state.

[2] While a proposed constitutional amendment is treated as a bill as it proceeds through the legislative process, it is a joint resolution once it has been passed by both houses of the legislature.

[3] N.Y. CONST. art. XIX, sec. 1 (McKinney 1987).

[4] 1959 Op. Att'y. Gen. 36.

[5] N.Y. CONST. art. XIX, sec. 1 (McKinney 1987).

[6] J.F. ZIMMERMAN, THE GOVERNMENT AND POLITICS OF NEW YORK STATE 58-59 (1981).

(2) Constitutional Convention. Under the constitutional convention method of amending the constitution, the proposed amendments originate with the delegates to a constitutional convention. The amendments are submitted to the people. If the majority of the voters approve the amendments, they become law on the "first day of January next after such approval."[7]

Since 1846, New York's Constitution has provided that the following question must be put to the voters every twenty years and also whenever the legislature so provides by law: "Shall there be a convention to revise the constitution and amend the same?"[8] The present constitution calls for that question to be put to the people in 1957 and every twenty years thereafter.

The major revisions of New York's constitution over the years have been accomplished through the work of constitutional conventions. The last major revision of the constitution as the result of a constitutional convention occurred in 1938. As of this writing, there has not been a constitutional convention called since 1967. All of that convention's proposals were rejected by the people. In 1977, the voters decided against calling a constitutional convention.

An overview of New York's constitutional revision from 1777 to the present is found in section 2 of this Chapter. A checklist of documents produced in connection with New York's ten constitutional conventions and four constitutional commissions is found in section 3 of this Chapter.

(3) Conflicts. If an amendment proposed by a constitutional convention conflicts with an amendment proposed by the legislature for approval by the voters at the same election, the amendment proposed by the constitutional convention is "deemed to supersede the amendment so proposed by the legislature."[9]

b) Publication of the Constitution. This section describes where to find the annotated and unannotated versions of the current Constitution, the text of constitutional amendments that were approved, those that failed to win approval, and superseded constitutions.

[7] N.Y. CONST. art. XIX, sec. 2 (McKinney 1987).
[8] *Id.*
[9] N.Y. CONST. art. XIX, sec. 3 (McKinney 1987).

(1) The Annotated Constitution. Book 2 (in 3 volumes) of ***McKinney's Consolidated Laws of New York Annotated***[10] and volumes 42 and 42A of ***New York Consolidated Laws Service***[11] contain annotated versions of the Constitution. They provide annotations of cases interpreting the Constitution as well as other research aids such as cross references to statutory law, references to law review articles, and references to legal encyclopedias. Since ***McKinney's*** and ***CLS*** also contain the unannotated Constitution, the researcher can choose whether to read the relevant constitutional provisions in the annotated or the unannotated portion of the volumes.

In ***McKinney's*** and ***CLS,*** an index to the Constitution follows the text. The Constitution is also indexed in the general ***McKinney's*** and ***CLS*** index volumes so that the researcher can search for references to the Constitution and the general statutes simultaneously. Unless the researcher is positive that only the Constitution needs to be consulted on a question, using the general index is preferable to using the Constitution volumes index. New York's Consolidated Laws contain many provisions that one might expect to find in a state constitution. For instance, a Bill of Rights is Article 2 of the Civil Rights Law[12] and a Human Rights Law is Article 15 of the Executive Law.[13] Conversely, the Constitution contains subjects that one might expect to find in the general statutes, e.g., general rules on wages and hours in public employment,[14] civil service merit system and veterans' preferences,[15] and the number of miles of ski trails allowed in the State Forest Preserve. Fortunately, both ***McKinney's*** and ***CLS*** provide liberal cross references from the Constitution to the general statutes and vice versa to alert the reader to related provisions.

The first volume of the ***McKinney's*** Constitution contains the following useful material: a short history of the Constitution, an annotated essay on constitutional interpretation in New York, and a distribution table showing where sections of the Constitution of 1894 were transferred as a result of the constitutional revisions of 1938.

[10] Hereinafter ***McKinney's.***
[11] Hereinafter ***CLS.***
[12] N.Y. CIV. RIGHTS LAW secs. 2-15 (McKinney 1976 & 1987 Supp.).
[13] N.Y. EXEC. LAW secs. 290-300 (McKinney 1982).
[14] N.Y. CONST. art. 1, sec. 17 (McKinney 1982).
[15] N.Y. CONST. art. 5, sec. 6 (McKinney 1982).

(2) The Unannotated Constitution. New York's Constitution is published periodically in unannotated format in the following sources:

* *Constitution of the State of New York,* (an annual pamphlet published by the Secretary of State);

* *Manual For the Use of the Legislature of the State of New York* (published biennially and called the "Legislative Manual" or the "blue book");

* *Gould's Consolidated Laws of New York* (published annually, Constitution is in volume 1); and

* *Michie's Consolidated Laws of New York* (published annually, Constitution is in volume 8).

As previously mentioned in Section 1(b)(1), both *McKinney's* and *CLS* contain unannotated versions of the Constitution that are updated with annual pocket parts and interim pamphlets. New York's current Constitution is also printed along with the other state constitutions in *Constitutions of the United States: National and State.*[16]

Finally, the unannotated Constitution is available online in the Legislative Retrieval System (LRS). Mead Data Central projects that the Constitution will once again be available on LEXIS when the Consolidated Laws file comes back online during 1988. The West Publishing Company projects that the Constitution will be available online on WESTLAW during 1988.

(3) Citator. *Shepard's New York Statute Citations* can be used to locate New York and federal cases from 1909 to date that cite the Constitution of 1894, as amended. Attorney General opinions, administrative opinions, and local laws citing the Constitution can also be located. More recently, law reviews and *American Law Reports* articles citing the Constitution have been included in the scope of *Shepard's New York Statute Citations.* This unit of *Shepard's* can also be used to locate New York cases since 1909 that cite the U. S. Constitution and to locate

[16] This seven-volume looseleaf service is published by Oceana Publications for the Columbia University Legislative Drafting Fund.

the text of proposed amendments that are printed in the session laws. Only amendments proposed by the legislature are printed in the session laws.

(4) Proposed Amendments. The text of constitutional amendments proposed in the current legislature carry bill numbers and can be located through the finding tools for researching bills. These finding tools are described in section 3 of Chapter 2. The text of amendments proposed by a constitutional convention can be found in the documents produced by the convention. Constitutional convention documents are listed in section 3 of this Chapter.

The text of constitutional amendments proposed by the legislature which have received their first or second approval in the legislature are printed in an appendix to the official session laws, the ***Laws of New York***. The status of the proposed amendments (first passage, second passage, approved or disapproved at the general election) is explained. Proposed amendments that would affect particular sections of the Constitution can be located by Shepardizing that constitutional section in ***Shepard's New York Statute Citations***. The citation in ***Shepard's*** gives the year and page number in ***Laws of New York*** where the proposed amendment is printed.

Proposed amendments are also printed in the ***McKinney's*** and ***CLS*** pocket parts for the Constitution volumes, but they only appear in pocket parts issued for use in the years when further action on the amendment is pending when the pocket part goes to press. For example, a proposed amendment which received first approval in the 1986 session and second approval in the 1987 session was printed in the 1987 and 1988 pocket parts. Since the text of the 1988 pocket part is finalized before the 1987 general election is held, the vote on the proposed amendment is not found in the 1988 pocket part. An amendment approved by the voters in 1987 would be printed in the 1989 pocket part ***as part of the Constitution.***

A convenient source for the text of all constitutional amendments proposed between 1895 and 1937 is the 1938 Constitutional Convention's report, popularly known as the Poletti Report.[17] The text of subsequent proposed amendments can be located in the session laws or in the superseded ***McKinney's*** or ***CLS*** pocket parts.[18]

[17] 2 NEW YORK (STATE). CONSTITUTIONAL CONVENTION COMMITTEE, 1938. REPORTS. (1938) [hereinafter POLETTI REPORT].

[18] Superseded ***McKinney's*** pocket parts are available in microform from the William S. Hein Co., Inc.

The *Legislative Manual* does not print the text of proposed constitutional amendments, but each volume does contain a list of proposed amendments to the Constitutions of 1821, 1846 and 1894. This list summarizes and gives the popular vote on each proposed amendment since 1821. The list is a useful finding tool to locate proposed amendments in *Laws of New York.*

(5) Prior Constitutions. New York's colonial charters and its constitutions of 1777, 1821, 1846 and 1894 are collected in ***The Federal and State Constitutions, Colonial Charters, and Other Organic Laws of the State, Territories, and Colonies,*** compiled by Francis Newton Thorpe in 1909.[19] They are also collected in the Poletti Report[20] and in ***Sources and Documents of United States Constitutions,*** compiled by William F. Swindler.[21]

New York constitutions are included in the microfiche set called ***State Constitutional Conventions, Commissions, and Amendments*** published by Congressional Information Service (CIS). Four bibliographies serve as indexes to this CIS set by including the microfiche number adjacent to the bibliographic entry. These bibliographies, in chronological order, are:

Browne, C. E., ***State Constitutional Conventions from Independence to the Completion of the Present Union, 1776-1959: a bibliography.*** Westport, Conn.: Greenwood Press, 1973;

Yarger, S. R., ***State Constitutional Conventions, 1959-1975: a Bibliography.*** Westport, Conn.: Greenwood Press, 1976;

Canning, B., ***State Constitutional Conventions, Revisions, and Amendments, 1959-1976: a bibliography.*** Westport, Conn.: Greenwood Press, 1977; and

State Constitutional Conventions, Commissions and Amendments, 1959-1978: an Annotated Bibliography, Nicholas Olcott, bibliography editor. Washington, D.C.: Congressional Information Service, 1981.

[19] 5 THORPE, THE FEDERAL AND STATE CONSTITUTIONS, COLONIAL CHARTERS, AND OTHER ORGANIC LAWS OF THE STATES, TERRITORIES, AND COLONIES 2623-2741 (1909).

[20] 1 POLETTI REPORT, *supra* note 17, in Part II at 1-155.

[21] 7 SWINDLER, SOURCES AND DOCUMENTS OF UNITED STATES CONSTITUTIONS 142-344 (1978).

From 1840 to date each *Legislative Manual*[22] includes the Constitution as currently in effect.

2. CONSTITUTIONAL HISTORY OF NEW YORK.

a) Period of Dutch Rule. The foundations for New York's constitutional development lie in the institutions of the Netherlands and England. The Dutch colonial period spanned the 55 years from Henry Hudson's discovery of Manhattan in 1609 to the English conquest in 1664. The colony's organic documents were contained in commercial charters. Some Dutch trading charters concerned only commercial matters. However, some granted extensive governmental powers and those charters, in effect, functioned as the organic law of New Netherland. An example of the latter was the charter granted to the Dutch West India Company in 1621. Additional governmental authority was granted to the patroons of New Netherland by the Dutch Assembly through charters of "Freedoms and Exemptions," dated 1649, 1640 and 1650. Selected passages from these major Dutch charters are reproduced in the first volume of the ***Legal and Judicial History of New York*** by Alden Chester[23] and in the first volume of ***Constitutional History of New York*** by Charles Z. Lincoln.[24] They are printed in full in E.B. O'Callaghan's ***Documents Relative to the Colonial History of the State of New York.***[25]

b) Period of English Rule. The course of New York's constitutional development changed with the conquest of New Netherland by the English. King Charles II granted a charter to his brother, James, Duke of York. It gave him full proprietary powers, provided that the government be consistent (or nearly so) with the laws of England. Twenty-one years after the conquest, the first colonial assembly passed the Charter of Liberties and Privileges, a document which could well have been called New York's original constitution.[26] The Charter was approved by the Duke of

[22] The *Legislative Manual* was published annually from 1840 to 1974; since 1975 it has been published biennially.

[23] 1 CHESTER, LEGAL AND JUDICIAL HISTORY OF NEW YORK 19-36 (1911).

[24] 1 LINCOLN, CONSTITUTIONAL HISTORY OF NEW YORK 6-16 (1906) [Hereinafter Lincoln].

[25] E.B. O'CALLAGHAN, DOCUMENTS RELATIVE TO THE COLONIAL HISTORY OF THE STATE OF NEW YORK [in 15 vol.] (1856).

[26] Lincoln *supra* note 24, at 433. The Charter of Liberties and Privileges is reproduced in Lincoln at pages 95-107 where annotations draw comparisons between the Charter's provisions and the provisions of New York's first constitution, the Constitution of 1777.

York and sent on to England for approval by the king. In the interim, King Charles died and the Duke of York's title merged in his new title, King James II. In this capacity, King James vetoed the Charter. For reforms of the breadth found in the Charter, the colonists of New York had to await independence.

c) **Period of Statehood.** A summary of the major constitutional provisions and changes from the first constitution, the Constitution of 1777, to the present follows.

Constitution of 1777

New York's Fourth Provincial Congress declared New York independent of the English on July 9, 1776. The Provincial Congress then changed its name to the Convention of the Representatives of the State of New York. The Convention of the Representatives was charged with designing a form of government for the new state and had to accomplish this charge under the most trying circumstances. The Convention

> was subjected to the danger of attack and possible capture by the British. To avoid this, it became necessary for the Convention to move from place to place. It went from White Plains to Harlem, where its sessions were held in the church. It afterwards met successively at King's Bridge, Odell's in Phillipp's Manor, Fishkill, Poughkeepsie, and finally at Kingston, where the Constitution was adopted.[27]

New York's first constitution was drafted by a committee of the Convention whose membership included John Jay, Gouverneur Morris, Robert R. Livingston, and Abraham Yates. John Jay is credited with being the principal author.[28] The draft constitution was presented to the Convention on March 12, 1777. Following debate and amendment, the Constitution of 1777 was adopted by the Convention at Kingston on April 20, 1777.

New York's first Constitution consisted of a preliminary section, which included the Declaration of Independence, and forty-five articles. Abstract rights asserted in this Constitution were: all power was derived

[27] *Id.* at 491-92.
[28] 1 CHESTER, *supra* note 23, at 363; I LINCOLN, *supra* note 24, at 471.

from the people; each citizen was entitled to full protection of his individual rights (essentially as such rights were described in the thirty-ninth article of the Magna Carta); the right of property owners to vote was established; and the rights of religious liberty and trial by jury were guaranteed.[29]

The Constitution continued many existing institutions of the colonial period, adapting them as necessary to the new democracy. Article 35 continued in force both the English common and statute law and the colonial law, "subject to such alterations and provisions as the legislature of this state shall, from time to time, make concerning the same."[30] The court system at the lower levels remained essentially unchanged.[31] The Assembly was continued, and the House of Lords and Colonial Council became the Senate. Other changes included popular election of the governor, establishing the Court for the Correction of Errors and Trial of Impeachment as the highest appellate court (replacing the colonial Court of Errors), creating a Council of Revision with veto power over legislation, and creating a Council of Appointment with power to appoint important non-elected officials. Many of these changes diluted the power of the governor and reflected lessons learned from the bitter conflict between the royal governors and the Assembly. The Constitution of 1777 continued in force without amendment until 1801.

Amendments of 1801

The Constitution of 1777 did not provide for its own amendment nor for future constitutional conventions. By 1800, a controversy was raging over the governor's appointment power in relation to the Council of Appointment. In order to deal with this matter and other desired constitutional changes, the legislature called for a constitutional convention which met in Albany on October 13, 1801. On October 27, the convention adopted five amendments. The first four amendments reorganized the legislature. The fifth amendment gave the governor and members of the Council of Appointment concurrent power to appoint non-elected officials.

[29] 1 LINCOLN, *supra* note 24, at 590-91.
[30] N. Y. CONST. of 1777, art. XXXV.
[31] The history of New York's colonial and state court system is outlined in Chapter 6 (Judicial System).

Constitution of 1821

Following public outcry in 1820 when the Council of Revision vetoed a legislative bill calling for a constitutional convention, the 1821 session of the legislature succeeded in submitting the question of holding a constitutional convention to the voters. The people voted for the convention, and it was convened in Albany on August 28, 1821. The proposed constitution went into effect on December 31, 1822. This was the first New York constitution to be submitted to the people for approval.

Historian Charles Z. Lincoln points out that this constitution could more accurately be called the "Constitution of 1822" since 1822 was the year in which it was approved and went into effect.[32] However, it is usually referred to as the Constitution of 1821.

The new constitution abolished the Council of Revision. While veto power over legislation was given to the governor, the new constitution provided that his veto could be overridden by legislative action. The Council of Appointment, hopelessly enmeshed in the spoils system, was also abolished. The power to nominate and appoint important state officers (the secretary of state, attorney general, treasurer, and the comptroller) was transferred to the legislature. The governor was given appointive power over lesser offices, subject to the consent of the senate. A Bill of Rights was written into the constitution for the first time. The Supreme Court of Judicature became the intermediate appellate court. It consisted of a chief justice and two associate justices. Judicial districts were established. The right to vote was expanded to include both personal and real property owners,[33] and the legislature gained the right to initiate proposed constitutional amendments.

Constitution of 1846

The Constitutional Convention of 1846 was called following a petition to the legislature from 24 counties asking the legislature to put the question of calling a constitutional convention to a popular vote. The legislature did so, the people voted in favor of the convention, and it was convened at Albany on June 1, 1846.

[32] 1 LINCOLN, *supra* note 24, at 637.

[33] The property qualification as it applied to white male voters was abolished by an amendment passed in 1826; the property qualification for holding public office was abolished in 1845. The property qualification for black male voters was not abolished until 1875.

The Constitution of 1846 made public officials more accountable to the voters. The offices of secretary of state, comptroller, attorney general, state engineer, canal commissioner and inspector of prisons became elective. Most judgeships also were made elective. Senators and assemblymen were to be elected from districts rather than at large. A requirement that every twenty years the legislature submit to the voters the question "Shall there be a Convention to revise the Constitution and amend the same?" was added.[34]

The Court of Errors was abolished and replaced by the Court of Appeals as New York's highest court. Concern over the state's solvency in the era of canal and railroad expansion led to a limitation on state debt and a prohibition on extending state credit to any private party or corporation.

The Constitution of 1846 was approved at an election held on November 3, 1846 and went into effect on January 1, 1847. In the interval between the adoption of the Constitution of 1846 and the Constitution of 1894 came the work of the Constitutional Convention of 1867, the Constitutional Commission of 1872, and the Judiciary Commission of 1890.

The Constitutional Convention of 1867 was authorized under article XII, sec. 2 of the 1846 Constitution. It convened in Albany on June 4, 1867. It proposed a new constitution but submitted its proposals to the people in several parts. Only the revised judiciary article was approved at the November 2, 1869 election. The Judiciary Article of 1869, which took effect on January 1, 1870, is described in Chapter 6 (Judicial System).

The Constitutional Commission of 1872 was created by the legislature[35] to propose amendments to the constitution. Many of the provisions recommended by the Commission were those rejected by the voters in 1869. Eleven amendments were approved by the voters in November, 1874 and went into effect on January 1, 1875. Notable changes wrought by these amendments included giving the governor a line-item veto power over appropriation bills and abolishing property qualifications for black voters.

[34] N.Y. CONST. of 1846, art. XII, sec. 2. That provision is found in sec. 2 of art. XIX of the present New York Constitution.

[35] 1872 N.Y. LAWS ch. 884.

The Judiciary Commission of 1890 was created[36] to amend the judiciary article. Its recommendations were submitted to the legislature on March 4, 1891, but they arrived too late for consideration in that session. The Commission's proposals were later adopted by the Constitutional Convention of 1894.[37]

Constitution of 1894

The question whether to hold a constitutional convention was put to the voters in 1886, and the voters answered in the affirmative. However, until a dispute between Governor David B. Hill and the legislature over the method of choosing the convention delegates was resolved, the convention was deferred. Finally, the Constitutional Convention of 1894 was convened in Albany on May 8, 1894. The revised constitution proposed by the convention was approved by the voters on November 6, 1894 and went into effect on January l, 1895. The Constitution of 1894, as amended, is the present constitution of the State of New York.

The Constitution of 1894 incorporated the changes in the judiciary article recommended by the Judiciary Commission of 1890, set up a merit-based civil service system, prohibited sale of the state forest preserve, founded the University of the State of New York, authorized the legislature to maintain and support free, public schools, and established home rule provisions for cities. It also established the present method of selecting delegates to a constitutional convention.

Since the Convention of 1894, there have been three general constitutional conventions. These were held in 1915, 1938 and 1967. There was also a Judicial Constitutional Convention in 1921. The Judiciary Amendment of 1925 is described in Chapter 6. The changes proposed by the Constitutional Conventions of 1915 and 1967 were defeated when presented to the voters.

The Constitutional Convention of 1938 convened at Albany on April 5, 1938. Of 694 proposals, 76 were reported out of committee and 58 were adopted by the Convention. These proposals were divided into nine parts, six of which were approved by the voters on November 8, 1938. Among the changes wrought by the 1938 amendments were the broadening of home rule protections for local governments, allowing use of state money and credit for social welfare, requiring public officers to testify

[36] 1890 N.Y. LAWS ch. 189.
[37] E. BREUER, CONSTITUTIONAL DEVELOPMENTS IN NEW YORK 1777-1958 37 (1958).

without immunity before grand juries, and authorizing the legislature to provide transportation to and from any school in the State. Over 50 other changes to the constitution were also approved. Among the defeated proposals were the judicial amendments.

3. DOCUMENTS OF CONSTITUTIONAL REVISION IN NEW YORK.

Both the successful and the unsuccessful attempts at constitutional revision since 1776 resulted in the production of hundreds of documents which are of immeasurable use to both the legal historian and the researcher seeking to interpret the State's fundamental instrument. This section is a checklist of reports, proceedings, journals, manuals and other documents of the constitutional conventions and constitutional commissions charged with the amendment of the constitution of the State of New York.

This checklist is adapted from ***Constitutional Developments in New York, 1777-1958*** by Ernest Henry Breuer,[38] ***New York State Documents: an Introductory Manual*** by Dorothy Butch,[39] and the state constitutional convention bibliographies compiled by Browne, Yarger, Canning and CIS and listed above in Section 1(b)(5).

Some of the constitutional documents listed below are included in multistate documents collections in microform. The documents that are reproduced in the CIS microfiche series, ***State Constitutional Conventions, Commissions and Amendments,*** are indicated by "CIS" and the CIS document number, e.g., CIS [NY 3]. Constitutional documents that are reproduced in the Library of Congress microfilm series, ***Records of the States of the United States of America,***[40] are indicated by "L.C." followed by class designation ("C" for Constitutional Records) and reel number, e.g., L.C. C: Reel 1.

[38] E. H. BREUER, ***supra*** note 37, at 24-58.

[39] D. BUTCH, NEW YORK STATE DOCUMENTS 10-16 (1987).

[40] U.S. Lib. of Congress, ***Records of the States of the United States of America, a Microfilm Compilation prepared by the Library of Congress in Association with the Univ. of North Carolina.*** William Sumner Jenkins, editor, 1949. Class C in this series collected early constitutional records of the states, including New York. New York coverage in this series is for the years 1776-1846.

a) Constitutional Conventions.

(1) Constitutional Convention of 1776-1777.

New York (State). Convention of the Representatives, 1776-1777.
An ordinance of the convention of the State of New York for organizing and establishing the government, agreed to by the said convention. Fishkill, 1777. 12pp.

CIS [NY 3]

New York (State). Convention of the Representatives, 1776-1777.
An address of the Convention of the Representatives of the State of New York to their constituents. Fishkill, 1776. 19 pp.

CIS [NY 2]; L.C. C: Reel 1.

New York (State). Legislature.
Journals of the Provincial Congress, Provincial Convention, Committee of Safety and Council of Safety of the State of New York. 1775-1776-1777. Albany, 1842. Reprinted by R. Weed. 2 v.

CIS [NY 1]
The Fourth Provincial Congress changed its name to the Convention of the Representatives and under that name it adopted New York's first Constitution on April 20, 1777.

(2) Constitutional Convention of 1801.

New York (State). Constitutional Convention, 1801.
Journal of the convention of the State of New York begun and held at the City of Albany, on the thirteenth day of October, 1801. Albany: John Barber, printer to the convention, 1801. 42 pp.

CIS [NY 5]

New York (State). Constitutional Convention, 1801.
Journal of the Convention of the State of New York began [sic] and held at the City of Albany, on the thirteenth day of October, 1801. Albany: reprinted by Cantine & Leake, printers to the State, 1821. 52 pp.

(3) Constitutional Convention of 1821.

New York (State). Constitutional Convention, 1821.
Documents, committee reports etc. Albany, 1821.

L.C. C: Reel 1.
These documents were printed separately and later bound together in one volume.

New York (State). Constitutional Convention, 1821.
Journal of the Convention of the State of New York. Begun and held at the Capitol in the City of Albany, on the twenty-eighth day of August, 1821. Albany: Cantine & Leake, printers to the State, 1821. 564 pp.

CIS [NY 7]; L.C. C: Reel 1.

New York (State). Constitutional Convention, 1821.
A report of the debates and proceedings of the convention of the State of New York, held at the Capitol, in the city of Albany, on the 28th day of August, 1821.... New York: Printed by J. Seymour, 1821. 367 pp.

L.C. C: Reel 1.

New York (State). Constitutional Convention, 1821.
*Reports of the proceedings and debates of the convention of 1821, assembled for the purpose of amending the Constitution of the State of New York: containing all the official documents, relating to the subject, and other valuable matter....*Albany: E. and E. Hosford, 1821. 703 pp.

CIS [NY 8]; L.C. C: Reel 1.
Nathaniel H. Carter and William L. Stone, reporters of the convention, and Marcus T. C. Gould, stenographer, prepared this indexed volume.

(4) Constitutional Convention of 1846.

New York (State). Constitutional Convention, 1846.
Manual for the use of the convention to revise the Constitution of the State of New York, convened at Albany, June 1, 1846. New York: Walker and Craighead, 1846. 371 pp.

CIS [NY 16]; L.C. C: Reel 3.
The *Manual* includes the text of constitutions of the United States, New Jersey, Louisiana, Florida, Texas, Missouri, and Iowa.

New York (State). Constitutional Convention, 1846.
Autograph album.

The album contains signatures and photographs of the convention membership.

New York (State). Constitutional Convention, 1846.
Debates and proceedings in the New York State convention for the revision of the Constitution. Albany: Printed at the Office of the Albany Argus, 1846. 948 pp.

L.C. C: Reel 2.
This volume was prepared by S. Croswell and R. Sutton who were reporters for the newspaper, the *Argus*.

New York (State). Constitutional Convention, 1846.
Documents of the convention of the State of New York, 1846.... Albany: Carroll & Cook, 1846. 2 v.

L.C. C.: Reel 3.
The convention documents were numbered. Volume one contained document nos. 1-63; volume two contained nos. 64-136.

New York (State). Constitutional Convention, 1846.
Journal of the convention of the State of New York, begun and held at the Capitol in the city of Albany, on the first day of June, 1846. Albany: Carroll and Cook, 1846. 1648 pp.

CIS [NY 13]; L.C. C: Reel 2.

New York (State). Constitutional Convention, 1846.
Report of the debates and proceedings of the Convention for the revision of the Constitution of the State of New York.... Albany: Printed at the Office of the *Evening Atlas*, 1846. 1143 pp.

CIS [NY 14]; L.C. C: Reel 3.
This volume was prepared by William G. Bishop and William H. Attree who were reporters for the Albany *Evening Atlas.*

(5) Constitutional Convention of 1867-1868.

New York (State). Constitutional Convention, 1867-1868.
The New York convention manual, prepared in pursuance of chapters 194 and 458, of the laws of 1867.... Albany: Weed, Parsons & Co., 1867.

CIS [NY 22]
The ***Manual*** was written by Franklin B. Hough under the direction of Francis C. Barlow, Secretary of State, Thomas Hillhouse, Comptroller, and John H. Martindale, Attorney General.

New York (State). Constitutional Convention, 1867-1868.
Documents of the Convention of the State of New York, 1867-68. Albany: Weed, Parsons and Company, 1868. 5 v.

CIS [NY 21]
Contains Document Nos. 1 to 185.

New York (State). Constitutional Convention, 1867-1868.
Journal of the convention of the State of New York, begun and held at the Capitol, in the city of Albany, on the 4th day of June, 1867. Albany: Weed, Parsons & Company, 1867. 1547 pp.

CIS [NY 19]

New York (State). Constitutional Convention, 1867-1868.
Photographs of the officers and members of the constitutional convention of the State of New York, 1867. With signatures. Albany: Jeffers & McDonald, 1867.

New York (State). Constitutional Convention, 1867-1868.
Proceedings and debates of the constitutional convention of the State of New York, held in 1867 and 1868, in the city of Albany. Albany: Weed, Parsons and Company, 1868. 5 v.

CIS [NY 20]
Edward F. Underhill, reporter of the convention, prepared this transcript of the convention proceedings.

New York (State). Constitutional Convention, 1867-1868.
Revision documents of the constitutional convention of the State of New York, 1867-68. Albany, 1868.

(6) Constitutional Convention of 1894.

New York (State). Constitutional Convention, 1894.
The convention manual for the sixth New York State constitutional convention, 1894.... Albany: Argus Co., 1894. 10 v.

CIS [NY 33]
The *Manual* was prepared by George A. Glynn under the direction of John Palmer, Secretary of State, James A. Roberts, Comptroller, and Theodore E. Hancock, Attorney General.

New York (State). Constitutional Convention, 1894.
Documents. Albany, 1894. 2 v.

CIS [NY 32]

New York (State). Constitutional Convention, 1894.
Documents and reports of the constitutional convention of the State of New York, 1894. Albany: The Argus Company, 1895. 395 pp.

Selected documents and reports revised and edited by George A. Glynn.

New York (State). Constitutional Convention, 1894.
Journal of the constitutional convention of the State of New York, begun and held at the Capitol, in the city of Albany, on Tuesday, the eighth day of May, 1894. Albany: The Argus Company, 1895. 1001 pp.

CIS [NY 30]

New York (State). Constitutional Convention, 1894.
[Proposed constitutional amendments]. Albany, 1894. 3v.

New York (State). Constitutional Convention, 1894.
Record. Albany, 1894. 6 v.

New York (State). Constitutional Convention, 1894.
Revised record of the constitutional convention of the State of New York, May 8, 1894 to September 29, 1894. Albany: The Argus Company, 1900. 5 v.

CIS [NY 31]
Revised and indexed by Hon. William H. Steele and published under the direction of Hon. Charles E. Fitch.

(7) Constitutional Convention of 1915.

New York (State). Constitutional Convention, 1915.
The convention manual of procedure, forms and rules for the regulation of business in the seventh New York State constitutional convention, 1915.... Albany: J. B. Lyon, 1915. 400 pp.

CIS [NY 40]

New York (State). Constitutional Convention, 1915.
Directory of delegates, post office addresses, committee assignments, seat numbers, and other information. Albany, 1915. 22 pp.

CIS [NY 41]

New York (State). Constitutional Convention, 1915.
Documents of the constitutional convention of the State of New York, 1915, begun and held at the Capitol in the city of Albany on Tuesday the sixth day of April. Albany: J. B. Lyon, 1915. 724 pp.

CIS [NY 38]

New York (State). Constitutional Convention, 1915.
Journal of the constitutional convention of the State of New York, 1915, begun and held at the Capitol in the city of Albany on Tuesday the sixth day of April. Albany: J. B. Lyon, 1915. 1018 pp.

CIS [NY 36]

New York (State). Constitutional Convention, 1915.
List of delegates. Proposals to be submitted. Record of Convention of 1894, being an index of all propositions introduced. Albany: Legislative Index Publishing Co., 1914. 61 pp.

New York (State). Constitutional Convention, 1915.
Proposed amendments of the constitutional convention of the State of New York, 1915, begun and held at the Capitol in the city of Albany on Tuesday the sixth day of April. Albany: J. B. Lyon Company, 1915. 2v.

New York (State). Constitutional Convention, 1915.
Record of the constitutional convention of the State of New York, 1915, begun and held at the Capitol in the city of Albany on Tuesday the sixth day of April. Albany: J. B. Lyon Co., 1916. 4 v.

New York (State). Constitutional Convention, 1915.
Revised record of the constitutional convention of the State of New York, April sixth to September tenth, 1915. Albany: J. B. Lyon Co., 1916. 4 v.

CIS [NY 37]

New York (State). Constitutional Convention, 1915.
Rules of the 1915 constitutional convention; reprinted. New York: Grosby Press. 36 pp.

CIS [NY 39] The convention rules revised to July 15, 1915.

New York (State). Constitutional Convention, 1915.
Proposed constitution of the State of New York as amended and revised, adopted by the convention September 10, 1915, with explanatory abstracts and form for submission to the voters, pursuant to chapter 668, Laws of 1915. Prepared under the direction of Francis M. Hugo, secretary of state. Albany, 1915. 79 pp.

CIS [NY 42]
The proposed 1915 constitution did not receive voter approval.

New York constitutional convention index; a complete record of all proposed amendments introduced in the convention beginning April 6, 1915. Albany: Legislative Index Publishing Company, 1915. 275 pp.

(8) Judiciary Constitutional Convention of 1921.

New York (State). Constitutional Convention, 1921.
Proceedings of the session of the executive committee of the judiciary constitutional convention of 1921. New York: Marshall & Munson, 1921.

The session lasted from May 31 to June 23, 1921 and was chaired by William D. Guthrie. These proceedings are reprinted in volume 9 of the Poletti Report.

New York (State). Constitutional Convention, 1921.
Report to Legislature dated January 4, 1922, and appendices. Albany: J. B. Lyon Company, 1922. 90 pp.

Legislative Document No. 37 (1922).

New York (State). Constitutional Convention, 1921.
Supplemental report of executive committee, Judiciary constitutional convention of 1921. Dated February 17, 1922. Albany: J.B. Lyon Co., 1922. 11 pp.

Legislative Document (1922) No. 67.

(9) Constitutional Convention of 1938.

New York (State). Constitutional Convention Committee.
Reports. New York and Albany, 1938. 12 v.

These Reports are collectively known as the "Poletti Report." The contents are:

Vol. I The New York State Constitution annotated.
Vol. II. Amendments proposed to the New York Constitution, 1895-1937.
Vol. III. Constitutions of the States and United States.
Vol. IV. State and local government in New York.
Vol. V. New York City government - functions and problems.
Vol. VI. Problems relating to Bill of Rights and general welfare.

Vol. VII.	Problems relating to legislative organizations and powers.
Vol. VIII.	Problems relating to executive administration and powers.
Vol. IX.	Problems relating to judicial administration and organization.
Vol. X.	Problems relating to taxation and finance.
Vol. XI.	Problems relating to home rule and local government.
Vol. XII.	General index to reports.

The twelve volume **"Poletti Report"** was created in preparation for the constitutional convention of 1938. It is an invaluable resource for research on New York constitutional history and government. Volumes 1-5 were written by outside experts; volumes 6-11 were written by the six subcommittees of the convention committee.

New York (State). Constitutional Convention, 1938.
Documents Nos. 1-18. Albany, 1938.

Document Nos. 1-15 are the committee reports; No. 16 is the revised and amended version of the constitution to be submitted to the voters; No. 17 concerns submission of proposed amendments; and No. 18 is the address of the delegates to the people of the State of New York concerning the revised constitution.

New York (State). Constitutional Convention, 1938.
Journal of the constitutional convention of the State of New York, April fifth to August twenty-sixth, 1938. Albany: J. B. Lyon Company, 1938. 1190 pp.

CIS [NY 47]
In addition to the Journal itself, this contains convention rules and documents of the convention.

New York (State). Constitutional Convention, 1938.
Proposed amendments of the constitutional convention of the State of New York, April fifth to August twenty-sixth, 1938. Albany: J. B. Lyon Company, 1938 3 v.

CIS [NY 49]

New York (State). Constitutional Convention, 1938.
Record of the constitutional convention of the State of New York, 1938, begun and held at the Capitol in the city of Albany, on Tuesday the fifth day of April. Albany: J. B. Lyon Company, 1938. 3 v.

New York (State). Constitutional Convention, 1938.
Revised record of the constitutional convention of the State of New York, April fifth to August twenty-sixth, 1938. Albany: J. B. Lyon Company, 1938. 4 v. 3542 pp.

CIS [NY 48]

New York constitutional convention record and index. A complete record issued weekly of all proposed amendments to the constitution with a complete history of action taken in the convention beginning April 5, 1938. Albany: Legislative Index Co., 1938. 165 pp.

(10) Constitutional Convention of 1967.

New York (State). Constitutional Convention, 1967.
Documents Nos. 1-60. Albany, 1967.

New York (State). Constitutional Convention, 1967.
Proceedings of the New York State constitutional convention. Albany, 1968. 12 v.

CIS [75A - 75F]
This set contains the journal, record, propositions, and documents of the 1967 constitutional convention.

New York (State). Constitutional Convention, 1967.
Rules of the 1967 New York State Constitutional Convention and Pertinent Resolutions and Statutes. Albany, 1967. 55 p.

CIS [NY 74]

New York (State). Dept. of Audit and Control.
Comptroller's studies for the 1967 Constitutional Convention. Albany, 1967. 5 v.

CIS [NY 72A - 72E]

New York (State). Temporary State Commission on the Constitutional Convention.
Reports Nos. 1-16. Albany, 1967. 16 v.

CIS [NY 56 - 71]

New York (State). Temporary State Commission on the Constitutional Convention.
Transcript of public hearings. New York: Ralph Fink, 1966. 5 v.

New York constitutional convention, 1967, record and index. Comprehensive summaries of all propositions introduced with history of action thereon; individual record of delegates; subject index of propositions; resolutions standing committees. Albany: Legislative Index Co., 1967. 309 pp.

b) Constitutional Commissions.

(1) Constitutional Commission of 1872.

New York (State). Constitutional Commission, 1872-1873.
Amendments proposed to the Constitution of the State of New York by the constitutional commission transmitted to the Legislature, March 25, 1873. Albany, 1873. 46 pp.

New York (State). Constitutional Commission, 1872-1873.
Journal of the constitutional commission of the State of New York. Begun and held in the common council chamber, in the city of Albany, on the 4th day of December, 1872-1873. Albany: Weed, Parsons and Company, 1873. 735 pp.

CIS [NY 25]

(2) Judiciary Commission of 1890.

New York (State). Constitutional Commission, 1890-1891.
Journal. Albany, 1891. 125 pp.

CIS [NY 28]

New York (State). Constitutional Commission, 1890-1891.
Photographic album containing photographs of the members of the commission. Albany.

New York (State). Constitutional Commission, 1890-1891.
Reports of the committees of the constitutional commission on various courts of the State and final report to the Legislature. Albany. 54 pp.

New York (State). Constitutional Commission, 1890-1891. Committee on the Court of Appeals.
Report. 1890. 36 pp.

New York (State). Judiciary Commission.
Report of the Judiciary Commission, appointed under chapter 189, Laws of 1890, dated January 23, 1891. In *Senate Documents*, 1890, no. 51, March 4, 1891. CHECK THIS CITE.

(3) Temporary Commission on the Constitutional Convention.

New York (State). Temporary Commission on the Constitutional Convention.
Interim Report, 1st-2nd. Albany, 1957. 2 v.

New York (State). Temporary Commission on the Constitutional Convention.
Transcript of public hearing, June 4-17, 1957. New York, 1957. 4 v. in 2

(4) Temporary Commision on the Revision and Simplification of the Constitution.

New York (State). Temporary Commission on the Revision and Simplification of the Constitution.
New York State Constitutional Revision and Simplification: 1957-1961. New York: 1957-1961.

New York (State). Temporary Commission on the Revision and Simplification of the Constitution.
Staff Report. No. 1-35. NewYork: 1958-1960. 14 v.

For a detailed description of these 35 reports, see item no. 97 in *New York State Documents: an Introductory Manual* by Dorothy Butch.

REFERENCES

Breuer, E. H. *Constitutional Developments in New York, 1777-1958.* Albany: Univ. of the State of New York, 1958. (New York State Library Bibliography Bulletin 82).

Butch, D. *New York State Documents: an Introductory Manual.* Albany: Univ. of the State of New York, 1987. (New York State Library Bibliography Bulletin 89).

Browne, C.E. *State Constitutional Conventions from Independence to the Completion of the Present Union, 1776-1959.* Westport, Conn.: Greenwood Press, 1973.

Chester, A. *Legal and Judicial History of New York.* New York: National Americana Society, 1911.

Dougherty, J. H. *Constitutional History of the State of New York.* 2d ed. rev. and enl. New York: Neale Pub. Co., 1915.

Ellis, D. M., et. al. *A History of New York State.* Ithaca: Cornell University Press, 1967.

Lincoln, C. Z. ***The Constitutional History of New York from the beginning of the colonial period to the year 1905 showing the origin, development and judicial construction of the constitution.*** Rochester: Lawyers Co-operative Publishing Company, 1906.

New York (State). ***Constitutional Records, 1776-1821 and 1846.*** Washington, D.C.: Library of Congress, 1949. 3 microfilm reels. (Records of the States of the United States of America series).

New York (State). Temporary State Commission on the Constitutional Convention. ***Introductory Report: 1967 Convention Issues.*** New York: The Commission, 1966.

State Constitutional Conventions, Commissions and Amendments, 1959-1978: a Bibliography. Project manager, Mark Vonderhaar; bibliography editor, Nicholas Olcott. Washington, D.C.: Congressional Information Service, 1981.

State Constitutional Conventions, Revisions, and Amendments, 1959-1976: a Bibliography. Compiled by Bonnie Canning. Westport, Conn.: Greenwood Press, 1977.

Swindler, W. F. ***Sources and Documents of United States Constitutions.*** Dobbs Ferry: Oceana Publications, 1978.

Thorpe, F. N. ***The Federal and State Constitutions, Colonial Charters, and Other Organic Laws of the States, Territories, and Colonies Now or Heretofore Forming the United States of America.*** Washington, D.C.: U.S. Government Printing Office, 1909.

Yarger, S. R. ***State Constitutional Conventions, 1959-1975: a Bibliography.*** Westport, Conn.: Greenwood Press, 1976.

Zimmerman, J. F. ***The Government and Politics of New York State.*** New York: New York University Press, 1981.

Chapter Two
STATE LEGISLATION: Legislative Process, Bills, Session Laws, and Resolutions

1. OVERVIEW OF NEW YORK LEGISLATION

a) Legislative Authority. Article III of the New York Constitution vests the legislative power of the State in the Senate and Assembly,[1] sets the size of the Senate and the Assembly,[2] and determines such basic matters as qualification and time of election of legislators and the assent required for passage of particular kinds of statutes. The Legislative Law, which is one of the Consolidated Laws, provides further authority for the legislative process.

Pursuant to article III, sec. 9, each house of the legislature determines its own procedural rules. There are also joint Senate and Assembly rules. The Senate, Assembly, and joint rules are published periodically by the Senate and Assembly.[3] They are available online on the Legislative Retrieval System (LRS).[4]

Pursuant to section 10 of article III, each house must keep and publish a journal of its proceedings.[5] Unfortunately for the researcher interested in debates[6] on legislation, the journals are not transcripts of proceedings in the two houses. They merely record summaries of each day's proceedings.

b) The Legislative Term. The legislature meets in annual sessions. The sessions are numbered consecutively starting with the first session in 1777. The two-session term of the legislature corresponds with the two-year terms of the members of the Senate and Assembly.

The two-session legislative term is called a Legislature. The comparable name at the federal level for the two-session legislative term is a Congress. The numbering system at the federal and New York levels differs. In New York, only the legislative sessions are numbered, e.g., 210th Session (1987). At the federal level, Congresses are numbered con-

[1] N.Y. CONST. art. III sec. 1 (McKinney 1987).

[2] N.Y. CONST. art. III sec. 2 (McKinney 1987). The Constitution sets the size of the Assembly at 150 members. While the Constitution sets the size of the Senate at 50 members, as the result of the U.S. Supreme Court's rulings on reapportionment, the Senate currently has 61 members selected from 61 senatorial districts.

[3] As of this writing the current rules were: New York (State). Assembly. ***1987-1988 Rules of the Assembly*** (Albany: 1987) and New York (State). Senate. ***Rules of the Senate: 1987-1988*** (Albany: 1987). The most up-to-date coverage of the house rules is found in the LRS database.

[4] The Legislative Retrieval System [hereinafter LRS] is a legislative database operated by the New York Legislative Bill Drafting Commission. LRS is more fully described in Chapter 12 (Databases for New York Legal Research).

[5] N.Y. CONST. art. III, sec. 10 (McKinney 1987). The Senate and Assembly journals have been published since 1777.

[6] Materials concerning legislative intent are described in Chapter 5 (Legislative History).

secutively, while sessions within a Congress are numbered as either the first or second session, e.g., 92nd Congress, first session.

The governor may call the legislature into extraordinary session. During such sessions, the agenda is set by the governor, and the legislature cannot consider any other matters.[7] The legislature, by a petition signed by two-thirds of the elected members of each house, may call itself into extraordinary session to act upon matters set forth in the petition.[8]

New York bills which do not pass in the first session of a Legislature are usually "deemed" to be reintroduced in the second session. They continue to carry the same bill number and are known as "carryover bills." The procedures for automatic reintroduction of bills in the second session of the legislature are found in the Senate and Assembly rules.[9]

New York bills which do not pass during a legislature "die." To be revived, they must be reintroduced in the next legislature with new bill numbers.

c) **Overview of Statutory Publication.** The term "statute" as used in this chapter means an act of the New York legislature "declaring, commanding or prohibiting something."[10] The pattern of statutory publication in New York is similar to that at the federal level. Using generic terms, that pattern is:

bill ⟶ slip law ⟶ session laws ⟶ "code" or compiled laws

Sections 1(c)(1)-(c)(4) below contain brief discussions of this statutory publication pattern using comparisons with the federal statutory publication pattern. Sections 3 and 4 of this Chapter describe research in New York bills and session laws. The next chapter, Chapter 3, presents an historical overview of the compiled laws or "codes" since colonial times. Chapter 4 describes the Consolidated Laws of New York, which is the current "code." New York legislative history is discussed in Chapter 5.

1) **Bills.** Bills are proposed statutes. When they are introduced in the Senate or Assembly they are assigned bill numbers that indicate their house of origin, i.e., S311 means Senate bill number 311 and A45 means

[7] N.Y. CONST. art. 4, sec. 3 (McKinney 1987).

[8] N.Y. CONST. art. III, sec. 18 (McKinney 1987) and N.Y. LEGIS. LAW secs. 34-39 (McKinney Supp. 1987)

[9] At this writing, these procedures are found in Senate Rule VI, sec. 8 and Assembly Rule III, sec. e(2).

[10] N.Y. Statutes sec. 1 (McKinney 1971).

Assembly bill number 45. Federal bill numbers also are identifiable by house of origin, i.e., S. 632 means Senate bill number 632 and H.R. 3672 means House of Representatives bill number 3672.

2) Chapter Laws. When a bill becomes a law in New York, the new law is called a chapter law. At the federal level, a new law is called a Public Law. Separately printed copies of chapter laws and federal public laws are known as slip laws.

Each New York chapter law is given a number that puts it in chronological order with the other new laws passed in the same session of the Legislature. That number is the chapter number (abbreviated "ch." or "c."). Each federal act is also given a number that puts it in chronological order with the other new laws passed in the same session of the Congress. That number is the Public Law number (abbreviated "Pub.L.").

3) Session Laws. The third step in the publishing pattern outlined above occurs at the end of each legislative session. The individual laws are arranged in order by number and printed in annual volumes called session laws. Session laws contain ***only*** the laws passed in that year's legislative session. The numbers of the new laws arrange the laws in chronological order by date of passage.

In New York, the session laws published by the authority of the government are the ***Laws of New York*** (abbreviated "N.Y. Laws" or sometimes simply "L."). New York's session laws are also published unofficially by the West Publishing Company and the Lawyers Co-operative Publishing Company.[11] The federal counterpart of ***Laws of New York*** is ***Statutes at Large.*** The federal session laws are published unofficially by the West Publishing Company in a publication called the ***U.S. Code Congressional & Administrative News (U.S.C.C.A.N.)*** and by Lawyers Co-op in a publication called ***U.S.C.S. Advance Service.***

4) Statutory Compilations or "Codes." The current laws of a general and permanent nature are published in a subject-arranged order called a "code"[12] or statutory compilation, and it is in this kind of

[11] See section 4 of this Chapter.

[12] Warthen's recent article, ***The Non-Emergence of the Anglo American Law Code*** in 6 ***Legal Reference Services Q.*** 129 (1986), explains the difference between a true code and a statutory compilation like New York's Consolidated Laws. A true code is a systematic and comprehensive enactment of a whole field of law that pre-empts all other law within that field. The usual American statutory compilation, of which our current Consolidated Laws is an example, is systematic but neither comprehensive nor pre-emptive. Reference to other statutory and case law is often necessary to fill in gaps in coverage or to determine issues. See Warthen at 133.

publication that most statutory research begins.

The New York subject arranged "code" is the Consolidated Laws of New York. The Consolidated Laws of New York have not been published by authority of the State since 1909/10. At this writing, the Consolidated Laws are published unofficially by four publishers: West Publishing Company, ***(McKinney's Consolidated Laws of New York Annotated),***[13] Lawyer's Co-operative Publishing Company ***(New York Consolidated Laws Service),***[14] the Michie Company ***(New York Consolidated Laws)***[15] and Gould Publications ***(Gould's Consolidated Laws of New York).***[16] New York's Consolidated Laws are also available online in full text in the Legislative Retrieval System (LRS). Mead Data Central projects that the Consolidated Laws will once again be available online on LEXIS during 1988. The West Publishing Company projects that the Consolidated Laws will become available online on WESTLAW during 1988.[17]

Continuing the analogy with federal publication patterns, the official federal "code" is the ***United States Code.*** The ***United States Code*** is also published unofficially by both West Publishing Company ***(U.S. Code Annotated)***[18] and the Lawyer's Co-operative Publishing Company ***(U.S. Code Service).***[19] The New York and federal publication pattern is summarized in the chart on the next page.

d) Statutory Construction. Statutory construction is governed by the General Construction Law, which is one of the Consolidated Laws. Secondary sources of guidance in construing New York statutes include Book 1 of ***McKinney's Consolidated Laws of New York Annotated***, entitled "Statutes," and the section entitled "Statutes" in the New York legal encyclopedia, ***New York Jurisprudence 2d.***

e) Legislative Process. Detailed descriptions of the legislative process in New York are found in Baaklini and Dawson's ***The Politics of Legislation in New York State: How a Bill Becomes a Law,*** in the annual ***New York Red Book***, in chapter 6 of J. F. Zimmerman's ***The Government and Politics of New York State***, in the ***Lenz & Reicker, Inc. New York State Government Reference Book***, and in "Formalities of Enactment

[13] Hereinafter ***McKinney's.***
[14] Hereinafter ***CLS.***
[15] Hereinafter ***Michie's.***
[16] Hereinafter ***Gould's.***
[17] LRS, LEXIS, and WESTLAW are described in Chapter 12 (Databases For New York Legal Research).
[18] Hereinafter ***USCA.***
[19] Hereinafter ***USCS.***

FEDERAL AND NEW YORK STATUTORY PUBLICATION PATTERN

BILLS	SLIP LAWS	SESSION LAWS	"CODE"
Fed.: bills (Senate and House of Representatives)	**Fed.:** Public Laws	**Fed.** *Statutes at Large*	**Fed.:** *U.S. Code*
		U.S.C.C.A.N. (West)	*U.S.C.A.* (West)
		U.S.C.S. Advance Service (Lawyers Co-op)	*U.S.C.S.* (Lawyers Co-op)
NY: bills (Senate and Assembly)	**NY:** Chapter Laws	**NY:** *Laws of New York*	**NY:** Consolidated Laws of N.Y.
		McKinney's Session Laws (West)	*McKinney's* (West)
		C.L.S. Session Laws (Lawyer's Co-op.)	*C.L.S.* (Lawyers Co-op)
			Michie's
			Gould's

and Approval," which is chapter 2 of *McKinney's,* Book 1 ("Statutes").[20] For details of the legislative process in each house, see the Senate Rules, the Assembly Rules, and the joint rules.

2. BILL DRAFTING

Many agencies and advisory committees are charged with assisting the legislators by proposing legislation and giving drafting assistance. These include the Law Revision Commission, the Legislative Bill Drafting Commission (LBDC), and other governmental entities. Several of the bar associations in New York are also influential in shaping legislation.

a) The Law Revision Commission. The Law Revision Commission was established in 1934[21] to examine the common law and statutes of the State of New York for areas needing reform or modernization and to recommend needed changes to the legislature. The Commission consists of the chairpersons of the Senate and Assembly Committees on Codes and Committees on the Judiciary (who serve as ex officio members of the Commission) and five members appointed by the governor.

Bills to carry out the Commission's proposals are drafted by the Commission and introduced in the legislature by the Commission's ex officio members. The purposes and composition of the Commission are set forth in detail in the Legislative Law.[22] The annual legislative recommendations of the Law Revision Commission can be found in the Commission's annual report. The report is issued by the State and also included in the unofficial session laws volumes, which are discussed in Section 4 of this Chapter.

b) The Legislative Bill Drafting Commission. The Legislative Bill Drafting Commission *(LBDC)* was created to assist legislators in drafting bills, to advise legislators as to the constitutionality, consistency or effect of proposed legislation, and to conduct research on subjects of proposed legislation.[23] There are two Commissioners who are appointed jointly by the Temporary President of the Senate and the Speaker of the Assembly. The Commissioners direct a staff of attorneys and are supported by a

[20] *Formalities of Enactment and Approval,* Chap. in N.Y. Statutes (Book 1) (McKinney 1971).

[21] 1934 N.Y. LAWS ch. 597.

[22] N.Y. LEGIS. LAW sec. 72 (McKinney 1952).

[23] N.Y. LEGIS. LAW sec. 24, 25 (McKinney Supp. 1987).

data processing and technical staff. The Commission's publication, the *Legislative Digest,* and its database, LRS, are described in sections 3 and 4 of this Chapter. LRS is described in more detail in Chapter 12 (Databases for New York Legal Research).

c) Other Governmental Agencies, Commissions, and Committees. Other bodies which draft proposed legislation and recommend it to the legislature include the Advisory Committee on Civil Practice, the Advisory Committee on Criminal Law and Procedure, the Commission on Uniform State Laws and the Office of Court Administration.

When major reform or modernization of an area of the law is called for, the governor or the legislature may appoint special committees to study and make recommendations for law revision. Examples of bodies so charged by the governor were the Governor's Committee to Review New York Laws and Procedures in the Area of Human Rights (1968) and the Governor's Temporary Commission to Review the Sales and Use Tax Laws (1979). Examples of bodies so charged by the legislature were the Joint Legislative Committee to Revise and Simplify the Education Law (1964-68) and the Select Committee to Study Revision of Corporation Laws (1957-75).

d) Bar Associations. The specialized committees of the New York State Bar Association,[24] the Association of the Bar of the City of New York,[25] and various other bar associations play an important role in shaping legislation by commenting at legislative hearings concerning areas in need of law reform, by drafting model legislation, and by analyzing proposed legislation.

The usefulness of legislative reports by governmental entities, special commissions and committees, and bar association committees, as well as research methods for locating such reports, in connection with the search for legislative intent are described in Chapter 5 (Legislative History).

3. BILLS

a) Introduction of Bills. Bills may be introduced in either house by a legislator, by a legislative standing committee, by message from the other house of the legislature, or by an order of the house in which the bill

[24] ***See generally*** the ***Legislative Report*** of the New York State Bar Association.

[25] ***See generally*** the ***Bulletin*** of the Association of the Bar of the City of New York's Committee on State Legislation and the ***Record*** (the Association's monthly journal).

originated. Bills also may be introduced jointly by a sponsor from each house. The one exception to the introduction of bills by legislative action is the executive budget. The executive budget is submitted in bill form by the governor pursuant to article VII of the New York Constitution.[26]

Bills may be "prefiled" for introduction at the beginning of the legislative session in January, or they may be introduced during the session. Bills prefiled at the beginning of the Legislature may be recognized by their low numbers, e.g., A22, S37;[27] bills prefiled at the beginning of the second session of the Legislature do not have low numbers. The word "prefiled" appears on the face of prefiled bills.

A bill to be introduced is deposited with the Revision Clerk in each house who works closely with the Legislative Bill Drafting Commission (LBDC) in examining the bill for technical flaws, proofreading it, assigning an identifying number (e.g. Senate bill 1023, Assembly bill 2413), and assigning an official date of introduction. The bill is sent to the printer, and the Legislative Bill Drafting Commission enters the text of the newly introduced bill and other relevant information in the LRS database for subsequent tracking. Bills enter LRS on a very current basis. New bills may be online in LRS within three hours of introduction; in all instances they are online within 24 hours of introduction.

Upon introduction, an Assembly bill is deemed to have had its first reading, while a Senate bill is deemed to have had its first and second readings.[28] With certain exceptions, article III, section 14 of the New York Constitution requires three "readings" before final action can be taken on a bill's passage. The requirement of three readings, also called "aging of bills," apparently was added to the Constitution in 1894 as a means to prevent premature voting on bills that were not yet printed and available to the legislators.[29]

Newly introduced bills are referred for study and legislative action to the appropriate standing or select committee of the house in which they were introduced. The names of the standing and select committees for the current session and the names of the members are available in the ***Legislative Digest***, the ***State Register,*** on LRS, and in the first issue of ***McKinney's Session Law News*** for each legislative session. Committee membership from prior sessions of the legislature is listed in the bound

[26] The budget process is described in section 4 of Chapter 4.

[27] Givens, ***A Primer on the New York State Legislative Process: How It Differs From Federal Procedure,*** 57 N.Y. ST. B. J. 8, 10 (April, 1985).

[28] A.I. BAAKLINI & C.S. DAWSON, THE POLITICS OF LEGISLATION IN NEW YORK STATE: HOW A BILL BECOMES A LAW 32 (1979) [hereinafter BAAKLINI AND DAWSON].

[29] J.F. ZIMMERMAN, THE GOVERNMENT AND POLITICS OF NEW YORK STATE 113 (1981).

volumes of the ***Legislative Digest*** and its predecessor, the ***New York Legislative Record and Index***. Legislative committee membership is also listed in the annual Senate and Assembly journals and, until 1975, in the Legislative Documents series.[30]

b) Bill Text and Accompanying Memorandum. Senate Rule VI, sec. 4, and Assembly Rule III, sec. 1, require that each bill be given a title which briefly states the subject matter of the bill. When a bill proposes to amend a Consolidated Law or a court act, the title must also refer to such law, e.g., "AN ACT to amend the vehicle and traffic law, in relation to parking permits for handicapped persons." When a bill proposes to amend existing law, all new matter to be added to or inserted in the existing law must be underlined; all matter proposed to be eliminated by amendment from existing law must be printed in its proper place in the bill but enclosed in brackets.

The rules of each house require each bill's sponsor to file an accompanying memorandum setting forth the intent of the proposed legislation. Senate Rule VI, sec. 1, and Assembly Rule III, sec. 1(f), prescribe the contents of legislative memoranda in the respective houses. Legislative memoranda are described more fully in Chapter 5 (Legislative History).

c) Amendment of Bills. Bills may be amended either in committee or on the floor any number of times before final legislative passage as long as the house rules are observed. When a bill is amended, a letter of the alphabet is appended to the bill identifying number to distinguish each amended version, e.g., Assembly bill as introduced, A1001; as amended once, A1001-A; as amended twice, A1001-B. Before 1969, successive print numbers were used to identify each printing of an amended bill.

There is no formal New York counterpart to the conference committee procedure that exists in the U.S. Congress for the purpose of resolving differences between the two legislative houses over the wording of a bill. However, a procedure for substituting bills does exist, and it can expedite compromise between the houses in the case of bills for which there is strong political support.

[30] New York's Legislative Documents series is described in section 6 of Chapter 5 (Legislative History).

d) Publication of Bills.

1) Current Session. At this writing, bills for the current session of the legislature can be obtained by subscription from Legislative Digest/Hamilton Printing Company of Rensselaer, New York and New York Legislative Service, Inc. of New York City. The latest amended versions of bills in the current and previous session are available online through both LRS and Legi-Tech. Individual copies of bills are available from the Assembly and Senate Document Rooms.[31]

2) Bound Bills. The legislature has issued sets of bound bills since 1830. From 1830 to 1841, the bills of the Senate and Assembly were issued together under the title ***Bills of the Senate and Assembly***. During that period, bills of both houses were numbered in a single sequence. Since 1842, the bills were issued by each house as ***Bills of the Assembly of the State of New York*** and ***Bills of the Senate of the State of New York***. There is a publication lag of several years in the issuance of the bound bills.

The volumes of bound bills are supposed to contain all versions of each bill, whether the bill passed into law or not. Probably due to the large number of bills introduced in each legislature and the sheer difficulty of locating all versions of every bill at the end of the legislature, it cannot be said that New York's bound bill volumes are complete. New York's Legislative Library should be contacted for information about bills not included in the bound bills volumes. The telephone number and address of the New York Legislative Library are included in Appendix F (New York Law Libraries).

e) Finding and Tracking Bills in the Current Session.

1) Finding Bills by Subject. Bills on a particular subject can be identified through ***Legislative Digest's*** "Index by Subject" or by performing an online subject search on LRS, Legi-Tech, or STATE NET. LRS, Legi-Tech, and STATE NET are databases that are described more fully in Chapter 12 (Databases for New York Legal Research). Both the New York Legislative Service, Inc. and the Legislative Department of Commerce Clearing House, Inc. provide bill searching services for subscribers to their legislative services.

31 Assembly Document Room, Room 305, State Capitol, Albany, N.Y. 12224 Tel. (518) 455-5165. Senate Document Room, Room 323, Mezzanine, State Capitol, Albany, N.Y. 12247. Tel. (518) 455-2311 or 455-2312.

The ***Legislative Digest*** is published annually by the New York Legislative Bill Drafting Commission. The ***Legislative Digest's*** subject index is arranged alphabetically by broad categories. The vast majority of "subject" entries are in reality merely the names of the Consolidated Laws (e.g. Civil Practice Law and Rules, Education Law). While the ***Legislative Digest's*** subheadings are quite detailed, finding the proper main subject heading is greatly facilitated when the researcher knows which Consolidated Law, unconsolidated law, or article of the Constitution will be amended if the bill passes.

This example illustrates the point. In the 1987 session of the legislature, a bill to merge New York's specialized trial courts into the supreme court was introduced. Researchers familiar with the issue of court merger would know that such a change in the court system would require a constitutional amendment. In fact, this bill was up for its second passage in the 1987 session, having already passed the legislature previously. Researchers who did not know this information might have been hard pressed to find this bill in the ***Legislative Digest's*** subject index.

While the concept behind the proposed amendment was popularly known as court reform or court merger, the bill to achieve these purposes was not indexed in the ***Legislative Digest*** under such topics as "Court Reform," "Courts," "Court Merger" or even "Judiciary." The bill was indexed under "Constitution, NYS" since, as was mentioned previously, court merger requires amendment of the judiciary article of the New York Constitution. The actual index entry was as follows:

Constitution, NYS
  Judiciary, Art 6
    Merging the court system with supreme court, Art
    6 generally A11

"A11" refers to Assembly bill number 11. As this example illustrates, effective use of the ***Legislative Digest's*** subject index requires a substantive grasp of New York law.

2) Finding Bills by Sponsor's Name. To find bills where the primary sponsor's name is known, consult the ***Legislative Digest's*** sections entitled "Senate Individual Record" and "Assembly Individual Record" or use the LRS, Legi-Tech, or STATE NET bill search features.

3) Determining Bill Status. During the current session, a bill's daily status can be determined online using the bill tracking features of LRS, Legi-Tech or STATE NET. Alternatively, the researcher can call the Bill Status Hotline (in New York State toll-free call to [800] 342-9860, or toll call to [518] 455-2255, or out-of-state [518] 455-7548).

The cumulative, weekly issues of the ***Legislative Digest*** also provide bill status but not as quickly as that information can be located online or by telephone. In the ***Legislative Digest,*** consult the sections entitled "Bill Action in Senate" and "Bill Action in Assembly."

Researching bills from prior sessions of the legislature is described in Chapter 5 (Legislative History).

f) Final Passage in the Legislature and Action by the Governor. Generally, a majority of the elected membership of each house is required to pass a bill. Bills that would appropriate funds for local or private purposes require a two-thirds vote for final passage.[32] Special laws which affect the property, affairs or government of a municipality (except the City of New York) and that are brought to the legislature on certificate of necessity by the governor also require a two-thirds vote for final passage.[33] Tax and appropriation bills require a majority, but there must be a quorum of three-fifths of the elected membership present for the vote.[34]

After a bill receives the required approval of both legislative houses, passage is certified by the presiding officer of each house pursuant to section 40 of the Legislative Law. The bill is returned to the house of origin to be engrossed. Engrossing a bill involves affixing to it the certifications of passage from each house and enclosing the bill in a jacket. The house of origin transmits the engrossed bill to the governor's office.

While the bill awaits gubernatorial action, the Governor's Counsel's Office solicits the views of parties interested in the bill and prepares a recommendation for final action by the governor. Views are solicited from key state officials such as the budget director and department and agency heads. The views of special interest groups are often solicited. Responses are placed with the bill in its "bill jacket." The contents and usefulness of bill jackets are described more fully in Section 4 of Chapter 5 (Legislative History).

[32] N.Y. CONST. art. 3, sec. 20 (McKinney 1987).

[33] N.Y. CONST. art. 9, sec. 2(b)(2)(b) (McKinney 1987).

[34] N.Y. CONST. art. 3, sec. 23 (McKinney 1987).

Action by the governor on legislative bills is governed by article 4, section 7 of the New York Constitution. Until the last ten days of the legislative session, the governor has ten days from receipt of a bill passed by the legislature to sign or veto it. The governor has thirty days to act on a bill passed by the legislature during the last ten days of its session. The governor can sign bills into law, veto them, or take no action on them. Bills that are neither signed into law by the governor nor delivered back to the legislature on a veto message during the ten day period while the legislature is in session automatically become law. Bills that are not signed by the governor within the thirty day limit at the end of the session are "pocket vetoed" and do not become law. If the governor vetoes a bill, a two-thirds vote in each house of the legislature is required to override the veto. A veto override rarely occurs in New York.

g) Chapter Laws. As previously mentioned above in Section 1(c)(2), the new laws, which are numbered in chronological order, are called chapter laws. The first official version of a new law is the engrossed bill bearing the governor's signature or, in the case of a law not signed by the governor, certification of how the bill passed (without signature during the ten day limitation period while the legislature was in session or on a veto override). At this writing, the chapter number is assigned to the new law in the office of the Legislative Secretary to the Governor.

The original engrossed bill is deposited with the Secretary of State pursuant to section 93 of the Executive Law. A copy is retained in the office of the Legislative Secretary to the Governor. Copies are sent to the Speaker of the Assembly, the Temporary President of the Senate, and the Legislative Bill Drafting Commission (LBDC). The LBDC enters the full text of new chapter laws in LRS daily. It maintains at least two years of the chapter laws in the LRS database.

Under current practice, New York does not print its chapter laws separately as slip laws for general distribution. However, publication of the slip laws, subject to the availability of funding, is authorized by section 49 of the Legislative Law. Individual copies of chapter laws are available from the LBDC and from the Department of State's Miscellaneous Records office.[35] Chapter laws are also available by subscription from Legislative Digest/Hamilton Printing Company of Rensselaer, New York, from the Legislative Department of Commerce Clearing House, Inc.,[36] and from the New York Legislative Service, Inc.

[35] Miscellaneous Records, New York Department of State, Third Floor, 162 Washington Ave., Albany, N.Y. 12231, Tel. (518) 474-4770.

[36] Legislative Department, Commerce Clearing House, Tel. (312) 583-8500.

in New York City.

McKinney's Session Law News of New York and the *Advance Legislative Service for the New York Consolidated Laws Service* are advance sheets for the *McKinney's* and *CLS* session laws. These advance sheets are pamphlets that contain the new chapter laws. They are described in the next section of this Chapter.

4. SESSION LAWS

a) Publication of the Session Laws. As previously mentioned above in Section 1(c)(3), session laws are the laws of each annual legislative session printed in chronological order (by chapter number). Official printed session laws for the state of New York exist from the first session in 1777 to date, except for 1975. In 1975, a fiscal crisis prevented publication of *Laws of New York*. For 1975, the certified, engrossed bills are the only official text of New York's laws. Fortunately, both of the unofficial session law services published session law volumes in 1975. Some of the laws passed during the 1975 extraordinary session are printed in the 1975 unofficial session laws. The remaining laws from the 1975 extraordinary session are printed in the 1976 session laws.

For a checklist of New York's legislative sessions and printed session laws from colonial times to the present, see Section I of *Pimsleur's Checklists of Basic American Legal Publications.*[37] *Pimsleur* lists both the official and the unofficial session laws. For a discussion of the history of New York's session laws until 1920, see *The Session Laws of the State of New York* by John T. Fitzpatrick.[38]

b) Laws of New York. Currently, there are three printings of New York's session laws: *Laws of New York*, published by the New York Legislative Bill Drafting Commission, *McKinney's Session Laws of New York,* published by West Publishing Company, and *New York Consolidated Laws Service Session Laws,* published by Lawyers Cooperative Publishing Company.

The official publication is *Laws of New York*. The printing, contents and distribution of *Laws of New York* are governed by sections 44-49 of the Legislative Law. Each volume of the *Laws of New York* bears notice

[37] PIMSLEUR'S CHECKLISTS OF BASIC AMERICAN LEGAL PUBLICATIONS, Section I, Session Laws, edited by M. Zubrow.

[38] 13 LAW LIBR. J. 80 (1921). When he wrote this article, Mr. Fitzpatrick was Law Librarian of the New York State Library.

of joint certification by the Temporary President of the Senate and the Speaker of the Assembly. Accordingly, pursuant to section 70-b of the Public Officers Law, the contents of ***Laws of New York*** are entitled to be read into evidence.

By statute,[39] ***Laws of New York*** must contain the session laws, any concurrent resolutions proposing amendments to the New York Constitution, and any concurrent resolutions proposing or ratifying amendments to the U.S. Constitution passed at each session. If any amendments to the New York Constitution were approved by the people at the last general election, they must be included in ***Laws of New York***. Finally, the publication must contain a list of specified government officials, tables showing the laws amended or repealed in the session, and it must contain an index to that session's laws and concurrent resolutions.

c) Unofficial Session Laws: *McKinney's and CLS Session Laws.* ***McKinney's Session Laws of New York*** has been published since 1951; ***New York Consolidated Laws Service Session Laws*** has been published since 1976. While these unofficial session laws publications are very accurately compiled, they are not certified. In case of discrepancy between wording in the unofficial session law publications and wording in ***Laws of New York,*** the latter prevails.

d) Comparison of the Official and Unofficial Session Laws Publications. All three session law publications provide subject indexes and tables of laws affected by the year's new chapter laws.

The three session law publications differ to some extent in their scope. ***Laws of New York*** is the most comprehensive of the three publications in covering the legislature's activity. In addition to the general laws, it includes concurrent resolutions, special laws, temporary laws, and the appropriation laws. By contrast, the unofficial session laws generally do not include appropriation laws. ***McKinney's Session Laws*** includes more special laws than does the ***CLS Session Laws.***

While ***McKinney's Session Laws*** and ***CLS Session Laws*** contain less primary source material than ***Laws of New York*** does, they print useful secondary source material that is not found at all in the ***Laws of New York.*** Both of the unofficial session laws publications typically include the annual reports of the Law Revision Commission, the Advisory Com-

[39] N.Y. LEGIS. LAW sec. 45 (McKinney 1987).

mittee on Civil Practice, the Advisory Committee on Criminal Law and Procedure, and the governor's annual message to the joint session of the legislature setting forth his legislative program for the year. The ***CLS*** and ***McKinney's*** session laws also include the governor's approval memoranda and memoranda of agencies such as the Office of Court Administration. The use of these publications in determining "legislative intent" is discussed in Chapter 5 (Legislative History).

e) Research in the Session Laws. Locating a law in the session laws can be done in several ways. If the year and either the date of approval or the chapter number are known, it is a simple matter to find a law in any of the three versions of New York's session laws, since the laws in the annual volumes are arranged in chronological order by their chapter numbers.

If only the year and the bill number of the law is known, the chapter numbers of newly enacted laws can be located in several ways through the ***Legislative Digest***. The "Cross Reference Table" leads from bill number to chapter number. In the Senate and Assembly "Bill Action" sections, the subsections entitled "Assembly Bills Signed by the Governor" and "Senate Bills signed by the Governor" cross refer from bill number to chapter number. Chapter numbers can be located on LRS and Legi-Tech by using the bill status feature.

If the section of the Consolidated Laws that is amended by the new law is known, the "Subject Index" for the chapter laws in the ***Legislative Digest*** provides subject access by the name of the Act and the name of the Consolidated Law that the new law amends.

f) Advance Session Laws Services and Databases. Both the West Publishing Company and the Lawyers Co-operative Publishing Company provide advance pamphlet services during the legislative session. These services are ***McKinney's Session Law News of New York*** (West) and the ***Advance Legislative Service for the New York Consolidated Laws Service*** (Lawyers Co-operative Publishing Company). The chapter laws are also available online on LRS.

The ***McKinney's*** and ***CLS*** advance services commence publication a few months after the January session of the legislature begins. Early pamphlets are quite slender, reflecting the fact that very little other legislation can be passed until the state budget is passed around April 1.

Each pamphlet of the session law services contains a cumulative subject index and cumulative tables indicating which sections of the Consolidated Laws and other laws are affected by the new enactments. These tables update the statutory portions of the pocket parts of ***McKinney's Consolidated Laws of New York Annotated*** and the ***CLS Consolidated Laws of New York*** and the annual volumes of ***Michie's*** and ***Gould's.*** The session law pamphlets include the governor's annual message to the joint session of the legislature, governor's memoranda of approval concerning the new laws, memoranda of government agencies concerning the new laws, and legislative highlights.

5. RESOLUTIONS

Resolutions are a kind of legislative action that does not require approval by the governor. Concurrent resolutions and joint resolutions require the approval of both the Assembly and the Senate. Single house resolutions require only approval in one house.

The most important kind of resolution is the concurrent resolution. Proposed amendments to the New York Constitution, proposed amendments to the United States Constitution, and ratification by the New York legislature of a proposed amendment to the United States Constitution all take the form of concurrent resolutions. While they are making their way through the legislative process, they have bill numbers and are treated procedurally like bills. Upon passage by both houses, concurrent resolutions are printed in ***Laws of New York*** pursuant to section 45 of the Legislative Law. They are also included in bound and unbound collections of bills (by bill number) and are available online in the bill files of LRS. Concurrent resolutions are the only kind of New York resolution for which the text is readily available and which bear bill numbers.

Summaries of the other kinds of resolutions can be found in the Senate and Assembly journals, in the ***Legislative Digest,*** and on LRS. The actual text of these resolutions is available only through the resolutions' sponsors or from the Senate or Assembly documents rooms. These resolutions have a detailed classification system as follows:

J	Senate joint resolution
B	Senate concurrent resolution
C	Assembly concurrent resolution
E	Assembly resolution
K	Legislative resolution
R	Senate resolution
L	Assembly joint resolution

Despite this elaborate scheme, in the ***Legislative Digest*** the resolutions of each house are numbered chronologically without regard to the alphabetical categories listed above. The first few resolutions listed for each house in the ***Legislative Digest*** are the "housekeeping" resolutions. The remaining resolutions are labelled "L," a generic designation for resolutions to distinguish them from bills in the ***Legislative Digest.*** These single house resolutions labelled "L" generally are of a ceremonial or commemorative nature. Summaries of these resolutions on LRS contain the classification designations shown above.

6. GLOSSARY

The following glossary of terms used in connection with New York bills is adapted primarily from Baaklini and Dawson's ***The Politics of Legislation in New York State***[40] and from the Senate and Assembly rules. For a humorous look at Albany's legislative jargon, see S. Weisman's "A Must List That Will Fly for Cliche Lovers."[41]

carryover bills — bills remaining "alive" (active) from the first annual (regular) session of the two-year legislative term to the second year's session, which eliminates the need to reintroduce and reprint bills.

chapter amendments — bills amending recently enacted bills, bills signed into law by the governor, or bills about to be enacted or signed, which are introduced when it is necessary to correct an oversight in the original bills or to make a change to insure legislative passage and/or gubernatorial approval.

companion bills — otherwise identical bills that are introduced and sponsored, numbered, and printed separately in each house. They may be individually or multi-sponsored.

co-sponsored or uni-bills — identical bills simultaneously introduced in both houses as one bill. They are only printed once, with the names of the Senate sponsor(s) and Assembly sponsor(s) and joint bill numbers appearing on the front of the bill.

[40] BAAKLINI & DAWSON, *supra* note 28, at 32-33, 91.
[41] N.Y. Times, June 7, 1976, at 13, col. 1.

enabling bills — bills which create a body or authorize an activity.

engrossed bills — bills which passed both houses and whose passage was certified by the appropriate officer of each house and which are jacketed and ready for transmission to the governor for approval.

home rule bills — bills which affect one or more but not every member of a class of municipality (county, city, town, or village) and which must be accompanied by a home rule request at introduction. Home rule legislation is discussed in Chapter 11.

licensing bills — bills which call for state or local regulation of an occupation or activity and possibly specify a fee and other requirements.

one-house bills — bills that for political reasons can only reasonably be expected to pass one house. These bills are most common when houses are split (controlled by an opposing political party).

private bills — bills introduced by a legislator which deal with limited concerns affecting one or more individuals.

program or department bills — bills which originate in the executive branch but must be sponsored by a legislator or committee.

starred bills — bills on which legislative action is suspended.

study bills — bills introduced for discussion or other purposes without intent to pass them immediately or at all.

ten day bills — bills passed by the legislature and transmitted to the governor during the regular legislative session; the governor has ten days in which to act upon such bills.

thirty day bills — bills passed by the legislature during the last ten days of its session; the governor has 30 days in which to act upon such bills. If the governor does not approve a thirty day bill, it is pocket-vetoed.

three-fifths bills — bills imposing, continuing, or reviving a tax, creating a debt or appropriating money. A quorum of three-fifths of the elected membership in each house is required for passage.

two-thirds bills — bills appropriating public money or property for local or private purposes. Passage of these bills requires a two-thirds vote in each house.

two-year bills — same as carryover bills.

REFERENCES

Baaklini, A. I. and C. S. Dawson. ***The Politics of Legislation in New York State: how a bill becomes a law.*** Albany: Comparative Development Studies Center, Graduate School of Public Affairs, State University of New York at Albany and the New York State Assembly, 1979.

Formalities of Enactment and Approval. Chap. in ***McKinney's Consolidated Laws of New York Annotated.*** Book 1, Statutes. St. Paul, Minn.: West Publishing Co., 1971.

Givens, R. ***A Primer on the New York State Legislative Process: How it Differs From Federal Procedure.*** 57 New York State Bar Journal 8 (April, 1985).

New York Jurisprudence 2d. Statutes. Rochester, N.Y.: Lawyers Cooperative Publishing Company (1967 & 1987 Supp.).

New York (State). ***The New York Red Book.*** Albany: Williams Press, 1986. (Annual).

Pimsleur's Checklists of Basic American Legal Publications. Ed. by M. Zubrow. Section I, Session Laws. Littleton, Co.: Fred B. Rothman, 1962- .

Zimmerman, J.F. ***The Government and Politics of New York State.*** New York: New York University Press, 1981.

Chapter Three
STATE LEGISLATION: Revisions and Compilations of New York Legislation from 1638-1950

1. OVERVIEW

Probably the lawyer's most essential need is access to a reliable, logically arranged compilation of the legislation currently in effect for his or her state. Today, New York researchers are served by no fewer than four printed compilations and one online data base[1] containing the Consolidated Laws of New York.[2] This abundance of sources for New York statutes is not new. New York lawyers, legislators and publishers have struggled mightily from the colonial period to publish usable, current editions of New York laws. Those efforts have produced the daunting list of statutory compilations, revisions, successive editions, and supplements which are the subject of this Chapter.

An evolving pattern of publication can be discerned in the mass of titles listed in Sections 2 and 3 of this chapter. This section traces that evolving pattern of publication from the initial practice of merely compiling all of the statutes in chronological order, through statutory revision of increasing complexity, and finally, in this century, to the development of our current compilation, the Consolidated Laws of New York.

[1] The Consolidated Laws of New York are available online in the Legislative Retrieval System (LRS). Mead Data Central projects that the Consolidated Laws will once again be available on LEXIS during 1988. The West Publishing Company projects that the Consolidated Laws will become available on WESTLAW in 1988.

[2] The printed compilations are described in Chapter 4.

a) Chronological Compilations. The ***Bradford Laws*** represented the first attempt by a contemporary publisher to compile and print all of the laws from several sessions together. William Bradford, public printer to the colony, compiled the acts of the colonial assembly for the years 1691-1694 in chronological order. He published subsequent, cumulative editions in 1710, 1713, 1719 and 1726.

The earliest laws of the New York colonial period were not systematically collected and arranged in chronological order until much after the fact. These collections are: ***Laws and Ordinances of New Netherland, 1638-1674*** (translated from the Dutch and published in 1868); ***Earliest Printed Laws of New York, 1665-1693*** (published by M. Glazier, Inc. in 1978); and ***Colonial Laws of New York, 1664 to the Revolution*** (published by the state printer, J.B. Lyon, in 1894).

Holt's Session Laws were the first compiled session laws printed after the Revolution. They contained all of the session laws of the new state passed in the years 1777-1783. Later, a compilation of all the session laws from 1777-1801 was authorized by chapter 341 of the Laws of 1885. It was printed in 1886-1887.

b) Edited Chronological Compilations. A more sophisticated compilation pattern than the examples mentioned above appeared in 1719 when the ***Baskett Laws*** were published. John Baskett's compilation contained the general and permanent acts of the colonial assembly that were in effect in 1718 in full text. Temporary, private, repealed and obsolete acts were listed by their title but were not printed in full. This editing resulted in a more convenient set of the statutes.

Following in the pattern developed with the ***Baskett Laws,*** subsequent chronological compilations of current, general laws included the ***Livingston and Smith Laws*** (laws of 1691-1762), ***Van Schaak's Laws*** (laws of 1691-1773), the ***Jones and Varick Revision*** (laws of 1777-1789), and the ***Greenleaf Session Laws*** (laws of 1777-1792).

c) The Revised Acts, Revised Laws and Revised Statutes. Revised laws, as that term was used in nineteenth century New York, were compilations of current statutes arranged by subject rather than by date passed. Revisers were directed by the legislature to comb through the session laws, compile the "live" law, edit the language when necessary, and present the revised laws to the legislature for re-enactment.

This procedure of revision produced the ***Kent and Radcliff Revision of 1801,*** also known as the Revised Acts of 1801, and the ***Van Ness and***

Woodworth Revision of 1813, also known as the Revised Laws of 1813. The ***Revised Statutes of 1827/28,*** also known as the Butler and Duer Revision, took the revision process a step farther by incorporating principles from the common law in the revised statutory law and by arranging the revised laws into five major divisions which were subdivided into chapters.[3] The ***Revised Statutes of 1827/28*** was the last official revision of New York's statutes until the incomplete revision of 1889-1900 produced the General Laws of New York.

Eight more editions of the ***Revised Statutes*** were published during the nineteenth century, but none of them were published by statutory authority or re-enacted by the legislature. Subject divisions became very unclear in these later editions, because the legislature was under no constraint to identify new enactments as amendments to the chapters of the ***Revised Statutes of 1827/28.*** Complicating the organization of the second through ninth editions of the ***Revised Statutes*** was the codification movement of the period which resulted in removing penal acts and civil and criminal procedure acts from the general statutes.[4]

Concern that the editions of the ***Revised Statutes*** were incomplete and no longer organized effectively for modern times led to the emergence of two more unofficial editions of the statutes. These compilations were: Edmond's ***Statutes at Large,*** first published in 1863, and Birdseye's ***Revised Statutes, Codes and General Laws of the State of New York,*** first published in 1889. Second and third editions of Birdseye followed in 1896 and 1901. Those editions of Birdseye reflected the revisions of the last decade of the century, known as the General Laws of New York, which are described below.

d) General Laws of New York. Sixty years after the last official statutory revision (the ***Revised Statutes of 1827/28*** went into effect in 1829) the 1889 legislature created a Statutory Revision Commission[5] to completely review and revise the general laws of the state and to present its proposed revisions to the legislature. The Commission decided to call the new revision the General Laws of New York to distinguish it from the Revised Acts, Revised Laws, and Revised Statutes.

[3] The five parts were: I. Territory, Political Divisions, Civil Polity, and the Internal Administration of the State; II. Property (real and personal), Domestic Relations, and Private Rights; III. Judiciary, Civil Procedure; IV. Crimes, Punishments, and Criminal Procedure; and V. Miscellaneous and Local Laws.

[4] The practice codes are described in Chapter 8 (Practice and Procedure Acts, Evidence, and Court Rules).

[5] 1889 N.Y. LAWS ch. 289.

Forty-eight general laws, called chapters, were proposed by the Statutory Revision Commission and enacted by the legislature between 1889 and 1897. Fifty-one bills were submitted to the 1900 legislature, but only four were passed. The failed bills would have added four additional chapters to the General Laws, amended the existing chapters, and codified various areas of the law, including evidence. Despite the unfinished state of the project of statutory revision, the legislature disbanded the Statutory Revision Commission in 1900.[6]

While the Statutory Revision Commission did not succeed in producing a complete revision of the statutes, it did establish a procedure for orderly amendment of statutes that is known as continuous consolidation. This is described in detail in succeeding paragraphs describing the Consolidated Laws.

The General Laws of New York were never published by authority of the State. There were three unofficial editions: Heydecker's ***General Laws and Revised Statutes*** (editions in 1899 and 1901), Cumming and Gilbert's ***General Laws and Other General Statutes of the State of New York,*** and the second and third editions of Birdseye's ***Revised Statutes,*** which appeared in 1896 and 1901. The ninth edition of the ***Revised Statutes,*** published in 1899, also included the General Laws. These unofficial versions of New York's "live" statutory law had to encompass the General Laws, the unrepealed Revised Statutes, general laws included in neither the Revised Statutes nor the General Laws, and the stream of new amendments to the General Laws. The Birdseye edition of the Revised Statutes included the civil and criminal practice and penal codes; the Heydecker and Cumming & Gilbert editions did not.

e) Consolidated Laws of New York. When the Statutory Revision Commission was abolished in 1900, the legislature established a Joint Committee on Statutory Revision Bills to build upon the work of the Commission and to report its recommendations concerning statutory revision to the legislature in 1901. Its report is printed as Assembly Document No. 72 (1901). Work on statutory revision continued in the legislature until, in 1904, the legislature created a Board of Statutory Consolidation[7] to undertake what has turned out to be New York's last comprehensive, official statutory revision. The Board chose selected lawyers throughout the state to perform a page-by-page examination of the session laws in order to discover all "live," permanent laws of a

[6] 1900 N.Y. LAWS ch. 664.
[7] 1904 N.Y. LAWS ch. 664.

general nature enacted since 1777. The Board's goal was to make the new compilation so accurate and complete that resort to session laws enacted in the past would be totally unnecessary. The Consolidated Laws were to form "a basis for a new starting point in general substantive legislation"[8] in the state.

The Board of Statutory Consolidation reported sixty-one chapters of the Consolidated Laws to the legislature. Forty-nine of these chapters bore the names of existing General Laws. Massive schedules of repeal accompanying the Board's report identified the disposition of every general law and also indicated where "live" general law was distributed in the proposed Consolidated Laws. These schedules are included as supplements to the 1909 ***Report of the Board of Statutory Consolidation.***

The proposed chapters did not include the codes of civil procedure and criminal procedure or the Condemnation Law, although chapter numbers were reserved for them. It was expected that those laws would be brought into the Consolidated Laws at a later time.[9] Fifty-nine of the proposed sixty-one chapters were passed by the legislature in 1909. The remaining two chapters, the Railroad Law and the Public Service Commission Law, were passed in 1910.[10]

To eliminate the need for further mass revision, the process of continuous consolidation, first adopted in connection with the General Laws, was continued with the Consolidated Laws. Each new bill that proposes to amend or repeal a section of one of the Consolidated Laws, or which proposes to add a new section, must clearly identify the law and section affected as part of its text. When that bill becomes law, there is no question where its provisions will be distributed among the Consolidated Laws. While the system is not perfect, it allows piecemeal revision of particular Consolidated Laws when there is sufficient political pressure to do so; no longer is the legislature and the law publishing community faced with the cumbersome and very expensive job of periodically revising and re-enacting the entire mass of New York's statutory law.

The state undertook to publish the ***Consolidated Laws of New York*** only once, in 1909/10. Since 1909/10, various commercial publishers have provided both annotated and unannotated versions of the Consolidated Laws.

[8] 1 REPORT OF THE BOARD OF STATUTORY CONSOLIDATION v (1909).

[9] The Code of Civil Procedure eventually was revised as the Civil Practice Act in 1920, which was in turn revised as the Civil Practice Law and Rules in 1962. The Code of Criminal Procedure was revised as the Criminal Procedure Law in 1971. The Condemnation Law was merged into the Eminent Domain Procedure Law in 1977.

[10] Today, the Consolidated Laws contain 89 Chapters. The names of the current Consolidated Laws are listed in section 8 of Chapter 4.

f) The Bibliography of Statutory Revision in New York. The most exhaustive record of the revisions and compilations of New York's statutory law is found in ***Pimsleur's Checklists of Basic American Legal Publications.***[11] A "Bibliography of Codification and Statutory Revision" and an essay entitled "Statute Law in New York from 1609 to 1901" are included in supplements to the ***Report*** of the New York Legislature's Joint Committee on Statutory Revision Bills.[12] John T. Fitzpatrick, when he was Law Librarian of the State Law Library, wrote a bibliographical essay entitled ***Revisions and Compilations of the Laws of New York*** in 1919[13] and another entitled ***Revised Statutes of 1826*** in 1921.[14] Still another treatment of this subject is found in the 1909 ***Report*** of the Board of Statutory Consolidation.[15] The history of New York's statutory revision is included in the excerpted Board of Statutory Consolidation's ***Report*** in ***McKinney's*** Book 1 (Statutes).[16]

The remaining sections of this Chapter provide full bibliographic information for the most important compilations and revisions of New York's statutory law until 1950. The compilations and revisions are listed in chronological order according to the time period included in the compilation rather than by date of publication. When compilations or revisions are known generally by a popular name or short title, the popular name or short title precedes the entry and is enclosed in quotation marks.

Some of New York's early statutory compilations are included in the Library of Congress microfilm series, ***Records of the States of the United States of America,*** New York Section. These are identified by "L.C." followed by class designation (B for Codes and Compilations) and reel number, e.g., L.C. B: Reel 2.

[11] 1 PIMSLEUR'S CHECKLISTS OF BASIC AMERICAN LEGAL PUBLICATIONS, edited by M. Zubrow. (1962-) This checklist is Publication No. 4 of the American Association of Law Libraries. It is published by the Fred B. Rothman Company of Littleton, Colorado.

[12] New York (State). Joint Committee on Statutory Revision Commission Bills. ***Report.*** 41-116, 126-167 (1901). (Assembly Document No. 72).

[13] 12 LAW LIBR. J. 21 (July, 1919).

[14] 19 LAW LIBR. J. 72 (1921).

[15] 1 REPORT OF THE BOARD OF STATUTORY CONSOLIDATION v-li (1909).

[16] MCKINNEY'S CONSOLIDATED LAWS OF NEW YORK ANNOTATED, Book 1, Statutes, vii-xxxvii (1971).

2. COLONIAL PERIOD, 1638-1775

New Netherland.

Laws and Ordinances of New Netherland, 1638-1674. Compiled and translated from the original Dutch records in the office of the secretary of state, Albany, N. Y., by E. B. O'Callaghan. Albany, N.Y.: Weed, Parsons and company, printers, 1868.

"The Duke's Laws"
New York (Colony)

...East-Hampton book of laws. June y 24th, 1665.

This compilation contains the laws introduced under the government of the Duke of York. These are reprinted in *Colonial Laws of New York* and in *The Earliest Printed Laws of New York, 1665-1693.*

"Earliest Laws of New York"
New York (Colony)

The Earliest Printed Laws of New York, 1665-1693, with an editorial note by John D. Cushing. Wilmington, Del: Michael Glazier, Inc., 1978. (Colony Laws of North America Series).

This facsimile volume contains: Laws and Acts of the General Assembly for their Majesties Province of New York, 1691-93 (the first printing of the "Bradford Laws"); A Catalogue of Fees Established by the Governour & Council, 1693; First Grant to the Duke of York, 1664; Second Grant to the Duke of York, 1674; and the Duke of York's Laws, 1665-75.

"The Bradford Laws"
New York (Colony)

The laws of Her Majesties colony of New York, as they were enacted by the governour, Council and General assembly for the time being, in divers sessions, the first of which began April the

9th, annoq; Dom. 1691.... to the 12th of November, 1709. [New York] Printed by William Bradford, printer to the Queens Most Excellent Majesty for the colony of New York, 1710.

L.C. B: Reel 2.

William Bradford was public printer to the colony. The edition listed here is the second edition of the Bradford Laws. The first edition included the laws of the assembly for the years 1691-1694. Later compilations were published by Bradford in 1713 (laws of 1691-1712), 1719 (laws of 1691-1719), and 1726 (laws of 1691-1725).

"The Baskett Laws"
New York (Colony)

Acts of the assembly, passed in the province of New York from 1691 to 1718. London. Printed by J. Baskett, printer to the king, 1719.

L.C. B: Reel 2.

In this compilation, only those laws still in force were printed in full text. The Baskett Laws was the first collection to reprint the current law in full but to include temporary, private, expired, repealed and obsolete laws by title only.

"Livingston and Smith Laws"
New York (Colony)

Laws of New York, from the year 1691 to 22d May 1762 inclusive. Published according to an act of the General assembly ... New York, Printed by James Parker, 1752-62. 2 volumes. Volume 2 has imprint: New York, Printed by William Weyman.

L.C. B: Reel 2.

Compiled by William Livingston and William Smith. This was the first compilation in which the compilers assigned a chronological chapter number to each act included.

"Van Schaak's Laws"
New York (Colony)

Laws of New York from the year 1691 to 1773 inclusive. Published according to an act of the General assembly .... New York, Printed by Hugh Gaine. 1774.

Compiled by Peter Van Schaack. Like the Livingston and Smith compilation, the Van Schaak Laws are arranged by chapter number.

"The Colonial Laws of New York"
New York (Colony)

Colonial Laws of New York from the Year 1664 to the Revolution, including the charters to the Duke of York, the commissions and instructions to colonial governors, the Duke's laws, the laws of the Dongan and Leisler assemblies, the charters of Albany and New York and the acts of the colonial legislatures from 1691 to 1775 inclusive ... Transmitted to the Legislature by the Commissioners of statutory revision pursuant to chapter 125 of the laws of 1891. Albany: J. B. Lyon, state printer, 1894.

The Colonial Laws follow the VanSchaak arrangement using chapter numbers. Index features allow tracing of each law's history.

3. REVISIONS AND COMPILATIONS PUBLISHED FROM THE REVOLUTION TO 1950

"Holt's Session Laws"
New York (State).

Laws of the State, commencing with the First Session of the Senate and Assembly, after the Declaration of Independence, and the Organization of the New Government of the State, Anno 1777. Printed by John Holt. Poughkeepsie, N.Y.: 1784.

L.C. B: Reel 4.

Holt's Session Laws contains laws from the 1st session, 1777, through the 5th session, 1783. The laws of each session are arranged in chronological order by chapter number. Session laws from the 6th session (1783) and 7th session (1784) are appended.

"Jones and Varick Revision"
New York (State)

Laws of the state of New York, comprising the Constitution, and the acts of the Legislature since the Revolution, from the first to the twelfth session, inclusive. Published according to an act of the Legislature, passed the 15th April, 1786... Printed by Hugh Gaine. New York: 1789.

L.C. B: Reel 4.

This revision contains the general statutes passed by the state legislature, arranged in chronological order, with an appendix containing the acts of the colony which "Are most necessary to be known."

By chapter 35 of the Laws of 1786, Samuel Jones, a member of the Assembly, and Richard Varick, the Speaker of the Assembly, were charged to collect, organize and revise the colonial laws and laws of the new state so that in the final product "none of the statutes of England or of Great Britain shall operate or be considered as laws of this State."

For an argument that the Jones and Varick revision not only accomplished this charge but also imported English law not before known in the colony, see Mark De Wolfe Howe's article entitled ***The Process of Outlawry in New York: a Study of the Selective Reception of English Law***, 23 Cornell L. Q. 559 (1937/38).

"Greenleaf Session Laws"
New York (State)
Laws of the state of New York, comprising the constitution, and the acts of the legislature, since the Revolution, from the first to the fifteenth session, [1777-1792] inclusive ... New York, Greenleaf, 1792.

The Greenleaf Session Laws contained session laws in force, "no notice being taken of those which are either repealed, expired, or obsolete; and this is the Reason why the Chapters do not always follow in regular Succession."

In 1797 a third volume extended the coverage of the Greenleaf Session Laws through the 20th session, 1797.

New York (State)
Laws of the State, 1777-1801. (Reprinted). Albany, New York: 1886-1887.

This reprint of the session laws was authorized by chapter 341 of the Laws of 1885.

"Kent and Radcliff Revision" or "Revised Acts of 1801"
New York (State)
Laws of the state of New York. Published by authority ... Albany: Printed by Charles R. and George Webster, 1802.

The Kent and Radcliff Revision is New York's first attempt at consolidating and re-enacting law in force. James Kent and Jacob Radcliff were authorized to undertake the revision by chapter 70 of the Laws of 1800. Publication was authorized by chapter 194 of the Laws of 1801.

"Van Ness and Woodworth Revision" or "Revised Laws of 1813"
New York (State)
Laws of the state of New York, revised and passed at the 36th session of the Legislature, with marginal notes and references, furnished by the revisors, William P. Van Ness and John Wood-

worth ... pursuant to the act, entitled "An act for publishing the laws of this state," passed April 13th, 1813. Albany: Southwick, 1813.

This revision was authorized by chapter 150 of the Laws of 1811.

"Revised Statutes of 1827-28" or the "Butler and Duer Revision"
New York (State)

The revised statutes of the state of New York, passed during the years one thousand eight hundred and twenty-seven, and one thousand eight hundred and twenty-eight: to which are added, certain former acts which have not been revised. Printed and published under the direction of the revisers [John Duer, B. F. Butler, and John C. Spencer] ... Albany, Printed by Packard and Van Benthuysen, 1829.

This is the first of nine editions of the Revised Statutes and the only one of them undertaken by statutory authority. Revision was authorized by chapter 336 of the Laws of 1824. This revision was necessitated by statutory changes following the 1821 revision of the New York Constitution.

"Revised Statutes, 2nd Edition (1836)"
New York (State)

The revised statutes of the state of New York, as altered by the Legislature; including the statutory provisions of a general nature, passed from 1828 to 1835 inclusive, with references to judicial decisions: to which are added, certain local acts passed before and since the revised statutes; all the acts of general interest passed during the session of 1836; and an appendix, containing extracts from the original reports of the revisers to the Legislature, all the material notes which accompanied those reports, and explanatory remarks. Prepared by and published under the superintendence of the late revisers [John Duer, B. F. Butler, John C. Spencer] ... 2nd ed. Albany, Printed by Packard and Van Benthuysen, 1836.

"Revised Statutes, 3rd Edition (1846-48)"
New York (State)

The revised statutes of the state of New York, as altered by subsequent enactments: together with statutory provisions of a general nature, passed between the years 1828 and 1845 inclusive, arranged in connection with the same or kindred subjects in the revised statutes; with notes of decisions by the courts upon the provisions contained in the text. Prepared by John Duer, B. F. Butler, and John C. Spencer, late revisers of the statutes... 3d ed. Albany: W. C. Little and Co., 1846-48.

"Revised Statutes, 4th Edition (1852)"
New York (State)

The revised statutes of the state of New York, as altered by subsequent legislation; together with the unrepealed statutory provisions of a general nature, passed from the time of the revision to the close of the second session of the Legislature in 1851... to which are added, all acts of general interest passed during the session of 1852, with references to judicial decisions in relation to their provisions, and explanatory notes. Prepared by Hiram Denio and William Tracy, 4th ed. Albany: Gould, Banks & Co.; New York: Banks, Gould & Co., 1852.

"Revised Statutes, 5th Edition (1859)"
New York (State)

The revised statutes of the state of New York, as altered by subsequent legislation, together with the unrepealed statutory provisions of a general nature, passed from the time of the revision to the close of the session of the Legislature of 1858... to which are added references to judicial decisions in relation to their provisions, and explanatory notes. Prepared by Amasa J. Parker, George Wolford and Edward Wade, 5th ed. Albany: Banks & Brothers, 1859.

"Edmonds' Statutes" or "Statutes at Large (1863)"
New York (State)

Statutes at large of the state of New York, comprising the Revised statutes as they existed on the 1st day of July, 1862, and all the general public statutes then in force, with reference to judicial decisions, and the material notes of the revisers in their report to the Legislature. Edited by John W. Edmonds... Albany, N.Y.: W.C. Little, 1863.

Judge Edmonds attempted to disentangle New York's mass of legislation by separating the Revised Statutes, together with the text of only those changes expressly denominated as amending the Revised Statutes, from the codes and other general legislation.

Judge Edmonds published a supplement to ***Statutes at Large*** in 1868 which covered the 1863-1866 sessions. A second edition of ***Statutes at Large*** was published in 1869 by Weed, Parsons & Company. In 1870, a supplement was published covering the 1867-1870 sessions. In 1875, Weed, Parsons & Co. published a supplement edited by Judge Edmonds and William Hildreth Field which covered the 1871-1874 sessions. The 1882 supplement was edited by A. G. Conant and covered the 1875-1880 sessions. The 1890 supplement was edited by J. C. Thomson and covered the 1881-1888 sessions.

"Revised Statutes, 6th Edition (1875)"
New York (State)

The revised statutes of the state of New York, as altered by subsequent legislation; together with the unrepealed statutory provisions of a general nature, passed from the time of the revision to the close of the session of the Legislature of 1875, arranged in the manner of the Revised Statutes. To which are added references to judicial decisions in relation to their provisions, and explanatory notes, and a full and complete index. Edited by George W. Cothran, 6th ed. Albany: Banks & Brothers, 1875.

"Revised Statutes, 7th Edition (1882)"
New York (State)

The revised statutes of the state of New York, as altered by subsequent legislation; together with the other statutory provisions of a general and permanent nature now in force, passed from the year 1778 to the close of the session of the Legislature of 1881, arranged in connection with the same or kindred subjects in the Revised Statutes; to which are added references to judicial decisions upon the provisions contained in the text, explanatory notes, and a full and complete index. Edited by Montgomery H. Throop, 7th ed. Albany: Banks & Brothers, 1882.

The 7th edition of the Revised Statutes omitted material deemed by Throop to be superseded by the 1881 Code of Criminal Procedure. A supplement to the 7th edition covering legislative sessions down to 1887 was published by J.C. Fowler in 1888.

"Revised Statutes, 8th Edition (1889)"
New York (State)

The revised statutes of the state of New York, as altered by subsequent legislation; together with the other statutory provisions of a general and permanent nature, (except the Code of Civil Procedure, the Code of Criminal Procedure, and the Penal Code), passed from the year 1778 to February 1, 1889, and now in force. Edited by Montgomery H. Throop. 8th ed. Albany: Banks, 1889-92.

Supplemental volumes covered the 1889-1892 sessions.

"Birdseye's Revised Statutes"
New York (State)

The revised statutes, codes and general laws of the state of New York. Containing the text, carefully compared with the original, of all the general statutory law of the state in force on January 1st, 1890, including the constitution of the state, the revised statutes, the codes of civil and criminal procedure and the penal code, alphabetically arranged by subjects, with references to the decisions, and with historical and explanatory notes and a complete system of cross references, supplemented with a full analytical index and table of the statutes contained herein. By Clarence F. Birdseye. New York: Strouse, 1889-90.

Arranging the laws alphabetically by subject represented still another attempt to bring order to New York's general laws and codes. A second edition of *Birdseye* was issued in 1896 (published by Baker) and a third edition was issued in 1901 (published by Baker, Voorhis & co.). Various supplements to each of the three editions were issued, the last of which covered the 1902-1905 sessions.

"Revised Statutes, 9th Edition (1896)"
New York (State)

The revised statutes of the state of New York, together with all the other general statutes, (except the civil, criminal and penal codes), as amended and in force on January 1, 1896. Ed. by Charles A. Collin. 9th ed. Albany: Banks & Brothers, 1896.

In this edition, the Revised Statutes were separated from the General Laws. Unrevised general statutes passed since 1777 were printed in chronological order.

"General Laws" (Heydecker)
New York (State)

General laws of New York, containing all amendments to the close of the session of 1900. Compiled and edited by Edward L. Heydecker. With topical and alphabetical index and Appendix of all general (uncodified) acts now in force, by titles. Albany: M. Bender, 1900.

The General Laws were the first state-authorized revision of the statutes in 60 years. The first edition of Heydecker contained the 46 chapters of the General Laws that had been passed by the legislature by 1900. An appendix contained all other general statutes in effect but not included in the General Laws. This included unrepealed fragments of the Revised Statutes. A second edition of Heydecker was published in 1901.

"General Laws" (Cumming and Gilbert)
New York (State)

The general laws and other general statutes of the state of New York, annotated, as amended and in force January 1, 1902. Containing the federal and state constitutions, the general laws and other general statutes, except the Civil, Penal and Criminal Codes. [Certified by the secretary of state as correct transcripts of the original laws.] With index and table of laws; compiled and annotated by Robert C. Cumming and Frank B. Gilbert. New York: The Banks Law Publishing Co., 1901.

Cumming and Gilbert were experienced legal editors who had served as assistants to the Statutory Revision Commission. Supplements to Cumming and Gilbert were issued in 1902, 1904 [some copies have a 1905 imprint] and 1906, all published by the Banks Law Publishing Company.

Consolidated Laws (1909)
New York (State)

The consolidated laws of the state of New York, prepared pursuant to Laws of 1904, chapter 664 by the Board of statutory consolidation, passed at the 132nd session of the Legislature begun Jan. 6, 1909, and ended April 30, 1909, in the city of Albany, as amended by the Legislature of 1909, together with the Public Service Commisions Law and the Railroad Law and published by the state under supervision of the Board, pursuant to Laws 1909, chapter 458. Official edition. Albany: Lyon, 1909-1910.

The term "Consolidated Laws" was adopted to distinguish this consolidation of New York's general statutes from the Revised Acts, Revised Laws, Revised Statutes, and General Laws which preceded it. It was the last general revision of the New York laws in the twentieth century.

Consolidated Laws of New York (Wadhams)
New York (State)

The consolidated laws of the state of New York, 1909; prepared under the direction and control of the Board of Statutory Consolidation, composed of Adolph J. Rodenbeck, William B. Hornblower, John G. Milburn and Adelbert Moot, comprised in 59 chapters, and the Public Service Commissions Law and the Railroad Law, constituting all the general statutory law of the state of New York, except that contained in the Code of Civil Procedure and Code of Criminal Procedure ... Edited by Frederick E. Wadhams ... With a complete analytical index, and the constitution of the state of New York. New York: The American Law Book Company, 1909.

"Birdseye's Cumming and Gilbert's" Consolidated Laws of New York Annotated

New York (State)

Annotated consolidated laws of the State of New York as amended to January 1, 1910 containing also the federal constitution with notes of Board of Statutory Consolidation, tables of laws and index. Edited by Clarence F. Birdseye, Robert C. Cumming and Frank B. Gilbert. New York: Banks Law Publishing Company, Baker, Voorhis & Co.; Albany: Matthew Bender & Co., 1909.

A second edition of Birdseye's Cumming & Gilbert was published in 1918. The set was supplemented periodically until 1925.

Consolidated Laws (Wadhams)

New York (State)

The consolidated laws of the state of New York passed at the one hundred and thirty-third session of the Legislature begun January 5, 1910, and ended May 27, 1910, in the city of Albany as amended by the Legislature of 1910 and published by the state under the supervision of Frederick E. Wadhams, secretary to the Board of Statutory Consolidation, pursuant to Laws 1910, chapter 373. Official ed. Albany: J.B. Lyon company, printers, 1910.

This edition contained technical corrections to the Consolidated Laws as passed in 1909 and also included the Public Service Commission Law and the Railroad Law, which passed in in 1910.

"McKinney's"

New York (State)

Consolidated laws of New York annotated as amended. Compiled under the editorial supervision of William M. McKinney. Northport, N.Y.: Edward Thompson Company, 1916-

Mr. McKinney was assisted in his editorial duties by Minor Bronaugh and Ralph Straub. The West Publishing Company acquired a majority interest in the Edward Thompson Company during the 1930's. Beginning in 1970, the West name replaced the Thompson name on newly issued ***McKinney's*** volumes. ***McKinney's*** is described in detail in Chapter 4 (State Legislation: Consolidated Law, Unconsolidated Laws, and Other Legislation).

"Cahill's Consolidated Laws"
New York (State)

Cahill's Consolidated laws of New York, being the Consolidated laws of 1909, as amended to July 1, 1923, compiled and edited by James C. Cahill. Chicago, Ill.: Callaghan and company, 1923.

A second edition was issued in 1930 and the work was supplemented until 1939.

"Baldwin's Consolidated Laws"
New York (State)

Baldwin's New York consolidated laws annotated, 1938, containing all laws to June 1, 1938. Edited by Edward Baldwin. Cleveland, Ohio: Banks, Baldwin Law Publishing Company, 1938.

This is a one-volume edition of the consolidated and unconsolidated laws that was also known as "Baldwin's Bluebook." The set was supplemented by ***Baldwin's New York Laws Service*** and a Decennial supplement. It ceased publication in 1948.

"Baldwin's Consolidated Laws Annotated"
New York (State)

Baldwin's Consolidated Laws annotated, lifetime edition. Cleveland, Ohio: Banks, Baldwin Law Publishing Company, 1938.

An 8-volume annotated set that was supplemented with pocket parts until 1943.

"Thompson's Laws"
New York (State)

Thompson's law of New York containing all laws of a general and permanent nature; consolidated, unconsolidated, criminal and civil practice, as well as miscellaneous related acts in force and effect January 4, 1939 with complete index and tables. Brooklyn, N.Y.: Edward Thompson Company, 1939.

Thompson's was designed to interact with *McKinney's* by providing an unannotated edition of the laws while *McKinney's* provided the annotated edition. Its index was very comprehensive and took up as many volumes as the 1939 volumes of the laws themselves. *Thompson's Laws* was updated annually until 1950.

"CLS or Consolidated Laws Service"
New York (State)

New York Consolidated Laws Service. Rochester, N.Y.: Lawyers Co-operative Publishing Company, 1950-

CLS was published as a looseleaf service from 1950-1975. The present hardbound format supplemented with pocket parts and cumulative pamphlets, was adopted in 1976. *CLS* is described in detail in Chapter 4.

REFERENCES

Fitzpatrick, J. T. *Revisions and Compilations of the Laws of New York.* 12 Law Library Journal 21 (July, 1919).

________*Revised Statutes of 1826.* 19 Law Library Journal 72 (1921).

New York (State). Board of Statutory Consolidation. *Report.* Albany: Lyon, 1909. (vol. 1, pp. v-li). Excerpted in *McKinney's Consolidated Laws of New York Annotated,* Book 1, Statutes (McKinney 1971) at vii-xxxvii.

New York (State) Legislature. Joint Committee on Statutory Revision Bills. ***Statute Law in New York from 1609 to 1901.*** Supp. to ***Report*** [of the Joint Committee]. Assembly Doc. No. 72 (1901).

Chapter Four
STATE LEGISLATION: Consolidated Laws, Unconsolidated Laws, and Other Legislation

1. CONSOLIDATED LAWS OF NEW YORK

a) Definition. The Consolidated Laws of New York make up New York's statutory "code" or statutory compilation. The terms "code" and statutory compilation as used in this chapter refer to sets of current statutes of a public, general, and permanent nature compiled from the session laws into subject areas. Statutory compilations provide ready access to the current laws. By contrast, session laws provide the text of the laws in chronological order exactly as they were passed in a particular year. Session laws do not reflect subsequent repeal or amendment.

b) Consolidation. The Consolidated Laws of New York were enacted in 1909/10. The process of consolidation in New York is described in section 1 of Chapter 3 (State Legislation: Revisions and Compilations of New York Legislation from 1638-1950). As is explained in Chapter 3, the Consolidated Laws of 1909 formed a new point of reference for New York's legislation. Since the Consolidated Laws of 1909 re-enacted all "live," permanent laws of a general nature enacted since 1777, it was no longer necessary to refer to earlier laws. Many current provisions of the Consolidated Laws were originally enacted before 1909, but the researcher will note that the historical notes in the annotated versions of the Consolidated Laws trace those laws back to the 1909 consolidation.

Since the enactment of the Consolidated Laws in 1909, whenever a law is enacted that affects one or more of the Consolidated Laws, the text of the session law contains the name, section(s) and subsection(s) of the affected Consolidated Laws. For example, chapter 210 of the 1985 Laws at section 1 provides:

> Subdivision three of section two hundred two-a of the town law, as amended by chapter five hundred nine of the laws of nineteen hundred fifty, is amended as follows...

This passage can be restated to read, "Section 1 of chapter 210, Laws of 1985, amends section 202-a(3) of the Town Law as follows... Section 202-a(3) was last amended by the Laws of 1950, ch. 509."

This process of embedding in the text of the chapter laws the citation to the new law's eventual location in the Consolidated Laws is called continuous consolidation. This process provides for orderly revision of the Consolidated Laws and forestalls the otherwise recurring need for expensive and disruptive general revision of the entire body of the laws.

New York's Consolidated Laws are compiled or consolidated into eighty-nine subject areas, called "laws." Examples of Consolidated Laws are: the Abandoned Property Law, the Business Corporation Law, and the General Municipal Law. The Consolidated Laws are subdivided into articles, sections and subsections.

In the years since the 1909 consolidation, many of the Consolidated Laws have been renamed, combined or eliminated. For example, when the Conservation Law was completely revised in 1972, it was renamed the Environmental Conservation Law. The Negotiable Instruments Law was repealed when the Uniform Commercial Code was adopted in 1964. The Estates, Powers and Trusts Law was created largely from the old Decedent Estate Law but also from parts of the Personal Property Law and the Real Property Law in 1967. The annotated versions of the Consolidated Laws, ***McKinney's Consolidated Laws of New York Annotated***[1] and ***New York Consolidated Laws Service,***[2] provide tables for revised Consolidated Laws that trace the section-by-section distribution of the old act or law into the new law.

Each Consolidated Law has a distinct chapter number. The chapter numbers of the Consolidated Laws bear no relation to the chapter numbers which arrange New York's chapter laws in chronological order in the session laws.[3] The chapter numbers of the Consolidated Laws originally arranged the names of the laws in alphabetical order.[4] That they no longer serve that purpose can be seen from the alphabetical list of the current eighty-eight Consolidated Laws found in section 8 of this Chapter. The chapter numbers do serve as a delimiter for statutory definitions. For example, when a term is defined "for purposes of this chapter," the researcher knows that the definition will operate within that Consolidated Law but may have another meaning when used in another chapter of the Consolidated Laws. The chapter numbers of the Consolidated Laws are not usually cited in legal writing.

Court acts are passed by the legislature but are not part of the Consolidated Laws of New York. Technically, they are included among the "unconsolidated" laws.[5] The four sets of the Consolidated Laws, discussed in section 1(c) below, include the court acts for the user's convenience. The court acts are:

Court of Claims Act	Uniform City Court Act
Family Court Act	Uniform District Court Act
New York City Civil Court Act	Uniform Justice Court Act
New York City Criminal Court Act	

1 Hereinafter ***McKinney's.***

2 Hereinafter ***CLS.***

3 Chapter laws and session laws are described in Chapter 2 (State Legislation: Legislative Process, Bills, Session Laws, and Resolutions).

4 The 61 original Consolidated Laws that passed in 1909/10 are listed by chapter number among the 64 chapters reported by the Board of Statutory Consolidation in ***McKinney's,*** Book 1 (Statutes) at xxvii-xxix.

5 Unconsolidated laws are described in section 3 of this Chapter.

The New York Constitution is also included in each of the four sets of the Consolidated Laws.

c) Publication of the Consolidated Laws of New York. Unlike the federal government and the governments of many states, New York does not publish a current, "official" edition of its statutory compilation. The last such effort was the publication of the original Consolidated Laws by the Board of Statutory Consolidation in 1909-10. With the advent of the Legislative Retrieval System,[6] the LRS online Consolidated Laws database could be said to approximate an "official" version in that it is maintained by statutory authority. However, it is not certified as containing the official text of the Consolidated Laws; the commercially published sets described in this section are so certified.

There are four comprehensive, unofficial sets of the Consolidated Laws: ***McKinney's Consolidated Laws of New York Annotated, New York Consolidated Laws Service, Michie's New York Consolidated Laws, and Gould's Consolidated Laws of New York.*** They are described below in the order in which their publication began.

(1) McKinney's Consolidated Laws of New York Annotated. Publication of ***McKinney's Consolidated Laws of New York Annotated*** by the Edward Thompson Publishing Company began in 1916. The West Publishing Company acquired a majority interest in the Edward Thompson Publishing Company during the 1930's. The West name replaced the Thompson name in all newly issued ***McKinney's*** volumes beginning in 1970. ***McKinney's*** is similar in format and features to the ***U.S. Code Annotated***, which is also published by the West Publishing Company.

Significant features of *McKinney's* are:

* annotations of federal and New York cases interpreting, construing or applying a section of a Consolidated Law, court act, or a selected unconsolidated law printed in McKinney's;

* cross references to ***West's McKinney's Forms;***

* annotated treatise on principles of New York statutory construction (in Statutes, Book 1);

[6] The Legislative Retrieval System [hereinafter LRS] is the New York statutory database created and maintained by the N.Y. Legislative Bill Drafting Commission. LRS is described in more detail in Chapter 12 (Databases for New York Legal Research).

* historical information on each section of the laws including source and derivation;

* signed practice commentaries that interpret the court acts and the Civil Practice Law and Rules (CPLR), Surrogate Court Practice Act (SCPA), Criminal Procedure Law (CPL), Estates, Powers and Trusts Law (EPTL), Domestic Relations Law (DRL), Business Corporation Law (BCL), and Environmental Conservation Law (ECL). The practice commentaries are essays by expert practitioners on practice under the particular section of the act or law. These commentaries sometimes include information on the section's legislative history;

* criminal sentencing pamphlet with references to the Criminal Procedure Law and Penal Law;

* references to West's legal encyclopedia, ***Corpus Juris Secundum (C.J.S.);***

* annual revision of the entire General Index;[7]

* research aids such as West topic and key numbers and references to articles in law reviews and legal periodicals;

* cross references to related federal and New York statutes, and the constitution;

* cross references to New York ***Official Compilation of Codes, Rules and Regulations (NYCRR);***

* distribution tables to aid tracing from old to new sections of a revised Consolidated Law;

* indexes to each title, court act, constitution (U.S. and N.Y.) at the end of those volumes; and

* popular name table at the end of the General Index.

[7] Until 1987, volumes of the ***McKinney's*** General Index were supplemented annually with pocket parts.

The West key numbers listed in ***McKinney's*** can lead the researcher to related cases in any West digest, including ***West's New York Digest 3d***[8] and can form the basis for a key number search on WESTLAW.

Method of Supplementing McKinney's

Each volume of ***McKinney's*** is updated annually by a pocket supplement (called a pocket part) issued in December, by interim cumulative pamphlets (called the Interim Annotation Service) issued in April and July, and by replacement volumes which are issued when the pocket parts for particular volumes become too cumbersome.

Updating Legislation Found in McKinney's

The pocket part for a ***McKinney's*** bound volume contains the text of legislation affecting the Consolidated Law in that bound volume down to the end of the last regular session of the legislature. For example, the 1987 pocket parts contained the legislation down to the end of the 1986 regular session of the legislature. The Interim Annotation Service pamphlets update the whole set of ***McKinney's.*** The April pamphlet contains legislation, if any, that passed after the end of the regular session of the legislature. For example, the April, 1987 Interim Pamphlet contained legislation that passed in the Extraordinary Session of the 1986 session of the legislature. To find whether a particular Consolidated Law is affected or amended by late-in-the-year legislation, consult the "Table of Consolidated Laws Affected" in the interim pamphlet.

To bring the search for the text of new statutes down to date, use the cumulative tables of Consolidated Laws affected that are found in either of the two advance session law services: ***McKinney's Session Law News of New York*** or ***Advance Legislative Service for the New York Consolidated Laws Service.***[9] The search for legislation in the current session of the legislature that affects a particular Consolidated Law can also be performed on LRS and Legi-Tech.[10]

[8] ***West's New York Digest 3d*** is described in detail in Chapter 7 (Court Reports and Case Finders).

[9] The advance session law services are described in section 4(f) of Chapter 2 (State Legislation: Legislative Process, Bills, Sessions Laws, and Resolutions).

[10] Legi-Tech is a statutory database that contains and tracks New York bills. Both LRS and Legi-Tech are described in detail in Chapter 12 (Databases for New York Legal Research.

Updating Annotations to Cases Found in McKinney's

The pocket parts for any bound *McKinney's* volume contain additional annotations that were reported after the cutoff point for the bound volume. The pocket part, too, has a cutoff point. The cutoff points are expressed as volume numbers of the court reports. For example, the cutoff point for the 1987 pocket parts was 502 N.Y.S.2d 668, 67 N.Y.2d, 117 A.D.2d, 131 Misc.2d, and so forth. Later annotations are found in the April and July Interim Annotation Service pamphlets, which also have cutoff points expressed as volume numbers of the court reports.

After using the pocket parts and making note of the cutoff point for the Interim Annotation Service pamphlets, further updating requires the use of court report advance sheets, *Shepard's Citations,* and database searching. Careful practice requires the use of all of the following methods:

* Use the statutory tables found in either the advance sheets for the official reports[11] or for *New York Supplement 2d* to identify cases construing particular Consolidated Laws. Start this process at the volume numbers immediately following the Interim Pamphlets' cutoff points;

* "Shepardize"[12] the statute. The most current paper supplements to *Shepard's New York Statute Citations* will identify recent cases that cite particular Consolidated Laws.[13]

* Use the statutory citation as a search term on LEXIS or WESTLAW.[14] The search can be limited by date so that only recent cases are located. On WESTLAW, the search could also utilize the West topic and key number associated with the Consolidated Law in *McKinney's.*

[11] The current, official New York court reports are: *New York Reports 2d, Appellate Division Reports 2d,* and *Miscellaneous Reports 2d.* One advance sheet reports new cases in all three of these reports. Current New York court reports are described in section 2 of Chapter 7 (Court Reports and Case Finders).

[12] "Shepardizing" a primary source, such as a statute or a case, is the process of verifying the statute's or case's current status by using the appropriate unit of *Shepard's Citations.* The appropriate unit for the Consolidated Laws is *Shepard's New York Statute Citations,* which is described in more detail in section 2 of this Chapter.

[13] *Shepard's New York Statute Citations* is described in section 2 of this Chapter.

[14] At this writing, it is not possible to Shepardize the Consolidated Laws using the *Shepard's* services on LEXIS and WESTLAW.

(2) New York Consolidated Laws Service Annotated Statutes With Forms (CLS). *New York Consolidated Laws Service Annotated Statutes With Forms (CLS)* is published by the Lawyers Co-operative Publishing Company of Rochester, New York. Publication of *CLS* in looseleaf format began in 1950. *CLS* changed to is present format using pocket part and pamphlet supplementation in 1976.

CLS is similar in format and features to *U.S. Code Service (U.S.C.S.),* which is also a Lawyers Co-operative publication.

Significant features of Consolidated Laws Service

* historical notes indicating the source and derivation of each section;

* contains legal forms directly related to the statutes;

* extensive cross references to the *NYCRR*, New York's administrative code;

* cross references to related federal and New York statutes;

* selected annotations of federal and New York cases interpreting the New York Constitution, consolidated and selected unconsolidated laws, and court acts;

* references to other Lawyers Co-op publications such as *New York Jurisprudence 2d, American Jurisprudence 2d, AmJur Pleading and Practice Forms, Carmody-Wait 2d, A.L.R., and AmJur Trials.* A *CLS* volume called "Statutory Guide" provides essentially the same references to Lawyers Co-operative Publishing Company publications in a handbook format;

* references to law review articles;

* references to jury instructions published by Lawyers Co-op.

Updating Legislation and Annotations Found in CLS

CLS volumes are updated annually by pocket parts issued in December, by an interim pamphlet, and by occasional bound replacement volumes. The interim pamphlet is called Midyear Statutory & Later Case Service, and it is issued in April. Like the ***McKinney's*** Interim Annotation Service pamphlets, the ***CLS*** Midyear Service pamphlet includes late-in-the-year legislation and new case annotations. The procedure for updating the ***CLS*** pocket parts and Midyear Service is essentially the same as the procedure described above for updating legislation and annotations in ***McKinney's***. The advance session law service coordinated with ***CLS*** is the ***Advance Legislative Service for the New York Consolidated Laws Service.***

Features of CLS and McKinney's Compared

A major difference between ***CLS*** and ***McKinney's*** is the number of annotations included in the respective sets. ***McKinney's*** contains more annotations, because it is the West Publishing Company's editorial policy that every case construing a Consolidated Law should be annotated in ***McKinney's. CLS*** contains fewer annotations, because it is the Lawyers Co-op's editorial policy that the attorney is best served by annotating only cases that are currently significant in ***CLS***. Because it includes fewer annotations, ***CLS*** takes up less shelf space than ***McKinney's*** does.

A second major difference between ***CLS*** and ***McKinney's*** is the number of cross references to the ***Official Compilation of Codes, Rules and Regulations (NYCRR)***. At this writing, ***CLS*** is a more comprehensive source for these cross references than is ***McKinney's.*** This ***CLS*** feature provides a useful entry point to the ***NYCRR,*** which is not well indexed.

A third major difference between these annotated sets is that ***CLS*** contains the official (and some unofficial) forms related to the court acts and Consolidated Laws. ***McKinney's*** does not contain forms. However, ***McKinney's*** does provide numerous cross references to a form set called ***West's McKinney's Forms***, which is available by separate subscription.

(3) Michie's New York Consolidated Laws. Michie's ***New York Consolidated Laws***[15] is an eight-volume, softbound, unannotated set of

[15] Hereinafter ***Michie's.***

the Consolidated Laws which began publication in 1987. It contains the text of the Consolidated Laws (arranged in alphabetical order), the court acts and the New York Constitution. The Michie Company, which is located in Charlottesville, Virginia, plans to issue a new edition annually. No intervening supplementation is planned.

(4) Gould's Consolidated Laws of New York. ***Gould's Consolidated Laws of New York***[16] is a nine-volume, unannotated set of the Consolidated Laws which, like ***Michie's*** also began publication in 1987. It contains the text of the Consolidated Laws, the court acts, and the New York Constitution. Unlike the other sets of the Consolidated Laws, ***Gould's*** does not print the Consolidated Laws in alphabetical order. Instead, they are grouped by subject.

Gould Publications, located in Binghamton, New York, makes this set available in either looseleaf or hardbound format. The publisher plans to issue a new edition annually with no intervening supplementation.

Gould also publishes selected, unannotated statutes. For example, the Gould ***Commercial Law Handbook*** contains the Uniform Commercial Code (with official comments) and other commercial statutes in one volume. One-volume statutory handbooks are also available from Matthew Bender & Co. and the West Publishing Company.

d) Databases Containing the Consolidated Laws. The Consolidated Laws are maintained on the LRS database as of this writing. Mead Data Central projects that the Consolidated Laws will once again be available online on LEXIS in 1988. The West Publishing Company projects that the Consolidated Laws will become available on WESTLAW in 1988. West also projects that the ***McKinney's*** annotations will be available on WESTLAW in the future.

e) Certification. Each of the four commercially published statutory compilations bears a joint certification signed by the Temporary President of the Senate and the Speaker of the Assembly that the text contained therein is accurate. Formerly, certification of statutes was the responsibility of the Secretary of State. The certification entitles the publication to be read into evidence pursuant to section 70-b of the Public Officers Law. The LRS Consolidated Laws database is not certified at this writing.

[16] Hereinafter ***Gould's.***

2. CITATORS

Shepard's New York Statute Citations provides information on the status of the Consolidated Laws. It provides citations to legislation, administrative opinions, judicial decisions, and selected periodicals and law reviews that cite the Consolidated Laws. Thus, ***Shepard's New York Statute Citations*** can be used to:

* check for amendment, repeal or addition of a section of the Consolidated Laws;

* locate New York and federal cases which cite a section of the Consolidated Laws and to quickly identify whether the constitutionality of the law was tested;[17]

* locate attorney general opinions which cite a section of the Consolidated Laws; and

* find a law review note citing a section of the Consolidated Laws.

The Consolidated Laws section[18] in ***Shepard's New York Statute Citations*** is arranged alphabetically by the name of the Consolidated Law, e.g., Abandoned Property Law, Agriculture and Markets Law, and then by section number and subsection number.

In order to fully appreciate the information conveyed in this unit of Shepard's, the researcher should study the detailed example found in that part of the ***Shepard's*** introductory material called "Illustrative Statutes." Note especially that the entry for a statutory section that has many subsections (called subdivisions in ***Shepard's***) first lists citations to the entire section and later lists citations to particular subdivisions. The researcher interested in a particular subdivision should not necessarily assume that citations to the whole section are without value.

Shepard's New York Statute Citations currently is printed in four bound volumes (three of which are called Supplements) plus several paperbound supplements. Every volume and supplement that chronologically could contain a particular law must be checked. For ex-

[17] Treatment of a section of the Consolidated Law in judicial decisions is analyzed using the following abbreviations: constitutionality upheld - "C"; held unconstitutional "U"; held unconstitutional in part - "Up."

[18] Other sections of this citator analyze citations to the U.S. and N.Y. Constitutions, local laws and the ***Official Compilation of Codes, Rules and Regulations.***

ample, a law that passed in 1976 need only be checked in volume 3 and the paperbound supplements, but a law that passed in 1935 must be checked in all of the volumes and supplements that cover the Consolidated Laws.

To a certain extent, the information provided in ***Shepard's New York Statutes Citations*** overlaps with information found in the ***McKinney's*** and *CLS* annotations and historical notes and in the statutory sections of the periodical indexes. In the case of very recent statutory change, LRS and Legi-Tech will provide the new law's citation before it appears in the ***Shepard's*** supplementary pamphlet. A properly constructed search on LEXIS or WESTLAW will locate a recent case construing a section of the Consolidated Laws before that case citation appears in the paper ***Shepard's*** supplement. Nonetheless, "Shepardizing" the statutory section is an essential step in legal research, and it almost always produces references not located through other research methods.

3. UNCONSOLIDATED LAWS

a) Definition. New York's unconsolidated laws are any laws passed by the legislature that are not part of the Consolidated Laws. This category includes court acts, the New York City Charter and Administrative Code, other special laws, and miscellaneous laws which don't "fit" the purview of the Consolidated Laws (or which didn't "fit" into the various statutory revisions which preceded enactment of the Consolidated Laws).

b) Publication of Current Unconsolidated Laws.

1) McKinney's Unconsolidated Laws. ***McKinney's*** Unconsolidated Laws is part of the ***McKinney's Consolidated Laws of New York*** set. The ***McKinney's*** editorial staff selects from the unconsolidated laws those laws that it deems to be of general interest and of a permanent nature. Those laws are grouped under unofficial titles and chapters which in turn are subdivided by unoffical section numbers. The usual ***McKinney*** editorial features (historical notes, annotations of cases and administrative decisions and library references) facilitate research. The volumes of the ***McKinney's*** Unconsolidated Laws have their own index and also are indexed in the General Index to ***McKinney's.***

Unconsolidated laws that are printed elsewhere in ***McKinney's,*** such as court acts, are not repeated in the unconsolidated laws volumes.

2) CLS Unconsolidated Laws. The *CLS* Unconsolidated Laws is part of the *New York Consolidated Laws Service*. Like the *McKinney's* Unconsolidated Laws volumes, the *CLS* volumes contain unconsolidated laws selected by the editors and arranged by unofficial titles, chapter numbers, and sections. The *CLS* Unconsolidated Laws titles, chapter numbers, and sections bear no relation to those found in *McKinney's* Unconsolidated Laws. The unconsolidated laws are indexed at the back of the last volume of unconsolidated laws and in the *CLS* General Index.

3) Laws of New York. The most comprehensive source for unconsolidated laws is the official session laws, *Laws of New York*. Since the session laws are annual and have no cumulative indexing, the *McKinney's* and *CLS* volumes of unconsolidated laws are of more practical use. However, as noted previously, *McKinney's* and *CLS* print only selected unconsolidated laws.

4) Legislative Retrieval System (LRS). The unconsolidated laws for the most recent two years are available online on LRS. Since there is no offical classification scheme for the unconsolidated laws, unconsolidated laws are retrievable in the LRS database by session law citation and not by either the *McKinney's* or the *CLS* classification system.

5) New York City Charter and Administrative Code. Three publishers currently publish the New York City Charter and Administrative Code. They are Williams Press, Lenz & Reicker, Inc., and Commerce Clearing House.

6) Court Acts. The Court Acts are included in all four current sets of the Consolidated Laws (*McKinney's, CLS, Michie's and Gould's*). They are also published with related practice statutes in various pamphlet editions described in Chapter 8 (Practice and Procedure Acts, Evidence and Court Rules).

c) Statutory Record of the Unconsolidated Laws, 1777-1928. The Board of Statutory Consolidation, after completing its project of consolidating New York's general laws and creating a statutory listing of all of the session laws that were incorporated into the Consolidated Laws, turned its attention to the "orphans" of statutory revision, the unconsolidated laws. The result was the *Statutory Record of the Unconsolidated Laws.*

The *Statutory Record* is a chronological listing in two massive volumes of all special, private and local laws enacted from February 1, 1778 to

January 1, 1912. This work was supplemented by two volumes which updated the *Statutory Record* to January 1, 1929. The supplemental volumes also included laws of a general nature which were not incorporated in the Consolidated Laws and which were enacted or amended between 1912 and 1928.

The *Statutory Record* captured the citations to the special, private, and local laws in one publication for the first time. For each law, it provides the citation to the *Laws of New York*, a brief description of the law, and citations to subsequent amending or repealing legislation. The *Official Index*, which gives subject access to the first three volumes of the *Statutory Record*, was published in 1920 by the Legislative Bill Drafting Commissioners. These publications were partially continued by New York *Local Laws*, which is discussed in Chapter 11 (Local Legislation).

4. THE EXECUTIVE BUDGET AND APPROPRIATION LEGISLATION

a) Executive Budget. Article VII of the New York Constitution governs State finances; implementing legislation is found in the State Finance Law. Preparation and presentation of the executive budget to the legislature are governed by sections one through three of article VII of the Constitution. The provision that suggests the desirability of a balanced budget is found in section 2 of article VII, which reads in pertinent part, "the governor shall submit to the legislature a budget containing a complete plan of expenditures proposed to be made before the close of the ensuing fiscal year and all moneys and revenues estimated to be available therefor...."[19]

The executive budget has been published annually by the governor's office since 1928/29. From 1928/29 to 1931/32, it was called ***Message From the Governor and the Budget Containing Financial Reports and Recommendations.*** Since 1932/33, the title has been ***The Executive Budget — State of New York.*** The executive budget was also collected in the *Legislative Documents* series until that series ceased publication in 1975. The governor's annual budget message to the legislature, which summarizes the executive budget, has been published separately as *State of New York Annual Budget Message* since 1962/63.

[19] N.Y. CONST. art. VII, sec. 2 (McKinney 1987).

b) Appropriation Bills. Each year, between mid-January and February 1, the governor submits the executive budget together with the related appropriation, revenue and other budget bills to the legislature. The governor also submits, with or without comment, the budget requests of the Legislature and the Judiciary. The legislature then has two months to work on the budget before the new fiscal year begins on April 1. Pursuant to section 23 of the Legislative Law, the budget bills, as well as all other bills that involve any appropriation from the State treasury, are referred to the Senate Committee on Finance and the Assembly Committee on Ways and Means.

Section 4 of article VII of the New York Constitution gives the legislature the power to strike out or reduce an item of appropriation in bills submitted by the governor. While the legislature can add other items of appropriation on other subjects, it cannot alter the governor's bills by replacing the governor's items with its own having the same object or purpose.

Appropriation items submitted by the governor become law once they are passed by both houses of the legislature. They do not have to go back to the governor for approval. Section 4 of article IV gives the governor a line-item veto over appropriation bills. This power encompasses legislative additions to the budget bills and all other appropriations proposed by the legislature.

Section 23 of article III of the New York Constitution requires a three-fifths quorum, a roll-call vote and a simple majority of the membership to pass an appropriation bill. Section 5 of article VII prohibits the legislature from considering any other appropriation bills until all appropriation bills submitted by the governor, either with the budget or by message of necessity, are finally acted upon.

Regarding appropriations other than those submitted by the governor and any supplemental appropriations for the support of the government, section 6 of article VII requires that "no appropriations shall be made except by separate bills each for a single object and purpose."[20] This provision is meant to eliminate "riders" unrelated to the subject of appropriation. It also ensures that a tremendous number of appropriations bills are passed in each term.

Section 7 of article VII prohibits spending state monies "except in pursuance of an appropriation by law."[21] It also requires that the appropria-

[20] N.Y. CONST. art. VII, sec. 6 (McKinney 1987).
[21] N.Y. CONST. art. VII, sec. 7 (McKinney 1987).

tion law shall "distinctly specify the sum appropriated, and the object or purpose to which it is to be applied."[22] This provision is meant to place a ceiling on expenditures for particular items, to limit transfering of funds between programs and departments in case of underexpenditure or overexpenditure, and to prevent the State from incurring indebtedness without an appropriation.

c) Publication of Appropriation Chapters. Budget and appropriation chapters are published annually in ***Laws of New York***, but they are not included in either the ***McKinny's*** or the ***CLS*** session laws.

All budget and appropriation chapters are also printed, together with comparative data on previous appropriations, in a publication called the "Black Book." The Black Book is compiled by the the Assembly Ways and Means Committee and the Senate Finance Committee. Its current official name is ***Classification of Appropriations by the Legislature of 19—***. Its titles over the years were: ***Appropriations***, (1919-1921); ***Financial Plan for the General Budget and Classification of Appropriations Made By the Legislature,*** (1922-1929); ***Classification of Appropriations,*** (1930); and ***Appropriations and Reappropriations,*** (1940-1945). The Black Book has been published under its current title since 1946.

LRS contains the budget chapters for the most recent two years, and its budget database serves as an online "Black Book."

The ***Report of the Fiscal Committees on the Executive Budget***, known popularly as the "Green Book," is an analysis of the executive budget produced annually by the Assembly Ways and Means and Senate Finance Committees. It expresses the legislature's budgetary findings. The findings are guidelines for administrative application for the forthcoming fiscal year. Similar reports are also issued concerning the supplemental and any deficiency budgets. The ***State of New York Budget Summary***, published by the Division of the Budget, is a mid-year evaluation of progress toward meeting the goals set forth in the governor's executive budget. This report was called ***Budget Summary*** or ***New York State Budget*** from 1965/66-1981/82. In 1982/83 it was called ***New York State Mid-Year Report.***

d) Certification of Appropriation Laws. Sections 42 and 44 of the Legislative Law describe certification and presumptive evidence of certification of laws which pass into law without action by the governor pursuant to sections three and four of article VII of the New York Constitution.

[22] ***Id.***

5. UNIFORM LAWS

The National Conference of Commissioners on Uniform State Laws has, since 1912, promoted the drafting and adoption of uniform laws in areas of the law where similarity in the laws of the several states is seen to be desirable. A notable example of such a uniform law is the Uniform Commercial Code, which has been adopted in all 50 states.

New York's Commission on Uniform State Laws was established in 1952 by chapter 597 of the Laws of 1952. It consists of five members appointed by and serving at the pleasure of the governor. New York's commissioners participate in the annual National Conference of Commissioners on Uniform State Laws. The annual publication of the Conference, the ***Handbook of the National Conference of Commissioners on the Uniform State Laws,*** contains a summary of the year's activities and also contains the text of uniform laws not yet adopted by any state. The text of uniform laws that have been adopted by at least one state are printed in ***Uniform Laws Annotated,*** a multi-volume set published by the West Publishing Company.

a) Uniform Laws Annotated. The text of the uniform laws, as adopted by the National Conference of Commissioners, is printed in ***Uniform Laws Annotated.***[23] The text is annotated with Commissioners' notes and annotations of cases interpreting the uniform laws in the various states.

Few states adopt uniform laws verbatim as drafted by the Commissioners and as printed in the text of the ***U.L.A.***. For New York researchers, it is important to be able to locate the text of the uniform law as it actually was passed in New York and to understand how New York's version of the uniform law differs from the text as adopted by the National Conference of Commissioners. The ***U.L.A*** provides both of these pieces of information.

To find variations in wording adopted by New York, consult the annotations supplementing the ***U.L.A.*** text of each uniform law adopted by New York. For each section, the variations are listed in alphabetical order by state, including New York.

When New York adopts a uniform law, the law is printed in the New York session laws and in the Consolidated Laws. To find the citation to the Consolidated Laws for a particular uniform law, turn to the beginning of the text of that uniform law in the ***U.L.A.*** An alphabetical list of states which have adopted some or all of that uniform law is printed

[23] Hereinafter *U.L.A.*

there. It identifies the citations in the states' statutory compilations where the uniform law is codified. Since New York is an adopting state, the list will contain the Consolidated Laws citation.

A complete survey of uniform laws adopted in New York can be found in the alphabetical list of the states printed in the index pamphlet for the *U.L.A.* The entry for New York indicates which of the uniform laws that are printed in the *U.L.A.* have been adopted by New York. This entry does not give citations to the Consolidated Laws; only the list found at the beginning of the text for each uniform law in *U.L.A.* provides that information.

b) Using Consolidated Laws Indexes to Locate Uniform Laws. The easiest method for locating the Consolidated Laws citation for a particular uniform law is to use *U.L.A.*, as described above. The researcher should be aware that there is some variation between the names chosen for individual uniform laws by the National Conference of Commissioners and those chosen for use in New York. These variations and variations in the indexing practices of the four publishers of the Consolidated Laws make location of a uniform law through the indexes to *McKinney's, CLS, Michie's* and *Gould's* difficult.

In *McKinney's*, look both under the full title (starting with the word "uniform") and in the popular name table. In *CLS* and in the *Michie's*, omit the word "uniform" and look under the rest of the words in the title. When all else fails and the *U.L.A.* is not available, look for the uniform law using a subject approach in the indexes to the Consolidated Laws.

c) Uniform Laws and Model Acts Adopted in New York. The following list identifies uniform laws and model acts adopted as of this writing by New York and it provides their citation to the Consolidated Laws.

Anatomical Gift Act (Public Health Law secs. 4300 to 4308)

Attendance of Witnesses From Without a State in Criminal Proceedings, Act to Secure (Criminal Procedure Law sec. 640.10)

Child Custody Jurisdiction Act (Domestic Relations Law secs. 75-a to 75-z)

Commercial Code (Uniform Commercial Code secs. 1-101 to 13-105)

Controlled Substances Act (Public Health Law secs. 3300 to 3396)

Criminal Extradition Act (Criminal Procedure Law secs. 570.02 to 570.66)

Disposition of Community Property Rights at Death (Estates, Powers and Trusts Law secs. 6-6.1 to 6-6.7)

Enforcement of Foreign Judgments Act (1964 Act) (Civil Practice Law and Rules secs. 5401 to 5408)

Fiduciaries Act (General Business Law secs. 359-i, 359-*l)*

Foreign Money-Judgments Recognition Act (Civil Practice Law and Rules secs. 5301 to 5309)

Fraudulent Conveyance Act (Debtor and Creditor Law secs. 270 to 281)

Gifts to Minors Act (1966 Act) (Estates, Powers and Trusts Law secs. 7-4.1 to 7-4.13)

Insurers Liquidation Act (Insurance Law secs. 7408 to 7415)

Interstate Compromise of Death Taxes Act (Tax Law sec. 249-o)

Joint Obligations Act (Model) General Obligations Law secs. 15-101 to 15-110)

Limited Partnership Act (1916 Act) (Partnership Law secs. 1 to 74)

Management of Institutional Funds Act (Not-for-Profit Corporation Law secs. 102, 512, 514, 522)

Motor Vehicle Certificate of Title and AntiTheft Act (Vehicle & Traffic Law secs. 2101 to 2135)

Partnership Act (Partnership Law secs. 1 to 74)

Photographic Copies of Business and Public Records as Evidence Act (Civil Practice Law and Rules sec. 4539)

Principal and Income Act (1962 Act) (Estates, Powers and Trusts Law sec. 11-2.1)

Reciprocal Enforcement of Support Act (1950 Act) (Domestic Relations Law secs. 30 to 43)

Reciprocal Transfer Tax Act (Tax Law sec. 960-a)

Simplification of Fiduciary Security Transfers Act (General Business Law secs. 359-m to 359-w)

Simultaneous Death Act (Estates, Powers and Trusts Law sec. 2-1.6)

State Administrative Procedure Act (1961) (Model) (State Administrative Procedure Act sec. 100 *et. seq.)*

Testamentary Additions to Trusts Act (Estates, Powers and Trusts Law sec. 3-3.7)

Vendor and Purchaser Risk Act (General Obligations Law sec. 5-1311)

Voting by New Residents in Presidential Elections Act (Elections Law secs. 11-102 to 11-112)

Where the date of an act is noted above, several dated versions of a particular uniform law currently exist. The version adopted in New York is identified by its date. For example, New York has adopted the 1916 Uniform Limited Partnership Act. There is also a Revised Uniform Limited Partnership Act of 1976, as amended in 1985, that was not adopted by New York. The text of each dated version usually is published in the *U.L.A.*

Two of the acts listed above are "model" acts. They are the Joint Obligations Act and the State Administrative Procedure Act. Model acts are promulgated by the National Conference of Commissioners in areas where there is demand among the states for guidance in drafting an act, but where uniformity is not necessary by the nature of the subject matter.

Not all laws bearing the title "uniform" are uniform laws which had their origin with the National Conference of Commissioners. For example, New York's "Uniform District Court Act" provides "uniform" procedure within district courts under the Unified Court System in New York State, but it is not the handiwork of the National Conference of Commissioners.

6. INTERSTATE COMPACTS AND AGENCIES

a) Interstate Compacts. Interstate compacts are agreements between or among states; the federal government can also be a compact party. For example, the federal government is a party to the Interstate Oil and Gas Compact and the New England Interstate Water Pollution Compact. The federal government of Canada and individual provinces can also be parties. For example, the provinces of New Brunswick and Quebec are parties to the Northeastern Forest Fire Protection Compact, and Canada is a party to the New York-Canada International Bridge Compact and the Ogdensburg Bridge and Port Authority Compact.

Interstate compacts must receive Congressional approval pursuant to article I, sec. 10 of the U.S. Constitution which provides, "No state shall, without the consent of Congress..., enter into any Agreement or Compact with another State...." As interstate compacts are legislative in nature, their texts are printed in both ***Statutes at Large*** and in the session laws of those states which are parties to the compact. The majority of compacts to which New York is a party are enacted as Consolidated Laws. However, some are not. Those that are not enacted as Consolidated Laws are usually among the unconsolidated laws selected for publication in ***McKinney's*** and ***CLS***.

Legislative efforts in this area proceed under the guidance of the New York Senate's Select Committee on Interstate Cooperation. The 1981 and 1985 editions of the Committee's ***Inventory of New York State Compacts*** are excellent resources for research. They provide subject, title and state indexes to New York compacts. For each compact, the ***Inventory*** lists the New York State statutory authority for the compact, its Department of State file number (if any), the administrative body for the compact, and other parties to the compact.

The other important resources for research in interstate compacts are the ***Book of the States*** (published annually) and ***Interstate Compacts and Agencies*** (published every several years). Both are publications of the Council of State Governments in Lexington, Kentucky.

To facilitate locating the text of New York compacts in the indexes of New York's four publications covering the Consolidated Laws, the titles of those compacts that are currently in effect are listed in Appendix H.

b) Interstate agencies. Compacts often establish interstate agencies or commissions to administer the agreements reached by the compact parties or to carry out federal statutory mandates affecting several states.

Examples of these are the International Joint Commission and the Port Authority of New York and New Jersey. These agencies are listed in Appendix H.

7. LEGISLATIVE CITATION FORM

The most widely accepted guide to legal citation form is the ***Uniform System of Citation*** (the "Blue Book" or "Harvard blue book"), now in its 14th edition. For use in New York briefs, Lawyers Co-op publishes the ***Official New York Law Reports Style Manual*** (1987). The official ***Style Manual*** is prepared by the Law Reporting Bureau of the State of New York. The editors of ***St. John's Law Review*** published ***New York Rules of Citation*** in 1978. This guide applied the Blue Book rules then in effect (12th edition) to New York examples. The following citation examples also adapt Blue Book rules to New York examples.

a) Unenacted Bills.

Senate: S. (or N.Y.S.) 10651, 209th Sess. (1986).

Senate — bill number

Assembly: A. (or N.Y.A.) 11505, 209th Sess. (1986).

Assembly — bill number

b) Session Laws.

1985 N.Y. Laws ch. 210 § 1

title of official session laws — section number

year law enacted — chapter number

c) Session Laws Service.

Ch. 32 § 1 1987 McKinney's Session Law News of New York 90.

chapter number — title of unofficial session laws service — section number — page number

d) Consolidated Laws

McKinney's:

N.Y. Educ. L. § 313(1) (McKinney Supp. 1987).

name of the Consolidated Law — publisher — year of pocket part — section number — cited section is in the pocket part

Consolidated Laws Service:

N.Y. Educ. L. § 313(1) (Consol. 1985).

name of the Consolidated Law — publisher — section number — year of bound volume

The example above illustrates one effect of the different revision schedules of ***McKinney's*** and ***CLS.*** The current text of section 313(1) of the Education Law happens to be printed in the ***McKinney's*** pocket part but in the ***CLS*** bound volume. As can be seen in this example, when material is in the pocket part, that fact is indicated by the abbreviation "Supp."

Michie's:

N.Y. Educ. L. § 313(1) (Michie 1986).

section number — year of the annual volume — name of the Consolidated Law — publisher

Gould: The citation would be the same as for *Michie's* except that the parenthetical would read (Gould 1986).

e) Memoranda

Memorandum of Assemblyman William B. Hoyt, *reprinted in* 1981 N.Y. Legis. Ann. 116.

Memorandum of State Department of Insurance, *reprinted in* 1981 N.Y. Laws (McKinney) 2416.

Governor's Memorandum on Approval of ch. 3, *reprinted in* 1981 N.Y. Laws (Consol.) Gm-33.

8. CHAPTERS OF THE CONSOLIDATED LAWS

Following is a list of the 89 laws that presently comprise the Consolidated Laws of New York together with their chapter numbers.

Abandoned Property Law, Ch. 1
Agricultural Conservation and Adjustment Law, Ch. 9-A
Agriculture and Markets Law, Ch. 69
Alcoholic Beverage Control Law, Ch. 3-B
Alternative County Government Law, Ch. 11-B
Art and Cultural Affairs Law, Ch. 11-C
Banking Law, Ch. 2
Benevolent Orders Law, Ch. 3
Business Corporations Law, Ch. 4
Canal Law, Ch.5
Civil Practice Law & Rules, Ch. 8
Civil Rights Law, Ch. 6
Civil Service Law, Ch. 7
Commerce Law, Ch. 7-A
Cooperative Corporations Law, Ch. 77
Correction Law, Ch. 43
County Law, Ch. 11
Criminal Procedure Law, Ch. 11-A
Debtor and Creditor Law, Ch. 12
Domestic Relations Law, Ch. 14
Education Law, Ch. 16
Election Law, Ch. 17
Eminent Domain Procedure Law, Ch. 73
Employers' Liability Law, Ch. 74
Energy Law, Ch. 17-A
Environmental Conservation Law, Ch. 43-B
Estates, Powers and Trusts Law, Ch. 17-B
Executive Law, Ch. 18
General Associations Law, Ch. 29
General Business Law, Ch. 20
General City Law, Ch. 21
General Construction Law, Ch. 22
General Municipal Law, Ch. 24
General Obligations Law, Ch. 24-A
Highway Law, Ch. 25
Indian Law, Ch. 26

Insurance Law, Ch. 28
Judiciary Law, Ch. 30
Labor Law, Ch. 31
Legislative Law, Ch. 32
Lien Law, Ch. 33
Local Finance Law, Ch. 33-A
Mental Hygiene Law, Ch. 27
Military Law, Ch. 36
Multiple Dwelling Law, Ch. 61-A
Multiple Residence Law, Ch. 61-B
Municipal Home Rule Law, Ch. 36-A
Navigation Law, Ch. 37
New York State Printing & Public Documents Law, Ch. 58
Not-for-Profit Corporation Law, Ch. 35
Parks, Recreation and Historic Preservation Law, Ch. 36-B
Partnership Law, Ch. 39
Penal Law, Ch. 40
Personal Property Law, Ch. 41
Private Housing Finance Law, Ch. 44-B
Public Authorities Law, Ch. 43-A
Public Buildings Law, Ch. 44
Public Health Law, Ch. 45
Public Housing Law, Ch. 44-A
Public Lands Law, Ch. 46
Public Officers Law, Ch. 47
Public Service Law, Ch. 48
Racing, Pari-Mutuel Wagering and Breeding Law, Ch. 47-A
Railroad Law, Ch. 49
Rapid Transit Law, Ch. 48-A
Real Property Law, Ch. 50
Real Property Actions and Proceedings Law, Ch. 81
Rural Electric Cooperative Law, Ch. 77-A
Real Property Tax Law, Ch. 50-A
Religious Corporations Law, Ch. 51
Retirement and Social Security Law, Ch. 51-A
Rural Electric Cooperative Law, Ch. 77-A
Second Class Cities Law, Ch. 53
Social Services Law, Ch. 55
Soil and Water Conservation Districts Law, Ch. 9-B
State Administrative Procedure Act, Ch. 82
State Finance Law, Ch. 56
State Law, Ch. 57

Statute of Local Governments, Ch. 58-A
Surrogate's Court Procedure Act, Ch. 59-A
Tax Law, Ch. 60
Town Law, Ch. 62
Transportation Law, Ch. 61-A
Transportation Corporations Law, Ch. 63
Uniform Commercial Code, Ch. 38
Vehicle & Traffic Law, Ch. 71
Village Law, Ch. 64
Volunteer Firefighter's Benefit Law, Ch. 64-A
Workers' Compensation Law, Ch. 67

Chapter Five
LEGISLATIVE HISTORY

1. OVERVIEW

a) Legislative History Defined. A legislative history is a compilation of documents produced in the course of the legislative process. Researchers compile legislative histories as an aid in interpreting a statute. For example, where statutory language is ambiguous, where a particular application of a statute to a set of facts is advocated, or where fact patterns now existing may not have been contemplated when a statute originally passed, a legislative history may be helpful in interpreting the statutory language in question.

Use of legislative documents as an aid to statutory construction is often called the search for legislative intent. As will be described more fully below, some New York documents commonly viewed as belonging to a law's legislative history are actually written after the law has passed both houses of the legislature. Since post-passage documents could not have been considered by legislators as they debated and voted on the bill in the legislature, it is difficult to maintain that the views expressed therein represented the intent of the legislators.

A discussion of the weight given to inquiries into legislative intent by the courts of New York is found in *Legislative Intent and Extrinsic Aids to Statutory Interpretation in New York* by Ernest Breuer[1] and *Legislative Intent in New York State: Materials, Cases and Annotated Bibliography* by R. Allan Carter.[2]

b) Federal and New York Legislative History Compared.

(1) Federal. A considerable amount of printed or microform material is available for the study of federal legislative history. The bills in each house and their amended versions are available both in paper format and microform. House and Senate reports, which explain each bill reported out of committee, and conference committee reports, which explain compromises reached between the houses of Congress on a bill, are available. If hearings were held on a bill, hearing transcripts are also available. The record of floor debates in the U.S. Senate and House of Representatives is published in the ***Congressional Record.***

These federal documents are widely disseminated through the federal government's Depository Library Program. House and Senate reports, hearings, and documents are also available commercially from Congressional Information Service (CIS). For major federal legislation, compiled legislative histories are often published separately or included in looseleaf services in the subject area of the legislation.

(2) New York. By contrast to materials available at the federal level for research in legislative history or intent, relatively little material is available for New York legislation. While New York bills and amendments are relatively widely available, Senate or Assembly committee reports are not required by the Senate and Assembly rules and are seldom written. If hearings or debates are held on a bill, and if transcripts exist, the transcripts are only available in Albany. There is no formal conference committee procedure in New York. Therefore, no conference committee reports exist to explain the compromises on a bill reached between the Senate and Assembly. There is no New York equivalent to the ***Congressional Record.*** The Senate and Assembly journals, like the U.S. Senate and House journals, merely summarize each day's transactions; they do not contain verbatim accounts of legislative proceedings. The kinds of historical materials that are generally available for New York laws are:

[1] Breuer, ***Legislative Intent and Extrinsic Aids to Statutory Interpretation in New York*** 51 LAW LIBR. J. 2 (1958).

[2] R. A. CARTER, LEGISLATIVE INTENT IN NEW YORK STATE: MATERIALS, CASES AND ANNOTATED BIBLIOGRAPHY 9-10, 12-24, 31 (1981) [hereinafter CARTER].

* bills (introduced bills and amendments are available for virtually all laws);
* legislative memoranda (available on microfiche from 1985/86; selectively printed in the *New York State Legislative Annual;*
* governor's memoranda (not written for all laws); and
* bill jackets.

Other sources, such as reports or recommendations of special agencies, committees, or commissions, may also be available. The role of these special bodies in the legislative process is described in section 2 of Chapter 2. As noted in the previous paragraph, for a small proportion of recent legislation, a record of debates and hearings may be available in Albany. These materials will be explained in more detail in sections 2-6 of this Chapter.

(c) Procedure for Compiling a Legislative History. As with all research, the procedure to follow in the search for legislative intent depends on what information the researcher already has. The procedural steps listed here may not all be necessary, or they may be followed more appropriately in a different order, depending upon the particular situation.

1) Locate the Session Law's Citation. Assuming that the only information known is the law's section number in the Consolidated Laws, the first step in compiling a legislative history is locating the law's citation in the session laws. That citation will consist of the law's chapter number and the year of passage.

For laws currently in effect, the chapter number and year of passage can be found in the source note printed immediately below the text of the statutory section in *New York Consolidated Laws Service*[3] or *McKinney's Consolidated Laws of New York Annotated.*[4] This is an example from section 101-a of the Executive Law as printed in *McKinney's:*[5]

> Added L. 1971, c. 275; amended L. 1979, c. 696, sec. 3, L. 1981, c. 748 secs. 1,2.

This source note indicates that section 101-a was added to the Executive Law by chapter 275 of the Laws of 1971. It was amended the first time by

[3] Hereinafter *CLS.*
[4] Hereinafter *McKinney's.*
[5] N.Y. EXEC. LAW sec. 101-a (McKinney 1982).

section 3 of chapter 696 of the Laws of 1979. It was amended again by sections 1 and 2 of chapter 748 of the Laws of 1981.

The session laws should be consulted because the legislature occasionally incorporates its official intent, usually called "legislative findings and purpose," at the beginning of a law, and these findings are printed in the session laws. As noted in the next section, legislative findings usually would be reprinted, or at least excerpted, in *CLS* and *McKinney's* also.

2) Check the CLS and McKinney's Historical Material and the McKinney's Practice Commentaries. The second step in compiling a legislative history is determining whether *McKinney's* or *CLS* contains references to or quotations from other useful documents. For example, the Historical Note for section 9-0109 of the Environmental Conservation Law (ECL) in *McKinney's* reprints from the session laws the legislative findings and purpose for that section. These findings are also printed in full in session laws, as mentioned in the previous paragraph. In the case of a major recodification of an entire title of the Consolidated Laws, such as the 1985 revision of the Insurance Law, the editorial introduction at the beginning of the first volume containing the revised law in *McKinney's* or *CLS* can lead the researcher to important documents.

McKinney's features "Practice Commentaries" for the practice acts and laws.[6] The Practice Commentaries may give the context of statutory change and may quote extensively from reports of legislative committees or commissions, the text of which is not readily available elsewhere.

3) Use the Legislative Digest. The third step in compiling a legislative history is to gain an overview of legislative activity on the bill. Armed with the chapter number and year of passage, go to the volume of the *New York Legislative Digest* (for years 1985 to date) or its predecessors, the *New York Legislative Record and Index* (for years 1913 to 1984) and the *New York Legislative Index* (for years 1907 to 1912), which covers the year in which the law in question passed.

First, use the Cross Reference Table to convert the chapter number to the bill number. Then, use the sections entitled "Senate Introductory Record" and "Assembly Introductory Record" to trace the dates of

[6] Practice Commentaries are found in: the Civil Practice Law and Rules (CPLR); Surrogate's Court Practice Act (SCPA); Criminal Procedure Law (CPL); Estates, Powers and Trusts Law (EPTL) Domestic Relations Law (DRL); Business Corporation Law (BCL) and the Environmental Conservation Law (ECL).

legislative activity in each house. The dates of hearings, if any, will be noted there, also. The dates can be useful in later checking chronologically arranged sources such as the Senate and Assembly journals, newspapers covering New York legislation (such as the *New York Times,* the *Albany Times-Union,* the *Knickerbocker News,* and the *New York Law Journal*), and the limited archival holdings of hearings and debates (described below at section 5).

Similar information to that found in the *New York Legislative Record and Index* also is available in the *New York Legislative Service* which was published from 1946 to 1980.

4) Use Documents Indexes. The fourth step in compiling a legislative history is to consult indexes to New York documents in order to determine whether any committee or commission reports were issued concerning the law in question. These indexes are described in section 6 of this Chapter.

5) Locate the Relevant Documents. The fifth step in compiling a legislative history is to search for memoranda and bill jackets, the amended bills, and any other documents that have been identified.

The remainder of this chapter describes bills, memoranda, bill jackets and other relevant documents and how to find them.

2. BILLS

Most bills that pass into law were amended at least once in the legislature. In New York, bills are given an introductory number which identifies the house of origin; e.g., A2011 is an Assembly bill and S292 is a Senate bill. When a bill is amended for the first time, the letter "A" is added to the introductory number, e.g., A2011-A, S292-A. The letter "B" denotes the second amendment of the bill, and so on. Prior to 1969, amendments were identified by successive print numbers. "Uni-bills"[7] carry both a Senate and Assembly introductory number.

Textual comparison of the originally introduced bill and all subsequent amendments in each house can be useful in determining what changes were necessary to make the bill acceptable to the legislature. To make these comparisons, the researcher needs to locate a library which

[7] Uni-bills are identical bills that are introduced simultaneously in each house. A glossary of legislative terms is found in section 6 of Chapter 2.

subscribes to the current bills in paper format or which maintains the bills for past years, depending on the year of the law being researched.

Bills and amendments for the current session and recent legislative sessions are available in slip format at the Legislative Library in Albany, the State Library, the SUNY at Buffalo Law Library and in other larger collections of New York documents. At this writing, bills for the current session are available by subscription from Hamilton Press of Rensselaer, New York.

Bills from the last two years (and sometimes the last three years) are also available online through New York's two full-text legislative databases, Legislative Retrieval System (LRS) and Legi-Tech.[8] However, only the latest amended version of each bill is maintained online, so comparison of the several versions of an amended bill is not possible on either LRS or Legi-Tech.

Bound volumes of bills are issued by the state several years after each session. The Legislative Library in Albany has incomplete holdings of Assembly bills for the years 1832-1877 and complete holdings from 1877 on. It has incomplete holdings of Senate bills for the years 1832-1897 and complete holdings from 1897 to date. However, this library does not serve the public directly. The State Library holds the Senate and Assembly bills from 1830-1980 in microform and bills in hard copy from 1981 to date. It does serve the public directly. Other New York depository libraries also have extensive retrospective holdings of bills in hard copy or microform.

3. MEMORANDA

a) Introductory Memoranda. Senate Rule VI, sec. 4 and Assembly Rule III, sec. 1 require every bill introduced in the Senate or Assembly to be accompanied by an introductory memorandum explaining the purpose of the bill. Although these memoranda often are quite general in approach, they can be useful, especially when the law for which legislative intent is sought made only minor changes in the Consolidated Laws.

Legislative memoranda are on file at the Legislative Library and are included in the bill jackets.[9] Introductory memoranda are selectively

[8] Legislative Retrieval System [hereinafter LRS] and Legi-Tech are New York legislative databases described more fully in Chapter 12 (Databases for New York Legal Research).

[9] Bill jackets are described in section 4 of this Chapter.

printed in the ***New York State Legislative Annual***, which has been published by the New York Legislative Service, Inc. of New York City since 1946. For the years 1985/86 to date, the legislative memoranda can be purchased in microfiche from Capitol Microfilm Services, Inc. of Schenectady. The State Library and the SUNY at Buffalo Law Library are among the libraries collecting the legislative memoranda on microfiche. At this writing, introductory memoranda are not available on LRS or Legi-Tech.

b) Governor's Memoranda. Article 4, section 7 of the New York Constitution requires the governor to write an explanatory memorandum setting forth the reasons for vetoing any bill. There is no requirement of a "veto memorandum" when a bill is "pocket vetoed." A bill is pocket vetoed when the governor neither signs nor vetoes a thirty-day bill.[10]

Upon signing a bill into law, the governor may write a memorandum of approval setting forth reasons for approving the bill, but there is no requirement that the governor do so. Since governor's memoranda are written after a bill has passed both houses of the legislature, they could not be said to have influenced the debate or vote of the legislature. Accordingly, governor's memoranda could not be said to reflect legislative intent.

Governor's approval memoranda are included in the ***New York State Legislative Annual, McKinney's Session Laws of New York,***[11] ***New York Consolidated Laws Service Session Laws,***[12] the ***New York Legislative Digest,*** and the ***Public Papers*** of the governors. Approval memoranda are also included in the bill jackets of laws for which approval memoranda were written. Governor's veto memoranda are included in the veto bill jackets and in the ***Public Papers*** of the governors.

c) Other Memoranda. Memoranda of state departments and agencies, such as the Office of Court Administration, concerning legislation are printed in the ***CLS Session Laws*** and ***McKinney's Session Laws***. They are also included in the bill jackets. The unofficial session laws also contain the annual report of the Law Revision Commission, which sets out the Commission's annual legislative recommendations.

[10] A thirty-day bill is one passed during the ten days before the legislature adjourns. For a discussion of the governor's role in the final passage of laws, see section 3(f) of Chapter 2 (State Legislation: Legislative Process, Bills, Resolutions and Session Laws.

[11] Hereinafter ***McKinney's Session Laws.***

[12] Hereinafter ***CLS Session Laws.***

4. GOVERNOR'S BILL JACKETS.

When a bill that has passed the Senate and Assembly is awaiting gubernatorial action, the Governor's Counsel's Office solicits expressions of interest concerning it. These are gathered in a packet which also contains the bill itself and the introductory memoranda. The packet is called a bill jacket.

A typical bill jacket might contain several letters from lobbyists and a letter from the Attorney General's Office concerning the bill's effect on existing law. While bill jackets do not contain a record of debate, a transcript of any hearings, or any committee reports of the sort available as a matter of course for federal legislation, no New York legislative history search is complete without them. As R. Allan Carter notes,

> [w]hile sometimes limited or even useless, bill jackets are nevertheless important, since they often contain the only available material on legislative intent. They are especially important when only one or two sections of a particular law are amended or added, and, conversely, become less helpful in regard to extensive revisions. They are also useful when ascertaining what individual, agency, committee, or group was the primary motivator for the bill.[13]

Bill jackets exist from 1921 to the present, with partial holdings for 1905.[14] The bill jackets for approved bills are arranged by year and chapter number.

Veto jackets also exist from 1921. When a bill is vetoed, the veto message is included in the veto jacket. This information can be useful for comparison with legislation on the same subject that does pass in the next legislature. Veto jackets are arranged by year and introductory number before 1964. Beginning in 1964, veto jackets are arranged by year and veto number. The veto number is found in the bill status information in the *New York Legislative Digest* and in its predecessor, the ***New York Legislative Record and Index.***

A third category of bill jackets, called "recall jackets," contains information on bills that were "recalled" from the governor's office to the legislature, usually for technical correction, but which did not subse-

[13] CARTER, *supra* note 2, at 9.
[14] CARTER, *supra* note 2, at 7.

quently pass into law. Recall jackets for the years 1936-1954 are microfilmed with the veto jackets in the collection described in the next paragraph. Recall jackets for more recent years are housed in the State Archives.

Collections of bill jackets for approved and vetoed bills are available in five locations: the New York State Archives (holds hard copy for all but the most recent two or three years), the New York State Library (microform), the New York Public Library (microform), the Legislative Secretary to the Governor's Counsel (holds hard copy for the most recent two or three years), and the SUNY at Buffalo Law Library (microform). At this writing, bill jackets have been converted to microform for the years 1905 and 1921 to 1982. Further conversion to microform is planned. The bill jackets in microform can be purchased from the State Archives in Albany.

5. TRANSCRIPTS OF DEBATES AND HEARINGS

a) Debates. At this writing, transcriptions of selected Senate debates from 1960 to the present are available at the New York State Senate Office of Microfilm and Records Storage, Room 500 HI, The Capitol, Albany, New York 12248. Telephone: (518) 455-2661.

Transcriptions of some Assembly debates from 1977 to the present are available from the New York State Assembly Public Information Office, New York State Assembly, Room 102, Legislative Office Building, Albany, New York, 12248. Telephone: (518) 455-4218. The State Archives houses transcriptions of debates for the years 1974-1976; telephone (518) 473-1203.

b) Hearings. At this writing, audiotapes of selected Assembly hearings from the past two years are available at the New York State Assembly Office of Program and Committee Staff, New York State Assembly, Room 518, The Capitol, Albany, New York 12248. Telephone: (518) 455-4433. No record of Senate hearings is available. The State Library contains a large number of printed hearings; however, not all of those holdings are cataloged.

6. OTHER SOURCES

Commissions, committees, and agencies of the government may be charged with assisting the legislature in drafting bills. The role of these agencies is described in connection with the bill drafting process in section 2 of Chapter 2. They include the Law Revision Commission and the Judicial Conference. When the language of the law as passed reflects the recommendations of such bodies, their reports, notes, or comments are "given pursuasive weight by the courts."[15] The Legislative Documents series and finding tools for legislative documents and other documents are listed below. For a more detailed description of these finding tools, consult ***New York State Documents: an Introductory Manual.***[16]

a) Legislative Documents Series. The four series of the New York State Legislative Documents are a rich source of reports containing legislative recommendations. Each series includes publications of the legislative, executive, and judicial branches of government for a particular time period. The four series are:

New York (State) Legislature. ***Legislative Documents of the Senate and Assembly of the State of New York.*** Albany. 1830. (Covers 1830 documents only).

New York (State) Legislature. Assembly. ***Documents of the Assembly of the State of New York, 1831-1918.*** Albany. (Annual).

New York (State) Legislature. Senate. ***Documents of the Senate of the State of New York, 1831-1918.*** Albany. (Annual).

New York (State) Legislature. ***Legislative Documents, 1919-1975.*** Albany. (Annual).

While documents are still issued in New York bearing Legislative Document numbers, the legislative documents have not been collected, bound together, and issued as an annual set since 1975.

[15] MARKE, ***State Legislative History.*** Chap. in J.J. MARKE and R. SLOANE, LEGAL RESEARCH AND LAW LIBRARY MANAGEMENT (1982) at 89.
[16] D. BUTCH, NEW YORK STATE DOCUMENTS 5-7, 33-34 (1987).

b) Indexes to State Publications Useful for Legislative History. Several indexes are useful in locating material relevant for legislative history both in the Legislative Documents series and among uncollected New York documents.

The following indexes are the standard tools for accessing New York documents of the nineteenth and early twentieth centuries.

New York (State) Legislature. ***General Index of the Documents and Laws of the State of New York.*** Albany: T. Weed, 1842. This indexes legislative documents issued from 1830 to 1842.

New York (State) Legislature. ***General Index to Documents of the State of New York 1855-1891.*** Albany. This index was published by the Legislature in 6 volumes and is popularly known as the ***General Index.***

Hasse, A.R. ***Index of Economic Material in Documents of the States of the United States: New York, 1789-1904.*** New York: Kraus Reprint Corp., 1965. This index was originally published in 1907 and is popularly known as ***Hasse.***

Bowker, R. R. ***State Publications: a provisional List of the Official Publications of the Several States of the United States From Their Organization.*** New York: The Publisher's Weekly, 1899-1908. New York documents are found in Part 2, which is entitled "North Central States" and is dated 1902.

Jewett, A. L. ***Official Publications of the State of New York Relating To Its History As Colony and State.*** Albany: University of the State of New York, 1917.

In the twentieth century, a very important index is the ***Cumulative Index To Joint Legislative Committees and Selected Temporary State Commissions, 1900-1950 and Supplement, 1951-1965*** published by the Legislature. The joint legislative committees and temporary state commissions indexed were responsible for proposing some of the most comprehensive revisions of New York's laws for the period covered in the ***Cumulative Index.***

A particularly useful feature in the ***Cumulative Index*** is the index to the names of the committee and commission chairpersons. The names of commission and committee chairpersons often became the names by which the reports of the committees or commissions were popularly known. For example, John D. Bennett chaired the New York State Temporary Commission on the Modernization, Revision and Simplification of the Law of Estates. That Commission created the Estates, Powers and Trusts Law (EPTL) out of the old Decedents' Estates Law and other laws. The Commission's report came to be known simply as the Bennett Commission Report. To locate the multi-volume report in most library catalogs, the researcher would need to know the "long" or "official" name of the commission. While searching under Bennett Commission might not locate the report in a library catalog, the official name can be located in the ***Cumulative Index*** by searching under Bennett. Then, the catalog can be searched using the official name. The ***Cumulative Index*** also gives the legislative document numbers so that reports can be found in the fourth series of the Legislative Documents.

A recently published six-volume index by R. Allan Carter, the ***Annotated List and Indices of the New York State Legislative Documents Series, 1919-1976,*** includes a subject index to the reports of temporary commissions and joint legislative committees, and also to governor's messages and other documents that are included in the fourth series of the Legislative Documents. A key word index and an index to the reports by the name of the chairperson are notable for the reasons described above. Another helpful listing compiled by R. Allan Carter is the ***Annotated List and Indexes of Reports of New York State Governors' Committees and Task Forces, 1925-1985***. The reports are listed in chronological order and are indexed by chairperson and key word.

The State Library has issued three bibliographical works which can be of great assistance in locating documents relevant to legislative history. First, the monthly ***Checklist of Official Publications of the State of New York***, which has been published since October, 1947, includes, among many other documents, studies, reports and public hearings of legislative committees and commissions important enough to merit publication by the State. There is an index to authors, committee chairpersons, and vice-chairpersons which covers volumes 1-23 (1947-1969). Unfortunately, the ***Checklist*** has no subject index. The monthly ***Checklists*** have been cumulated in various ways over the years. The cumulation entitled ***Official Publications of the State of New York*** cumulates volumes 1-15 (1947-1962) of the ***Checklists***. Two cumulations cover volumes 16-21 (1962-1967) and volumes 22-27 (1968-1973). Annual cumulations were issued for the years 1968-1971.

Second, the ***Dictionary Catalog of Official Publications of the State of New York***, which has been published annually since 1973, lists monographs cataloged by the State Library. Access is by author, title and subject.

Third, the ***Serial Supplement*** to the ***Dictionary Catalog***, which was published in 1985, lists the bulk of the serials cataloged by the State Library from its inception through June 22, 1984. Since many committee and commission reports that are useful in discovering legislative intent were issued as serials, this is still another possible source for that information.

c) Records and Briefs. Records and Briefs are the record on appeal at the Appellate Division and Court of Appeals.[17] They contain the court records and briefs filed with the appellate court. During the course of compiling the legislative history of a law, the researcher may discover that the appellate courts have had occasion to use documents of legislative history to interpret that law. This can be an important research lead, because the briefs filed with the appellate court may well contain very useful information on the statute's legislative history. The briefs may even include copies of otherwise hard-to-find documents.

To locate collections of Cases and Points in New York libraries, consult ***A Union List of Cases and Points, 3d ed.,*** compiled by J. White and D. Tybur.[18]

REFERENCES

Breuer, E. H. ***Legislative Intent and Extrinsic Aids to Statutory Interpretation in New York*** 51 Law Library Journal 2 (1958).

Breuer, E. H. ***Source Material Relating to Legislation in the State of New York: an Annotated Bibliography of Legislative History and Legislative Intent.*** rev. by R. A. Carter. Albany: State University of New York, 1977.

[17] Under the Civil Practice Act, which preceded the Civil Practice Law and Rules, Records and Briefs were called Cases and Points.

[18] UNION LIST OF CASES AND POINTS/RECORDS AND BRIEFS IN NEW YORK STATE LAW LIBRARIES (comp. by J.L. White & D.M. Tybur) (3d ed. 1987).

Butch, D. *New York State Documents: an Introductory Manual.* Albany: State University of New York, 1987.

Carter, R. A. *Legislative Intent in New York State: Materials, Cases and Annotated Bibliography.* Albany: State University of New York, 1981.

Fairfield, D. A. *Background Materials for Statutory Interpretation in New York*. Chap. in *New York State Legislative Annual.* New York: New York Legislative Service, Inc., 1963.

Marke, J. J. *State Legislative History*. Chap. in J. J. Marke and R. Sloane. *Legal Research and Law Library Management*. New York: Law Journal Seminars-Press, 1982.

Chapter Six
JUDICIAL SYSTEM

1. HISTORY OF NEW YORK'S COURTS

Taking into account both the colonial period and the period of statehood, New York's court system has been in existence for over three hundred and sixty years. The court system, at first a distinctly Dutch institution, became a predominantly English institution by about 1670. Until well after the Revolution, New York's highest court resembled the judicial functions of the English House of Lords. Not until the reforms of 1846, when the Court of Errors was abolished and the Court of Appeals created, did New York have a court of last resort that was separate from the legislative branch of government. The Court of Chancery, an institution originally based on the royal prerogative of the king, was also abolished in 1846.

In addition to the landmark changes of 1846, many other changes in the court structure took place in the nineteenth century. New York's burgeoning population and rapidly increasing commercial activity placed great burdens on the court system. In response to these demands, new courts were created, older courts were combined, merged, or abolished, and various devices were created to deal with case backlogs of enormous proportion.

There have been many attempts to win political and popular approval for simplifying New York's court system and modernizing its administration during the twentieth century. For example, the framework of a statewide unified court system was created in 1962. Since then, there have been extensive changes in the way the courts are financed and administered. On the other hand, efforts to reduce the sheer number of courts led to only minor modifications. As a result, the organization of the major courts has remained essentially the same since the Constitution of 1894 went into effect.

Section 1 of this Chapter briefly outlines the chronological development of New York's major courts and serves as an introduction to Section 2, which describes the present court system.

a) The Colonial Period. The following description of New York's major courts during the colonial period is quite simplified. It cannot begin to describe the people's opposition to proprietary and royal prerogative that fuelled most of the structural changes here so dispassionately described.

1) Courts Under Dutch Rule (1624-1664). The province of New Netherland was under the control of the Dutch West India Company from 1624 to 1664. The Company dominated the judicial system as well as every other aspect of civil life in New Netherland. Eight of the Company's nineteen-member board of directors were in charge of New Netherland, and they appointed a Director General to govern the colony. The board of directors also appointed a Council which had administrative, legislative and judicial responsibilities. The Council was the first judicial tribunal in New Netherland. It decided both criminal and civil cases.[1] A "schout-fiscal" acted as both sheriff and prosecuting officer. Appeal of decisions to the Amsterdam chamber of the Dutch West India Company was virtually impossible.[2]

[1] D. ELLIS, A HISTORY OF NEW YORK STATE 22 (1967) [hereinafter ELLIS].

[2] J. GOEBEL, THE COURTS AND THE LAW IN COLONIAL NEW YORK, in 3 FLICK, HISTORY OF THE STATE OF NEW YORK 5 (1933) [hereinafter GOEBEL].

In 1647, Governor Peter Stuyvesant grudgingly responded to popular dissatisfaction by changing the judicial tribunal to a board of nine men whom he selected from an elected panel of eighteen,[3] but this reform was not long-lived. In 1652, further reforms created a municipal government in New Amsterdam composed of a schout, two burgomasters and five schepens. In Holland, these officials had quite separate duties. The schout performed the functions of prosecutor and bailiff. The burgomasters served in rotation as mayor. The schepens functioned as aldermen. In New Netherland, these officials sat together as a combined administrative, legislative and judicial body.[4] Under Dutch rule, appeals from the Court of Schout, Burgomasters and Schepens lay to the supreme Council in Amsterdam.[5]

In 1664, Peter Stuyvesant, lacking the support of the people in resisting the English, surrendered to the Duke of York.

2) Courts Under English Rule 1664-1776. On March 1, 1665, less than one year after the Duke of York was granted the proprietorship of New York, Governor Richard Nicolls promulgated the Duke's Laws. The Duke's Laws was a code derived from the statutes of Massachusetts and New Haven.[6]

The judicial system established under the Duke's Laws consisted of the Court of Assizes, courts of sessions, and town courts. The highest court, the Court of Assizes, consisted of the governor, his Council, and justices of the peace. The Court of Assizes had original jurisdiction in major civil and criminal cases and in equity. There was a limited right of appeal from lower courts. In the case of capital offenses, the governor could issue a special commission of oyer and terminer to handle the case.

Under the Duke's Laws, the bulk of the civil and criminal cases were heard in circuit courts called courts of sessions. All sessions cases were taken to juries.[7] The Mayor's Court of New York functioned as the City's court of sessions, having transformed itself from its former identity as the Court of Burgomasters and Schepens. Minor local matters were heard in town courts where panels usually were presided over by justices of the peace.

In 1683, the "Dongan Judiciary," named for Governor Thomas Dongan, was established. The Act for the Reform of the Judicial System

[3] *Id.* at 5.

[4] 1 Chester, Legal and Judicial History of New York 59 (1911).

[5] Goebel, *supra* note 2, at 5.

[6] D. Ellis, *supra* note 1, at 30. The Duke's Laws are reprinted in I Colonial Laws of New York 6-73 (1894 ed.).

[7] Goebel, *supra* note 2, at 14.

(November 1, 1683) created a regular Court of Oyer and Terminer to handle the more serious civil and criminal cases. This court also had transfer and appellate jurisdiction. The 1683 Act vested equity jurisdiction in a Court of Chancery that consisted of the governor and his Council.

The Court of Chancery became the highest court when the Court of Assizes was abolished in 1684 and its pending cases were transfered to Chancery. Under the Dongan Judiciary, the Mayor's Courts in New York and Albany lost their criminal jurisdiction but were continued as civil courts. Criminal jurisdiction in the cities was transferred to a court of quarter sessions.

The Supreme Court of Judicature was created in 1691 by an Act[8] that established the court structure that persisted, with minor changes, until well after the Revolution. The Supreme Court of Judicature was given original jurisdiction over both civil and criminal cases. It was the predecessor of today's Supreme Court.[9] The Supreme Court of Judicature was composed of a chief justice and four puisne judges. The court sat in New York City and at circuit sessions in the state's counties. In connection with the circuit sessions, the justices also held Courts of Oyer and Terminer to hear the more serious civil and criminal cases. Once a year, in each county, a judge of the Supreme Court and three specially commissioned justices of the peace sat as a court of common pleas to hear matters triable at common law.[10]

Appeal of major cases from the Supreme Court of Judicature lay to the governor and his Council sitting as a Court of Errors. The King and his Privy Council comprised the court of last resort.[11]

At the local level, town courts were replaced by justices of the peace sitting with one local freeholder to hear cases. The justices of the peace came together periodically to sit as a court of sessions to hear more serious criminal or administrative matters. The Mayor's Courts were continued by the 1691 Act to function as the commercial courts and the courts of common pleas in New York and Albany.

[8] Act of May 6, 1691, reprinted in I Colonial Laws of New York 226 (1894 ed.).

[9] The court of last resort in today's federal court system and in the court systems of most states is the supreme court. In New York, the court of last resort has never been called the supreme court. The New York Supreme Court has always functioned as either a trial court with some appellate functions (1691-1821), an intermediate appellate court (1821-1846), or a court comprised of two levels so as to discharge both trial and appellate responsibilities (1846 to the present).

[10] J. GOEBEL, *supra* note 2, at 22-23.

[11] R. MACCRATE, APPELLATE JUSTICE IN NEW YORK 18 (1982) [hereinafter MACCRATE].

A Court of Chancery, previously abolished, was recreated by the 1691 Judiciary Act. It was seldom used and was allowed to expire in 1699. The Provincial Assembly would not approve the revival of that unpopular court, but it was revived by the governor in 1701 and was retained in the court structure until finally abolished in 1846.

b) The Period of Statehood.

1) The Constitution of 1777 and the Court of Errors. The Revolutionary Constitution was adopted on April 20, 1777. The judiciary article, article XXIV, mandated creation of a Court for the Correction of Errors and Trial of Impeachments. At the end of the Revolutionary War, the legislature carried out the constitutional mandate by an Act of November 24, 1784. The Court, commonly known as the Court of Errors, was made up of the president of the Senate, the senators, the chancellor, and the judges of the existing Supreme Court. The Court of Errors replaced the colonial governor and his Council as the court of last resort and was continued until 1846.

The other features of the post-1691 colonial court structure, described in the previous section of this Chapter, remained essentially unchanged until 1821.

2) Constitution of 1821 and Intermediate Appellate Review. Under the Constitution of 1821, the Supreme Court became the intermediate appellate court subject to final review by the Court of Errors. Eight judicial circuits were created and circuit judges were appointed by the governor from each circuit to handle trials.

These changes at the appellate level provided short-lived relief for the steadily increasing workload of the appellate courts.[12] It could take as long as 10 years for an appeal to be heard in Chancery.[13] In addition, there was dissatisfaction with the mixed judicial and legislative composition of the Court of Errors. The ratio of senators to judges on the Court of Errors was 32 to 4,[14] and many judges and attorneys believed that politics intruded into too many of the Court's decisions. Popular dissatisfaction with the judicial system fuelled the drive for a constitutional convention in 1846.

[12] F. BERGAN, THE HISTORY OF THE NEW YORK COURT OF APPEALS, 1847-1932 14 (1985) [hereinafter BERGAN].

[13] N.Y. STATE CONSTITUTIONAL CONVENTION. PROCEEDINGS 450 (1846).

[14] BERGAN, *supra* note 12, at 10.

3) The Constitution of 1846 and the Creation of the Court of Appeals, the General Term of Supreme Court, and an Expanded Supreme Court. The Constitution of 1846 and the implementing legislation of 1847[15] brought sweeping changes for New York's judicial system. An eight member Court of Appeals was created to replace the Court of Errors.[16] Four of the Court of Appeal's members, including the Chief Judge, were elected; the other four members were selected from among the Supreme Court justices with the shortest remaining terms. The Constitution of 1846 abolished the Court of Chancery. Its jurisdiction was transferred to Supreme Court.

The Supreme Court, which had been performing the function of the intermediate appellate court since 1821, was reconstituted as a statewide court with original jurisdiction over both law and equity.[17] General Terms of Supreme Court were created as the courts of intermediate appellate review. The General Terms were composed of three Supreme Court justices from each of eight newly created judicial districts. The General Terms heard appeals from the special terms and trial terms of Supreme Court and from the lower courts. Single justices sat in special term of Supreme Court to hear non-jury matters. Four Supreme Court justices sat in each judicial district except in the first district, New York City, where there were five justices.

As noted above, the changes in court structure under the Constitution of 1846 included the creation of eight judicial districts. The arrangement of judicial districts, bounded by county lines, is still in effect today. However, the present number of districts is twelve.

4) The Judiciary Amendment of 1869 and the Creation of Four General Terms of Supreme Court. The Judiciary Amendment of 1869 reduced the number of General Terms of Supreme Court from a maximum of eight to a maximum of four. That structure was the foundation for the present organization of the Appellate Division of Supreme Court into four judicial departments. The Amendment also provided for election of the judges of the Court of Appeals and reduced the size of the Court from eight to seven, which is its present size.

15 N.Y. CONST. of 1846, art. XXIV; 1847 N.Y. LAWS ch. 280.

16 The enormous appeals backlog of the Court of Errors was not transferred to the Court of Appeals. Instead, it was handled by a five-member Commission of Appeals appointed by the governor.

17 For a summary of the debate in the 1846 Constitutional Convention over the propriety of calling this court "Supreme Court," see BERGAN, *supra* note 12, at 25.

The continuing pressure of calendar problems also led to creation of a temporary Commission of Appeals in 1870 to handle the backlog of Court of Appeals cases. It remained in existence until 1875.[18]

5) The Judiciary Amendment of 1888 and the Creation of a Second Division of the Court of Appeals. The Judiciary Amendment of 1888 permitted the creation of a second division of the Court of Appeals to help reduce that Court's backlog. Seven Supreme Court justices were designated as Associate Court of Appeals Judges for this purpose. Volumes 118, 120, 122, 124, 127, 130, 132 and 134 of ***New York Reports*** contain the Second Division decisions.[19]

6) The Constitution of 1894 and the Creation of the Appellate Division. The Constitution of 1894 and its implementing legislation[20] created the Appellate Division of Supreme Court to supplant the General Terms of Supreme Court as the state's intermediate appellate court. As is the case today, one court sat in each of four judicial departments. The number of justices could vary according to each department's caseload.

Appellate Division justices were designated by the governor from among the membership of the Supreme Court. The Appellate Division assumed the jurisdiction not only of the General Terms of Supreme Court but also the jurisdiction of the General Terms of the Superior Courts of Buffalo and New York City, the New York City Court of Common Pleas and the Brooklyn City Court. Those courts were abolished and their pending cases were transferred to Supreme Court.

In the continuing effort to reduce the number of appeals to the Court of Appeals, the Constitution of 1894 limited the Court's jurisdiction to questions of law and reduced the number of circumstances where appeal in civil cases could be had. The new Constitution also provided that the governor could designate as many as four Supreme Court justices to serve as associate judges on the Court of Appeals upon certification by the Court that it was unable to hear and dispose of its cases with reasonable speed. That provision is found in today's Constitution at article VI, sec. 2(b).

The judiciary article was numbered XXIV in the constitutions of 1777, 1821 and 1846. It became article VI in the Constitution of 1894. While the judiciary article has been amended many times since 1894, the struc-

[18] BERGAN, *supra* note 12, at 119.

[19] Moore, ***One Hundred Fifty Years of Official Law Reporting and the Courts in New York,*** 6 SYRACUSE L. REV. 273, 284 (1955).

[20] 1895 N.Y. LAWS ch. 376.

ture of the major courts that was put in place by the Constitution of 1894 exists in substantially the same form today.

7) Judiciary Amendment of 1925. The Judiciary Amendment of 1925 implemented many of the recommended changes in article VI that were originally proposed by the Constitutional Convention of 1915 and the Judicial Constitutional Convention of 1921. Among these changes were the following. The Appellate Terms were given constitutional recognition. The jurisdiction of the Court of Appeals was broadened to include review of cases where the Appellate Division, on reversing or modifying a final judgment, made new findings of fact. Direct appeal to the Court of Appeals from the trial court was allowed where the death penalty was imposed. Direct appeal also was allowed in cases where only a constitutional question was involved. As to the lower courts, the jurisdiction of the courts in the City of New York was modified and the City Court was made a constitutional court.

The Judiciary Amendment of 1925 accomplished the last wholesale revision of the judiciary article until 1962. The revisions to article VI proposed by the Constitutional Convention of 1938 were not approved. For an historical survey of the changes in the judiciary article from 1821 to 1937, see the ninth volume of the 1938 Constitutional Convention Committee Reports (the "Poletti Report.")

8) Judiciary Amendment of 1962. A revised judiciary article was approved at the November 7, 1961 general election. Implementing legislation was drafted by the Joint Legislative Committee on Court Reorganization and became chapters 684-705 of the Laws of 1962. The legislation included the Family Court Act, the New York City Civil Court Act and the New York City Criminal Court Act.

The Judiciary Amendment of 1962 created the framework for a unified court system. A Family Court was created, which replaced the Domestic Relations Court of the City of New York and the Children's Courts in the counties outside the City. The City of New York's court system was completely reorganized. Supreme Court was given jurisdiction over matters formerly heard by the Court of General Sessions of the County of New York and the County Courts in the Bronx, Kings, Queens, and Richmond counties. Those courts were abolished and their caseload, judges, and personnel were transferred to Supreme Court. A citywide Civil Court was created to replace City Court and Municipal Court. A citywide Criminal Court was created to replace the Court of Special Sessions and the City Magistrate's Court.

2. THE PRESENT JUDICIAL SYSTEM

a) Overview. Viewed most simply, New York's judicial system consists of two functional levels of courts: appellate courts and courts of original jurisdiction. The list below merely categorizes the courts according to function and should not be viewed as a literal representation of the route of appeal in the court system.

NEW YORK'S COURTS

APPELLATE COURTS

Court of Appeals
Appellate Division of Supreme Court
Appellate Terms (1st and 2nd Depts.)
County Courts, appellate session (3rd and 4th Depts.)

COURTS OF ORIGINAL JURISDICTION

"Superior Trial Courts"
- Supreme Court
- Court of Claims
- Family Court
- Surrogate's Court
- County Court

"Inferior Trial Courts"
- New York City Civil and Criminal Courts and other City Courts
- Town and Village Courts (Justice Courts)
- District Courts (exist only in 2nd Dept.)

The route of appeal in New York is fairly complex. In general, the Appellate Terms and appellate sessions of County Court hear civil and criminal appeals from the local "inferior trial courts." The Appellate Division hears appeals from the "superior trial courts" in civil matters and from the County Courts and Supreme Court in criminal matters. As designated by statute, the departments of the Appellate Division hear appeals from administrative determinations. Only about ten per cent of the cases heard by the Appellate Division are subsequently reviewed by the Court of Appeals.[21] For a discussion of New York appellate practice, see Newman's *New York Appellate Practice*, published by Matthew Bender.

A recent study on New York's appellate court system, known as the MacCrate Report, reached the following conclusion on the complexity of New York's present appellate system:

> Today New York has possibly the most complex structure of appellate justice of any state in the nation. This situation is due to a variety of factors, among them the large number and variety of trial courts and administrative agencies that produce appealable decisions; the lack of usual restrictions on appealability of interlocutory decisions to the intermediate appellate courts; an intricate concept of finality with regard to the jurisdiction of the Court of Appeals; unorthodox standards of appellate review and a maze of pathways for appeal from various inferior courts and administrative agencies.[22]

While restrictions on access to the Court of Appeals went into effect in 1986,[23] a proposed constitutional amendment to simplify the court system, which passed both houses of the legislature in 1986,[24] was not reported out of committee in the 1987 legislature.[25] At this writing, it would appear that the New York court system will retain many of the features complained of in the MacCrate Report for the foreseeable future.

b) New York's Appellate Courts.

(1) The Court of Appeals. New York's court of last resort is the Court of Appeals. There are seven members of the Court: a chief judge and six associate judges. Since 1977 the judges have been appointed by the governor to fourteen year terms according to procedures set forth in article VI, section 2, of the Constitution.

[21] NEW YORK (STATE). DEPT. OF STATE. LOCAL GOVERNMENT HANDBOOK 33 (4th ed. 1987) [hereinafter LOCAL GOVERNMENT HANDBOOK].

[22] MACCRATE, *supra* note 11, at 14.

[23] N.Y. CIV. PRAC. L. & R. sec. 5601 as amended by 1985 N.Y. LAWS ch. 300. See Gleason and S. D. Ferlazzo, ***The Court of Appeals Moves Towards "Certiorari" Status*** 58 N.Y. ST. B. J. 8 (May, 1986).

[24] Con. Res. [S.9618], 209th Sess., 1986 N.Y. LAWS 3570.

[25] A11, 210th Sess. (1987).

NEW YORK STATE JUDICIAL SYSTEM
CIVIL APPEALS STRUCTURE

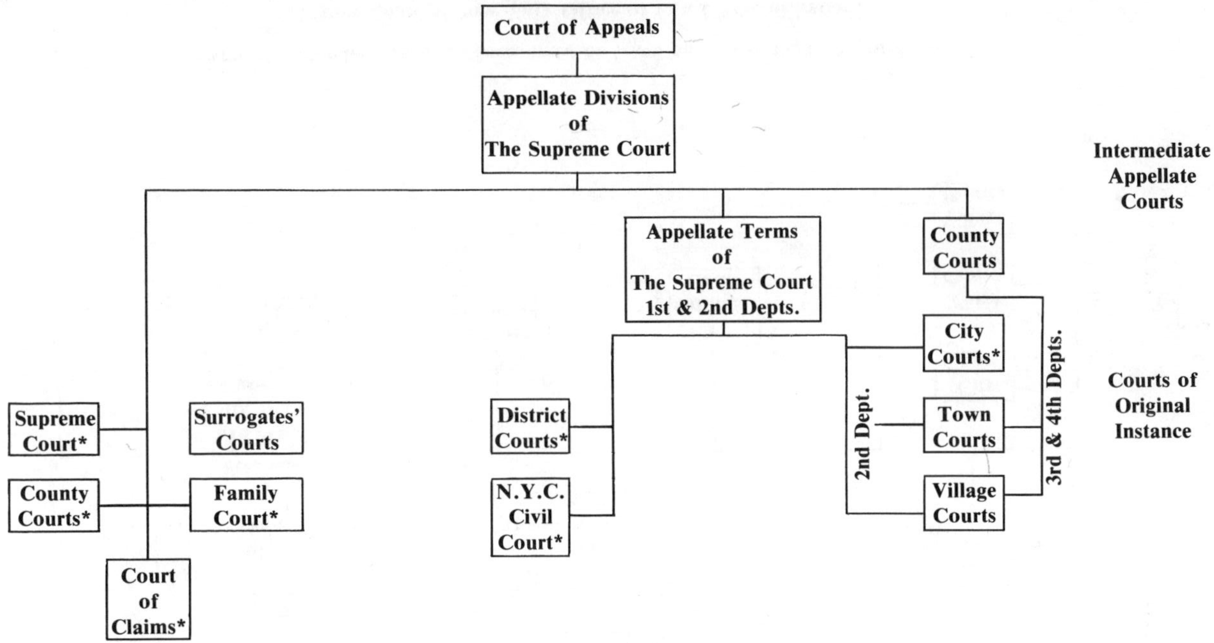

*Appeals from judgments of courts of record of original instance that finally determine actions where the only question involved is the validity of a statutory provision under the New York State or United States Constitution may be taken directly to the Court of Appeals. Only some of the City Courts are courts of record.

Source: State of New York Office of Court Administration.

NEW YORK STATE JUDICIAL SYSTEM CRIMINAL APPEALS STRUCTURE

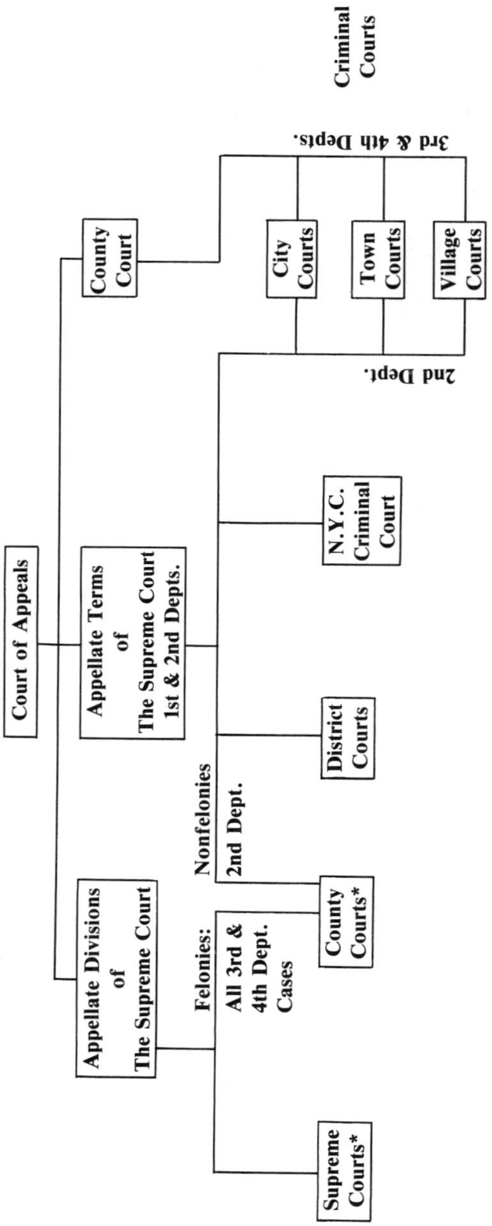

*Appeals involving death sentences must be taken directly to the Court of Appeals.

Source: State of New York Office of Court Administration.

The jurisdiction of the Court of Appeals is limited to appellate review of questions of law, with certain exceptions as set forth in article VI, section 3. These exceptions (when the Court has the power to review findings of fact) include criminal cases involving the death sentence, matters from the Commission on Judicial Conduct and non-jury civil cases in which the Appellate Division reversed or modified a lower court judgment after it found new facts.

In addition to its function as the state's court of last resort, the Court of Appeals also has certain administrative powers. These include the power to promulgate rules of court, to regulate admission of attorneys to the bar, and to appoint the members of the State Board of Law Examiners. The Court also has the responsibility for approving policy proposed by the Chief Judge for the unified court system.

The Chief Judge of the Court of Appeals is the Chief Judge of the State of New York and is the chief judicial officer of the unified court system. For a discussion of court administration, see Section 3 of this Chapter.

(2) The Appellate Division of Supreme Court. The principal intermediate appellate court in New York is the Appellate Division of Supreme Court. It has the power to review both the law and facts in civil and criminal cases. It also serves as a court of original jurisdiction in limited areas that include actions concerning the admission,[26] discipline and disbarment of attorneys,[27] and Article 78 proceedings brought against a Supreme Court justice.[28]

While the Appellate Division is a division of Supreme Court, New York's statewide court of original jurisdiction, the Appellate Division acts through four separate courts, one sitting in each of the four judicial departments.[29]

Each judicial department is made up of judicial districts. Distribution of districts among the departments is governed by article VI, section 4(a) of the Constitution. The map on the next page illustrates the boundaries of the judicial departments and the judicial districts. Similar maps illustrating these boundaries appear in every ***New York Supplement 2d*** bound volume and advance sheet, in the annual reports of the Chief Administrator of the Courts, and in the New York ***Legislative Manual.***

[26] N.Y. Civ. Prac. L. & R. secs. 9401-9407 (McKinney 1981 & 1987 Supp.).

[27] N.Y. Jud. Law sec. 90 (McKinney 1983 & 1987 Supp.)

[28] Civ. Prac. L. & R. sec. 506(b) (McKinney 1976 & 1987 Supp.). An article 78 proceeding is an action brought under article 78 of the Civil Practice Law and Rules to obtain judicial review of administative decisions.

[29] N.Y. Const. art. VI, sec. 4(a) (McKinney 1987).

JUDICIAL DEPARTMENTS AND JUDICIAL DISTRICTS

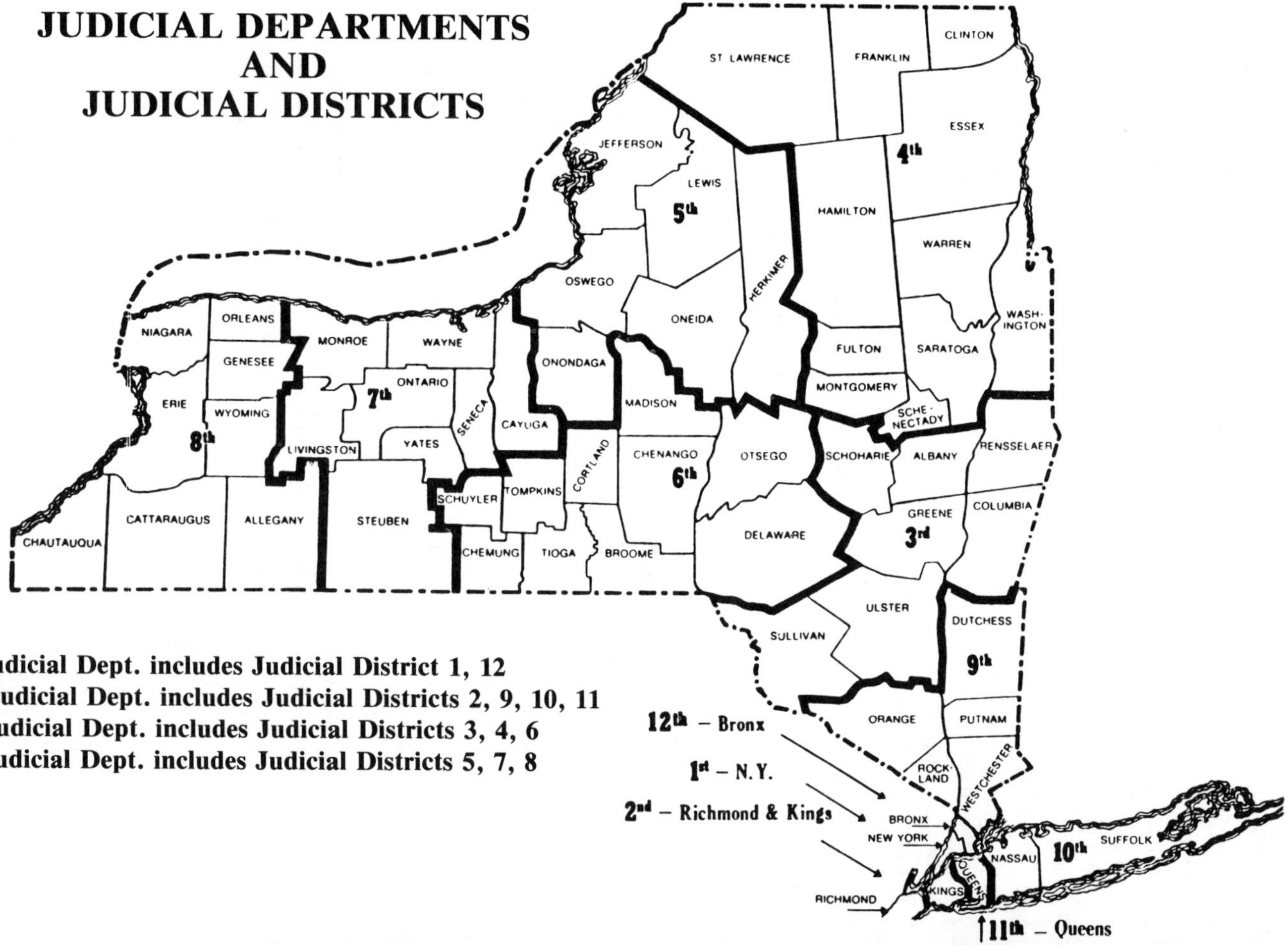

1st Judicial Dept. includes Judicial District 1, 12
2nd Judicial Dept. includes Judicial Districts 2, 9, 10, 11
3rd Judicial Dept. includes Judicial Districts 3, 4, 6
4th Judicial Dept. includes Judicial Districts 5, 7, 8

Each department of the Appellate Division takes appeals from the "superior" trial courts in its Department. The superior trial courts are Supreme Court, Surrogate's Court, Family Court, County Court and the Court of Claims. Appeals from determinations of administrative agencies are taken to the department designated by statute to hear them.

Since the Appellate Division is a branch of Supreme Court, its justices are designated by the governor from the ranks of the elected Supreme Court justices[30] to serve for five year terms. The governor also designates one presiding justice to serve in each of the four judicial departments.[31] Section 4(e) of article VI allows the designation of additional justices when needed, so the total number of justices presiding in each department of the Appellate Division is not fixed. At this writing, the First and Second Departments each have fifteen justices sitting; the Third and Fourth Departments each have nine justices.[32] The Appellate Division justices usually sit in panels of five. However, in the Second Department, only four justices usually sit on a panel.[33]

(3) The Appellate Terms and Appellate Session of County Courts. Appeals from the superior trial courts are taken to to the Appellate Division. Appeals from the lower trial courts are handled differently in the departments.

In the First and Second Departments, the inferior courts include the Civil Court and Criminal Court of the City of New York. In the Second Department there are also district, city, town and village courts. Appeals from these courts are taken to the appropriate Appellate Terms of Supreme Court in the First and Second Departments. In addition, the Appellate Term, Second Department, hears appeals from the county courts in all civil and non-felony cases.

The Appellate Terms consist of from three to five Supreme Court justices who are designated to serve on that court by the chief administrator of the courts with the approval of the presiding justice of the Appellate Division.[34] While the New York Constitution authorizes each judicial department to establish an Appellate Term,[35] only the First and

[30] N.Y. CONST. art. VI, sec. 4(c) (McKinney 1987).
[31] *Id.*
[32] T. NEWMAN, NEW YORK APPELLATE PRACTICE sec. 1.04(1), n.2.
[33] *Id.* at sec. 1.04(1).
[34] N.Y. CONST. art. VI, sec. 8(a) (McKinney 1987).
[35] N.Y. CONST. art. VI, sec. 8 (McKinney 1987).

Second Departments have done so. Orders of the Appellate Term can only be appealed to the Appellate Division by permission.[36]

In the Third and Fourth Department, appeals from the lower trial courts are taken to one of the judges in the appropriate County Court, sitting in appellate session. The inferior courts in the Third and Fourth Departments are the city, town and village courts. Orders of the county courts' appellate sessions may be appealed as of right to the Appellate Division.[37]

c) New York's Trial Courts. Brief descriptions of New York's numerous trial level courts follow. For each court, reference is provided to the appropriate section of the judiciary article establishing the court as well as to the major statutory provisions concerning the court's jurisdiction and the practice act, if any. More detailed descriptions of these courts can be found in the civil and criminal practice treatises listed in Chapter 13. Court rules are discussed in section 5 of Chapter 8 (Practice and Procedure Acts, Evidence, and Court Rules).

(1) Supreme Court. Supreme Court is a single court of statewide jurisdiction with a branch in each of the State's 62 counties. Supreme Court has jurisdiction under the Constitution to hear any criminal or civil action or proceeding, regardless of the amount of money involved, except for claims against the State.[38] In practice, outside of the City of New York, Supreme Court hears principally civil matters, while the County Courts hear the criminal matters. Within the City of New York, Supreme Court sits in both civil and criminal parts. Supreme Court justices are elected to Supreme Court from the judicial districts and serve for fourteen-year terms.

References: Constitution, article VI, §§ 6,7; Judiciary Law § 140-b.

(2) Court of Claims. The Court of Claims has exclusive jurisdiction to determine private claims against the State of New York and claims against certain agencies of the State. Claims against political subdivisions of the State, such as cities and counties, are heard in Supreme Court. Court of Claims judges are appointed by the governor for nine-year terms.

[36] N.Y. Civ. Prac. L. & R. sec. 5703(a) (McKinney 1978).
[37] N.Y. Civ. Prac. L. & R. sec. 5703(b) (McKinney 1978).
[38] Only the Court of Claims has jurisdiction to hear claims against the State.

References: Constitution, article VI, § 9; Court of Claims Act §§ 8,9.

(3) Family Court. Family Court has jurisdiction over family matters such as juvenile delinquency, persons in need of supervision (PINS); paternity proceedings, and crimes or offenses between spouses or between parents and their children. It does not have jurisdiction over matrimonial actions: Supreme Court has exclusive jurisdiction over matrimonial actions.

There is a Family Court in each county. Outside of the City of New York, Family Court judges are elected; they are appointed by the mayor within the City of New York. Family Court judges serve for ten-year terms.

Reference: Constitution, article VI, § 13; Family Court Act § 115.

(4) Surrogate's Court. The Surrogate's Court has jurisdiction over the property of decedents, probate and construction of wills, administration of estates, and guardianship of minors. There is a Surrogate's Court in each county. Surrogates are elected for fourteen years; in some counties the County Court judge may also serve as surrogate and Family Court judge.

References: Constitution, article VI, § 12; Judiciary Law § 189-c Surrogate's Court Practice Act § 201.

(5) County Court. The County Court has both criminal and civil jurisdiction. Generally, the County Court functions as the criminal trial court, while Supreme Court functions as the general civil trial court for the county. There is a County Court in each county outside of the City of New York. In the less populous counties, the County Court judge may also function as the surrogate and Family Court judge. County Court judges are elected for ten-year terms.

As noted previously, in the Third and Fourth departments, County Courts hold appellate sessions to hear appeals from decisions of the local "inferior courts."

References: Constitution, article VI, §§ 10, 11; Judiciary Law § 183 et. seq., §§ 190, 190-a.

(6) New York City Civil Court. The New York City Civil Court has jurisdiction over actions to recover money and property up to a value of $25,000 and various landlord-tenant matters. The judges are elected from the judicial districts within the City of New York and serve for ten-year terms.

References: Constitution, Article VI, § 15(a),(b); N.Y.C. Civil Court Act § 202 et. seq.

(7) New York City Criminal Court. The New York City Criminal Court is the busiest criminal court in the world.[39] It has jurisdiction over misdemeanors and may conduct preliminary hearings in felony cases. The judges are appointed by the mayor for ten-year terms.

References: Constitution, article VI, § 15(a),(c); N.Y.C. Criminal Court Act.

(8) District Courts. The District Courts have both civil and non-felony criminal jurisdiction. Section 16 of the judiciary article authorizes creation of District Courts throughout the state. At this writing, there are only two District Courts; one covers all of Nassau County and the other covers the western part of Suffolk County. Judges are elected for six-year terms.

The District Courts discussed in this section are state courts. There are district courts in the federal court system which are also trial level courts. The federal courts in New York State are discussed in section 6 of this Chapter.

References: Constitution, article VI, § 16; Uniform District Court Act.

(9) City Courts Outside of the City of New York. City courts have both civil and non-felony criminal jurisdiction. The extent of a city court's civil jurisdiction varies from city to city. Judges are elected for terms of six years.

References: Constitution, article VI, § 17; Uniform City Court Act.

[39] LOCAL GOVERNMENT HANDBOOK, *supra* note 21, at 38.

(10) Town and Village Courts (the Justice Courts). Outside of the City of New York, each county is divided into towns, many of which contain villages. The town and village courts can be collectively called the justice courts. The judges of the town courts are called town justices or justices of the peace; the judges of the villages are called village justices or village police justices.

The justice courts have both civil and non-felony criminal jurisdiction. In addition, the justice courts, together with the city and district courts, also handle basic preliminary criminal functions irrespective of the seriousness of the crime. Examples of this function are bail-setting, warrant issuance and preliminary hearings to determine probable cause for detention pending grand jury action.[40]

The method for selecting judges and the length of their terms are determined by the legislature. Generally, the town and village judges are elected for terms of four years.

References: Constitution, article VI, § 17; Uniform Justice Court Act.

d) Jurisdiction Over "Small Claims" Actions. New York has no "small claims courts" as such. Most of the lower courts (district courts, town and village courts, the New York City Civil Court and the city courts outside the City of New York) maintain a small claims part or session. At this writing, the monetary ceiling for small claims is $2,000 in most courts.[41] Procedure is governed by Article 18 of the appropriate court act (New York City Civil Court Act, Uniform City Court Act, Uniform District Court Act and Uniform Justice Court Act).

e) Alternative Dispute Resolution. New York has several mechanisms for resolving civil and criminal disputes without resort to formal judicial proceedings. Civil arbitration programs through the courts have been established in at least 31 countries.[42] Arbitration is also used in the Small Claims parts.

[40] NEW YORK (STATE). LEGISLATURE. SENATE SELECT TASK FORCE ON COURT REORGANIZATION. PRELIMINARY REPORT 33 (1983).

[41] 1987 N.Y. LAWS ch. 254.

[42] W. Greenawalt, ***Alternatives to Court Resolution of Disputes: Report of NYSBA's Special Committee,*** 56 N.Y. ST. B. J. 36, 37 (Oct. 1984). See the N. Y. City Civil Court Act, sec. 206(c), the Uniform District Court Act, sec. 206(c) and 22 NYCRR Part 28.

The Office of Court Administration's Community Dispute Resolution Centers Program was established in 1981.[43] These state-funded centers can provide conciliation, mediation, arbitration or other forms of dispute resolution. Matters typically handled in the Community Dispute Resolution Centers include neighborhood disputes concerning pets, nuisances and noise, trespass, juvenile delinquency, and vandalism.

3. COURT ADMINISTRATION

Court administration is governed by article VI, section 28, of the New York Constitution and sections 210 through 217 of the Judiciary Law. The responsibility for court administration is divided among the Chief Judge of the Court of Appeals, the Chief Administrator of the Courts, the Administrative Board of the Courts, and the Judicial Conference. The present administrative structure is the result of constitutional amendments and legislation which went into effect in the 1960's and 1970's.[44]

a) The Chief Judge and the Administrative Board of the Courts. New York has had the framework for a "unified court system" since 1961.[45] The Chief Judge of the Court of Appeals is the unified court system's chief judicial officer and Chair of the Administrative Board of the Courts. Members of the Administrative Board of the Courts are the presiding justices from each judicial department. The Chief Judge, after consultation with the Board, establishes standards and administrative policies applicable to the unified court system. These must be approved by the Court of Appeals.

b) The Chief Administrator of the Courts. The Chief Administrator of the Courts is appointed by the Chief Judge with the advice and consent of the Board. If the Chief Administrator is a judge or justice in the unified court system, he or she holds the title of Chief Administrative Judge. The Chief Administrator supervises the administration and operation of the unified court system.

[43] 1981 N.Y. LAWS ch. 847, codified at N.Y. JUD. LAW secs. 849-a through 849-g.

[44] For an historical overview of New York court administration from 1953 to 1986, see Bellacosa, ***Judicial Administration — Spell it O-C-A Not O-R-C-A*** 58 N.Y. ST. B.J. 6 (July, 1986) [hereinafter Bellacosa].

[45] N.Y. CONST. art. VI, sec. 1 (McKinney 1987).

The Chief Administrator's annual report to the governor on the activities of the unified court system is the best source for statistics on the courts and for current descriptions of the court structure and administration. Additional useful information included in the annual report are the number of registered attorneys by county and judicial department, personnel and budgetary information on the court system, a summary of educational and training programs conducted during the year, and a summary of legislation sponsored by the Chief Administrator.

The current series of annual reports covers 1978 to date. Prior to 1978, the above-described annual information on the court system was published in the annual reports of the Administrative Board of the Judicial Conference (1955-1977) and the annual reports of the Judicial Council (1934-1954).

c) **Office of Court Administration.** The Office of Court Administration (OCA) was established in 1974.[46] The OCA assists the Chief Administrator in the operation of the unified court system. Its responsibilities include budget preparation and management for the unified court system, attorney registration, and administration of the Community Dispute Resolution Centers Program.

The OCA Counsel's Office has an important legislative role. Its legal staff advises the legislative committees on the Civil Practice Law and Rules, Criminal Law and Procedure, and Family Court. The Counsel's Office was very involved in the development of the uniform rules for the trial courts,[47] which went into effect in 1986.

d) **The Judicial Conference.** The Judicial Conference is a large body composed of: the Chief Judge of the Court of Appeals; the presiding Appellate Division justice and one Supreme Court justice from each of the four judicial departments; representative judges from the other courts; and representatives from the state bar. The chairpersons and ranking minority members of the Senate and the Assembly Committees on the Judiciary and Committees on Codes are ex officio members of the Judicial Conference.

The Judicial Conference studies and makes recommendations for changes in laws and rules relating to civil, criminal and family law practice. The Judicial Conference also advises the Chief Administrator of the

[46] 1974 N.Y. LAWS ch. 615.
[47] Bellacosa, *supra* note 44, at 9.

Courts on education programs for the judicial and non-judicial personnel of the unified court system. When requested to do so, it consults with the Chief Judge and Chief Administrator on the administration and operation of the court system. Many of the functions now performed by the Administrative Board of the Courts were performed by the Judicial Council (from 1934-1954) and the Judicial Conference (from 1955-1977).

4. COMMISSION ON JUDICIAL CONDUCT

The Commission on Judicial Conduct came into existence on April 1, 1978 as the result of amendment of article VI, section 22, of the New York Constitution. The eleven-member Commission has the responsibility to investigate and make initial determinations concerning complaints against any judges or justices in the unified court system. It can determine that the subject judge or justice be admonished, censured or removed from office. The Commission transmits its determinations to the Chief Judge of the Court of Appeals for delivery to the judge or justice. Upon request of the subject judge or justice, the Commission's determination will be reviewed by the Court of Appeals.

Prior to 1978, judicial conduct was reviewed and judges or justices were disciplined by the Court on the Judiciary.

5. REGULATION OF ATTORNEYS

a) Rules for Admission to Practice. Section 53(1) of the Judiciary Law authorizes the Court of Appeals to promulgate rules on admission to practice in the courts of New York State. These rules are found in 22 NYCRR part 520. They include age, educational and examination requirements, and the rules on reciprocity (admission without examination of attorneys from other jurisdictions).

The State Education Department also issues standards for law curriculum within the State. The Department rules are found in 8 NYCRR 52.6.

The State Board of Law Examiners administers the New York State bar examination twice each year. Board rules are found in 22 NYCRR part 6000. The Board must certify to the appropriate Appellate Division that each applicant for admission to practice either has passed the required bar examination or that the bar examination was not required for that applicant.

Section 90(1) of the Judiciary Law gives the Appellate Division the responsibility for determining whether the applicants meet standards of character and fitness to practice law and whether the applicants have fulfilled all other requirements for bar admission. When all standards are met, each Appellate Division admits attorneys resident in its judicial department to practice in the courts of the State.

Regulations governing bar admission are found in the NYCRR as follows:

First Department - 22 NYCRR part 602
Second Department - 22 NYCRR part 690
Third Department - 22 NYCRR part 805
Fourth Department - 22 NYCRR part 1022.34

New York State does not have an "integrated bar." In states which do have an integrated bar, joining the bar association is synonymous with admission to practice in the courts. In New York State, an attorney does not have to join a bar association in order to practice law.

b) Rules of Conduct for Attorneys. Section 90(2) of the Judiciary Law gives the responsibility for control of attorneys and "all persons practicing or assuming to practice law"[48] to the Supreme Court. Section 90(2) also vests the authority to discipline attorneys in the Appellate Division. Each Appellate Division has adopted rules for the professional conduct of attorneys in its judicial department and for discipline of attorneys who violate those standards of conduct. These rules are found in the NYCRR as follows:

First Department - 22 NYCRR part 603
Second Department - 22 NYCRR part 691
Third Department - 22 NYCRR part 806
Fourth Department - 22 NYCRR part 1022

c) Ethics Opinions. The New York State Bar Association, the Association of the Bar of the City of New York, the New York County Bar Association and the Bar Association of Erie County publish the opinions of their Committees on Professional Ethics. In addition to the sources of

[48] N.Y. JUD. LAW sec. 90(2) (McKinney 1983).

opinions listed below, the issues of the *New York State Bar Journal* publish the latest New York State Bar Assocation ethics opinions on a monthly basis.

Association of the Bar of the City of New York. Committee on Professional Ethics. ***Opinions / Committees on Professional Ethics*** [of] the Association of the Bar of the City of New York, the New York County Lawyers' Association, New York State Bar Association. Edited by Eugene Wypski. London; New York:

5v. Loose-leaf supplementation.

Bar Association of Erie County. Ethics Committee. ***Ethics Committee Opinions.*** no. 1- Buffalo: Erie County Bar Association, 1974-

National Reporter on Legal Ethics and Professional Responsibility, Frederick, Md.: University Publications of America, 1983. Looseleaf supplements.

Now edited by Professor David Luban, this reporter is organized alphabetically by state. The New York section contains the Code of Professional Responsibility, formal and informal opinions of the New York State Bar Association's Committee on Professional Ethics, and the full text of New York court decisions interpreting the Code. Each issue contains topical commentary by Professor Luban.

New York State Bar Association. Committee on Professional Ethics. ***Formal Opinions.*** No. 1-500. Albany: New York State Bar Association, 1974-1979.

______ ***Opinions.*** No. 501- . Albany: New York State Bar Association, 1979

Looseleaf supplementation.

6. THE FEDERAL COURTS IN NEW YORK

Article III of the U.S. Constitution is the foundation of our federal court system. The highest court in the United States is the U.S. Supreme

Court. The intermediate appellate court in the federal judicial system is the Court of Appeals. The Court of Appeals is organized into twelve regional, numbered circuits. The Thirteenth Circuit, which is the Court of Appeals for the Federal Circuit has national jurisdiction. Each circuit except the District of Columbia Circuit and the Thirteenth Circuit includes three or more states. New York is included in the Second Circuit along with Connecticut and Vermont. The judges for the Second Circuit sit in New York City.

There are several kinds of trial level courts in the federal court system. The courts of general jurisdiction are the District Courts. Each state contains at least one federal District Court, and the more populous states have more than one. New York is divided into four districts: Northern, Southern, Eastern and Western. Court for the Northern District is held at Albany, Auburn, Binghamton, Malone, Syracuse, and Utica. Court for the Southern District is held at New York and White Plains. Court for the Eastern District is held at Brooklyn, Hauppauge, and Hempstead. Court for the Western District is held at Buffalo, Canandaigua, Elmira, Jamestown, and Rochester.

In addition to the District Courts, there are various specialized trial level courts: U.S. Claims Court, U.S. Court of International Trade, (which sits in New York City and other major ports) and the U.S. Tax Court. Bankruptcy matters are handled by bankruptcy judges under the jurisdiction of the District Courts.

REFERENCES

Bellacosa, J.W. ***Judicial Administration — Spell it O-C-A- Not O-R-C-A.*** 58 New York State Bar Journal 6 (July, 1986).

Bergan, F. ***The Appellate Division at Age 90: Its Conception and Birth, 1894.*** 57 New York State Bar Journal 7 (January, 1985).

Bergan, F. ***The History of the New York Court of Appeals, 1847-1932.*** New York: Columbia University Press, 1985.

Chester, A. ***Courts and Lawyers Of New York.*** New York: American Historical Society, 1925.

Chester, A. ***Legal and Judicial History of New York.*** New York: National Americana Society, 1911.

The Courts of New York. New York State Bar Association, comp. Albany: N.Y.S. Bar Association, 1987.

Daly, C. P. *Historical Sketch of the Judicial Tribunals of New York From 1623 to 1846,* in 1 *E.D. Smith Common Pleas Reports* (1855).

Ellis, D. M. et. al. *A History of New York State.* Ithaca: Cornell University Press, 1967.

Flaherty, D. H. *A Select Guide to the Manuscript Court Records of Colonial New England.* 11 American Journal of Legal History 107 (1967).

Goebel, J. *The Courts and the Law in Colonial New York.* Chap. in 3 Flick, *History of the State of New York.* New York: Columbia University Press, 1933.

Goebel, J. and T. R. Naughton, *Law Enforcement In Colonial New York: a Study in Criminal Procedure.* New York: Commonwealth Fund, 1944.

Hamlin, P.M. *Legal Education in Colonial New York.* New York: New York University, Law Quarterly Review, 1939.

Hamlin, P.M. and C.E. Baker. *Supreme Court of Judicature Of the Province Of New York, 1691-1704.* New York: New York Historical Society, 1959.

MacCrate, R. *Appellate Justice In New York.* Chicago: American Judicature Society, 1982.

Moore, J.H. *One Hundred Fifty Years of Official Law Reporting and the Courts in New York.* 5 Syracuse Law Review 273 (1955).

New York (City). Mayor's Court. *Select Cases of the Mayor's Court of New York City, 1674-1784.* Washington: American Historical Association, 1935.

New York (State). Dept. of State. ***Local Government Handbook,*** 4th ed. Albany: N.Y. Dept. of State, 1987.

New York (State). Legislature. Select Task Force on Court Reorganization. ***Preliminary Report.*** Albany: N.Y. Legislature, 1983.

New York (State). Senate. Judiciary Committee. ***Order in the Courts: Weighing the Impact of Court Merger, Appellate Reform and Judicial Selection Proposals in New York State.*** Albany: N.Y. Legislature, 1986.

Newman, T. ***New York Appellate Practice.*** New York: Matthew Bender, 1985- .

Note, ***Law In Colonial New York: the Legal System of 1691.*** 80 Harvard Law Review 1757 (1967).

Pennypacker, M. ***The Duke's Laws: Their Antecedents, Implications and Importance.*** New York: New York University School of Law, 1944. Also printed in the Anglo-American Legal History Series. Series 1, no. 2.

Chapter Seven
COURT REPORTS AND CASE FINDERS

1. OVERVIEW OF NEW YORK COURT REPORTS

The complexity of New York's court system, past and present, was described in Chapter 6. That complexity is reflected in the number and scope of court reports, official and unofficial, published in New York since 1801. Section 1 of this Chapter provides a brief account of the highlights of court reporting in New York. It is intended to introduce section 2, which is a detailed description of the current court reports, and section 7, which is a checklist of New York's 105 current and discontinued court reports and major reprint sets.

In order to present this material concisely, references to court report volumes in this Chapter are often abbreviated in the following manner: 2 N.Y. means volume 2 of *New York Reports*; 183 N.Y.S.2d means volume 183 of *New York Supplement*, second series; 1 N.Y.2d (1956) means volume one of *New York Reports*, second series, which reported decisions handed down in 1956. A list of New York legal abbreviations, including court report abbreviations, is found in Appendix G.

a) Nominative Reports. The earlier New York court reports were compiled and published by individuals. Those reports were known as "nominatives" because they bore the name of and were cited by the name of their compiler. Usually, the compiler was the court reporter. Some nominative reports were totally private endeavors ("unofficial") while some were "official," i.e., published by authority of the state.

New York's first court report was a nominative, ***Coleman's Cases***, published in 1801. It included cases decided in the Supreme Court of Judicature between 1791 and 1800.

b) Establishment of the Official Court Reports. By the Act of April 7, 1804, the legislature provided for the appointment of an official reporter to publish the decisions of the Supreme Court of Judicature. George Caines was appointed to serve as the state's first official reporter. The first official report of New York decisions was ***Caines' Reports*** (also known as the ***New York Term Reports***),[1] which included cases decided in the Court of Errors and the Supreme Court of Judicature between 1803 and 1805.

In 1814, the official reporter's duties were enlarged to include reporting Chancery decisions.[2] The separate position of Chancery Reporter was created in 1825[3] and continued until Chancery was abolished in 1846.

[1] Moore, ***One Hundred Fifty Years of Official Law Reporting and the Courts in New York,*** 6 Syracuse L. Rev. 273, 288 (1955) [hereinafter Moore].

[2] 1814 N.Y. Laws ch. 193.

[3] 1815 N.Y. Laws ch. 263.

c) **Establishment of the Current Official Reports.** The Court of Appeals succeeded the Court of Errors as the State's highest court under the new Constitution of 1846. That Constitution[4] provided for the appointment of a State Reporter to be responsible for publishing the decisions of the Court of Appeals in the new official report series, the ***New York Reports***. The first volume of ***New York Reports*** was published in 1847.

Volumes of ***New York Reports,*** first series, carry both the official volume numbers of ***New York Reports*** and the nominative titles and volume numbers. So, for example, 1 N.Y. is also 1 ***Comstock***; 5 N.Y. is also 1 ***Selden***. This "double identity" continues until 309 N.Y., which is the last volume in the first series of ***New York Reports***. Modern citation practice uses only the citation from ***New York Reports,*** but the nominative names and volume numbers are of historical interest and can be found in the checklist of court reports in Section 7 of this Chapter.

The Constitution of 1846 established the General Term of Supreme Court as the State's intermediate appellate court. This court had no official series of reports until 1869. The unofficial report was ***Barbour's Supreme Court Reports***, which reported decisions of the General Term from 1847 to 1877. ***Barbour's*** actually was a more comprehensive report of General Term decisions than was the first official report, ***Lansing's***, described below.

The scope of New York's official reporting was extended to the General Term of Supreme Court in 1869 when the office of Supreme Court Reporter was created.[5] The resulting reports, ***Lansing's Supreme Court Reports*** and ***Hun's Supreme Court Reports,*** were published until the Constitution of 1894 abolished the General Term and replaced it with the Appellate Division of Supreme Court. At that time, the ***Appellate Division Reports***[6] supplanted the ***Supreme Court Reports*** as the official report for New York's intermediate appellate court.

The lack of an official statewide report series for the lower courts of record was remedied in 1892 by the creation of the office of Miscellaneous Reporter and the beginning of the ***Miscellaneous Reports*** series.[7]

Coordination among the official reports began in 1895 with the publication of a weekly advance sheet reporting new decisions from all three of the official reports under one cover.[8] The pattern of coordina-

[4] N.Y. CONST. 1846, art VI, sec. 22; 1847 N.Y. LAWS ch. 277 and ch. 280 and 1848 N.Y. LAWS ch. 224 (enacting legislation).

[5] N.Y. CONST. 1869 art. VI, sec. 23; 1869 N.Y. LAWS ch. 99 (enacting legislation).

[6] 1895 N.Y. LAWS ch. 946 sec. 248-49.

[7] 1892 N.Y. LAWS ch. 598.

[8] Moore, *supra* note 1, at 300.

tion and consolidation continued in the twentieth century as the offices of court reporting were gradually merged. The office of Miscellaneous Reporter was eliminated in 1924[9] and responsibility for producing the ***Miscellaneous Reports*** was shifted to the Supreme Court Reporter. The present organization of official reporting in New York was established in 1938 when the duties of the State Reporter and Supreme Court Reporter were merged and the State Law Reporting Bureau was created.[10]

The creation of the various official series of reports did not at first discourage private individuals from printing unofficial reports. In ***One Hundred Fifty Years of Official Law Reporting and the Courts in New York***, John H. Moore of the State Law Reporting Bureau, describes the lively competition between the official and unofficial reporters.[11]

d) Emergence of the Current Unofficial Reports. Today, unofficial law reporting in New York is dominated by the West Publishing Company. The West Publishing Company began to publish ***North Eastern Reporter*** in 1885. It includes cases included in 99 N.Y. (1885) to the present. The second series of ***North Eastern Reporter*** began in 1936.

The West Publishing Company began publication of ***New York Supplement*** in 1888. While it was originally conceived of as a supplemental reporter to ***North Eastern Reporter***, its scope was soon expanded to include all three levels of the New York court system. A more detailed description of this development is found in Section 2(b)(2) of this Chapter. The second series of ***New York Supplement*** began in 1938.

2. THE PRESENT COURT REPORTS

As noted previously, New York currently is served by three official court reports and two unofficial court reports. In addition to these reports, the legal newspaper, the ***New York Law Journal***, selectively reports otherwise unreported downstate lower court decisions.

In addition to the printed sources of court reports, there are two online sources for New York cases. Both LEXIS and WESTLAW provide comprehensive, current and retrospective coverage of New York Court of Appeals cases. Coverage of current Appellate Division and reported trial

[9] 1924 N.Y. LAWS ch. 173.
[10] 1938 N.Y. LAWS ch. 494.
[11] Moore, *supra* note 1, at 293-98.

level cases is also comprehensive. For details of retrospective coverage, see the discussion of LEXIS and WESTLAW in Chapter 12 (Databases for New York Legal Research).

a) Current Official Reports. New York's current official reports are: ***New York Reports 2d, Appellate Division Reports 2d,*** and ***Miscellaneous Reports 2d.*** Published by authority of Article 14 of the Judiciary Law, the second series for all three official court reports began with volume one in 1956. While publication of the reports is authorized by the State, the reports are commercially printed. The printing contract is put out to bid periodically pursuant to section 434 of the Judiciary Law[12]. At this writing, the reports are published by Lawyers Co-operative Publishing Company of Rochester, New York.

Each volume of New York's official reports contains an index-digest and case name table giving access to decisions reported in that volume. Each opinion has a syllabus, which contains numbered summaries of the main points of law in the case. These are developed by the editors of the official reports, and they do not correspond to the topic and key numbers found in the headnotes of reports published by the West Publishing Company. The numbers in the syllabus are useful in Shepardizing[13] the particular points of law in the syllabus using ***Shepard's Citations***, but only in ***Shepard's*** divisions for New York's official reports.[14] It bears repeating that the syllabus numbers in the official reports and the headnote numbers in the West reports are not interchangeable.

(1) New York Reports 2d. The second series of ***New York Reports***, cited N.Y.2d, reports all decisions of New York's highest court, the Court of Appeals.

(2) Appellate Division Reports 2d. The second series of the ***Appellate Division Reports***, cited A.D.2d, reports all decisions of the four Appellate Divisions of Supreme Court.

(3) Miscellaneous Reports 2d. The second series of the ***Miscellaneous Reports***, cited Misc.2d, reports selected opinions of Supreme Court, other trial courts, and the Appellate Terms. For an opin-

[12] N.Y. JUD. LAW sec. 434 (McKinney 1983 & Supp. 1987)

[13] Shepardizing is the use of ***Shepard's Citations*** to verify the authority of a case.

[14] Shepardizing New York cases is described in Section 5 of this Chapter.

ion to be selected for reporting, it must be one that "the State Reporter, with the approval of the Court of Appeals, considers worthy of being reported because of its usefulness as a precedent or its importance as a matter of public interest."[15] Relatively few trial level opinions are selected for publication; one authority states that only 10% of them are published.[16]

(4) Advance Sheets. One weekly pamphlet, called an advance sheet, updates all three of the official court reports. Any individual advance sheet may contain new matter from all three of the court reports, or from only one or two of them. Each of the three official reports has its own volume numbers and page numbers. Accordingly, when an advance sheet includes reports from two or three official reports, it will include several sets of page numbers. While the volume and page contents of each advance sheet are clearly shown on its cover and spine, a few examples may serve to clarify the internal organization of the official advance sheets.

Contents of Advance Sheet No. 500 (August 12, 1987)

70 N.Y.2d 146-150
129 A.D.2d 28-99
135 Misc. 2d 631-687

Contents of Advance Sheet No. 501 (August 19, 1987)

129 A.D.2d 100-144
135 Misc. 2d 688-745

Contents of Advance Sheet No. 502 (August 26, 1987)

70 N.Y.2d 151-192
128 A.D.2d 128-1031

In the example above, notice that the volume numbers of the reports are not always published in numerical order in the advance sheets. For example, Advance Sheet No. 500 contains pages from 129 A.D.2d and Advance Sheet No. 502 contains pages from the previous volume, 128

[15] N.Y. JUD. LAW sec. 431 (McKinney 1983).
[16] M.L. COHEN & R.C. BERRING, HOW TO FIND THE LAW 19 n.3 (1983).

A.D.2d. Notice also that the advance sheets vary considerably in their size. For example, Advance Sheet No. 502 contains many more pages than Nos. 500 or 501. No. 502 contains almost 1,000 pages of memorandum decisions, mainly from the Second Department, no full opinions from the Appellate Division, only a few opinions from the Court of Appeals, and no opinions at all from the *Miscellaneous Reports*.

Each advance sheet contains a number of helpful features provided by the publisher, Lawyers Co-op. These include:

* digest-index and table of cases for decisions reported in the advance sheet;

* table of statutes construed and rules construed;

* signed current awareness commentaries that summarize and give citations to significant new legislation, court decisions, and attorney general, comptroller, and Tax Appeals opinions; and

* lists of new filings at the Court of Appeals and other lists that are useful in determining whether a case is being appealed.

Orange-colored, cumulative Index-Digest and Case Table pamphlets are published as extra issues of the official advance sheets in February, April, June, August, October, and December. Distribution tables indicate in which advance sheet the various report volume and page numbers fall.

b) Current Unofficial Reports. New York's current unofficial reports are: *North Eastern Reporter 2d and New York Supplement 2d.*

(1) North Eastern Reporter 2d. The *North Eastern Reporter* is a unit of the West Publishing Company's National Reporter System. It is one of seven "regional reporters" in the National Reporter System. A regional reporter reports the decisions of the highest courts of the states within its scope. The *North Eastern Reporter* reports all New York Court of Appeals decisions and the decisions of the highest courts of Illinois, Indiana, Massachusetts and Ohio.

Since it is a West Publishing Company reporter, the *North Eastern Reporter* contains West topic and key number references that coordinate its headnotes with the West digests, including the *Abbott's* and *West's* digests described in Section 3 of this Chapter. The headnote numbers can be used to Shepardize particular points of law digested in the headnotes. As mentioned in Section 2(a) above, the headnote numbers in the West reports and numbers in the syallabi of the official reports are not interchangeable. Shepardizing is described in Section 5 of this Chapter.

Coverage of New York Court of Appeals decisions in the *North Eastern Reporter* began with 99 N.Y which was included in 1 N.E. (1885). The *North Eastern Reporter* is now in its second series, which began with volume 1 in 1936 and is cited N.E.2d.

(2) New York Supplement 2d. Like the *North Eastern Reporter,* the *New York Supplement* is a unit of the West Publishing Company's National Reporter System. *New York Supplement* includes all ***reported*** decisions of New York's courts (Court of Appeals, Appellate Division, and those decisions selected for reporting from the Supreme Court and other lower courts). *New York Supplement* is now in its second series, which began with volume 1 in 1938 and is cited N.Y.S.2d.

Since it is a West reporter, *New York Supplement* possesses the West topic and key number features described above in connection with the *North Eastern Reporter*. Unlike *North Eastern Reporter, New York Supplement* has "star pagination," a feature that enables the researcher to cite to the appropriate page of the official reporters while actually using *New York Supplement.*

Questions frequently arise over how and when Court of Appeals decisions came to be included in *New York Supplement*, and why, since they were included, there were no parallel citations for Court of Appeals decisions from *New York Reports* citations to *New York Supplement* until 150 N.Y.S.2d. The publishing history for *New York Supplement* that follows will answer those questions.

New York Supplement began in 1888 as a reporter of the New York intermediate appellate and lower courts of record and was intended to be a supplemental reporter to the *North Eastern Reporter*. The desirability of making *New York Supplement* a comprehensive reporter by including Court of Appeals decisions became apparent to the West Publishing Company editors. At some point, Court of Appeals decisions were added in separately paginated appendices to all new sets of *New York Supplement* that were printed and sold. Thus, some printings of the first series of *New York Supplement* (bearing the 1888 imprint) contain Court of Appeals decisions in an appendix, and some (also bearing the 1888 imprint) do not.

In the editions of *New York Supplement* that do contain Court of Appeals decisions from volume 1 on, 1 N.Y.S. (1888) has an appendix containing 1-3 N.Y, (1847-1850), 2 N.Y.S. (1889) has an appendix containing 4-6 N.Y. (1850-1852), and so on. By the time 183 N.Y.S. (1920) was printed, inclusion of Court of Appeals decisions had been made current. From 183 N.Y.S. (1920) through 148 N.Y.S.2d (1955), Court of Appeals decisions were included on a current basis, although still in a separately paginated appendix.

Decisions of the Court of Appeals were integrated into the regular pagination of ***New York Supplement 2d,*** starting with 150 N.Y.S.2d. (1956). This change in ***New York Supplement 2d*** corresponded with the issuance of volume one of the second series of ***New York Reports.***

Once the Court of Appeals decisions were included in the regular pagination of ***New York Supplement 2d,*** a parallel citation[17] for a New York Court of Appeals case could and did include all three court reports instead of only ***New York Reports*** and ***North Eastern Reporter.***

For a time, the ***New York Supplement*** included decisions that were not approved for reporting by the State Law Reporting Bureau.[18] Another interesting feature of ***New York Supplement*** is that it absorbed and continued the ***New York State Reporter,*** which was another unofficial reporter for New York courts of record.[19]

The bound volumes of ***New York Supplement 2d*** are kept up-todate by pamphlets called advance sheets. The spine of each advance sheet indicates the volume number of which the particular pamphlet is a part. Each advance sheet contains a cumulative digest for the volume of which it is a part. The digests are arranged by West topic and key number. They can be used to update the pocket parts of ***West's New York Digest 3d*** and to further verify the authority of a case after Shepardizing it. To use the advance sheet digest features to accomplish those tasks:

1. Shepardize your case, taking note of the last N.Y.S.2d volume covered in ***Shepard's;***

2. Note the relevant West topics and key numbers from your case (you would already know them if you were updating the ***West's New York Digest 3d*** pocket parts);

[17] Parallel citations are citations to two or more reports in which the ***same*** opinion can be found. This is an example of a parallel citation for an Appellate Division case in both ***Appellate Division Reports 2d*** and ***New York Supplement 2d: Bowers v. Zaimes,*** 59 A.D.2d 803, 398 N.Y.S.2d 766 (3d Dept 1977).

[18] For a description of the complications ensuing when unofficially reported cases were cited to the courts, see J.J. MARKE and R. SLOANE, LEGAL RESEARCH AND LAW LIBRARY MANAGEMENT 57-58 (1982).

[19] The ***New York State Reporter*** (v. 1-75, 1886-1896) began publication in 1886, two years before West issued the first volume of ***New York Supplement.*** Beginning with volume 76, it was merged into ***New York Supplement.***

3. Trace the relevant West topics and key numbers through the digests in only those N.Y.S.2d advance sheets for volumes NOT covered in your ***Shepard's*** search (or NOT covered in the digest pocket part); or

4. ALTERNATIVELY, perform the Shepardizing online through WESTLAW, then update ***Shepard's*** for your case by performing a West topic and key number search on WESTLAW. The search should be limited by date so that only the most recent cases are retrieved; and

5. Locate the cases identified in step 3 or 4 either in the advance sheets of *New York Supplement 2d* or online.

In addition to the digest feature, *New York Supplement 2d* advance sheets contain other useful editorial features such as: legislative highlights and court news; the text of new court rules; summaries of new decisions of the Commissioner of Education, the Counsel for the State Board of Equalization and Assessment, attorney general and comptroller; and cumulative tables indicating cases in that volume of the advance sheets which cite the Consolidated Laws.

(3) New York Law Journal. The *New York Law Journal* has been published since 1888.[20] It is the official legal newspaper for the First and Second Departments. In addition to printing and digesting notable cases from the Court of Appeals and First and Second Departments, the *New York Law Journal* publishes downstate trial court opinions not published elsewhere. These may be cited to the *N.Y.L.J.* in New York courts. It is available by hardcopy subscription from New York Law Publishing Co. of New York City. It is also available on microfilm from University Microfilms International, 300 North Zeeb Road, Ann Arbor, Michigan.

Cases reported in *N.Y.L.J.* are digested in the *New York Law Journal Digest-Annotator* (formerly *Clark's Digest-Annotator*). This digest is described in Section 3 of this Chapter. Substantive articles in the *New York Law Journal* are indexed in ***Legal Resource Index (LRI).*** That index is described in Chapter 15 (Reference Books and Periodical Indexes).

[20] The *New York Law Journal* absorbed and continued the *Daily Register* (1872-1888), which had absorbed and continued the *New York Daily Transcript* (1859-1872).

(4) Upstate Legal Record. The *Upstate Legal Record* began publication in 1986. It prints selected, significant cases with emphasis on the Third Department of the Appellate Division. It also digests other important New York and federal cases.

(5) Buffalo Law Journal. The *Buffalo Law Journal* began publication in 1929. It contains local court calendars and legal notices. It was known as the *Buffalo Daily Law Journal* from 1929-1978. When its publishing frequency changed to twice weekly, the title was changed to *Buffalo Law Journal.*

(6) Daily Record [Rochester]. The *Daily Record* began publication in 1908. Like the *Buffalo Law Journal* it contains local court information and legal notices.

3. DIGESTS AND OTHER CASE FINDERS

Digests are case finders which classify case summaries (also called digests or annotations) by subject.[21] Digests that are published by the West Publishing Company offer the advantage of West topic and key number compatibility with West reporters, including *New York Supplement*, West statutes, including *McKinney's Consolidated Laws of New York Annotated*, West digests in all jurisdictions (federal and state), including *West's New York Digest 3d,* and WESTLAW, a legal research database. Sections 3(a)-(c) below describe the West digests for New York cases and how to use them.

Specialized digests produced by other publishers offer a focused approach. One digests only cases reported in *New York Law Journal.* Others digest current New York cases in particular areas such as jury verdicts, matrimonial law, civil practice, and criminal law. These specialized digests are described in Section 3(d) and (e) below.

a) The Basic Uses of West Digests. Following is a functional summary of how to find basic information about cases in a West digest.

* to find cases on a subject — use the Descriptive Word Index, which is a subject index to the Digest.

[21] W. STATSKY, LEGAL RESEARCH, WRITING, AND ANALYSIS 27 (2d ed. 1982).

* to find citations or parallel citations of cases when only the case name is known — use the Table of Cases which lists digested cases in alphabetical order, gives the full citation to the court reports, and gives the West topic and key numbers for each case. There is also a Defendant-Plaintiff table, which is an alphabetical list by defendant's name.

* to find cases in which legal terms are defined — use the digest's Words and Phrases volume. It lists legal words and phrases, under which are found digested cases in which the words or phrases are defined.

* to find groups of cases under a particular West key number — turn to the body of the digest volumes, which are arranged alphabetically by digest topic and then numerically by key number. Under the key number will be found the digested cases. Since each case digest contains the case name and citation, the researcher can easily locate the desired cases in the court reports.

b) The Abbott/West New York Digest Series. The major digest for New York cases from the earliest court reports to the present is divided into three chronological series, each bearing a distinct title. The titles are: ***Abbott New York Digest, Consolidated Edition*** (coverage is 1794-1929); ***Abbott New York Digest 2d*** (coverage is 1930-1961); and ***West's New York Digest 3d*** (coverage is 1961 to date).

(1) Abbott New York Digest, Consolidated Edition. ***The Abbott New York Digest, Consolidated Edition*** digests New York cases reported between 1794 and 1929. It was published cooperatively by three companies: West Publishing Company, Baker, Voorhis & Company, and Lawyers Cooperative Publishing Company. The classification system used in this series was a combination of a system first devised by Benjamin Vaughan Abbott and a system developed by the editors of West's ***American Digest*** and ***New York Digest.***

The main set is comprised of 42 volumes in 43 books and includes a Words and Phrases volume, a Table of Cases, a Defendant-Plaintiff Table and a Descriptive Word Index (the subject index).

An eight volume cumulative supplement to the ***Consolidated Edition*** of ***Abbott's*** digested New York cases reported between 1929 and 1944. Its coverage ended with the following reporter volumes: 292 N.Y.; 54 N.E.2d; 47 N.Y.S.2d; 267 A.D.; and 181 Misc.

(2) Abbott New York Digest 2d. ***Abbott New York Digest 2d*** digests New York cases reported between 1930 and 1961. Between 1930 and 1944, its coverage overlaps with that of the Cumulative Supplement to the Consolidated Edition. ***Abbott's 2d*** digests decisions reported in ***New York Reports, Appellate Division Reports, Miscellaneous Reports*** and ***New York Supplement*** for the period 1930 through 1961.

Abbott's is comprised of 28 volumes in 61 books plus 14 unnumbered volumes. The case digests in ***Abbott's 2d*** are arranged by West topic and key number. It contains references to ***American Law Reports*** (A.L.R.) annotations,[22] law review articles, and major New York statutes. The Descriptive Word Index, Table of Cases, Defendant-Plaintiff Table, and Words and Phrases volumes cumulate references to both the first and second series of ***Abbott's. Abbott New York Digest 2d*** was published by West Publishing Company and Lawyers Cooperative Publishing Company.

(3) West's New York Digest 3d. ***West's New York Digest 3d*** digests New York cases decided since 1962 and federal cases arising in New York which were decided since 1962. The ***Abbott's*** first and second series did not include federal cases which arose in New York. ***Abbott's 3d*** arranges the case digests by the West topic and key number and also gives references to ***Corpus Jurus Secundum (C.J.S.),***[23] New York attorney general opinions and law review articles. Unfortunately, ***Abbott's 3d*** does not give references to either A.L.R. or ***New York Jurisprudence 2d,***[24] since those sources are published by Lawyers Co-operative Publishing Company and not by West.

The ***West's New York Digest 3d*** is comprised of 43 volumes in 48 books. The Table of Cases, Defendant-Plaintiff Table, Words and Phrases volumes and Descriptive Word Index cover ***only*** the third series and not the earlier two ***Abbott's*** series. This digest covers the three official New York reports for the period 1962 to date and cases reported in 232 ***New York Supplement 2d*** to date. Federal cases arising in New York that are reported in ***Federal Supplement, Federal Rules Decisions, Federal Reporter 2d, West's Bankruptcy Reports*** and ***Supreme Court Reporter*** are also digested from 1962 to date.

[22] ***American Law Reports*** [hereinafter A.L.R.] is an annotated series of court reports. The annotations are extensive and a citation to one can be a useful research lead. A.L.R. is a general reporter and not limited to New York cases.

[23] ***Corpus Juris Secundum*** is a general legal encyclopedia published by the West Publishing Company.

[24] ***New York Jurisprudence 2d*** is a legal encyclopedia for New York which is described in Chapter 15 (Reference Books and Indexes).

Like the other West digests for federal and state jurisdictions, each volume of ***West's New York Digest 3d*** is updated by annual pocket parts. In turn, the pocket parts are updated about midway through the annual publishing cycle by a supplementary pamphlet covering the whole set. Each pocket part and pamphlet indicates its cutoff point, which is the last volume number for each of the covered reporters digested in that pocket part or pamphlet.

To determine whether even more recent cases in the New York state courts have been reported, update the digest using the "Key Number Digests" found in each of the advance sheets for ***New York Supplement 2d***. To determine whether more recent New York cases in the federal courts have been reported, update the digest using the "Key Number Digests" found in each of the advance sheets for the appropriate West reports for the federal courts. The updating process can also be done as a topic and key number search on WESTLAW. To retrieve both federal and New York cases (in other words, to duplicate the coverage of ***West's New York Digest 3d*** on WESTLAW), the particular key number search should be performed in both the appropriate New York and the appropriate federal databases.

c) Other West Digests. New York cases are also digested in West's digest system (***American Digest***, the ***Decennial Digests*** and the ***General Digests***). These massive sets digest federal and state cases reported in West's National Reporter System. New York cases are not digested in a regional digest; West publishes digests for all of the West regional reporters ***except North Eastern Reporter***. As noted previously, ***North Eastern Reporter*** includes all decisions of the New York Court of Appeals.

d) New York Law Journal Digest-Annotator. The ***New York Law Journal Digest-Annotator***[25] digests cases reported in the legal newspaper, the ***New York Law Journal.*** As mentioned above in section 2(b)(3), the ***New York Law Journal*** reports selected opinions of both the First and Second Judicial Departments and the lower courts in those Departments. Few of the lower court opinions are reported in ***New York Supplement*** and, therefore, they are not digested in ***Abbott's 2d*** or ***West's 3d*** digests.

[25] The ***New York Law Journal Digest-Annotator*** continues ***Clark's Digest-Annotator,*** v. 1-45, 1937-1981.

The New York Law Journal Digest-Annotator's digesting system is keyed to New York's statutory classification and is not related to the West topic and key number system. Unlike the ***Abbott's*** and ***West's*** digests, the ***Digest-Annotator*** is published in monthly pamphlets that are cumulated into annual volumes. To locate a particular case by name, the researcher must know in which year it was reported in the ***New York Law Journal.***

The ***Digest-Annotator's*** digests are divided into four broad categories: surrogate's practice, civil practice, substantive civil law, and criminal law. Since volume 41 (1977), the ***Digest-Annotator*** also includes an index to substantive articles in the ***New York Law Journal***, a realty law digest, a subject index to major opinions (opinions printed on the front page of the ***New York Law Journal***), and an index to Second Circuit opinions printed in the ***New York Law Journal***. Substantive articles in ***N.Y.L.J.*** are also indexed in ***Legal Resource Index***, which is described in Chapter 15 (Reference Books and Periodical Indexes).

References in the ***Digest-Annotator*** case table direct the researcher both to the case report in the ***New York Law Journal*** and to the topic and section where the case is digested in the ***Digest-Annotator***. The reference to "Schacter v. Kass -(4-21-60) 13, 4F -550:476(1)" is analyzed as follows:

> ***Schacter v. Kass*** was reported in the April 21, 1960 issue of the ***New York Law Journal*** at page 13, column 4 at the bottom (foot) of the column. Schacter v. Kass is digested in the ***Digest-Annotator*** under topic 550 (Personal Property) at classification line number 476 (Partnership agreements). It is the first case analyzed at classification line number 476 in the 1960 volume.

The ***Digest-Annotator*** index indicates the location of a case in a ***New York Law Journal*** column by the letters T (top), M (middle), or F (foot) following the column number.

e) Specialized Digests. The following specialized digests are published in looseleaf or newsletter format.

(1) Arbitration

New York No-Fault Arbitration Reports.
v. 1 Jan. 1977-
New York: American Arbitration Association.

A monthly newsletter.

(2) Class Actions

New York Class Action Digest.
v. 1, no. 1 (Spring 1986)-
Albany: New York State Bar Association.

(3) Civil Practice

New York State Law Digest. Albany: New York State Bar Association. 1965-

This monthly digest of significant practice cases was edited from October, 1977 to October, 1987 by David D. Siegel, author of ***Handbook on New York Practice*** (West 1978), the West hornbook on New York civil practice. Beginning in November 1987, notably others will share editorial responsibility on a rotating basis.

New York Civil Motion Citator. Edited by N. D. Adler and S. A. Hovani. 6th ed. East Setauket, N.Y.: National Attorneys' Publications, Inc., 1985-

This digest is arranged under topics such as article 78 proceedings, bill of particulars, discovery and inspection, and summary judgment.

(4) Criminal Law and Procedure

New York Criminal Case Citator. Edited by C. E. Von Schmidt. 2nd ed. East Setauket, N.Y.: National Attorneys' Publications, 1986-

This digest is arranged under topics such as search and seizure, arrest, discovery, speedy trial, jury instructions, identification and accusatory instruments.

Paton, William D.
Criminal Trial Manual - New York. Lancaster, Pa.: Hanford Pub. Co., 1983-
Looseleaf supplementation.

This digest of New York cases on criminal procedure is updated six times a year.

(5) Family Law

Family Litigation Manual - New York. Lancaster, Pa.: Hanford Pub. Co., 1988-
Looseleaf supplementation.

This digest of New York family law cases is updated six time a year.

New York Family Law Reporter. Garden City, N.Y.: Brian J. Barney, 1984-

(6) Jury Verdicts

New York Jury Verdict Reporter [Metropolitan Edition]. East Islip, N.Y.: New York Jury Verdict Reporter, Inc., 1981-

A monthly looseleaf digest that summarizes civil jury verdicts in Supreme, Civil and County courts in New York City and Nassau, Suffolk and Westchester counties. It also digests federal cases from the Southern and Eastern districts of New York.

New York Jury Verdict Reporter [Upstate Edition]. East Islip, N.Y.: New York Jury Verdict Reporter, Inc., 1983-

A monthly looseleaf digest that summarizes civil jury verdicts in Supreme and County courts north of Westchester County.

Appellate Supplement. East Islip, N.Y.: New York Jury Verdict Reporter, Inc., 1984-

This digest supplements the metropolitan and upstate editions of the *New York Jury Verdict Reporter*. It summarizes the decisions on appeal for cases that were first digested in either the metropolitan or the upstate editions. The 1984 softbound edition is kept up-to-date with looseleaf supplementation.

New York State Jury Verdict Review and Analysis. Newark, N.J.: Jury Verdict Review, 1983-

This monthly digest provides statewide coverage of New York Supreme Court and federal district court civil jury verdicts.

(7) Land Use

New York Land Report. v. 1- Albany: New York Land Institute, 1980-

The tab entitled "this month" contains digests of New York cases on land use and zoning.

(8) Matrimonial Actions

New York Matrimonial Case Citator. Edited by P.D. Sereduke. 4th ed. East Setauket, N.Y.: National Attorneys' Publications, 1986-

This digest is arranged under topics such as grounds for dissolution and annulment, pre-trial procedure, equitable distribution, support and maintenance, custody and visita tion, stipulations, and separation agreements.

(9) Real Estate

New York Real Estate Law Reporter. New York: Leader Publications, 1987-

A monthly newsletter digesting new cases on topics such as landlord and tenant, wetlands, municipal immunity, cooperatives and condominiums, lis pendens, and other areas of interest to the real estate practitioner.

f) LEXIS and WESTLAW. Both LEXIS and WESTLAW contain New York cases in full-text. The New York databases can be searched using words chosen by the researcher, thus freeing the search from the hierarchical indexing categories found in the traditional case digests. LEXIS and WESTLAW are described in Chapter 12 (Databases for New York Legal Research).

g) New York Jurisprudence 2d and the Annotated Codes. New York's legal encyclopedia, *New York Jurisprudence 2d*, summarizes New York administrative, statutory, and case law. The footnotes accompanying the text for each topic contain references to cases on that topic. *New York Jurisprudence 2d* is described in Chapter 15 (Reference Books and Indexes). Following each statutory section in New York's annotated statutory codes, *McKinney's Consolidated Laws Annotated* (*McKinney's*) and *New York Consolidated Laws Service* (*CLS*), are digests of cases in which that statutory section was applied or interepreted. *McKinney's* and *CLS* are described in Chapter 4 (State Legislation: Consolidated Laws, Unconsolidated Laws, and Other Legislation).

4. APPELLATE RECORDS AND BRIEFS

Briefs are the legal arguments submitted to a court in support of each party's position in a case. Records are the trial transcript and other court papers constituting the record on appeal. Appellate records and briefs can have considerable value as a research starting point on the points of law being argued in the appeal. They are also useful as illustrative forms for appeal papers.

Collections of New York records and briefs (formerly known as cases and points) can be located through the ***Union List of Cases and Points/ Records and Briefs In New York State Law Libraries.***[26]

5. CITATORS

Dominating the citator field are the citators of Shepards/McGraw Hill, Inc. ***Shepard's Citations*** provide accurate, timely, and comprehensive citation coverage for New York cases both in hardcopy and online (through LEXIS and WESTLAW).

Shepard's citators for cases allow the researcher to verify whether a case (the **cited case**) has been affirmed, overruled, cited in dissenting opinions, criticized, or distinguished in **citing cases**. Depending on the citator unit consulted, citators may also refer the researcher to the pages in law review articles, ***American Law Reports*** (***A.L.R.***), attorney general

[26] UNION LIST OF CASES AND POINTS/RECORDS AND BRIEFS IN NEW YORK STATE LAW LIBRARIES, compiled by J.T. White and D. M. Tybur (3d ed. 1987).

opinions, out-of-state cases and other sources where the cited case is mentioned.

The process of verifying case authority using ***Shepard's*** citators is called "Shepardizing." The general legal research guides listed in this book's Preface and in ***How To Use Shepard's Citations***, an instructional pamphlet published by Shepard's/ McGraw-Hill, Inc., provide instruction in the mechanics of Shepardizing in the hardcopy ***Shepard's*** citators. The online training features and hardcopy manuals made available by Mead Data Central (for use with LEXIS) and West Publishing Company (for use with WESTLAW) provide instruction in Shepardizing online.

A detail concerning the mechanics of Shepardizing is worth elaborating upon here. The syllabus numbers in the official reports and the headnote numbers in the West reports can be useful in Shepardizing. Assume that you are interested in headnote number 2 in the case reported in 437 N.Y.S.2d 75. Assume that when you Shepardize 437 N.Y.S.2d 75, you find a small, superscript number 2 appearing between the report abbreviation and the page number of a ***citing*** case: 505 N.Y.S.2d^{2} 2. The presence of that superscript number (Shepard's calls them "superior" numbers) indicates that the ***citing*** case deals with the point of law digested in headnote 2 of the ***cited*** case ***as reported in New York Supplement 2d***. Since the syllabus number in the official reports and the headnote number in the West reports are not interchangeable, the syllabus headnote for the particular point of law would have to be identified in order to locate that point of law when Shepardizing the official citation.

a) The Units of Shepard's New York Cases Citations.[27] Six units of ***Shepard's Citations*** are currently published in hardcopy for use in verifying authority of New York cases:

* ***Shepard's New York Court of Appeals Citations;***
* ***Shepard's New York Supreme Court Citations;***[28]
* ***Shepard's New York Miscellaneous Citations;***
* ***Shepard's New York Supplement Citations;***
* ***Shepard's New York Court of Appeals Case Names Citator;*** and
* ***Shepard's New York Appellate Division Case Names Citator.***

[27] Descriptions of other Shepard's publications relevant for New York legal research, e.g., ***Shepard's New York Statute Citations*** and ***Shepard's Acts and Cases By Popular Name***, can be located in the index.

[28] ***Shepard's New York Supreme Court Citations*** is the division for Shepardizing Appellate Division cases.

Each of the first three citators listed above contains several divisions. For example, ***Shepard's New York Court of Appeals Citations*** contains divisions for Shepardizing citations from N.Y., N.Y.2d, N.E., N.E.2d, N.Y.S.2d, the common law reports and Chancery reports.

As mentioned above, Shepard's Citations are also online services available through WESTLAW and LEXIS. However, Shepard's case name citators are not available online, presumably because case names and corresponding citations are readily found through field or segment searches on WESTLAW and LEXIS, respectively.

b) Basic Rules for Shepardizing.

1) Shepardize All Parallel Citations.[29] It is a mistake to assume that only one of the two or more parallel citations to New York cases need to be Shepardized. To obtain all citations for the cited case, all parallel citations for the case must be Shepardized for the following reasons.

First, the citing scope varies from one unit of ***Shepard's*** to another and from one division within a unit of ***Shepard's*** to another. Take the example of a New York Court of Appeals case with parallel citations in ***New York Reports, North Eastern Reporter***, and ***New York Supplement***. Law review articles and A.L.R. annotations citing that Court of Appeals case can be located by Shepardizing the ***New York Reports*** and the ***New York Supplement*** citation for the case, but they would not be located by Shepardizing the ***North Eastern Reporter*** citation. State cases from outside New York[30] that cite the New York Court of Appeals case can be located by Shepardizing the ***North Eastern Reporter*** citation in ***Shepard's North Eastern Reporter Citations***, but they would not be located by Shepardizing the ***North Eastern Reporter*** citation in ***Shepard's New York Court of Appeals Citations*** or by Shepardizing the ***New York Reports*** citation.

The second reason for Shepardizing all parallel citations of a case is that a citation appears in a ***Shepard's*** citator only if it appears in a citing document. If a particular document cites only the official report of a case,[31] the citing document will be located as a citing source by Shepardizing the official citation for the case but not by Shepardizing the unof-

[29] The term "parallel citation" is defined in ***supra*** note 17.

[30] Out-of-state cases that cite New York cases can be useful as persuasive authority in arguing what New York law should be.

[31] The preference for the official citation in New York's ***Official New York Law Reports Style Manual*** is noted in Section 6 of this Chapter.

ficial citation. While the reverse of this proposition is also true, the preference for citation from the official report means that more citing authority is likely to be located by Shepardizing the official citation for a case than will be located by Shepardizing the unofficial citation. Also, different publication cutoff points for the various divisions of Shepard's can result in the inclusion of one of the parallel citations and not the other in a given advance pamphlet. Accordingly, careful practice dictates Shepardizing all parallel citations for a case.

2) Study the Introductory Material for Each Unit of Shepard's and for Each Division Within a Unit. The scope of the various Shepard's units for New York will become clearer after study of the introductory material in each of the four New York units for New York cases. Within each of these units, each division has introductory notes. These division notes are especially important for Shepardizing nineteenth century cases.

3) Use All Volumes and Supplementation. A given unit of *Shepard's* contains several volumes and paper supplements. For example, at this writing, a complete set of *Shepard's New York Court of Appeals Citations* contains six bound volumes (called parts) and several paperbound supplements. In a busy library, some of these parts may be temporarily missing from the shelf. It is important to assemble all of them before beginning to Shepardize a case so that no citations are missed inadvertently. The front cover of the most recent supplement provides an up-to-date checklist of volumes and supplements for that division of *Shepard's*. Shepardizing online eliminates the need to physically assemble all relevant *Shepard's* volumes.

c) Shepardizing a New York Court of Appeals Case.

1) Reported in New York Reports, first series. A Court of Appeals case that is reported in the first series of *New York Reports* is also reported in *North Eastern Reporter*. The N.Y. citation should be Shepardized in the *New York Reports* division and the N.E. citation should be Shepardized in the *North Eastern Reporter* division of *Shepard's New York Court of Appeals Citations*. The latter division contains citing authority from New York Court of Appeals cases reported in *North Eastern Reporter*. To locate out-of-state cases citing the Court of Appeals case, the N.E. citation should also be Shepardized in a separate unit, *Shepard's North Eastern Reporter Citations*.

While Court of Appeals decisions reported in 1-309 N.Y. were included in volumes 1 N.Y.S. through 150 N.Y.S.2d, they were only included in an appendix and did not have *New York Supplement* page numbers.

As mentioned above in Section 2(b)(2), those earlier Court of Appeals opinions cannot be cited from *New York Supplement*. They cannot be Shepardized in ***Shepard's New York Supplement Citations*** nor in the N.Y.S. section in ***Shepard's New York Court of Appeals Citations***.

2) Reported in New York Reports, second series. A Court of Appeals case that is reported in the second series of ***New York Reports*** is also reported in ***North Eastern Reporter 2d*** and ***New York Supplement 2d.*** The N.Y. 2d, N.E. 2d, and N.Y.S. 2d citations should each be Shepardized in the three divisions of ***Shepard's New York Court of Appeals Citations*** that correspond with those three reports. The N.E. division only yields New York cases reported in N.E.2d. Out-of-state cases can be located using the N.Y.S. 2d citation or by Shepardizing the N.E. citation in ***Shepard's North Eastern Reporter Citations***. The N.Y.S.2d citation could also be Shepardized in ***Shepard's New York Supplement Citations***.

d) Shepardizing an Appellate Division Case. Appellate Division cases are reported in ***Appellate Division Reports*** and ***New York Supplement***. An Appellate Division case should be Shepardized in both the A.D. or A.D.2d division and in the N.Y.S. or N.Y.S.2d division of ***Shepard's New York Supreme Court Citations***. The N.Y.S. citation can also be Shepardized in ***Shepard's New York Supplement Citations***.

There is no unit of ***Shepard's*** carrying the name Appellate Division in its main title. The name Supreme Court in the title of ***Shepard's New York Supreme Court Citations*** reflects the historical structure of New York's court system. Recall that New York's intermediate appellate court was the Supreme Court between 1821 and 1846, that the General Term of Supreme Court was the intermediate appellate court from 1846 to 1894, and that when the present Appellate Division was established in 1894, it was created as a branch of Supreme Court. While today's researcher might appreciate a title change from ***Shepard's New York Supreme Court Citations*** to a title such as "Shepard's New York Appellate Division Citations," the present title does have firm roots in history.

e) Shepardizing a Miscellaneous Reports Citation. Cases from Supreme Court, the Appellate Terms, and various other lower courts of original jurisdiction are selectively reported in ***Miscellaneous Reports*** and ***New York Supplement***. A case reported in ***Miscellaneous Reports*** should be Shepardized in both the Misc. division and in the N.Y.S. (Misc. cases) division of ***Shepard's New York Miscellaneous Citations***. The N.Y.S. citation can also be Shepardized in ***Shepard's New York Supplement Citations***.

f) Using Shepard's New York Supplement Citations. Any *New York Supplement* citation can also be Shepardized in ***Shepard's New York Supplement Citations***. This citator does not have divisions by court; the references for cited cases run in consecutive volume and page number order throughout the first and second series of *New York Supplement*.

g) Shepardizing Nominative Reports. New York's official and unofficial nominative reports are analyzed in the divisions of ***Shepard's New York Citations*** that analyze the citations of the analagous courts in the modern period. For example, reports of cases decided in the General Term of Supreme Court are analyzed in ***Shepard's New York Supreme Court Citations***. Reports of trial level courts are analyzed in ***Shepard's New York Miscellaneous Citations***.

To determine which reports are analyzed in a division of ***Shepard's***, consult the list of cited material found in the preface to each division.

h) Locating Parallel Citations. Parallel citations are citations to two or more reports in which the **same** opinion can be found. The units of ***Shepard's Citations*** list parallel citations for a case only the first time that the case is analyzed in ***Shepard's***. The parallel citations are enclosed in parentheses in ***Shepard's*** and are at the top of the column of citations for the cited case.

Other sources for parallel citations are:

* the Table of Cases in the ***Abbott's*** and ***West's*** digests (see Section 3 of this Chapter);

* the *New York Blue and White Book*[32] published by the West Publishing Company;

* *New York Supplement* and *North Eastern Reporter*, which give parallel citations at the head of each case; and

* the ***Shepard's New York*** case name citators, which are described in section 5(i) below;

* LEXIS (the Shepard's and Autocite services);

* WESTLAW (the Shepard's and Instacite services).

[32] The *Blue and White Book* cross refers from citations for the official reports to citations for *New York Supplement* (blue pages) and vice versa (white pages).

i) Locating Citations From Case Names. Sources for citations when only the case name is known are:

* the Table of Cases in the *Abbott's* and *West's* digests;

* *Shepard's New York Court of Appeals Case Names Citator* (1940-1985 plus supplements) and *Shepard's New York Appellate Division Case Names Citator* (1960-1985 plus supplements);

* LEXIS (segment search by name); and

* WESTLAW (field search by title).

Shepard's Acts and Cases By Popular Name can be used to find citations to cases that have acquired a "popular name." For example, ***Trustees of Columbia College v. Thatcher*** is known as the "Columbia College Case" and ***Brown v. McGinnis*** is known as one of the "Black Muslim Cases." The citations to these cases can be found under their popular names in this unit of ***Shepard's***.

6. CASE CITATION FORM

Two current authorities provide guidance for New York case citation form. These are: ***A Uniform System of Citation, 14th ed.*** (1986),[33] published by the Harvard Law Review Association, and the ***Official New York Law Reports Style Manual*** (1987),[34] prepared by the State Law Reporting Bureau and published by Lawyers Co-Op. The ***Official Style Manual*** is designed to provide guidance for citation form in briefs and other papers submitted in the courts of the State. It is directed toward writing where footnotes are not used. The ***Bluebook*** is designed as a comprehensive guide to footnoting domestic, foreign, and international legal materials. It is the standard source for citation form used by academic writers.

Two other authorities exist regarding New York case citation form. Section 5529(e) of the Civil Practice Law & Rules provides, "New York decisions shall be cited from the official reports, if any."[35] Despite this rule, brief writers generally cite from both the official reports and from ***New York Supplement*** for the reader's convenience. Finally, ***New York***

[33] Hereinafter ***Bluebook.***

[34] Hereinafter ***Official Style Manual.***

[35] N.Y. Civ. Prac. L. & R. sec. 5529(e) (McKinney 1978).

Rules of Citation, prepared by the St. John's Law Review editors in 1978, provides many examples of citation to New York cases according to the 12th edition of the ***Bluebook***.

The ***Official Style Manual*** and the ***Bluebook*** differ regarding case citation form in several ways. In general, the ***Bluebook*** requires full punctuation, parallel citation,[36] and identification of the decision date and names of lower courts in parenthetical phrases.[37] Case names are either underscored (in typewritten work) or typeset in italics. The ***Official Style Manual*** requires minimal punctuation and no parallel citation for New York cases. Case names are typeset in italics. The ***Bluebook*** uses the abbreviations "A.D." and "A.D.2d" for the two series of ***Appellate Division Reports***, while the ***Official Style Manual*** uses the abbreviation "App Div" for the first series and "AD2d" for the second series.

Following are examples of case citations which contrast the ***Bluebook*** and ***Official Style Manual*** rules for New York citations.

Court of Appeals.

Bluebook: ***Spano v. Perini Corp.***, 25 N.Y.2d 11, 250 N.E.2d 31, 302 N.Y.S.2d 527 (1969).

Official Style Manual:
Spano v Perini Corp., 25 NY2d 11.

Appellate Division of Supreme Court.

Bluebook: ***Hennigan v. Buffalo Courier Express Co.***, 85 A.D.2d 924, 446 N.Y.S.2d 767 (4th Dept. 1981).

Official Style Manual:
Hennigan v. Buffalo Courier Express Co., 85 AD2d 924 [4th Dept].

[36] Parallel citations are citations to two or more reports in which the same opinion can be found. Any current New York Court of Appeals decision can be found in ***New York Reports, North Eastern Reporter, and New York Supplement.*** Current cases reported in ***Appellate Division Reports*** and ***Miscellaneous Reports*** are also reported in ***New York Supplement.*** The ***Bluebook*** (14th ed.) requires parallel citations for all New York cases. The examples of citation in this section illustrate parallel citation according to the ***Bluebook*** rules. The ***Official Style Manual*** requires citation only to the official reports.

[37] See Rule 10 and the New York examples at App. H of the ***Bluebook*** (14th ed.)

Citations to Decisions Reported in *Miscellaneous Reports*.

Bluebook: ***People v. Rollins***, 35 Misc.2d 14, 233 N.Y.S.2d 580 (Sup. Ct. Crim. Tm., Queens Co. 1962).

Brayman v. Stevens, 54 Misc.2d 974, 283 N.Y.S.2d 933 (Sup. Ct., Dutchess Co. 1967), ***aff'd. mem.,*** 28 A.D.2d 1090, 285 N.Y.S.2d 280 (2d Dept. 1967), ***aff'd. mem.,*** 20 N.Y.2d 868, 231 N.E.2d 787, 285 N.Y.S.2d 97 (1967).

Official Style Manual: ***People v Rollins***, 35 Misc2d 14.

Brayman v Stevens, 54 Misc2d 14, ***affd*** 28 AD2d 1090, ***affd*** 20 NY2d 868.

Citations to New York Law Journal.

Bluebook: ***Schacter v. Kass***, N.Y.L.J., April 21, 1960, at 13, col. 5 (Sup. Ct., Bronx).

Official Style Manual: ***Schacter v. Kass,*** NYLJ, April 21, 1960, p. 13, col. 5.

7. BIBLIOGRAPHY OF NEW YORK COURT REPORTS

This Section contains skeletal bibliographical information on New York court reports and major reprint sets from ***Coleman's Cases*** (1801) to the present. This checklist is adapted, by permission of the publisher, from the New York section of ***State Report Checklist*** to be published in 1988 by the William S. Hein & Co., Inc.

Earlier checklists of New York's court reports can be found in three sources (now out-of-print): 2 ***Abbott New York Digest, Consolidated ed.*** (1929),[38] ***Materials and Methods of Legal Research 3d ed.*** (1942) by Frederick C. Hicks, and ***Effective Legal Research*** (1953) by Miles O. Price and Harry Bitner.

For a bibliographic essay on the history of New York's courts and their reports, see "Law Reporting in New York," which is Chapter 4 of ***Legal Research and Law Library Management*** (1982) by Julius Marke and Richard Sloane. For an account of New York's official reports and

[38] ***Abbott's*** list includes both a description of the major courts and an alphabetically arranged description of almost all of the many reports.

reporters, see ***One Hundred Fifty Years of Official Law Reporting and the Courts of New York*** by John H. Moore (1955). Full bibliographic information on these sources is found at the end of this Chapter.

The dates listed for the court reports in the following checklist refer to the years of the decisions included in the reports and not to the years in which the court reports were published.

CHECKLIST OF NEW YORK COURT REPORTS

a) COURT REPORTS FROM 1846 TO DATE

Official Reports

COURT OF APPEALS

New York Reports 1st Series, v. 1-309.................. 1847 - 1956

v. 1-4	***Comstock's Reports***, v. 1-4	1847 -1851
v. 5-10	***Selden's Reports***, v. 1-6	1851 -1854
v. 11-14	***Kernan's Reports***, v. 1-4	1854 -1856
v. 15-27	***E.P. Smith's Reports***, v. 1-13	1857 -1863
v. 28-39	***Tiffany's Reports***, v. 1-12	1863 -1868
v. 40-45	***Hand's Reports***, v. 1-6	1869 -1871
v. 46-146	***Sickel's Reports***, v. 1-101	1871 -1895
v. 147-162.....	***E.H. Smith's Reports***, v. 1-16	1895 -1900
v. 163-191.....	***Bedell's Reports***, v. 1-29	1900 -1908
v. 192-193	***Newcomb's Reports***, v. 1-2	1908 -1909
v. 194-255	***Fiero's Reports***, v. 1-62	1909 -1931
v. 256	***Fiero & Rezzemini's Reports***, v. 1	1931

v. 257-288..... *Rezzemini's Reports*, v. 1-32 .... 1931 -1942

v. 289 .... *Rezzemini & Dimock's Reports*, v. 1 . 1942 -1943

v. 290-293..... *Dimock's Reports*, v. 1-4 .... 1943 -1944

v. 294 .... *Dimock & Coss's Reports*, v. 1 ...... 1944 -1945

v. 295-305 ..... *Coss's Reports*, v. 1-11 .... 1945 -1953

v. 306 .... *Coss & Flavin's Reports*, v. 1 .... 1953 -1954

v. 307-309 ..... *Flavin's Reports*, v. 1-3 .... 1954 -1956

New York Reports 2nd Series, v. 1-(1956 to date).

APPELLATE DIVISION OF SUPREME COURT

Appellate Division Reports
1st Series, v. 1-286 .... 1896 -1955

2nd Series, v. 1-(1956 to date).

SUPREME COURT AND MISCELLANEOUS TRIAL COURTS

Miscellaneous Reports.
1st Series, v. 1-208 .... 1892 -1956

2nd Series, v. 1-(1956 - date).

Unofficial Reports

New York Supplement
1st Series, v. 1-300 .... 1888 -1938

2d Series, v. 1-(1938 to date).

North Eastern Reporter
1st Series, v. 1-200 .... 1885 -1935

2nd Series, v. 1-(1936 - date).

b) EARLIER COURT REPORTS AND DISCONTINUED SERIES

COURT FOR THE CORRECTION OF ERRORS AND SUPREME COURT OF JUDICATURE

******Coleman's Cases***, 1 v. .... 1791 -1800

******Coleman and Caines' Cases***, 1 v. .... 1794 -1805

******Johnson's Cases***, v. 1-2 .... 1799 -1803

******Caines' Cases***, v. 1-2 .... 1796 -1805

******Caines' Reports***, v. 1-3 .... 1803 -1805
(Also known as ***Caines' New York Term Reports***)

******Johnson's Reports***, v. 1-20 .... 1806 -1823

******Anthon's Nisi Prius Cases***, 1 v .... 1807 -1851
(1st ed., 1808-1816; 2nd ed., 1807-1831; only the 1st ed. is reprinted in ***New York Common Law Reports***).

******Yates' Select Cases***, 1 v. 1809

******Cowen's Reports***, v. 1-9 .... 1823 -1829

******Wendell's Reports***, v. 1-26 .... 1828 -1841

******Hill's Reports***, v. 1-7 .... 1841 -1844

******Denios Reports***, v. 1-5 .... 1845 -1848

Lalor's Supplement to Hill and Denio, 1 v. .... 1842 -1844
(Also known as ***Hill and Denio's Supplement***)

Edmond's Select Cases, v. 1-2 .... 1834 -1853

******Lockwood's Reversed Cases***, 1 v. .... 1799 -1847

*Reprinted in ***New York Common Law Reports.***

New York Common Law Reports, (reprint) v. 1-18 . . . . . 1791 -1848

v. 1	Coleman's Cases, 1 v.; Coleman & Caines' Cases, 1 v.; Johnson's Cases, 3 v.
v. 2	Caines' Reports, 3 v.; Caine's Cases in Error, 2 v.
v. 3-6	Johnson's Reports, 20 v.
v. 7	Anthon's Nisi Prius, Yates' Select Cases, Lockwood's Reversed Cases, Cowen's Reports, v. 1-2.
v. 8	Cowen's Reports, v. 3-6.
v. 9	Cowen's Reports, v. 7-9; Wendell's Reports, v. 1.
v. 10-14	Wendell's Reports, v. 2-26.
v. 15	Hill's Reports, v. 1-4.
v. 16	Hill's Reports, v. 5-7; Denio's Reports v. 1.
v. 17	Denio's Reports, v. 2-5.
Index	

CHANCERY

**Johnson's Chancery Reports*, v. 1-7 . . . . 1814 -1823

**Hopkins Chancery Reports*, 1 v. . . . . 1823 -1826

Lansing's Select Cases in Chancery, 1 v. 1824, 1826

**Paige's Chancery Reports*, v. 1-11 . . . . 1828 -1845

**Edwards' Chancery Reports*, v. 1-4 . . . . 1831 -1850

**Hoffman's Chancery Reports*, 1 v. . . . . 1839 -1840

**Clarke's Chancery Reports*, 1 v. 1839 -1841

**Chancery Sentinel* (Saratoga), 6 v. in one . . . . 1841 -1847

**Sanford's Chancery Reports*, v. 1-4 . . . . 1843 -1847

**Barbour's Chancery Reports*, v 1-3 . . . . 1845 -1848

*Reprinted in *New York Chancery Reports Annotated.*

New York Chancery Reports Annotated (reprint),
v. 1-7 1814-1847

v. 1	Johnson's Chancery Reports, v. 1-5.
v. 2	Johnson's Chancery Reports, v. 6-7; Hopkins Chancery Reports, v. 1; Paige's Chancery Reports, v. 1-2.
v. 3	Paige's Chancery Reports, v. 3-6.
v. 4	Paige's Chancery Reports, v. 7-10.
v. 5	Paige's Chancery Reports, v. 11; Barbour's Chancery Reports, v. 1-3; Chancery Sentinel (Saratoga), v. 1-6.
v. 6	Edward's Chancery Reports, v. 1-4; Hoffman's Chancery Reports, 1 v.
v. 7	Clarke's Chancery Reports, v. 1; Sandford's Chancery Reports, v. 1-4.

COURT OF APPEALS

New York Court of Appeals Reports (reprint), v. 1-22 .. 1847 -1888

Comstock's Reports, v. 104 (1-4 N.Y.) .... 1847 -1851

Howard's Appeal Cases, 1 v. .... 1847 -1848
(Also known as ***Howard's Court of Appeals Cases***)

Selden's Reports, v. 1-6 (5-10 N.Y.) .... 1851 -1854

Keyes' Court of Appeals Reports, v. 1-4 .... 1863 -1868

Abbott's Court of Appeals Decisions v. 1-4 .... 1850 -1869

Selden's Notes of Cases, 1 v. .... 1852 -1854

Kernan's Reports, v. 1-4 (11-14 N.Y.) .... 1854 -1856

Transcript Appeals, v. 1-7 .... 1867 -1868

New York Condensed Reports, 1 v. .... 1881 -1882

Silvernail's Court of Appeals Reports, v. 1-4 .... 1886 -1892

COMBINED REPORTS

New York State Reporter v. 1-75 ....1886 -1896

SUPREME COURT

Barbour's Supreme Court Reports, v. 1-67 ....1847 -1877

Lansing's Supreme Court Reports, v. 1-7 ....1869 -1873
(Also known as *Lansing's Reports*)

Thompson and Cook's Supreme Court Reports, v. 1-6 ..1873 -1875

Hun's Supreme Court Reports, v. 1-92 ....1874 -1895

Silvernail's Supreme Court Reports, v. 1-5 ....1889 -1890

Winer, Unreported Opinions, 1 v. ....1912 -1940
(Printed in Dennis' *Buffalo City Court Act Annotated* (1940).

PRACTICE AND CODE CASES

Howard's Practice Reports, v. 1-67 ....1844 -1884

Howard's Practice Reports (*New Series*), v. 1-3........1884 -1886

Code Reporter, v. 1-3 ....1848 -1851

Code Reports (*New Series*), 1 v. ....1850 -1852

Abbott's Practice Reports, v. 1-19 ....1854 -1865

Abbott's Practice Reports (*New Series*), v. 1-16 ....1865 -1875

Abbott's New Cases, v. 1-32 ....1876 -1894

New York City Court Reports, v. 1-2 ....1874 -1888

New York Civil Procedure Reports, v. 1-40 ....1881 -1907

New York Civil Procedure Reports (New Series), 4 v...1908 -1913

McCarty's Civil Procedure Reports, 1 v 1882
Also known as 2 Civ. Pro. Rep.)

New York Monthly Law Record, v. 1-3 . . . . 1896 -1898

New York Annotated Cases, v. 1-20 . . . . 1894 -1908

New York Leading Cases Annotated, v. 1-2 . . . . 1912 -1914

Noble's Current Court Decisions, v. 1-3 . . . . 1908 -1910

Bradbury's Pleading and Practice Reports, v. 1-5 . . . . 1910 -1919

SURROGATE'S COURT

Bradford's Surrogate's Reports, v. 1-4 . . . . 1849 -1857

Redfield's Surrogate Reports, v. 1-5 . . . . 1857 -1882

Tucker's Surrogate Reports, 1 v. . . . . 1864 -1869

Demarest's Surrogate Reports, v. 1-6 . . . . 1882 -1888

Connoly's Surrogate Reports, v. 1-2 . . . . 1888 -1891

Power's Surrogate Reports, 1 v. . . . . 1890 -1894

Gibbons' Surrogate Reports, v. 1-2 . . . . 1893 -1898

Mills Surrogate's Reports, v. 1-18 . . . . 1899 -1917

SUPERIOR COURT

**Hall's Superior Court Reports*, v. 1-2 . . . . 1828 -1829

**Sandford's Superior Court Reports*, v. 1-5 . . . . 1847 -1852

**Duer's Superior Court Reports*, v. 1-6 . . . . 1852 -1857

**Bosworth's Superior Court Reports*, v. 1-10 . . . . 1856 -1863

**Robertson's Superior Court Reports*, v. 1-7 . . . . 1863 -1868

***Sweeney's Superior Court Reports**, v. 1-2 . . . . 1869 -1870

***Jones and Spencer's Super. Ct. Reports**, v. 1-29 . . . . 1871 -1892

***Buffalo Superior Court, Sheldon's Reports**, 1 v. . . . . . . 1854 -1875

* Reprinted in *New York Superior Court Reports*

New York Superior Court Reports,(reprint)v. 1-61 . . . . 1828 -1829

v. 1-2	Hall's Super. Ct. Rep., v. 1-2
v. 3-7	Sandford's Super. Ct. Rep., v. 1-5
v. 8-13	Duer's Super. Ct. Rep., v. 1-6
v. 14-23	Bosworth's Super. Ct. Rep., 1-10
v. 24-30	Robertson's Super. Ct. Rep., v. 1-7
v. 31-32	Sweeney's Super. Ct. Rep., v. 1-2
v. 33-61	Jones and Spencer's Super. Ct. Rep., 1-29

COMMON PLEAS

E. D. Smith's Common Pleas Reports, v. 1-4 . . . . 1850 -1858

Hilton's Common Pleas Reports, v. 1-2 . . . . 1855 -1860

Daly's Common Pleas Reports, v. 1-16 . . . . 1859 -1891

CITY COURT REPORTS

Select Cases of the Mayor's Court, 1 v. . . . . 1674 -1784

Livingston's Opinions (Marine), 1 v. 1802

Jacobs' City Court Reports, 1 v. . . . . 1874 -1889

Skillman's New York Police Reports, 1 v. . . . . 1828 -1829

Marine Court; City Court Reports, v. 1-2 . . . . 1874 -1889

v. 1	Robertson's City Court Reports (Marine); Supplement to v. 1 by E. Jacobs (1879-1884).
v. 2	Jacobs' City Court Reports.

CRIMINAL CASES

Wheeler's Criminal Cases, v. 1-3 . . . . 1791 -1825

Rogers' City Hall Recorder, v. 1-6 . . . . 1816 -1822

New York Judicial Repository, 1 v. . . . . 1818 -1819

Parker's Criminal Reports, v. 1-6 . . . . 1823 -1868

Cowen's Criminal Reports, v. 1-2 . . . . 1867 -1878

New York Criminal Reports, v. 1-41 . . . . 1878 -1924

ADMIRALTY

Hough's Vice-Admiralty Reports, 1 v. . . . . 1715 -1788

ELECTIONS

Armstrong's Contested Election Cases, 1 v. . . . . 1777 -1871

Baxter's Contested Election Cases, 1 v. . . . . 1777 -1899

REFERENCES

Abbott New York Digest, Consolidated Edition. Rochester: Lawyers Cooperative Publishing Co., 1929. (Vol. 2, pp. vii-xxvii).

Hicks, F. C. *Materials and Methods of Legal Research, 3d. ed.* Rochester: Lawyers Cooperative Publishing Co., 1942. (Pp. 500-502).

Marke, J. J. and R. Sloane. *Law Reporting in New York*. Chap. in *Legal Research and Law Library Management*. New York: Law Journals Seminars-Press, 1982.

Moore, J. H. *One Hundred Fifty Years of Official Law Reporting and the Courts in New York*, 6 Syracuse Law Review 273 (1955).

Price, M. O. and H. Bitner. ***Effective Legal Research***. Boston, Mass.: Little, Brown & Co., 1953. (Pp. 396-399).

State Report Checklist. Buffalo: William S. Hein & Co., Inc., 1988. (New York section).

Chapter Eight
PRACTICE AND PROCEDURE ACTS, EVIDENCE, AND COURT RULES

1. OVERVIEW

During the colonial period, practice in the courts was governed by the technicalities of English common law pleading and practice. The situation was perpetuated under New York's Revolutionary Constitution of 1777. Piecemeal statutory change prevailed until the efforts of reformers such as David Dudley Field, Arphraxed Loomis, and Montgomery Throop pressed for codification of the laws of practice. During the middle and later years of the nineteenth century, the procedural reforms proposed (but not always adopted) in New York were viewed as models for change in both the federal courts and in the states.

New York's current criminal and civil procedure laws are no longer found in separate "codes." The Civil Practice Law and Rules, replacing the 1920 Civil Practice Act, became part of the Consolidated Laws in 1962 (effective in 1963). The Criminal Procedure Law, replacing the 1881 Code of Criminal Procedure, was added to the Consolidated Laws in 1971. However, to this day, no separate law or code of evidence has ever been adopted. New York's court acts are "unconsolidated laws,"[1] while New York's court rules, since they are promulgated by administrative authority, are included in the administrative code, the ***Official Compilation of Codes, Rules and Regulations.***[2]

This Chapter highlights the major revisions of New York's practice and procedure acts from the ***Revised Statutes of 1827/1828*** to the present.

2. CIVIL PROCEDURE

a) Codification of Civil Procedure Before the CPLR.

1) Revised Statutes of 1827/1828, Part III. Part III of the ***Revised Statutes*** was comprised of over 2,500 sections containing most of the substantive and procedural law relating to courts and practice. This revision was organized after the manner found in treatises on British civil practice by William Tidd.

2) The Code of Procedure of 1848. The Constitution of 1846 required the legislature to appoint three commissioners whose duty it would be to revise, reform and simplify the rules and practice, forms, and proceedings of the State's courts.[3] The Commissioners on Practice and Pleading quickly produced, and the legislature quickly adopted, the Code of Procedure in 1848.[4] It is known as the "Field Code" after one of its principal draftsmen, David Dudley Field.

The Commissioners went on to draft a more comprehensive code, called the Code of Civil Procedure, which was presented to the legislature in 1850 but never adopted. This comprehensive code included not only the basic principles of procedure, pleadings, jurisdiction and court functions that were contained in the Field Code, but it also included the law of civil remedies, evidence, and expedited proceedings. Although it was rejected in New York, this code was adopted in whole or in part in the federal court system, and in virtually all of the states.[5]

[1] Although the court acts technically are unconsolidated laws, they are printed in comprehensive sets of the Consolidated Laws.

[2] Hereinafter ***NYCRR.***

[3] N.Y. CONST. OF 1846 art. XXIV, sec. 17.

[4] 1848 N.Y.LAWS ch. 379, amended form passed as 1849 N.Y. LAWS ch. 438.

[5] H. PETERFREUND and J. MCLAUGHLIN, NEW YORK PRACTICE: CASES AND OTHER MATERIALS 2 (1978)[hereinafter PETERFREUND]; Fitzpatrick, ***Procedural Codes of the State of New York*** 17 LAW LIBR. J. 12, 16 (1924) [hereinafter Fitzpatrick].

Since New York never adopted the proposed 1850 Code of Civil Procedure, lawyers had to contend with the Field Code plus over 2,000 sections still remaining in Part III of the ***Revised Statutes*** until 1877.

3) The Code of Civil Procedure (1877). This Code of Civil Procedure was originally the product of the Commission for the Revision of the Statutes, which had named it the Code of Remedial Justice. Substantial opposition in the legislature to the Commission's code forced the commissioners to make major revisions to their original proposal.[6]

The Code of Civil Procedure revised and consolidated the provisions of the 1848 Code of Procedure and Part III of the Revised Statutes. This Code is often called the "Throop Code" after one of the leading commissioners, Montgomery H. Throop.

4) The Civil Practice Act and the Rules of Civil Practice. The Civil Practice Act (C.P.A.) was adopted in 1920.[7] It was supplemented by the Rules of Civil Practice (R. Civ. P.) which were also adopted in 1920. However, they were adopted by a convention of judges, lawyers, and legislators rather than by the legislature. The Rules were "to consist of the former General Rules of Practice and some 200 new rules, mostly derived from sections of the Code [of Civil Procedure]."[8] The C.P.A. and the Rules of Civil Practice were amended by the legislature and Appellate Division justices, respectively, until the Civil Practice Law and Rules went into effect in 1963.

Court acts for the specialized courts also were enacted by the legislature in 1920 to supplement the C.P.A. Those court acts were: the Surrogate's Court Act (Laws of 1920, ch. 928), the Justice Court Act (Laws of 1920, ch. 937) the Court of Claims Act (Laws of 1920, ch. 922), and the New York City Court Act (Laws of 1920, ch. 935).

b) The Civil Practice Law and Rules (CPLR).

By 1954, there was sufficient interest in revising the C.P.A. for a Temporary Commission on the Courts to hold hearings on the subject. The

[6] The short-lived Code of Remedial Justice was a code of civil procedure in 13 chapters. It was passed and became chapter 448 of the Laws of 1876. However, the legislature suspended it by chapter 318 of the Laws of 1877, renamed it the Code of Civil Procedure by chapter 416 of the Laws of 1877, and, by chapter 449 of the Laws of 1877, the legislature compelled the Code's amendment to conform with chapter 416. Chapters 14-22 were added to the Code of Civil Procedure by chapter 178 of the Laws of 1880.

[7] 1920 N.Y. Laws ch. 925.

[8] Fitzpatrick, *supra* note 5, at 19.

Temporary Commission then appointed an Advisory Committee on Practice and Procedure to propose a revised civil practice act to the legislature. The Advisory Committee, chaired by Jackson A. Dykman, issued four preliminary reports to the legislature between 1937 and 1961. A fifth report was issued by the Senate Finance Committee and the Assembly Ways and Means Committee. The sixth and final report was issued by the Senate Finance Committee, chaired by Austin W. Erwin.

These six reports provide important background information on the Civil Practice Law and Rules. They were collected and issued as: New York (State) Legislature. Senate. Committee on Finance. ***Report to the Legislature Relative to the Revision of the Civil Practice Act, 1st-6th*** (1957-62). They were also included in the Legislative Document series as follows: 1957 Leg.Doc. No. 6-b, 1958 Leg.Doc. No. 13, 1959 Leg.Doc. No. 17, 1960 Leg.Doc. No. 20, 1961 Leg.Doc. No. 15, and 1962 Leg.Doc. No. 8.

(1) Description of the CPLR. The Civil Practice Law and Rules (CPLR) was passed by the legislature in 1962 and went into effect on September 1, 1963[9] as Chapter 8 of the Consolidated Laws. The CPLR replaces the former Civil Practice Act and the Rules of Civil Practice, which were not part of the Consolidated Laws. The CPLR is considerably shorter than the combined length of the old C.P.A. and the Rules of Civil Practice due to simplification of procedure and to the transfer of many specialized provisions and sections of substantive law to other, appropriate chapters of the Consolidated Laws.[10] Derivation and distribution tables are included with the CPLR that indicate the relationship of present CPLR sections and former CPA sections. Generally, CPA sections not distributed to the CPLR were transferred to appropriate sections of the Surrogate's Court Practice Act (SCPA), the Domestic Relations Law (DRL) and the Real Property Actions and Proceedings Law (RPAPL).

The CPLR is divided into 100 articles. Each article contains both sections and rules. Sections and rules are interspersed and the provisions are numbered consecutively without regard to their status as a section or a rule. Since 1978, as clarified by 1986 legislation,[11] both sections and rules may be changed by the legislature. Until 1978, sections of the CPLR

[9] 1962 N.Y. Laws chs. 308-318.

[10] Peterfreund, *supra* note 5, at 6.

[11] *See* D. Siegel. Handbook of New York Practice sec. 2 (1987 Supp.).

could be adopted or amended only by the legislature, while rules could be adopted or amended only by the Judicial Conference.

The CPLR governs most procedure in civil actions in Supreme Court and in the county courts and other courts "except where the procedure is regulated by inconsistent statute."[12] For an explanation of the applicability of the CPLR in various courts, see Weinstein-Korn-Miller, ***CPLR Manual*** sec. 1.02.

(2) Publication of the CPLR. ***McKinney's Consolidated Laws of New York Annotated***[13] and the ***New York Consolidated Laws Service***[14] contain the CPLR supplemented with annotations of cases. ***McKinney's*** also provides signed practice commentaries to provide assistance in interpreting many of the sections of the CPLR. The unannotated Consolidated Laws published by the Michie Company and Gould Publications also contain the CPLR.

Each section of both the Weinstein-Korn-Miller ***CPLR Manual*** and the Weinstein-Korn-Miller ***New York Civil Practice-CPLR*** treatise is preceded by the text of the relevant CPLR section or rule. The treatise, which comprises volumes 1 through 8 of the New York Civil Practice series (Matthew Bender), provides extensive commentary on the CPLR.

Annual, unannotated printings of the CPLR are found in: McKinney's C.P.L.R. pamphlet; Bender's C.P.L.R. pamphlet (the Redbook); Bender's ***Civil Practice Annual of New York;*** (essentially the same as Cahill-Parson's ***New York Civil Practice***, also published by the Matthew Bender Company); the ***New York Standard Civil Practice Deskbook*** (Lawyer's Co-op.); and the Michie's and Gould's sets of Consolidated Laws, as mentioned above. A one-volume looseleaf edition of the CPLR is also available from Gould.

The CPLR is available online on Legislative Retrieval System (LRS). Mead Data Central projects that the CPLR will again be available on LEXIS in 1988. The West Publishing Company projects that the CPLR will become available on WESTLAW during 1988.

[12] N.Y. CIV. PRAC. L. & R. sec. 101 (McKinney 1972).
[13] Hereinafter ***McKinney's.***
[14] Hereinafter ***CLS.***

3. CRIMINAL PROCEDURE

a) Codification of Criminal Procedure Before the Criminal Procedure Law (CPL).

1) Revised Statutes of 1827/1828. Before 1881, criminal procedure was governed by the common law and a patchwork of legislation concentrated in Part IV of the ***Revised Statutes of 1827/1828*** and its successors. The same Commissioners on Practice and Pleading who produced the Code of Procedure of 1848 also produced a proposed Code of Criminal Procedure in 1849 and a revised proposal in 1850.[15] Neither of these proposals was adopted by the legislature.

2) The Code of Criminal Procedure of 1881 (C.C.P.) In 1879, the 1850 draft Code of Criminal Procedure and an 1857 draft Penal Code were revised by David Dudley Field, James Emott, and Benjamin K. Phelps and submitted to the legislature. While they passed in both houses, they were not approved by the governor. Finally, in 1881, the Code of Criminal Procedure[16] and the Penal Code[17] were approved. As revised from time to time, the Code of Criminal Procedure (C.C.P.) remained in effect for 90 years. Sometimes cited as 66 ***McKinney*** (because it was printed in the 66th book of ***McKinney's),*** it was replaced by the Criminal Procedure Law in 1971. The Penal Code was replaced by the Penal Law in 1909 (1909 Consolidated Laws, ch. 40), which in turn was replaced by the Revised Penal Law in 1965.

b) The Criminal Procedure Law (CPL)

1) Description of the Criminal Procedure Law. The Criminal Procedure Law[18] went into effect on September 1, 1971 as Chapter 11-a of the Consolidated Laws. It is designed to mesh with the revised Penal Law as the old C.C.P. was supposed to mesh with the old Penal Code and the more recent Penal Law.

The Criminal Procedure Law was the product of the Temporary Commission on Revision of the Penal Law and Criminal Code that was created by the legislature in 1961. The Commission is often referred to as the Bartlett Commission after its chair, Assemblyman Richard J. Bartlett.

[15] J.T. Fitzpatrick, *supra* note 5, at 20.
[16] 1881 N.Y. LAWS ch. 442.
[17] 1881 N.Y. LAWS ch. 676.
[18] 1970 N.Y. LAWS ch. 996.

2) Publication of the Criminal Procedure Law. The Criminal Procedure Law is published with case annotations in ***McKinney's*** and ***CLS***. Signed practice commentaries are included in ***McKinney's***. Annual, unannotated printings of the C.P.L. are found in ***Michie's*** and ***Gould's*** sets of the Consolidated Laws, ***Gilbert Criminal Law and Procedure*** (Bender), and ***Bender's Criminal Law*** pamphlet (the Graybook). A one-volume looseleaf edition of the CPL is also available from Gould. The CPL is available online on Legislative Retrieval System (LRS). Mead Data Central projects that the CPL will again be available on LEXIS in 1988. The West Publishing Company projects that the CPL will become available on WESTLAW during 1988.

4. EVIDENTIARY LAW

a) Attempts at Codifying the Law of Evidence. Possibly the first effort to consolidate the rules of evidence was David Dudley Field's proposed Code of Civil Procedure of 1850. The rules of evidence were consolidated in Part IV of the proposed code. In 1886, David Dudley Field argued before the governor in favor of a revised Part IV, but to no avail. In 1887, the legislature established a Commission to Report a Code of Evidence.[19] The commissioners were David Dudley Field and Justices William Rumsey and David L. Follett. Their proposed code of evidence resembled the Indian Evidence Act and Sir James Fitzjames Stephen's ***Digest of the Law of Evidence***.[20] The draft code passed the legislature but was not approved by the governor. In the last decade of the nineteenth century, the Statutory Revision Commission proposed an evidence "code bill" that would have become chapter 56 of the General Laws of New York had it been adopted.

Most recently, a Proposed Code of Evidence was submitted to the 1982 and 1987 sessions of the legislature.[21] However, the proposed code never came up for a vote. If the Proposed Code of Evidence is adopted, it will become new Chapter 9-A of the Consolidated Laws.

[19] 1887 N.Y. LAWS ch. 124. The Commission's life was extended by chapter 99 of the Laws of 1888.

[20] ***Statute Law in New York from 1609 to 1901,*** Suppl. to NEW YORK (STATE). JOINT COMMITTEE ON STATUTORY REVISION BILLS. REPORT. 111. (Assembly Doc. No. 72) (1901).

[21] The Proposed Code of Evidence was introduced in the 1982 Session of the Legislature as S8875 and A11279 (1982). It was resubmitted by the Law Revision Commission in a revised version in the 1987 session as S4413A and A6200 (1987).

A pamphlet copy of the 1982 version of the Proposed Code of Evidence was distributed to all subscribers to the 1982 *McKinney's Session Laws*.

b) Current Law of Evidence. In the absence of a code or consolidated law of evidence, evidentiary law in New York is governed by common law and statutory evidentiary provisions. The statutory provisions are clustered mainly in Article 45 of the CPLR and Article 60 of the CPL. The Federal Rules of Evidence are often referred to for guidance in interpreting New York's law of evidence. The treatises on New York evidence are also useful sources for interpretation. These treatises are listed under the heading "Evidence" in Chapter 13 (Treatises, Practice Books, and Other Sources).

5. COURT RULES

a) Definition. Court rules govern practice before a specific court. They also govern internal court practices and procedures. They are judge-made, not legislative, rules which are promulgated pursuant to rule-making power derived from article VI of New York's Constitution.

b) Publication of Court Rules. New court rules are printed in the advance sheets of *New York Supplement 2d* and in the *State Register*. The current court rules are published officially in 22 *NYCRR* (see list below). However, the publication lag time for *NYCRR* indicates caution in rely ing solely on that publication. New York court rules can be found in volumes 43-45 of *CLS*. They are also published annually in pamphlet form in *McKinney's New York Rules of Court, State and Federal*. In addition to the New York court rules, the latter publication includes court rules for the U.S. Court of Appeals for the Second Circuit and the U.S. district courts in the four New York federal districts.

Civil court rules are published annually in *Bender's Civil Practice Annual*. The status of a particular court rule should be verified with the court clerk when there is any doubt about its currency.

The current New York rules of court, as arranged in *NYCRR*, are listed below.

Title 22. NYCRR. Judiciary.

(a) Court of Appeals. Rules of Practice. 22 NYCRR part 500.

(b) Supreme Court. Appellate Division.
- (1) First Department. 22 NYCRR part 600.
- (2) Second Department. 22 NYCRR part 670.
- (3) Appellate Term, Second Department. 22 NYCRR part 730.
- (4) Second, Ninth, Tenth and Eleventh Judicial Districts, Second Department. 22 NYCRR parts 754 - 799.
- (5) Third Department. 22 NYCRR part 800.
- (6) Fourth Department. 22 NYCRR part 1000.

(c) Uniform Rules for the Trial Courts of the Unified Court System.
- (1) Uniform Rules for the Engagement of Counsel. 22 NYCRR part 125.
- (2) Uniform Rules for Courts Exercising Criminal Jurisdiction. 22 NYCRR part 200.
- (3) Uniform Civil Rules for the Supreme Court and County Court. 22 NYCRR part 202.
- (4) Uniform Rules for the Family Court. 22 NYCRR part 205.
- (5) Uniform Rules for the Court of Claims. 22 NYCRR part 206.
- (6) Uniform Rules for the Surrogate's Court. 22 NYCRR part 207.
- (7) Uniform Rules for the New York City Civil Court. 22 NYCRR part 208.
- (8) Uniform Rules for the City Courts Outside of the City of New York. 22 NYCRR part 210.
- (9) Uniform Civil Rules for the District Courts. 22 NYCRR part 212.
- (10) Uniform Civil Rules for the Justice Courts. 22 NYCRR part 214.

The Uniform Rules For the New York State Trial Courts were promulgated by the Chief Administrative Judge and became effective on January 6, 1986. Simultaneously, numerous local court rules were repealed. While some variation in practice remains, substantial uniformity has been achieved consistent with the goals of New York's unified court system.

6. CITATORS

Cases, law review articles, and A.L.R. annotations citing the CPLR, the CPL and the statutory evidence provisions can be located by Shepardizing them using the "Consolidated Laws" section of ***Shepard's New***

York Statute Citations. The older ***Shepard's New York Statute Citations*** volumes contain citations to the superseded civil and criminal procedure acts.

Cases citing current New York court rules can be located using the *NYCRR* citation in the "New York Codes, Rules and Regulations" section of ***Shepard's New York Statute Citations***. Cases decided between 1961 and early 1985 construing New York court rules can be located using the *NYCRR* citation in the one-volume looseleaf entitled ***Shepard's Citations To New York Codes, Rules and Regulations***. This service ceased publication in August, 1985.

Selected annotations of cases citing current New York court rules can be located behind the orange tab ("Annotations — Case Notes and Administrative Notes") at the back of 22 *NYCRR* (volume A). Citations to earlier court rules, whether or not they were printed in 22 *NYCRR*, can be located in the "New York Court Rules" section of ***Shepard's New York Statute Citations***.

REFERENCES

Fitzpatrick, J. T. ***Procedural Codes Of the State of New York***. 17 Law Library J. 12 (1924).

New York (State). Legislature. Joint Committee on Statutory Revision Commission Bills. ***Statute Law in New York From 1609 to 1901***. Supplement 2 of the Committee's ***Report***. (Assembly Doc. No. 72). Albany: 1901.

Newman, T. ***New York Appellate Practice***. New York: Matthew Bender, 1985.

Peterfreund, J. & J. McLaughlin. ***New York Practice: Cases and Other Materials***. Mineola, N.Y.: Foundation Press, 1978.

Siegel, D. ***Handbook of New York Practice***. St. Paul, Minn.: West Publishing Company, 1978.

Chapter Nine
ADMINISTRATIVE CODES, RULES, AND REGULATIONS

1. OVERVIEW

Administrative rules and regulations are issued by executive departments and agencies pursuant to rulemaking authority granted by the statutes governing those departments and agencies. New York's Constitution requires the filing of regulations with the Department of State (they are not effective until so filed). The Constitution further requires the legislature to provide for the timely publication of New York rules and regulations. The relevant provision reads,

> [n]o rule or regulation made by any state department, board, bureau, officer, authority or commission, except such as relates to the organization or internal management of a state department, board, bureau, authority or commission shall be effective until it is filed in the office of the department of state. The legislature shall provide for the speedy publication of such rules and regulations by appropriate laws.[1]

[1] N.Y. CONST. art. IV, sec. 8 (McKinney 1987).

Article IV, section 8 was added to New York's Constitution in 1938. Legislation implementing article IV, section 8 is found in the State Administrative Procedure Act[2] and the Executive Law, as discussed below.

New York's codes, rules and regulations[3] are published in its administrative code, the ***Official Compilation of Codes, Rules and Regulations***.[4] Notice of current state rulemaking activity is published in the weekly issues of the ***New York State Register***.

2. THE RULEMAKING PROCESS AND THE STATE REGISTER

a) Rulemaking. The impetus for administrative rulemaking can come from statutory mandate, from an emergency situation that affects public health, safety or welfare, from an expressed public need which may be ascertained through hearings, from a desire within an agency to change its procedures, or from other sources.

Staff of the executive departments and agencies draft and file proposed regulations following procedures and guidelines set out in SAPA, in 19 *NYCRR* part 260, and in the ***State Register Manual.***[5] For an analysis of the effectiveness of New York's rulemaking process, see ***The New York Rulemaking Process*** by Professor R. A. Herman.[6]

b) Notices of Proposed Rulemaking. Article 2[7] of SAPA requires rulemaking notices to be published in the ***State Register***. The ***State Register*** has been published weekly since 1979[8] by the Department of State pursuant to sections 145-49 of the Executive Law.[9] By statute, rulemaking notices must include:

[2] Hereinafter SAPA in the text and N.Y. A.P.A. in the notes.

[3] Hereinafter codes, rules and regulations will be referred to simply as regulations.

[4] Hereinafter ***NYCRR.***

[5] N.Y. (STATE). DEPT. OF STATE, NEW YORK STATE REGISTER [MANUAL] [1986].

[6] 47 ALB. L. REV. 1061 (1983).

[7] N.Y. A.P.A. sec. 201-06 (McKinney Supp. 1987).

[8] The predecessor of the ***State Register*** was the ***State Bulletin,*** a much less comprehensive publication issued from 1928-1976. The history of the ***State Bulletin*** and the ***State Register*** is traced in R.A. CARTER, THE OFFICIAL COMPILATION OF CODES, RULES AND REGULATIONS OF THE STATE OF NEW YORK AND THE STATE REGISTER: THEIR HISTORY AND USE (1984)and in D. BUTCH, NEW YORK STATE DOCUMENTS: AN INTRODUCTORY MANUAL 25 (1987).

[9] N.Y. EXEC. L. secs. 145-49 (McKinney 1982, Supp. 1987).

* the statutory authority for the proposed regulation;
* the date, time and place of hearings, if any;
* a regulatory flexibility analysis and regulatory impact statement;
* either the text of the proposed regulation or a summary; and
* the name, public address and telephone number of the agency representative who can be contacted for further information.

Unlike the ***Federal Register***, which is the federal counterpart of New York's ***State Register***, the ***State Register*** contains the text of very few proposed regulations. In New York, publication of the full text of proposed regulations is required only if the text contains fewer than 2,000 words.[10] For proposed regulations that exceed 2,000 words,[11] only publication of a summary of the proposed regulation's subject, purpose and substance is required. Even when the text of the proposed regulation does not exceed 2,000 words, administrative agencies have the discretion to substitute publication of a summary of the proposed regulation for publication of the full text in the ***State Register***.[12]

The full text of proposed regulations, the text of the accompanying regulatory impact statement required by section 202-a of SAPA,[13] the regulatory flexibility statement required by section 202-b of SAPA,[14] and the location and date of any hearings concerning the proposed regulation can be obtained from the agency representative whose name, address and telephone number is set out in the notice of proposed rule making. The agency representative is also the person to whom written data, views and arguments concerning the proposed regulation are to be submitted.

The notices of rulemaking activities in the ***State Register*** are arranged alphabetically by agency. Each proposed regulation receives an identification ("I.D.") number when it is listed for the first time in the ***State Register***. The number consists of a three letter abbreviation for the agency, the issue number of the rule, the last two digits of the year, and a Department of State number. The abbreviation for the rulemaking activity at hand, called the "activity code," is added at the end of the I.D. number. These activity codes are:

[10] N.Y. A.P.A. secs. 202(1)(f)(iv), 5(b)(ii), and 6(d)(vi) (McKinney Supp. 1987).
[11] ***Ibid.***
[12] N.Y. A.P.A. sec. 202(b)(i) (McKinney Supp. 1987).
[13] N.Y. A.P.A. sec. 202-a (McKinney Supp. 1987).
[14] N.Y. A.P.A. sec. 202-b (McKinney Supp. 1987).

E = Emergency Rule Making with no permanent action intended;
A = Adoption;
P = Proposed Rule Making;
EP = Combined Emergency and Proposed Rule Making;
EA = Permanent Emergency Rule Making; and
PR = Renewal of Proposed Rule Making.

The following regulation number, CVS-52-85-00004-P, indicates the following:

CVS — Dept. of Civil Service

52 — Issue of ***State Register*** in which the text or summary of the proposed regulation was printed.

85 — year in which Notice of Rule Making appeared.

00004 — Dept. of State number.

P — Activity code. "P" indicates regulation was proposed.

When the proposed regulation in this example was later adopted, it was listed in the ***State Register*** as CVS-52-85-00004-A. The activity code "P" (for proposed) was changed to "A" (for adopted) in the I.D. number in that later listing.

The I.D. numbers used by the Department of State for proposed and adopted regulations do not identify which titles and sections of the ***NYCRR*** would be affected by adoption of a proposed regulation. The researcher must look in the ***State Register*** at each individual item of proposed rulemaking in order to find that information. Each item contains a line captioned "Proposed action" that identifies which ***NYCRR*** title and part(s) would be affected by adoption of the proposed rule. Similarly, the researcher must find the individual notice of adoption in order to identify *NYCRR* titles and parts affected by a newly adopted rule. Each notice of adoption contains a line captioned "Action taken" that identifies titles and parts affected by that newly adopted rule.

Tracking of proposed regulations is described in section 2(d) below.

c) Notices of Adoption. When regulations are adopted, notices of adoption must be published in the ***State Register***.[15] The full text of rules adopted under non-emergency procedures, the revised regulatory impact statement, and the agency's assessment of comments on issues raised by public comment on the proposed rule can be obtained from the agency representative identified in the notice of adoption.[16] The same procedure is followed to obtain the text of and information about rules adopted under emergency procedures.[17] As previously mentioned in section 2(b) above, the "Action Taken" line in the Notice of Adoption indicates the *NYCRR* title and part affected by the new regulation.

Eventually, the full text of newly adopted regulations is published in the *NYCRR*.

d) Tracking the Status of Proposed Regulations. Proposed regulations can be tracked in the ***State Register***, on the database known as STATE NET, and by requesting notification by an agency of rule-making in particular subject areas.

(1) State Register. The researcher can find current rulemaking notices in the ***State Register*** by scanning the weekly issues for rulemaking by particular agencies and by scanning the "Action Pending Index." The Action Pending Index provides a brief description of all proposed rules being considered for adoption.

Quarterly indexes to the ***State Register*** also provide access to the rulemaking notices. Both the Action Pending Index and the quarterly indexes are arranged by agency and then by I.D. number. The quarterly indexes are cumulated annually.

Unfortunately, there is neither a subject index to the ***State Register*** nor a table of *NYCRR* titles and parts affected by rulemaking activity.

[15] N.Y. A.P.A. sec. 202(5)(a) (McKinney Supp. 1987).
[16] N.Y. A.P.A. sec. 202(5)(b) (McKinney Supp. 1987).
[17] N.Y. A.P.A. sec. 202(6) (McKinney Supp. 1987).

(2) STATE NET. Online tracking of New York's current rulemaking activity is possible on the STATE NET database. STATE NET is available from Information for Public Affairs, Inc. of Sacramento, California. Using STATE NET, summaries of proposed New York regulations can be tracked by subject and rule number. Searches of summaries of proposed federal regulations in the ***Federal Register*** and summaries of proposed regulations in the 49 other states can also be performed on STATE NET. This database is described more fully in Chapter 12 (Databases for New York Legal Research).

(3) Agency notification. Researchers and lobbyists can request personal notification from a regulatory agency of all proposed rules which may affect them by submitting a written request to the agency.[18] Requests for notification must be renewed annually.

3. THE OFFICIAL COMPILATION OF CODES, RULES AND REGULATIONS (NYCRR)

The full text of New York's current administrative regulations is published in the 60 volume looseleaf set entitled ***Official Compilation of Codes, Rules and Regulations of the State of New York***. As the title indicates, the text of the ***NYCRR*** is "official." For evidentiary purposes, the ***NYCRR*** presumptively establishes the codes, rules and regulations of the State of New York.[19] The NYCRR is issued by the Department of State pursuant to sections 102-106 of the Executive Law.[20] At this writing, it is printed and distributed by Lenz & Riecker, Inc. of Albany.

Neither an "unofficial" nor a fully annotated version[21] of the ***NYCRR*** exists. As of this writing, the ***NYCRR*** is not available online in the LEXIS, WESTLAW, Legislative Retrieval System (LRS), or the STATE NET databases.[22]

a) Organization of the NYCRR. The administrative regulations in the ***NYCRR*** are compiled into the following numbered subject areas called titles:

[18] N.Y. A.P.A. sec. 202(1)(b) (McKinney Supp. 1987).
[19] N.Y. A.P.A. sec. 102(5) (McKinney Supp. 1987).
[20] N.Y. EXEC. L. secs. 102-106 (McKinney Supp. 1987).
[21] The ***NYCCR*** does contain citations to recent selected cases interpreting the regulations, but it does not provide references to law review articles or other secondary sources in - terpreting the regulations.
[22] These databases are described in Chapter 12 (Databases for New York Legal Research).

Title	Name
1	Agriculture and Markets
2	Audit and Control
3	Banking
4	Civil Service
5	Commerce
6	Environmental Conservation
7	Correctional Services
8	Education
9	Executive
10	Health
11	Insurance
12	Labor
13	Law
14	Mental Hygiene
15	Motor Vehicles
16	Public Service
17	Transportation
18	Social Services
19	State
20	Taxation and Finance
21	Miscellaneous
22	Judiciary

Each title is subdivided into parts. The statutory authority for each part is given at the head of that part. *NYCRR* parts are divided into decimally numbered sections. There is a two-volume key word index to the *NYCRR*. Officially sanctioned practice forms are found in the appendices of many *NYCRR* titles.

b) Finding NYCRR citations. While there are several access tools which can be used to find *NYCRR* citations, determining whether there are New York regulations on a given subject can be quite difficult. Finding tools for the *NYCRR* include the *NYCRR* key word index, the tables of contents of individual *NYCRR* titles and parts, and the annotated statutory compilations for New York, ***New York Consolidated Laws Service***[23] and ***McKinney's Consolidated Laws of New York Annotated.***[24]

[23] Hereinafter *CLS.*
[24] Hereinafter *McKinney's.*

(1) The NYCRR Index. The key word index volumes may yield the desired citation. However, the index could profit from expansion of the number of key words indexed. The index should be searched under the name of the administrative department or agency as well as under key word for best results.

(2) The NYCRR Tables of Contents. Scanning the detailed tables of contents found at the head of relevant *NYCRR* titles and parts can sometimes produce quicker results than using the *NYCRR* index.

(3) CLS and McKinney's Cross References to the NYCRR. Both *CLS* and *McKinney's* often cross-refer from statutory sections to the *NYCRR*. *CLS* provides more *NYCRR* cross references than does *McKinney's*. If there is a cross reference from a particular statutory section in *CLS* or *McKinney's*, the cross reference will be found in the editorial material located after the historical notes and before the case annotations.

c) Supplementation of the NYCRR. The *NYCRR* and its index are kept up-to-date by monthly looseleaf supplements. Supplementation for frequently revised titles is filed temporarily behind red tab cards labelled "Cumulative Supplement" at the back of the appropriate binder(s) for that title. Material which supplements less frequently revised titles is filed directly into the main body of material of that title by part number.

There is a publication delay of several months for the monthly *NYCRR* supplements. For example, a regulation adopted in August will be printed in the *NYCRR* supplement marked "August," but the August supplement might not be received by an *NYCRR* subscriber until December.

d) Updating the NYCRR. To determine whether a section of the *NYCRR* has been affected by rulemaking not yet filed into the *NYCRR*, consult the ***State Register***, the STATE NET database, or the regulatory department or agency itself.[25] As previously mentioned, the ***State Register*** does not provide a table of new regulations that would allow tracking by *NYCRR* titles and part numbers. Sections 2(b)and 2(d) above describe the procedure for determining whether any newly adopted rules affect particular *NYCRR* titles and parts.

[25] See section 2(d) above.

The text of a new, unpublished regulation usually can be found in several locations. Every effort should be made to identify its I.D. number through the ***State Register***. The researcher then can contact the agency representative listed in the notice of adoption in the ***State Register*** to obtain a copy of the full text. The text of a new regulation is also available in many regional offices of the issuing agency, in the State Library in Albany, and also in the Supreme Court law library within each judicial district designated by the Chief Administrator of the Courts to receive new regulations.[26]

e) Citation Form. A citation to the ***NYCRR*** following the ***Official New York Law Reports Style Manual*** (1987) consists of the title number, the abbreviation NYCRR, and the section or part number. For example, 19 NYCRR 130.7 means title 19 of the ***Official Compilation of Codes, Rules and Regulations of the State of New York***, section 130.7. When the entire part is referred to, the word "part" precedes the part number, e.g., 22 NYCRR part 205. For writers following the New York citation examples in ***A Uniform System of Citation, 14th ed.***,[27] citation form would be quite different, e.g. N.Y. COMP. CODES R. & REGS. tit. 19, §130.7 (1964). The date used when following the ***Uniform System of Citation*** form is the date of the regulation's adoption,[28] not the date at the bottom of the ***NYCRR*** page.

4. SUPERSEDED CODES, RULES AND REGULATIONS

The need to locate superseded sections of the ***NYCRR*** arises in connection with litigation concerning regulations which are no longer in effect, when a researcher is tracing changes in administrative law over a period of time, and when a researcher wishes to determine the purpose behind a current regulation by comparing the current text with repealed provisions.

The process of locating superseded material is complicated by the looseleaf format of the ***NYCRR***. When new ***NYCRR*** supplementation arrives in a library, the pages containing superseded regulations are withdrawn from the set and stored in bundles or looseleaf binders. These bundles or binders are usually arranged by the date the pages were withdrawn from the ***NYCRR***.

[26] N.Y. EXEC. LAW sec. 102(4)(c) (McKinney Supp. 1987).

[27] A UNIFORM SYSTEM OF CITATION 202 (14th ed. 1986)

[28] *Id.* at 110 (Rule 18.1[d]).

To determine which dated bundle of superseded ***NYCRR*** pages contains the desired superseded regulation:

1. find the "Historical Note" following the title and part number of the superseded regulation in the ***NYCCR;***

2. identify the date of repeal or amendment from the "Historical Note;"

3. find the dated bundle that falls immediately after that date of repeal or amendment.

That is the bundle that contains the superseded regulation.

Because of the large volume of superseded ***NYCRR*** pages and the difficulty of preserving them in meaningful order, there are not many complete sets of these pages. The New York State Library in Albany has a complete collection of the superseded pages from 1960 to date.[29] Other libraries in the state have quite extensive holdings, and the researcher may be able to locate the desired superseded pages in a local law library.

Before 1960, New York's administrative code was not published in looseleaf format. A five-volume compilation of the regulations was published in 1945. That set was supplemented with annual volumes. There is a complete set of the 1945 edition and all supplements in the New York State Library[30] and in many other law libraries in the state.

5. "PURPOSE" OR "INTENT" OF REGULATIONS

Very little published information is available on the "purpose" or "intent" of regulations. The notice of proposed rule making and notice of adoption that are published in the ***State Register*** should be consulted to identify the contact person at the department or agency who was responsible for providing information on the regulation at the time of its proposal and adoption. That contact person should be able to provide background information, especially when the text of a proposed regulation was changed because of comment received at the agency, either in written form or at public hearings.

[29] R.A. CARTER, ***supra*** note 8, at 7.
[30] ***Ibid.***

If it is difficult to find the notice of adoption by using the indexes to the ***State Register***, use the "Historical Note" which follows the text of the regulation in the *NYCRR*. Identify the date on which the adopted regulation was filed with the Department of State. The notice of adoption should have appeared in the ***State Register*** within two weeks after the date of filing with the Department of State.

Newspaper articles can be a source of background information on rulemaking. The time period when articles would be most likely to appear are around the dates when the notice of proposed rulemaking appeared in the ***State Register***, the dates when any hearings on the proposed regulation were held, and the time period around the date of adoption and the effective date of the regulation. Searches on the NEXIS and VU/TEXT newspaper databases could possibly locate relevant information. These databases are discussed in Chapter 12 (Databases for New York Legal Research).

When there are significant differences between the text of a proposed regulation and the final regulation as adopted, textual comparison of the two can contribute to the researcher's understanding of the purpose of the regulation. The notice of adoption in the ***State Register*** indicates whether the proposed and final versions of a regulation differ significantly.

Where the regulation in question is an amendment, comparison with the superseded regulation can be very useful. The procedure for locating the text of superseded regulations is described in section 4 of this Chapter.

6. CITATORS

At this writing, there are two printed sources that provide citations to judicial and administrative decisions and opinions interpreting sections of the *NYCRR*. These sources are the *NYCRR* annotations in the *NYCRR* itself and the *NYCRR* division in ***Shepard's New York Statute Citations***.

The *NYCRR* contains selected annotations of court decisions and administrative decisions interpreting the *NYCRR* found in federal and New York cases, the Education Department Reports, the opinions of the attorney general and the opinions of the comptroller. The annotations for particular regulations are located behind orange tabs found at the end of the *NYCRR* volume containing those regulations. The tabs are marked "ANNOTATIONS - Case Notes and Administrative Notes." Retrospective coverage in the annotations varies from volume to volume. The earliest decisions annotated are from 1981.

When using these annotations, as with using any annotated decision, the researcher should both read the full text of the decision and verify the decision's current status before relying on that decision to support a legal proposition.

The second source that provides citations to judicial and administrative decisions and opinions interpreting the *NYCRR* is ***Shepard's New York Statute Citations***, which has a separate *NYCRR* division. Coverage of the *NYCRR* in ***Shepard's New York Statute Citations*** began in 1985 when ***Shepard's Citations to New York Codes, Rules and Regulations*** ceased publication.[31] ***Shepard's New York Statute Citations*** includes references to secondary sources, such as law reviews, which cite the *NYCRR*.

The ***Shepard's Citations*** services available through WESTLAW and LEXIS do not include coverage of the *NYCRR*. However, cases and law reviews which cite the *NYCRR* can be located in the WESTLAW and LEXIS databases by using the *NYCRR* citation as a search term.

REFERENCES

Carter, R. A. ***The Official Compilation of Codes, Rules and Regulations of the State of New York and the State Register: their history and use***. Albany: The State University of New York, 1984.

Herman, R. A. ***The New York Rulemaking Process.*** 47 Albany Law Review 1061 (1983).

[31] ***Shepard's Citations to New York Codes, Rules and Regulations*** included citing materials from 1980-85. It was published in looseleaf format.

Chapter Ten
ADMINISTRATIVE DECISIONS, OPINIONS AND RULINGS, AND DOCUMENTS OF THE GOVERNOR

1. OVERVIEW

The determinations of state administrative agencies affect the life of seemingly every citizen at one time or another. To paraphrase Frank E. Cooper in his introductory chapter in ***State Administrative Law***, many people can avoid "court trouble," but few indeed can avoid the administrative agencies.[1] Examples of state agencies with pervasive effects on the citizenry are labor relation boards, departments of taxation, health departments, unemployment insurance appeal boards, and education departments.

The "judiciary-like" power of state agencies is derived from legislation. For example, the power of the New York's Workers' Compensation Board to hear disputed cases and render decisions is derived from the Workers' Compensation Law. Article 3 of the State Administrative Procedure Act (SAPA) governs adjudicatory proceedings of New York State agencies. A simplifed definition of an adjudicatory proceeding for purposes of SAPA is one "... in which a determination of the legal rights, duties or privileges of named parties thereto is required by law to be made only on a record and after an opportunity for a hearing."[2]

Judicial review of actions by state and local officers or agencies is commenced by a proceeding under article 78 of the Civil Practice Law and Rules. However, not all agency actions are subject to review under article 78.

[1] 1 Cooper, ***State Administrative Law*** 3 (1965).
[2] N.Y. A.P.A. sec. 102(3) (McKinney 1984).

General information on the purposes, activities and personnel of New York's departments, boards, commissions and other bodies can be found in the ***Manual For the Use of the Legislature of the State of New York*** (the Blue Book). The Blue Book gives the session law citation for the establishment of the administrative body. Similar information on New York's administrative bodies is found in the ***New York State Red Book***. Neither the ***Legislative Manual*** nor the ***Red Book*** contain bibliographical information concerning administrative decisions, opinions and rulings.

The most comprehensive study of New York's quasi-legislative and quasi-judicial agencies is the "Benjamin Report." The full citation to this report is: New York (State) Commissioner to Study, Examine and Investigate the Exercise of Quasi-Judicial Functions by Any Board, Commission or Department of the State, ***Administrative Adjudication in the State of New York. Report to Honorable Herbert H. Lehman, Governor of the State of New York, by Robert M. Benjamin, as commissioner***. Issued in 1942 in six volumes, the Benjamin Report greatly influenced administrative law reforms in the State.

The most comprehensive bibliography of New York administrative decisions, opinions and rulings is ***Sources of Published and Unpublished Administrative Opinions in New York State*** by Robert Allan Carter. Another helpful bibliography is ***New York Legal Documents: a Selective Annotated Bibliography*** by Susan Dow and Karen Spencer. The Dow and Spencer bibliography concentrates on current materials. The Carter bibliography describes both current and older materials and is especially useful since it analyzes New York's ***State Department Reports*** (***SDR***). The full name of the ***SDR*** is: ***Department Reports of the State of New York, containing the decisions, opinions and rulings of the state departments, officers, boards and commissions***. It is a 78-volume set that was issued from 1914 to 1958. The ***State Department Reports*** are often referred to as the "Department Reports."

The decisions, opinions and rulings listed in sections 2 and 3 of this Chapter are grouped by office or subject, i.e., Attorney General, Banking. Under the office or subject, the latest agency name is listed followed by the title or titles of the reports. New York document classification numbers follow many of the entries. Brief annotations follow some entries.

2. CURRENT DECISIONS, OPINIONS AND RULINGS

Administrative agencies and the titles under which they publish decisions, opinions and rulings change frequently. An asterisk (*) before the name of an agency in this section indicates that previous publishing history will be found in section 3 (Non-Current Decisions, Opinions and Rulings).

ATTORNEY GENERAL

*New York (State). Dept. of Law.
Opinions of the Attorney General. 1959-
LAW 119-3 OPIAG.

Includes both formal and informal opinions. Formal opinions are rendered to state officials concerning their powers and duties under the New York Constitution and laws of the State. Informal opinions are the unofficial views of the Attorney General rendered to counsel for local government upon request.

The opinions are available on microfilm from Trans-Media Publishing Co. of Dobbs Ferry, N.Y. and are also available on LEXIS and WESTLAW (retrospective coverage varies).

Analyzed in *Shepard's New York Miscellaneous Citations*.

BANKING

*New York (State). Banking Dept.
Annual Report of the Superintendent of Banks, State of New York 1940-
1851BAN 350-1

Includes published opinions on bank merger and holding company applications. The title of the Department varied slightly over the years.

The Banking Department's Legal Division maintains a file of unpublished legal opinions from approximately 1930 to date.

COMPTROLLER

*New York (State). Comptroller's Office.
Opinions of the New York State Comptroller. 1979-
R/RN AUD 050-3 OPINY 84-57133

Published in looseleaf format by Lenz & Reicker. Vol. 1 is incomplete; State Library holds slip opinions which fill in missing opinions in that volume.

Continues ***Opinions of the Comptroller Relating to Municipal Government***.

CORRECTIONS

New York (State). Department of Correctional Services.

Unpublished legal opinions are filed in the Department's Office of Counsel.

EDUCATION

University of the State of New York.
Education Department Reports. vol. 1 - 1962 -
UNI 068-3 EDUR 77-551550.

Each volume contains a case table, decision digest and statutory reference table. Often called the ***EDR***, it is analyzed in ***Shepard's New York Miscellaneous Citations***. Selected, current decisions are digested in the ***New York School District Law Letter***, published by Doran Publications, Inc.

ELECTIONS

New York (State). State Board of Elections.
NYS Board of Elections Formal Opinions. 1974?-

ENVIRONMENTAL CONSERVATION

*New York (State). Department of Environmental Conservation.

Unpublished declaratory rulings are maintained in the Department's Office of General Counsel. Rulings to 1983 were collected and published by the Office in 1983 under the title ***Declaratory Rul-***

ings: 6 NYCRR, Environmental Conservation Law. The New York Land Institute provides excerpts of the Department's administrative decisions in its publication, ***New York Land Report.*** The ***New York Land Report*** is a looseleaf service that is updated monthly.

FREEDOM OF INFORMATION LAW

New York (State). Committee on Open Government.
Advisory Opinions on the Freedom of Information Law. 1983 -
REC 500-3 FOIAO (1974-1983); OPE 500-3 FOIAO 84-5681 (1984-

Published by the Committee on Public Access to Records from 1974-83, the opinions consist of letters from the executive director of the Committee to individuals concerning their FOIL requests.

Individual letters are numbered as follows: FOIL - AO - 2942, where FOIL identifies the Freedom of Information Law, AO identifies the document as an advisory opinion, and where 2942 identifies the 2942nd letter in the series.

HEALTH

New York (State) Department of Health.

Opinions of counsel are obtainable through the Department's Records Access Office. Requests for certain materials may only be made by Freedom of Information Law request.

HEALTH PROFESSIONS

New York (State). Office of Professional Medical Conduct.
Annual Report. 1982-

The Office of Professional Medical Conduct investigates complaints concerning physicians and physicians' assistants. The annual report lists cases reviewed by the Board of Professional Medical Conduct and gives a digest of the complaint and the result.

HUMAN RIGHTS

New York (State). Division of Human Rights.

Decisions of the Division and its predecessor, the Commission for Human Rights, back to approximately 1960, are available in the Division's Office of Counsel. The Division's annual report contains summaries of the year's significant regional office conciliations and summaries of the commissioner's orders after hearings.

INSURANCE INDUSTRY

New York (State). Insurance Department.

Unpublished opinions are obtainable by written request from the Department's Office of General Counsel in New York City.

JUDICIARY

New York (State). Commission on Judicial Conduct.
Determinations of the New York State Commission on Judicial Conduct. v. 1- 1978/79-

LABOR RELATIONS

New York (State). Dept. of Labor. Division of Research and Statistics.
Collective Bargaining Settlements in New York State.
vol. 1 - 1947 -
LAB 580-3 COLBS

Volumes 1-8 were issued under the title ***Collective Bargaining Settlements Reached in New York***. This series consists of summaries of settlements reached.

New York (State). Dept. of Labor. Labor Relations Board.
Decisions and Orders. vol. 1 - 1937/38-
LAB 845-3 DECON

Bound volumes were published to vol. 37 (1974). Decisions and orders are now issued in slip format.

New York (State). Public Employment Relations Board.
Official Decisions, Opinions and Related Matters.
vol. 1 - 1968 -
RR PUB 114-4 OFDO

Currently published by Lenz & Reicker. Formerly published by Labor Relations Press. Kept up-to-date by looseleaf filing and annual bound volumes.

Cumulative digest covers volumes 1 - 10. The popular name is *PERB Reports.*

New York (State). Governor's Office of Employee Relations.
Grievance and Disciplinary Arbitrations. vol. 1-4?
1974-78?

The arbitration reports were published in looseleaf format and cited as *OER* reports. The arbitration reports are now kept internally at the Governor's Office of Employee Relations.

OPEN MEETINGS LAW

New York (State). Committee on Open Government.
Advisory Opinions on the Open Meetings Law. 1983 -
REC 500-3 OMLAO (1976-1983); OMLAO 84-56752 (1984-).

Published by the Committee on Public Access to Records from 1976-1983.

The advisory opinions consist of letters from the executive director of the Committee to individuals concerning their Open Meetings Law requests.

Individual letters are numbered as follows: OML - AO - 1295, where OML identifies Open Meeting Law opinions, AO identifies advisory opinions, and where 1295 identifies the 1295th letter in the series.

PERSONAL PRIVACY LAW

New York (State). Committee on Open Government.
Advisory Opinions on the Personal Privacy Protection Law.
1984-

Advisory opinions are issued to members of the public only. Personal Privacy Protection Law (PPPL) letters are issued by the Committee upon request from government agencies.

TAXATION OF CORPORATIONS, ESTATES & GIFTS, INDIVIDUALS, SALES, ETC.

*New York (State). Division of Tax Appeals. Tax Appeals Tribunal.

After August 31, 1987, taxpayer proceedings are commenced before administrative law judges in the Division of Tax Appeals and are subject to review by the new Tax Appeals Tribunal. At this writing, no decisions of the Tribunal have been released. The Department of Taxation and Finance projects that they will be distributed to publishers and LEXIS and WESTLAW, following past practice for Tax Commission opinions.

*New York (State). Taxpayer Services Division. Technical Services Bureau.

Since 1978, the Technical Services Bureau has published advisory opinions, decisions and memoranda on New York's income, estate and gift, corporation, sales and miscellaneous taxes. These are known as "TSB's" since they are issued by the Technical Services Bureau. Effective on September 1, 1987, the State Tax Commission was abolished and all of the adjudicatory functions of the Department of Taxation and Finance, which had been delegated to the Technical Services Bureau, have been transferred to the Division of Tax Appeals.

TSB's are numbered according to a numbering system that identifies series, year, type of TSB, and item number. For example, "TSB - H - 85- (160) - I," is the 160th Tax Commission opinion in the income tax series in the year 1985; "TSB - H - 87 (15) C" is the 15th opinion in the corporation tax series in the year 1987; and "TSB

- A - 86 (1) S'' is the first advisory opinion in the sales tax series for the year 1986.

TSB's are available on WESTLAW and LEXIS; retrospective coverage varies. TSB's are also available in the CCH *New York Tax Reports*, P-H *State and Local Taxes: New York*, and Comeau, Helm and Murphy's *New York Tax Service*.

TAXATION OF REAL PROPERTY

*New York (State). State Board of Equalization and Assessment.
Opinions of Counsel. v. 1 - 5 (1972 - 1976)
EQU 050-3 OPICO 76-56204.

Opinions of Counsel and Reports. v. 6, (1977/80-
EQU 050-3 OPICO 84-57340.

Since 1984, the opinions have been issued in slip format.

Proceedings of the State Board of Equalization and Assessment. 1984-??

The annual proceedings contain the text of Board resolutions which include subjects such as special equalization rates and ratios and state-owned land assessments. There is a subject index. The resolutions are numbered to identify year and item number. For example, Resolution 84-16 is the 16th resolution in the year 1984.

UNEMPLOYMENT INSURANCE

New York (State). Department of Labor. Unemployment Insurance Division. Adjudication Services Office.
Interpretation Service Index - Benefit Claims. 1987-

This is a subject-arranged digest of Unemployment Insurance Appeal Board and court decisions interpreting the Unemployment Insurance Law. It was revised in 1987 and is kept up-to-date with slip interpretations.

*New York (State). Unemployment Insurance Appeal Board.
Decisions. 1938-

Issued in slip format.

UTILITIES

*New York (State). Public Service Commission.
Public Service Commission Reports: Opinions, Orders, Rules and Regulations. v. 1- 1961-
PUB 146-3 REPOO 75-51102

WORKERS' COMPENSATION

*Department of Labor. Workers' Compensation Board.
Board Decisions and Administrative Rulings. v. 34-?, 1979-1983.

All decisions of the Full Board (13-member panel) and selected decisions of the three-member panel issued after 1983 are now reported in the *New York Worker's Compensation Law Reporter* published by LRP Publications. Publication of this reporter began in 1987.

Statistical analysis of workers' compensation and volunteer firefighter cases closed annually appear in *Compensation Cases Closed*, a Research & Statistics Bulletin published by the Board since 1945.

3. NON-CURRENT DECISIONS, OPINIONS AND RULINGS

As previously mentioned in section 1, a major source of non-current opinions, decisions, and rulings for the period 1914-1958 is the 78-volume *State Department Reports (SDR)*. The *SDR* contains opinions, decisions and rulings of a number of agencies as well as governor's messages, lists of state officials, and, occasionally, governor's memoranda. Three or four volumes were published each year. Publication of the *SDR* was suspended between 1943 and 1945. Volume 44 consists of a case name table arranged by agency which covers volumes 1 to 41.

Opinions and decisions reported in the *SDR* are cited by volume and page numbers, as in any case reporter. Decisions in the *SDR* are analyzed in *Shepard's New York Miscellaneous Citations*. Agency opinions, decisions, and rulings in this section of the Chapter are arranged by office or subject. A double asterisk (**) indicates that the current series is listed in section 2 of this Chapter.

AGRICULTURE AND MARKETS

Opinions of the Department of Farms and Markets and its successor, the Department of Agriculture and Markets, are found in volumes 31-34 and volumes 36-38 and 40 of the SDR, respectively.

ATTORNEY GENERAL

New York (State). Attorney General's Office.
Opinions of the Attorneys General of the State of New York From the Formation of the State Government to February, 1872. Compiled and arranged by Hiram E. Sickels. New York: Banks & Brothers, 1872.
ATT 950-4 OPIAG 1796-1872.

Indexed by subject and section of the law interpreted.

**New York (State). Attorney General's Office.
Annual Report of the Attorney General. 1893-1927.
ATT 950-1

The annual reports contain the formal opinions of the Attorney General for the years indicated. Attorney General opinions are also included in the Legislative Documents series and in the ***SDR***.

New York (State). Department of Law.
Annual Report of the Attorney General. 1928-1958.
LAW 119-1

The annual reports contain the formal opinions of the Attorney General for the years indicated.

Formal attorney general opinions are also found in nearly every volume of the ***SDR*** from volume 1 to volume 38. These volumes include opinions issued from 1914 to 1921 and 1924 to 1928.

New York (State). Department of Law.
Informal Opinions of the Attorney General. 1932-40, 1943-1958.

Informal opinions also were published in the 1941 and 1942 annual report of the attorney general and in eight volumes of the ***SDR***. Following is a list of the ***SDR*** volume numbers containing informal attorney general opinions and the year of the opinions included therein:

45 (1932), 48 (1933), 51 (1934), 54 (1935), 57 (1936),
58 (1937), 59 (1938), 61 (1939) and 63 (1940).

Informal Opinions of the Attorney General merged in 1959 with the section on Formal Opinions of the Attorney General in the Department's Annual Report to form ***Opinions of the Attorney General.***

BANKING

*New York (State). Banking Dept.
Annual Report. 1852-1939.

CIVIL SERVICE

New York (State). Civil Service Commission.
Annual Report of the New York State Civil Service Commission. 1883-1953.
CIV 214-1

The annual reports from 1896 to 1898 contain rulings of the Commission; the annual reports from 1899-1912 contain digests of the rulings. Volume 19 of the ***SDR*** also contains Commission rulings.

COMPTROLLER

State Board of Audit.
Annual Report. 1876-1883.

Comptroller opinions are found in the annual reports for 1876-1883.

Department of Audit and Control.

Between 1914 and 1932, Comptroller opinions were found in the *SDR*. *SDR* volumes and dates of Comptroller opinions printed therein are: 1 (1914), 9-21 (1916-1919), 23 (1920), 25 (1921), 28 (1922), 30-32 (1923-1925), 34 (1926), 36-38 (1926-1929), 41 (1931) and 42 (1932).

**Department of Audit and Control.
Opinions of the Comptroller Relating to Municipal Government. 1945-1978.
AUD 500-3 OPICM

ENVIRONMENTAL CONSERVATION

New York (State). Conservation Commission

Volumes 16-25 of the *SDR* contain opinions of the Commission.

EDUCATION

New York (State). Dept. of Public Instruction.
Annual Report of the Secretary of State as Superintendent of Common Schools. 1842/44 - 1851/52.

New York (State). Dept. of Public Instruction.
Annual Report of the State Superintendent of Public Instruction. 1853-1902/1903.
E379.747 N552

Reports issued between 1887 and 1902 contained decisions of the Superintendent of Public Instruction.

**University of the State of New York.
Report of the Education Department. 1903/04-1960/61.
E379.747 N556re

Decisions of the Commissioner of Education are contained in the 1903 - 1913 annual reports.

The Tenth Annual Report is entitled *Judicial Decisions of the State Superintendent of Common Schools, State Superintendent of*

Public Instruction, State Commissioner of Education from 1822-1913. This Report is also Assembly Document 1914, No. 42, Part F.

From 1914 to 1958, the decisions of the Commissioner are printed in the ***SDR***. They are found in volumes 1-43, 46, 49, 50, 52, 53, 55-58, 62, and 64-78.

From 1962 to the present, decisions of the Commissioner are printed in the ***Education Department Reports***.

ENGINEER AND SURVEYOR

The opinions of the State Engineer and Surveyor are found in volume 18 of the ***SDR***.

HEALTH

The Opinions of the Department of Health are published in volume 21 of the ***SDR*. The opinions of the Public Health Council are in volume 35 of the ***SDR***.

HOUSING

New York (State). State Rent Administrator.
Opinions of the State Rent Administrator Relating to Rent and Eviction Regulations of the Temporary State Housing Rent Commission. [1st ed.] June 1, 1951-
HOU 650-3 OPSRA

A third edition of collected opinions of the State Rent Administrator was issued between 1951 and 1957.

INSURANCE

New York (State). Insurance Dept.
Annual Report of the Superintendent of Insurance. v. 1-? 1859-?
INS 626-1

Insurance Commissioner opinions for 1906 through 1915 are printed in Part V of the Department's annual report. Opinions for the years 1918 and 1932 are found in volumes 15, 16, and 42 of the *SDR*.

LABOR

**New York (State). State Labor Relations Board.
Annual Analysis of Decisions. vol. 1-36, 1937-1972.
AB 845-3 ANNAD
Published by Williams Press.

MOTOR VEHICLES

Decisions of the Motor Vehicles Bureau are contained in volume 33 - 36 of the *SDR*.

PUBLIC WORKS

Decisions of the Dept. of Public Works are contained in volume 31 of the *SDR*.

SOCIAL SERVICES

The opinions of the State Board of Charities and its successor, the Department of Social Services, are published in volume 26 and volume 31 of the *SDR*, respectively.

TAXATION OF CORPORATIONS, ESTATES & GIFTS, INDIVIDUALS, SALES, etc.

**New York. (State) State Tax Commission.

Decisions of the State Tax Commission are contained in volumes 18, 32-42, 46, 49, 50, 52, 53, 55-57, 60, 64, 65, and 67-70 of the *SDR*.

New York State Tax Bulletin. 1965-1968.
TAX 770-3 NEWYS

The *Tax Bulletin* contain State Tax Commission decisions and opinions of counsel for 1965-1968.

UNEMPLOYMENT INSURANCE

New York (State). Division of Placement and Unemployment Insurance.

Guides to Interpretation and Procedure, Series B: Codification and Text of Selected Decisions. 1938-1939.
PLA 025-3 GUIIP

Contains text of selected decisions for the years indicated.

Weekly Digest of Opinions. 1938-1940.
PLA 025-3 WEEDD

This contains summaries of opinions for the years indicated. This agency was succeeded by the Unemployment Insurance Appeal Board.

UTILITIES

New York (State). Public Service Commission. 1st District.
Reports of Decisions of the Public Service Commission, First District. v. 1-12, 1907/09-1921.
PUB 178-3 REPDP

Reports for 1921 are also in the 1st annual report of the Commission.

New York (State). Public Service Commission. 2nd District.
Reports of Decisions of the Public Service Commission, Second District of the State of New York. v. 1-9, 1910-1921.
PUB 306-3 REPDP

Includes decisions for the Second District for the years 1907 to 1921. Reports for 1921 are also included in the Commission's annual report for 1921.

New York (State). Public Service Commission.
***Annual Report*. 1921-1960.
PUB 146-1

This report was formed by the union of the Reports of Decisions for the First and Second Districts. Decisions of the Commission for the years 1921-1960 are contained in the ***Annual Report*** and in the legislative documents series.

Decisions for this period are also found in volumes 13-37, 47 and 52 of the ***SDR***. Volume 47 contains selected opinions for the years 1928-1933.

WATER

Decisions of the Water Power and Control Commission and its predecessors, the Water Control Commission and the Water Power Commission, are found in the ***SDR*** as follows:

Water Control Commission, vols. 29-35.

Water Power Commission, vols. 36-43, 46, 49, 50, 51, 53, 55-58, 60, 62, and 64-68.

Water Power and Control Commission, vols. 36-43, 49, 50, 53, 55-58, 60, 62, and 64-78.

WORKERS' COMPENSATION

Decisions of the Industrial Commission are contained in vols. 4-25 of the ***SDR***.

Decisions of the Industrial Board are contained in vols. 26-37 of the ***SDR***.

Court decisions concerning the Workmen's Compensation Law are summarized in the following publications:

Compensation Court Decisions. New York State Workmen's Compensation Board. 1946/47-1966.

Court Decisions. 1966/67 - 1971.

Court Decisions in Workmen's Compensation Cases. v. 34-? 1971-?

Indexed by section of the Workmen's Compensation Law.

New York (State). Workmen's Compensation Board.

Board Decisions and Administrative Rulings, v. 26-33, 1971-1979.

Title varies over the years as follows:

Workmen's Compensation Board Decisions. vol. 1-14, 1946-1959;

Workmen's Compensation Board Reports. vol. 15-21, 1960-1967;

Board Decisions and Reports - Workmen's Compensation Board. v. 21 (no. 8) - v. 25, (1967-1971).

4. DOCUMENTS OF THE GOVERNOR

a) Executive Orders. Executive orders issued since 1960 are printed in the ***State Register*** and cumulated in 9 *NYCRR* Part 1. Executive orders issued before 1960 are included in most of the compilations of the public papers of the governors. The executive orders usually are indexed only by subject in those compilations.

b) Governor's Messages to the Legislature. The governors' annual messages to the legislature are printed in the ***CLS Session Laws*** (1976 to date) and the ***McKinney's Session Laws*** (1950 to date) and their advance sheets, in the Assembly and Senate journals, and in the public papers of the governor series. The journals and public papers series carry a publication lag of several years, however. The Office of the Governor has published ***Messages to the Legislature*** since 1777. It includes the annual messages, special messages and messages of necessity.

Governor's annual messages to the legislature were collected and published by Charles Z. Lincoln in 1909. The eleven-volume compilation is: New York (State) Governor. State of New York. ***Messages from the governors, comprising executive communications to the Legislature***

and Other Papers Relating to Legislation from the organization of the first colonial Assembly in 1683 to and including the year 1906. This work includes memoranda on approval of bills and an index of vetoes by subject. The ***Index of New York Governor's Messages 1777-1901***, by Malcolm Glenn and Charlotte Goves, indexes and includes digests and quotations from governor's messages delivered from 1777-1901. From 1830 to 1974, the annual messages to the legislature were included in the Legislative Documents series.

The governor's budget messages and executive budget are described in section 4 of Chapter 4 (State Legislation: Consolidated Laws, Unconsolidated Laws, and Other Legislation).

5. CITATORS

Shepard's New York Miscellaneous Citations analyses the decisions and opinions in the ***SDR***, the New York attorney general opinions and the ***Education Department Reports***. Citations to these sources are not presently analyzed in the LEXIS or WESTLAW Shepard's services, presumably because the sources themselves (with the exception of relatively recent attorney general opinions) are not part of the LEXIS or WESTLAW databases. However, by using the WESTLAW and LEXIS databases themselves as citators, citations to the SDR, attorney general opinions and ***Education Department Reports*** in New York cases can be located online.

REFERENCES

Butch, D. ***New York State Documents: an Introductory Manual.*** Albany: University of the State of New York, 1987.

Carter, R. A. ***Sources of Published and Unpublished Administrative Opinions in New York State.*** Albany: University of the State of New York, 1984.

Dow, S. and K. Spencer. ***New York Legal Documents: a Selective Annotated Bibliography.*** Chicago: American Association of Law Libraries, 1985. (AALL Occasional Paper Series, No. 3-21).

Chapter Eleven
LOCAL LEGISLATION

1. ENTITIES OF LOCAL GOVERNMENT

a) Outside of the City of New York. The entities of New York local government outside of the City of New York are counties, cities, towns and villages. All of these governmental units are corporate entities known as municipal corporations.[1]

The State of New York is divided into 62 counties, five of which comprise the City of New York. All of the counties outside of the City of New York have towns and villages within their borders.[2] Towns can contain villages within their borders but many do not. Thirty-six counties contain cities and twenty-one do not.

[1] The definition of a municipal corporation varies in New York Law. It can contract or expand, depending upon the applicable statute. For example, the definition of a municipal corporation in sections 65-66 of the General Construction Law includes the four general purpose governments (cities, counties, towns, and villages) as well as school districts. Section 2 of the General Municipal Law limits the term municipal corporation to the four general purpose governments for purposes of the General Municipal Law. Section 100(1) of the General Municipal Law expands the definition of municipal corporation, for purposes of section 100(1), to include not only the four general purpose governments but also school districts and district corporations.

[2] New York (State). Dept. of State. Local Government Handbook 59 (4th ed. 1987) [Hereinafter Local Gov't. Handbook].

b) The City of New York. The City of New York was consolidated from a number of counties, cities, towns, and villages by the state legislature in 1897. Unlike the multi-tier local governments prevailing outside its borders, New York City, although it includes five counties (Bronx, Kings, New York, Queens and Richmond), contains no county, town or village governments. Since they are units of the City, the five boroughs of the City of New York (Bronx, Brooklyn, Queens, Manhattan and Staten Island) have no powers of self-governance under the State home rule powers granted to local governments. Their powers are derived from the Charter of the City of New York.

c) Sources. For descriptions of current local government structure and local law in New York, see the latest editions of the Department of State's ***Local Government Handbook***[3] and ***Adopting Local Laws.***[4] Over the years, the Division of Local Government and Community Services and its predecessor, the Office of Local Government, produced many useful studies and handbooks on local law in New York, which should be readily available in New York State document collections. For a discussion of the evolution of local government in New York, see "State Mandates" in the ***Report*** of the New York State Commission on State and Local Finance. The section entitled "Counties, Towns and Municipal Corporations" in ***New York Jurisprudence 2d*** is also useful.

For discussions of local government law not limited to New York, see ***Antieau's Local Government Law*** (published by Matthew Bender), McQuillin's ***Law of Municipal Corporations 3d ed.*** (published by Callaghan & Company), and ***The Law of Local Government Operations*** by Charles S. Rhyne.

2. OVERVIEW OF HOME RULE

Generally speaking, home rule refers to powers granted by the state to units of local government enabling them to perform, without undue interference by the state and in a manner most suitable to local conditions, those governmental functions traditionally local in nature.

Home rule in New York has evolved gradually.[5] New York's Constitu-

[3] LOCAL GOV'T. HANDBOOK, ***supra*** note 2.

[4] ADOPTING LOCAL LAWS (1983) [Hereinafter ADOPTING LOCAL LAWS].

[5] ***See*** Comment, ***Home Rule, a Fresh Start*** 14 BUFFALO L. REV. 484, 485 (1964-65); Hyman, ***Home Rule in New York, 1941-1965, retrospect and prospect*** 15 BUFFALO L. REV. 335, 337-45 (1965-66); and Note, ***Home Rule and the New York Constitution*** 66 COLUM. L. REV. 1145, 1147 (1966).

tion has contained a "Home Rule" article since 1894. The present constitutional and statutory scheme took shape with the revision of article IX of the New York Constitution (known as the "Home Rule Article" or the Local Government Article) in 1963 (effective January 1, 1964). Implementing legislation in the form of the Municipal Home Rule Law was passed in 1963, which also became effective on January 1, 1964. The Statute of Local Governments, which also implemented the constitutional mandate, became effective on July 1, 1965. Despite its brevity, the Statute of Local Governments is a chapter of the Consolidated Laws. It is printed in the same volume as the Municipal Home Rule Law in ***McKinney's Consolidated Laws of New York Annotated*** and ***Gould's Consolidated Laws of New York***. In ***New York Consolidated Laws Service and Michie's Consolidated Laws of New York***, it is printed in alphabetical order with the other chapters of the Consolidated Laws.

Article IX, section 1, of the New York Constitution consists of a Local Government Bill of Rights. Among the enumerated rights are the right of every local government[6] to have a popularly elected legislative body, the right to enact local laws, as provided in article IX, the right of counties to adopt, amend and repeal alternative forms of county government, and the power of eminent domain.

Sections 2(b)(2) and 2(c) of article IX allocate lawmaking power between the state and units of local government.[7] Section 2(b)(2) prohibits the legislature from passing a law affecting the "property, affairs or government" of any local government except by a general law. A general law applies to ***all*** municipalities of the same type. The legislature may pass a special law, which is a law that affects the "property, affairs or government" of ***only one or less than all*** municipalities of the same type, upon a home rule request from the affected locality or localities. A simple majority is required for passage of a special law. Except in the case of the City of New York, the legislature also may pass a special law on certificate of necessity from the governor. A two-thirds vote of each house is required for passage following a certificate of necessity.

Section 2(c)(i) of article IX makes an affirmative grant of power to local governments to enact local laws relating generally to their "property, affairs or government" as long as the local laws are consistent with the general laws of the state and the Constitution. This grant is supplemented in section 2(c)(ii) of article IX by the grant of authority to

[6] Excepted from the phrase "every local government" is a county wholly included within a city, i.e., the counties of the City of New York.)

[7] ADOPTING LOCAL LAWS, ***supra*** note 4, at 2.

local governments to enact local laws on specific subjects, whether or not they relate to local "property, affairs or government," as long as they are consistent with general laws and not expressly restricted by special state law.

The Municipal Home Rule Law and Statute of Local Governments, implementing article IX of the Constitution, grant specific powers to and place specific limitations on the powers of both local governments and the legislature. Two important limitations on the local lawmaking power are that a county, city, town or village may not pass a local law that is inconsistent with the New York Constitution or any general law,[8] nor may it pass a law that impairs the powers of any other public corporation.[9]

The Municipal Home Rule Law contains the procedures for the adoption of local laws by counties, cities, towns and villages, the procedures for enactment and revision of county and city charters, and the procedures for initiating home rule requests.

3. CHARTERS.

Charters establish the basic form of organization and administration for cities and for those counties that have adopted charters. Under present home rule law, charters and their amendments can be comprised of local laws, or special laws, or a combination of these. Formerly, charters had to be approved by the legislature as special laws, although amendments could be made by local law.

At least nineteen counties in New York State have adopted their own charters.[10] In the absence of a charter, county operations are governed by the County Law in combination with local and special laws.

All cities in New York are governed by city charters. Procedures for adoption and revision of city charters are found in sections 36 and 37 of the Municipal Home Rule Law. Drafting of a new or revised city charter is usually the function of a charter commission. If the desired charter revision goes beyond the powers granted to the cities in section 10 of the Municipal Home Rule Law, it may be necessary to seek state legislation to effect the desired charter changes.

[8] N.Y. MUN. HOME RULE LAW sec. 10(1)(i) (McKinney 1969).

[9] N.Y. MUN. HOME RULE LAW sec. 10(5) (McKinney 1969).

[10] LOCAL LAW HANDBOOK, *supra* note 2, at 64.

4. LOCAL LAWS AND SPECIAL LAWS

a) **Local Laws.** The subject matter of local laws must fall within the general or specific grants of power contained in article IX of the New York Constitution, the Municipal Home Rule Law, Statute of Local Governments, or other state statutes delegating particular powers to local governments.

A local law properly enacted within the scope of the municipality's lawmaking authority has the same quality as a law enacted by the legislature, since both kinds of legislation derive from the New York Constitution.[11] Since a local law is an exercise of power derived from the New York Constitution, it is superior to a local ordinance or resolution that is an exercise of power derived from authority delegated by the legislature to municipalities.

Following are a sampling of typical local laws taken from the ***Local Laws of the Cities, Counties, Towns and Villages*** of 1972: a local law reducing the present speed limit on Winchell Road, Town of Camillus ... from fifty miles per hour to forty miles per hour; a local law providing for a four-year term of office for the town superintendant of highways; a local law authorizing increases in salaries of elective and appointive officials in the City of Amsterdam; and a local law establishing sewer rents for the Town of Ramapo.

(1) **Filing Local Laws.** A local law is not effective until certified copies of the law are filed locally and also with the Secretary of State and the State Comptroller.[12] The filing is to occur within five days after the law's final adoption and or approval.

(2) **Publication of Local Laws.** The first publication of a local law is in the newpaper(s) designated by the municipality for that purpose. The Secretary of State is charged by section 27(5)[13] of the Municipal Home Rule Law with the responsibility for publishing the local laws annually as a supplement to the session laws.

The changing titles of the Secretary of State's local law publications over the years reflect the expansion of local lawmaking power. Between 1924 and 1939, the title was ***Local Laws of the Cities in the State of New York.*** Between 1940 and 1942, the title was ***Local Laws of the Cities and Villages in the State of New York.*** Between 1943 and 1963, the title was ***Local Laws of the Cities, Counties and Villages in the State of New***

[11] LOCAL GOV'T. HANDBOOK, ***supra*** note 2, at 53; ADOPTING LOCAL LAWS, ***supra*** note 4, at i-ii.

[12] N.Y. MUN. HOME RULE LAW sec. 27 (McKinney 1969); 19 NYCRR 130.

[13] N.Y. MUN. HOME RULE LAW sec. 27(5) (McKinney 1969).

York. From 1964 to the present, the title is ***Local Laws of the Cities, Counties, Towns and Villages in the State of New York***.

The ***Local Laws*** series was published in bound annual volumes until 1973. It has been published on microfilm since 1974. At this writing, there is a delay of several years in the State's publishing program. To obtain copies of local laws for years not yet published, contact the unit of local government that passed the local law or the State Records Office, Department of State, 162 Washington Avenue, Albany, New York 12231.

For local laws filed between 1974 and 1982, the Secretary of State published an ***Index of Local Laws of the Counties, Cities, Towns and Villages By Municipality***. It was both a subject index and an index by the name of municipality. In the ***Index,*** local law notation contains the name of the municipality, the law number and the last two digits of the year in which the law was passed. For example, the first local law passed in 1977 in the Town of Lafayette is Lafayette Local Law 1-77. At this writing, budgetary constraints prevent continuation of this index.

b) Special Laws. When a municipality desires the enactment of legislation that is beyond its local lawmaking authority, it initiates a home rule request in order to have a "special law" passed by the New York legislature. A special law is defined in section 2(12) of the Municipal Home Rule Law as:

> [A] state statute which in terms and in effect applies to one or more, but not all, counties, counties other than those wholly included within a city, cities, towns or villages.[14]

In order for the legislature to pass a special law, the affected municipality (or municipalities) must first approve the proposed law by one of the methods outlined in section 40 of the Municipal Home Rule Law.[15] Following local approval, the proposed law is introduced in the state legislature with a Home Rule Request. Also pursuant to section 40, a Home Rule Request must declare that there is a necessity for enactment of the legislation, either because the local government does not have the power to enact such legislation by local law or by reason of other facts that must be set forth in the request. If the bill passes, it is published in ***Laws of New York***. A recent important example of a special law is the ***Administrative Code of the City of New York*** which is Chapter 907 of the 1985 ***Laws of New York***.

14 N.Y. MUN. HOME RULE LAW sec. 2(12) (McKinney 1969).
15 N.Y. MUN. HOME RULE LAW sec. 40 (McKinney 1969).

5. ORDINANCES

Counties, cities and towns may legislate in the form of ordinances as well as by local laws. While counties generally exercise their powers through local laws or resolutions,[16] they sometimes legislate by ordinance.[17]

As noted above, the distinction between local laws and ordinances is based upon the difference in their source; local laws stem from a constitutional grant, while ordinances stem from a delegation of legislative power from the legislature. However, the distinction is blurred by the virtual elimination of the ordinance form of village legislation[18] and by the option of other municipalities to legislate by local law on subjects they may also act on by ordinance.[19]

6. RESOLUTIONS

Resolutions are actions taken by a municipality of a temporary, special, or ministerial nature. They can be characterized broadly as administrative. By contrast, local laws and ordinances prescribe general, uniform and permanent rules of conduct. Local laws and ordinances can be characterized broadly as legislative.[20]

An example of the use of a resolution is found in section 10(32) of the General City Law[21] authorizing the creation by resolution of a commission or department of traffic control.

7. PUBLICATION OF CHARTERS, ORDINANCES, AND CODES

Researchers in New York local law are fortunate in that the charters, ordinances and codes for hundreds of New York municipalities are printed commercially. At least five companies are currently publishing various charters, codes and ordinances of New York local governments. Both the Williams Press of Albany and Lenz & Reicker, Inc., also of Albany, publish the ***New York City Charter and Administrative Code.***

[16] See N.Y. COUNTY LAW sec. 153 (McKinney 1972).

[17] See N.Y. MUN. HOME RULE LAW sec. 33(4).

[18] N.Y. VILLAGE LAW sec.20-2000 (McKinney 1987). Since 1974, villages may adopt orders, rules or regulations containing penalties only by local law.

[19] N.Y. MUN. HOME RULE LAW sec. 10(2) (McKinney 1969).

[20] Informal Op. Att'y Gen. No. 81-99 (1981).

[21] N.Y. GEN. CITY sec. 20(32) (McKinney Supp. 1987).

Commerce Clearing House (CCH) published the New York City Administrative Code in 1985 and projects that the volumes will be updated. The New York City Charter and Administrative Code is also maintained online in the New York Legislative Retrieval System (LRS).

The Municipal Code Corporation of Tallahassee, Florida publishes the ***Kenmore Municipal Code,*** the ***Charter and Ordinances of the City of Buffalo,*** the ***Charter, Revised General Laws, Local Laws, Special Acts and Miscellaneous Provisions of the City of Syracuse*** and the codes for many other municipalities in New York State. General Code Publishers Corporation of Rochester, New York publishes over 300 codes for New York municipalities including the cities of Albany, Rochester, Kingston, Schenectady, Mount Vernon, Peekskill and Plattsburgh. At this writing, notable omissions from the list of municipalities with commercially printed materials include Nassau County, Erie County, and the city of Niagara Falls.

Appendix E lists New York municipalities for which commercially published charters, ordinances and codes are available. Names and addresses of publishers are listed in Appendix D. In many cases, even where codes are commercially printed, the codes are only available for purchase through the municipality.

To obtain information on codes, it may be necessary to contact the clerk of the municipality to determine what arrangements can be made for local government research on that municipality. There is a Supreme Court library in almost all New York counties. These libraries generally maintain a current set of the codes and ordinances for their region. Appendix F lists New York law libraries, including the Supreme Court libraries.

8. CITATORS

Shepard's New York Statute Citations provides citations to New York and federal cases, agency decisions, and opinions of the attorney general in which the ***Local Laws,*** the ***New York City Charter, the New York City Administrative Code*** and the ordinances of the municipalities have been cited. For more recent years, the scope of ***Shepard's New York Statute Citations*** has been broadened to include citations appearing in selected law reviews, legal periodicals, and ***Laws of New York.***

The section in ***Shepard's New York Statute Citations*** covering citations to ordinances is arranged alphabetically by municipality. Within the municipality, topics such as "Fire Department," "Traffic," and "Zoning" are listed in alphabetical order. Citations to resolutions follow citations to ordinances under the name of the particular municipality.

An index to ordinances is another feature of this citator. The index provides an alphabetical list of subject headings derived from the more frequently cited provisions of New York ordinances. The index is a tool which allows researchers to identify and compare ordinances on similar subjects across municipalities.

Another useful feature in ***Shepard's New York Statute Citations*** is the Table of New York Acts by Popular Name or Short Title. This is the only popular name access tool for ***Local Laws*** and the ***New York City Administrative Code.*** However, its scope is quite limited. Only acts cited in ***Shepard's New York Statute Citations*** are included in this table. Like the index to ordinances, it provides a means to identify local legislation on similar subjects across municipalities. The importance of this table and the index to ordinances has increased since the publication of the ***Index of Local Laws*** ceased in 1982.

REFERENCES

Adopting Local Laws. Edited by John F. Eramo. Albany: New York State Dept. of State, 1983.

Emery, R. A. ***Where To Find Local Laws In New York State: a note*** 15 Government Publications Review 49 (1988).

New York (State). Dept. of State. ***Local Government Handbook***. 4th ed. Albany: New York State Dept. of State, 1987.

Chapter Twelve
DATABASES FOR NEW YORK LEGAL RESEARCH

1. OVERVIEW

This Chapter describes the databases that are currently among the most useful for New York legal and law-related research. While New York coverage is highlighted here, the jurisdictional scope of these databases (with the exception of LRS) extends beyond New York to various other jurisdictions: state, federal, foreign, and international.

a) Overview of the Databases. Readers who are unfamiliar with computer-assisted research, or who are familiar mainly with WESTLAW and LEXIS, should find this preliminary overview of the databases helpful.

Online databases are collections of information or data which are computer readable. Search capability, type and format of information retrievable, and search strategy vary from database to database. Most databases are available through one or more "online services," which are organizations or vendors that provide access to a number of different databases.

The two giants of the online legal research services are, of course, WESTLAW and LEXIS. Their New York databases provide full text coverage of cases and statutes[1], an increasing number of administrative decisions, and information from secondary sources and services such as law reviews and ***Shepard's Citations***.

Four other law-oriented databases offer research support for pending New York legislation: LRS, Legi-Tech, STATE NET and ELSS. STATE NET also provides research support for pending New York administrative regulations. Summarized New York tax law is included in PHINet through its Prentice-Hall ***All States Tax Guide*** database.

News and business databases offer a wealth of information on legal and law-related news such as settled cases, securities and corporate matters, and regional, statewide and national economic trends. Wire services and national legal newspapers and the ***New York Times***, which often include news about New York law and law firms, are online in full-text through NEXIS. Articles from selected state capital newspapers, including two papers that cover Albany, are available on VU/TEXT in full-text. VU/TEXT also includes business news articles from selected city newspapers and regional business newspapers, including many located in New York State. The Dow Jones news service offers news and business information including the full text of the ***Wall Street Journal***.

Access to these databases and to the other databases described in this chapter expand the researcher's "law library." Such access provides the capability to locate information quickly and to locate kinds of information that formerly could be acquired only after great effort, expense and delay, if it could be acquired at all. Computer searches readily performed for New York information on these databases include:

* locating cases tried by particular New York judges (LEXIS and WESTLAW);

[1] At this writing, Mead Data Central projects that the Consolidated Laws of New York will once again be available on LEXIS in 1988. WESTLAW projects that the Consolidated Laws will become available on WESTLAW in 1988. Both WESTLAW and LEXIS contain subsets of selected statutes for New York.

* locating cases settled out of court by searching the ***New York Times*** and the wire services (NEXIS);

* creating a user-defined file of bills pending in the New York legislature and checking their status daily (LRS, Legi-Tech, STATE NET and ELSS);

* identifying expert witnesses by searching selected national legal newspapers online (NEXIS);

* checking the status of proposed New York administrative regulations (STATE NET);

* gathering details on corporations from information filed with the Securities and Exchange Commission (Exchange, a service available through NEXIS);

* creating a bibliography of books on a particular topic in New York law (RLIN); and

* researching a medical condition in connection with a malpractice case (MEDIS service available through LEXIS).

For a more extensive overview of databases useful for general legal research, see the legal research guides listed in this book's preface and ***Electronic Databases in Legal Research: Beyond LEXIS and WESTLAW***[2] by S. Blair Kauffman. For a sobering analysis of the limitations of computer assisted legal research, see ***Full-Text Databases and Legal Research: Backing Into the Future*** by Robert C. Berring.[3]

b) Search Charges and Access to Databases . Any researcher who can afford to subscribe to the services that provide access to these databases can gather the kinds of information described above and much more using a database-compatible home or office computer, modem, telephone, and communication software package. Some services offer equipment leasing arrangements as an alternative to subscriber provided equipment.

[2] Kauffman, ***Electronic Databases in Legal Research: Beyond LEXIS and WESTLAW*** 13 RUTGERS COMPUTER & TECHNOLOGY L. J. 73 (1987) [hereinafter Kauffman].

[3] Berring, ***Full-Text Databases and Legal Research: Backing Into the Future*** 1 HIGH TECHNOLOGY LAW JOURNAL 27 (1987).

Search charges and subscription rates for access to databases change rapidly and may vary according to the category into which the subscriber fits. Some databases are available through more than one service; the cost for searching them may vary according to the online service through which they are accessed. In light of these facts, no attempt is made in this Chapter to describe search charges or subscription rates. However, it may be helpful to realize that some services provide discounted rates for special groups such as bar associations, government agencies, and law schools or other educational institutions. Some services provide subscription rate packages tailored to the amount of expected use or special low rates for evening-only searching. For up-to-date pricing information, contact the services directly. Their addresses and phone numbers (as of September, 1987) are included in the database and service descriptions in Sections 2-19 of this Chapter.

Researchers who have only occasional need for database searching and researchers for whom subscription or equipment costs are prohibitive may find that it can be cost-effective to use the services of information brokers who have access to the desired databases. Information brokers usually are listed in the classified pages of telephone and other local directories under headings such as "Information Services & Bureaus."

c) Current Awareness and Databases. It is a constant challenge to stay abreast of database changes and of the emergence of new, relevant databases. Most services provide an electronic bulletin board to acquaint subscribers with changes in the databases accessed through their services. This news may appear on the screen as part of the sign-on procedures. The services also produce brochures and provide other customer assistance to explain changes in the data bases. Many also provide looseleaf manuals for subscribers which document database contents.

In addition to information accessible mainly to subscribers, various printed sources can help the researcher keep up-to-date on the existence of databases relevant for New York legal research. The ***Directory of Online Databases***, published by Cuadra Associates of New York City, lists and provides subject access to over 2,900 commercially available databases. The hard copy version of this directory is updated three times a year. The ***Directory of Online Databases*** is also searchable online through WESTLAW. The ***Directory of Periodicals Online: Indexed, Abstracted, & Full-Text, News, Law and Business,*** produced by Federal Document Retrieval, Inc., indicates online availability of specific periodical titles. Finally, ***Ulrich's International Periodicals Directory*** includes a section listing periodicals available online and a section listing which periodicals are available from which online services.

Periodicals which have recently included articles on law-related databases include: the ***Legal Reference Services Quarterly,*** the ***Law Library Journal,*** the ***Rutgers Computer and Technology Law Journal,*** the ***Practical Lawyer, High Technology Law Journal***, and ***Legal Economics***. The ***Newsletter*** of the American Association of Law Libraries carries a column entitled "Law Library Hi-Tech" which provides current information on legal databases. The ***Legal Information Alert***, a newsletter, also tracks current news on legal databases. The ***New York Law Journal***, the ***New York State Bar Journal***, and the national legal newspapers also carry advertisements for and articles about relevant databases from time to time. To locate current articles on computer assisted legal research, consult the ***Legal Resource Index (LRI), Current Law Index (CLI)***, or the ***Index to Legal Periodicals (ILP)***. Consult the ***Directory of Online Databases*** to determine which services currently provide access to ***LRI*** and ***ILP*** online.

The remainder of this Chapter consists of descriptions of databases that are useful for New York legal research.

2. LEXIS

LEXIS is an online service available from Mead Data Central. Among its databases are the full text of reported New York cases. Retrospective coverage of cases as of September 4, 1987 is as follows:

Court of Appeals - 97 N.Y. (1884 to date)
Appellate Division - 189 A.D. (1919 to date)
Misc. Courts - 1 Misc.2d. (1955 to date).

New York cases and some administrative decisions are also available in specialized LEXIS libraries that cover taxation, securities, corporation law, employment, health, and public utilities cases for the states. Coverage of New York administrative material on LEXIS as of September 4, 1987 is as follows:

New York Tax Commission decisions, memoranda, adopted regulations and advisory opinions (1979 to date);
New York State Comptroller's opinions (1979 to date);
New York Public Service Commission slip opinions (1977 to date); and
New York Attorney General opinions (1977 to date).

Determinations of the new Tax Appeals Tribunal (successor to the Tax Commission) will be put online when issued. Mead Data Central projects that the full text of the New York Constitution and the Consolidated Laws will once again be available on LEXIS in 1988.

The LEXIS law review library contains the full text of articles from selected law reviews. Law reviews published in New York that are included in this LEXIS library as of September 4, 1987 are: ***Brooklyn Law Review, Columbia Law Review, Cornell Law Review, Fordham Law Review, Hofstra Law Review,*** and the ***New York University Law Review***. Besides law reviews, valuable secondary sources available through LEXIS include: ***American Law Reports*** (A.L.R.2d, A.L.R.3d, A.L.R.4th, and A.L.R. Fed.); state-oriented services such as the ***Environmental Law Reporter*** and the ***CCH Blue Sky Reporter***; and state-oriented newsletters, such as the ***CCH State Tax Week***. Both the ***Index to Legal Periodicals*** and the ***Legal Resource Index*** are also available through LEXIS.

Selected ***Shepard's Citations*** services and the Auto-Cite service are available through LEXIS for updating and verifying citations for cases included in the LEXIS libraries.

The Eclipse (Electronic Clipping Service) function on LEXIS provides automatic updating of customer-designed searches at daily, weekly or monthly intervals.

More information on LEXIS is available from Mead Data Central, 9393 Springboro Pike, P.O. Box 933, Dayton, Ohio 45401, Tel. (800) 227-4908 or (513) 865-6800.

3. WESTLAW

WESTLAW is an online service available from the West Pub-Publishing Company. Its databases include the full text of all New York cases reported in the West National Reporting System. Retrospective coverage of cases as of December 24, 1987 is as follows:

> Court of Appeals - 1 N.E. (1885 to date);
> Appellate Division - 172 N.Y.S. (1918 to date);
> Supreme Court - 172 N.Y.S. (1918 to date; and
> Misc. Courts of Record - 174 N.Y.S. (1919 to date).

West describes its case coverage as "full text plus" to indicate that case text is enhanced by the West topic and key number features that are used in the printed version of the West National Reporter System. ***West's***

N.Y. Digest 3d and *New York Supplement 2d* can be updated very efficiently by performing topic and key number searches on WESTLAW. This procedure is described in Chapter 6 (Court Reports and Case Finders).

New York cases are also searchable in specialized WESTLAW databases that cover New York corporation, education, family, insurance, and securities law.

According to its online listing, as of December 24, 1987, WESTLAW also includes the full text of the following additional material:

> New York Insurance Law (*McKinney*) as amended through May 10, 1985;
> New York Attorney General opinions - (1977 to date); and
> New York Comptroller opinions - (1977 to date).

The West Publishing Company projects that the Consolidated Laws will be available on WESTLAW during 1988.

Secondary sources searchable through WESTLAW include a law review database that contains the full text of selected articles from selected law reviews. Law reviews and legal periodicals published in New York that are included in this WESTLAW database as of September 8, 1987 are: ***Buffalo Law Review, Columbia Human Rights Law Review, Columbia Journal of Environmental Law, Columbia Journal of Law and Social Problems, Columbia Journal of Transnational Law, Cornell International Law Journal, Cornell Law Review, Fordham Law Review, Fordham Urban Law Journal, Hofstra Law Review, New York State Bar Journal, New York University Journal of International Law and Politics, New York University Law Review, New York University Review of Law and Social Change, Pace Law Review, Saint John's Law Review, Syracuse Journal of International Law and Commerce, Syracuse Law Review***, and the ***Westchester Bar Journal***. Both the ***Index to Legal Periodicals*** and the ***Legal Resource Index*** are also available through WESTLAW.

The ***Shepard's Citations*** and Insta-Cite services can be used to update and check case citations for most of the New York cases included in the WESTLAW databases. The online version of the ***Directory of Online Databases***, previously described in section 1 above, is searchable on WESTLAW.

Other specialized services which can be accessed through WESTLAW (through separate subscriptions) include DIALOG, VU/TEXT, and DOW JONES Text - Searches Services. These services are described below.

More information on WESTLAW is available from West Publishing Company, P.O. Box 64526, St. Paul, Minnesota 55164-9979, Tel. (800) 328-9352.

4. VERALEX

VERALEX is a database produced by Mead Data Central and VERACORP. As part of its federal and multi-state coverage, it contains the full text of reported New York court opinions and attorney general opinions. It also contains the full text of ***American Law Reports*** (A.L.R.). Unlike LEXIS and WESTLAW, VERALEX is not fulltext searchable; searches must be performed by citation to the desired document. Auto-Cite is also available on VERALEX.

For more information on VERALEX, contact Lawyers Co-operative Publishing Company, 50 Broad Street East, Rochester, N.Y. 14694, Tel. (716) 546-5530 or (800) 462-6807.

5. LEGISLATIVE RETRIEVAL SYSTEM (LRS)

The Legislative Retrieval System (LRS) is a New York legislative database developed and operated by the New York Legislative Bill Drafting Commission. Intended originally for use by the legislature and state agencies, it became commercially available in late 1984.

LRS maintains full text databases of bills and resolutions introduced and amended in the last two years (updated daily, latest amendment only), the Consolidated Laws (updated quarterly), the Chapter Laws passed in the current legislative term (updated as received from the governor's office), the Senate and Assembly rules (in the Consolidated Laws database), the New York City Charter and Administrative Code (updated quarterly), and budget chapters passed in the current legislative session.

In addition to the full text databases, other databases on LRS include bill summaries, bill status, Senate and Assembly floor calendars, standing committee agenda and hearing calendars, and the Senate and Assembly introductory record. The introductory record is searchable by a particular legislator's name. At this writing, LRS does not include the legislators' introductory memoranda.[4]

[4] Introductory memoranda are described in Chapter 2 (State Legislation: Legislative Process, Bills, Session Laws and Resolutions) and in Chapter 5 (Legislative History).

The subscriber can create and maintain one or many bill tracking files. Each bill file can be organized by subject. Capability includes report generation for either on-screen viewing or downloading to disk for later editing and printing.

More information on LRS is available from the New York Legislative Bill Drafting Commission, 55 Elk Street, Albany, New York 12207, Tel. (518) 455-7672 or (800) 356-6566.

6. LEGI-TECH

Legi-Tech is available through Legi-Tech, Inc. It contains the full-text of the New York bills (latest amendment only) from the current legislative term. The bills file can be searched by key word. The researcher can track bills, search the Senate and Assembly calendars, search for bills by sponsors' names, and determine voting records of legislators. Current campaign contribution reports, which legislators and constitutional officers must file with the Board of Elections, are also searchable.

Legi-Tech does not maintain a file of Chapter laws or Consolidated Laws. However, the bill tracking feature indicates whether a bill has become law. If it has, the chapter number is listed and the last amended version of the bill can be located in the bills file.

The subscriber can create customized "user-defined files" in order to track selected bills by subject or sponsor.

In addition to its New York State legislative database, Legi-Tech maintains similar databases for California and the U.S. Congress.

More information on Legi-Tech is available from Legi-Tech, Inc., 1 Steuben Place, Albany, New York, Tel. (513) 434-2242.

7. STATE NET (Information for Public Affairs)

STATE NET is a database available from Information for Public Affairs (IPA).[5] STATE NET contains summaries of all bills for the current term of Congress and the 50 state legislatures. The bill summaries can be searched using any combination of states and subjects. Searching access is by key word.

STATE NET also includes abstracts of proposed administrative regulations, information on hearings on proposed rulemaking, addresses

[5] In 1985, PAI Legislative Services changed its name to Information for Public Affairs.

for officials designated to receive comment, and other information contained in the ***Federal Register*** and in the state registers, including the ***New York State Register***. Abstracts of proposed administrative regulations in states which do not publish a state register are obtained directly from the administrative agencies by STATE NET staff. The administrative regulations abstracts can be searched using any combination of states and subjects. Unfortunately, STATE NET's administrative coverage is limited to proposed rulemaking. It does not maintain the ***Official Compilation of Codes, Rules and Regulations (NYCRR)*** online, nor does it include the ***Code of Federal Regulations*** or the administrative codes of the other states.

STATE NET's subscribers can create tracking files to follow New York legislative and administrative proposals, pending hearings, and action on proposals. STATE NET also contains the names and addresses of all of the current state legislators and members of Congress.

More information on STATE NET is available from Information for Public Affairs, 1900 - 14th Street, Sacramento, California 95814, Tel. (916) 444-0840.

8. ELECTRONIC LEGISLATIVE SEARCH SYSTEM (ELSS)

ELSS is a federal and state legislative bill tracking system produced by Commerce Clearing House (CCH) and available through the General Electric Information Service (GEIS). Selected bills in the areas of taxation, business, and education are summarized in the database. Status and other information on this selected legislation for the 50 states and Congress is searchable online.

More information on ELSS is available from local CCH representatives or from Commerce Clearing House, Inc., 4025 W. Peterson Ave., Chicago, Illinois 60646, Tel. (312) 346-9134.

9. NEXIS

NEXIS is an online service of Mead Data Central. It can be accessed through a LEXIS terminal or a microcomputer. Its NEXIS "library" contains newspapers, newsletters, magazines and wire services. Among the newspapers included in full-text are the ***New York Times*** (from June 1, 1980 to date), the ***National Law Journal*** (from January 3, 1983 to date), and ***Legal Times*** (from January 4, 1982 to date). At this time, the

NEXIS library contains the full text of approximately 150 business, news, government and trade publications which could provide information relevant in New York legal research. The NEXIS service also contains, in a separate library, selected biographical stories from the *New York Times* from June 1, 1980 to date.

Other services that are relevant for New York law and law-related research and that are available on NEXIS include Exchange, NAARS, and APOLIT.

The Exchange service contains research reports on U.S. and national companies, many of which are incorporated in or do business in New York. Exchange also contains the full text of Securities and Exchange Commission 10-Q and 10-K filings for more than 1,500 companies plus abstracted annual reports and SEC filings for more than 10,300 companies.

The NAARS service contains corporate annual reports, proxy reports and accounting information. It is made available on NEXIS through an arrangement with the American Institute of Certified Public Accountants.[6]

The Associated Press Political Service (APOLIT) contains information on political campaigns, issues and candidates, including information on statewide referenda.

For ideas on effectively using NEXIS for legal research, see ***NEXIS for Academic Law Librarians***[7] and ***Electronic Databases in Legal Research: Beyond LEXIS and WESTLAW.***[8]

More information on NEXIS is available from Mead Data Central, 9393 Springboro Pike, P.O. Box 933, Dayton, Ohio 45401, Tel. (800) 227-4908 or (513) 865-6800.

10. VU/TEXT

VU/TEXT is a service available through VU/TEXT Information Services. VU/TEXT's Newspapers database contains the full text of articles in the ***Albany Times Union*** and the ***Knickerbocker News*** (publication ceased in April, 1988). Business databases available through VU/TEXT contain selected, business-related articles from New York newspapers and regional business papers. Included in this category are: ***Business First*** (Buffalo), ***Buffalo News, Capital District Business Review***

[6] Kauffman, ***supra*** note 2, at 79.

[7] Cascio, ***NEXIS for Academic Law Librarians*** 6 Legal Reference Services Q. 47 (Spring/Summer 1986).

[8] Kauffman, ***supra*** note 2, at 75-81.

(Albany), Crane's New York Business, Democrat & Chronicle (Rochester), Long Island Business Journal, New York City Business, New York Times (National Edition), Newsday, Syracuse & Central Business Review, Syracuse Business, Syracuse Herald-American and Post Standard, Syracuse Herald Journal, the ***Journal of Commerce,*** and the ***Reporter Dispatch (White Plains).***

More information on VU-TEXT is available from VU/TEXT Information Services, Inc., 325 Chestnut Street, 1300 Mall Building, Philadelphia, Pennsylvania 19106, Tel. (800) 258-8080.

11. DOW JONES TEXT - SEARCHES SERVICES

DOW JONES Text - Searches Services offers online search service for business and financial information. Among the newspapers included in this service are the ***Wall Street Journal*** (1984 to date) and the ***Washington Post*** (1984 to date) in full-text.

More information on DOW JONES TEXT - SEARCHES SERVICES is available from the Dow Jones Company, Inc., P.O. Box 300, Princeton, N.J. 08543, Tel. (800) 522-3567 or (609) 520-8349 (in New Jersey).

12. NEWSNET

NEWSNET is an online service that provides access to the full text of over 300 professional and trade newsletters. Examples of newsletters emphasizing state regulation and included on NEWSNET that are of potential interest to the New York researcher are: ***CCH Tax Day - State, Solid Waste Report, State Regulation Report: Toxics,*** and ***Ground Water Monitor.***

More information on NEWSNET is available from NewsNet, Inc., 945 Haverford Road, Bryn Mawr, Pennsylvania 19010, Tel. (215) 527-8030 or (800) 345-1301.

13. DIALOG

DIALOG is a service which provides access to over 250 separate databases. Among the most directly useful databases for New York legal research available through DIALOG is the ***Legal Resource Index***. This online index covers virtually all of the law reviews and legal periodicals published in New York from 1980 to date. Online searching eliminates searching separate indexes for various time periods and provides searching by keyword as well as by author, case name, and subject. The ***Legal Resource Index*** also indexes the ***New York Law Journal.*** Other relevant DIALOG databases can be located by consulting the "Law and Government" section of the latest issue of the DIALOG ***Database Catalog*** or the ***Directory of Online Databases.***

More information on DIALOG is available from DIALOG Information Service, Inc., Marketing Department, 3460 Hillview Ave., Palo Alto, California, 94304, Tel. (800) 334-2564.

14. BRS

BRS is a service that provides access to over 100 databases, including the ***Legal Resource Index***, and many business, social science, and news databases that are also available through DIALOG.

More information on BRS, BRS/After Dark and BRS/BRKTHRU is available from BRS Information Technologies, 1200 Route 7, Latham, N.Y. 12110, Tel. (800) 345-4277 or (518) 783-1161.

15. HUMAN RESOURCE INFORMATION NETWORK

Human Resource Information Network is an online service of Executive Telecom System, Inc., a subsidiary of the Bureau of National Affairs (BNA). The service specializes in personnel and human resources issues. Its topical, multistate coverage includes online equivalents of selected BNA publications such as ***AIDS Policy and Law*** and ***Benefits Today.***

More information on the Human Resource Information Network is available from Executive Telecom System, Inc., Human Resource Information Network, 9585 Valparaiso Court, Indianapolis, Indiana 46268, Tel. (317) 872-2045 or (800) 421-8884.

16. WILSONLINE

WILSONLINE is an online service providing access to the H.W. Wilson Company's indexes. Among the databases that would be useful for New York legal research are: the ***Index to Legal Periodicals, Readers' Guide to Periodical Literature, Social Sciences Index,*** and the ***Business Periodicals Index.***

More information on WILSONLINE is available from the H.W. Wilson Company, 950 University Avenue, Bronx, N.Y. 10452, Tel. (800) 462-6060 (in New York State), (800) 367-6770 (outside of New York State), or (212) 588-8400.

17. RLIN

Research Libraries Information Network (RLIN) is a bibliographic database available through Research Libraries Group, a membership corporation of the nation's leading research libraries. RLIN contains over 25 million bibliographic records. Bibliographic records for books and serials can be searched online by access points that include subject heading, personal author, corporate author, title and key words in titles.

Very large academic law libraries with major New York collections whose holdings are at least partially represented in the RLIN database include the law libraries of Columbia University, Cornell University, Harvard University, New York University, and Yale University. It is projected that the bibliographic records of the SUNY at Buffalo Law Library will be loaded into the RLIN database in the near future. The collections of the New York Public Library, the Association of the Bar of the City of New York, the New York Historical Society, and the New York State Archives are also at least partially represented on RLIN.

Of great importance for research in New York legal history is the availability of New York's Historical Documents Inventory (HDI) in the RLIN Archival and Manuscripts Control file (AMC). This inventory contains records that describe over 12,000 manuscripts and manuscript collections located in approximately 600 repositories throughout New York State. The Historical Documents Inventory is a statewide survey project being conducted by the New York Historical Resources Center at Cornell University.

More information on RLIN is available from Research Libraries Group, Inc., Jordan Quadrangle, Stanford, California 94305, Tel. (415) 328-0920.

18. OCLC

OCLC Online Computer Library Center, Inc. is a bibliographic database with over 7,000 participating libraries. The New York State Library's holdings as well as the holdings of many other New York academic and public libraries, including law libraries, are at least partially represented on OCLC.

More information on OCLC is available from OCLC Online Computer Library Center, Inc., 6565 Frantz Road, Dublin, Ohio 43017, Tel. (614) 764-6000 or (800) 848-5878.

19. PHINet

PHINet is a database available through Prentice-Hall Information Network. Of particular interest for New York research is the file that contains a large New York City and New York State section comparable in content to the Prentice-Hall ***All States Tax Guide*** looseleaf service. The Vertex Sales Tax file contains sales, use, and rental tax rates for the 50 states and all cities and counties. Prentice-Hall Information Network projects that a New York file comparable to the New York unit of the Prentice-Hall ***State and Local Taxes*** looseleaf service will be online during 1988.

More information on PHINet is available from Prentice-Hall Information Network, 292 Madison Avenue, 4th Floor, New York, N.Y. 10017, Tel. (212) 373-8600.

REFERENCES

Berring, R.C. ***Full-Text Databases and Legal Research: Backing Into the Future.*** 1 High Technology Law Journal 27 (1987).

Cascio, N. ***NEXIS for Academic Law Librarians.*** 6 Legal Reference Services Quarterly 47 (Spring/Summer 1986).

Kauffman, S. B. ***Electronic Databases in Legal Research: Beyond LEXIS and WESTLAW.*** 13 Rutgers Computer & Technology Law Journal 73 (1987).

Chapter Thirteen
TREATISES, PRACTICE BOOKS, AND OTHER SOURCES

1. OVERVIEW

Treatises are "expositions by legal writers on case law and legislation."[1] Treatises on New York law range in depth from multi-volume works, such as ***White on New York Corporations***, to one-volume handbooks for the practitioner, such as Bowmar's ***Lien Priorities in New York***. Treatises written primarily for attorneys are often called practice books.

Section 1 of this chapter lists treatises and practice books in a subject arrangement. The subject headings used are in almost all cases the same headings assigned to these books by the Library of Congress, except that the subheading "New York" is omitted here. One exception to the practice of using Library of Congress headings is found in the family law area. Books that the Library of Congress lists under Domestic Relations Courts are listed here under either Matrimonial Actions or Family Court.

New York no longer has any treatise that attempts to cover all of New York law. The last treatise to attempt that feat was ***The Substantive Law of New York: with appropriate comments on evidence and procedure*** by Abraham L. Sainer, first published in 1969. Supplementation for that two-volume treatise ceased in 1985. At this writing, only the multi-volume legal encyclopedia for New York, ***New York Jurisprudence 2d,*** provides comprehensive coverage of New York subjective and adjective law. ***New York Jurisprudence 2d*** does provide a starting point for research in many topics of New York law, and it is a serviceable case finder. However, it is an encyclopedia and does not offer the depth or

[1] J.M. Jacobstein and R.M. Mersky. Fundamentals of Legal Research 345 (1987).

analysis of particular topics traditionally associated with multivolume legal treastises. ***New York Jurisprudence 2d*** is described in Chapter 15 (Reference Books and Indexes).

Many of the treatises and practice books listed in this chapter contain forms. Those works are indicated with an asterisk (*) next to the entry for the book. Chapter 14 describes works that are primarily form books. Practice works containing forms that are listed here are not listed again in Chapter 14.

This list does not include statutory handbooks or digests. Handbooks that primarily contain civil and criminal practice laws, court rules, and court acts are described in Chapter 8 (Practice and Procedure Acts, Evidence and Court Rules). Digests, including specialized digest-newsletters, such as the ***New York Law Digest*** and the ***Matrimonial Case Citator,*** are described in Chapter 7 (Court Reports and Case Finders).

The emphasis in this Chapter is on current works. However, selected older works and works that are no longer being supplemented are included in section 2 when no successor work covers the particular subject area. Section 3 describes currently available print and media sources for continuing legal education and for maintaining current awareness of trends in New York politics and government.

2. TREATISES AND PRACTICE BOOKS

APPELLATE PROCEDURE

Cohen, Henry,

The Powers of the New York Court of Appeals, by Henry Cohen and Arthur Karger, with a foreword by John T. Loughran. Rev. ed. New York: Baker Voorhis, 1952.

*Newman, Thomas R.

New York Appellate Practice by Thomas R. Newman with the assistance of Louis G. Adolfsen, Lissa Griffin, Ignatius J. Melito. New York: M. Bender, 1985-

2 v. (Loose-leaf).

This service provides guidance for civil and criminal appeals. It includes diagrams of New York's appellate court structure, forms, court rules, and statutes governing appeals.

BILLS OF PARTICULARS

*Greenfield, Benita
Callaghan's Bills of Particulars in New York, 1984 rev. ed., by Benita Greenfield. Wilmette, Ill.: Callaghan & Co., 1984-
Loose-leaf supplementation.

BURIAL LAW

Padula, Fred
The Last Word, a Consumer Guide to Funeral Planning. Albany, N.Y.: New York State Consumer Protection Board, 1983.

BUSINESS LAW

**New York Practice Guide. Business and Commercial.* Eileen M. Lach, general editor, Robert I. Kantowitz, tax editor. New York: M. Bender, 1987-
3 v. Looseleaf supplementation.

Contents of this set include: forms of business organization, purchase and sale of a business, bankruptcy, sales, bulk transfers, secured transactions, commercial arbitration, the employment relationship, and liquor licensing.

CIVIL PROCEDURE

Byer, Edward I.
A Guide to Civil Motions in New York State Courts. Albany, N.Y.: Williams Press, 1984.
Cover title: *Civil Motions*. Kept up-to-date by pocket supplements.

A one-volume, extensively annotated handbook for New York motion practice. Contains a table of statutes and an index.

Carmody-Wait 2d: Cyclopedia of New York Practice With Forms. Rochester: Lawyers Co-operative Publishing Co.
30 v. in 35 books. Kept up-to-date with pocket parts and replacement volumes.

The text covers civil practice and evidence. Six entire volumes are devoted to surrogate's court and estate practice. The scope of the textual portion of this set is approximately the same as that of the *New York Practice* set of treatises published by the Matthew Bender company. Approximately one-half of this set is made up of practice and legal forms.

Chase, Oscar G.

Civil Litigation in New York, by Oscar G. Chase. New York: M. Bender, 1983.

(Cases and Materials)

Peterfreund, Herbert

New York Practice: Cases and other Materials, by Herbert Peterfreund and Joseph M. McLaughlin. 4th ed. Mineola, N.Y.: Foundation Press, 1978.

(University casebook series)

Siegel, David D.

Handbook on New York Practice, by David D. Siegel. St. Paul, Minn.: West Pub. Co., 1978.

(Hornbook series)

Kept up-to-date with pocket supplements.

Wachtell, Herbert M.

New York Practice Under the CPLR, by Herbert M. Wachtell and Theodore N. Mirvis. 6th ed. New York: Practising Law Institute, 1986.

A one-volume handbook on New York civil practice designed to be "a working tool for the practicing lawyer and a succinct text for the law student" [Preface]. Contains tables of statutes and cases.

Weinstein, Jack B.

New York Civil Practice - CPLR, by Jack B. Weinstein, Harold L. Korn, and Arthur R. Miller. New York: M. Bender, 1963-

Vols. 1, 2, 2A, 3, 3A, 4, 5, 6, 7, 7A, and 8 of *New York Civil Practice*. Loose-leaf supplementation.

A comprehensive treatise on New York civil practice under the Civil Practice Law and Rules (CPLR). It currently fills 12 binders. An unnumbered binder contains a table of cases construing the CPLR. Tables of statutes and an index are at the back of vol. 8.

Weinstein, Jack B.
Weinstein-Korn-Miller CPLR Manual, by Oscar G. Chase. Rev. ed. New York: M. Bender; 1980-
Loose-leaf supplementation.

A one-volume condensation of the comprehensive Weinstein, Korn and Miller treatise on the CPLR. Like the treatise, the *Manual* discusses the Civil Practice Law and Rules in their section number order. While the internal section numbers of the Manual do not correspond with the internal section numbers of the treatise, the *Manual* provides numerous cross-references to the treatise. The 1987 revision of chapters 2 and 3 is by Jay C. Carlisle.

For related works, see also under Bills of Particulars, Class Actions (Civil Procedure), Discovery (Law), and Special Proceedings.

COLLECTION LAWS

**Collections and the Enforcement of Money Judgments*. [New York]: New York State Bar Association, 1986.

*Rubin, Joseph
New York Collections, By Joseph Rubin. Rochester, N.Y.: Lawyers' Co-operative Pub. Co., 1986.
Loose-leaf supplementation.

*Sherwin, Sidney
How to Collect a Money Judgment, by Sidney Sherwin. 2nd rev. ed. Kew Gardens, N.Y.: Attorney's Aid Publications, 1984.

CONDOMINIUMS AND COOPERATIVES

*DiLorenzo, Vincent
New York Condominium and Cooperative Law, by Vincent DiLorenzo. Rochester, N.Y.: Lawyers Co-operative Pub. Co., 1984.
Kept up-to-date by pocket supplements.

Taishoff, Louis C., ed.
Cooperative Housing Conversions. New York, N.Y.: Praeger in Cooperation with the Association of the Bar of the City of New York, 1981.

CONTRACTS

Simpson, Laurence Packer

Contracts, by Laurence P. Simpson and Richard W. Duesenberg. Brooklyn, N.Y.: Edward Thompson Co. 1963-82.

(*Encyclopedia of New York Law*, v. 6-8) Pocket part supplementation by the West Pub. Co. ceased in 1982.

CORPORATION LAW

***Israels, Carlos L.**

Israels on Corporate Practice, by Alan M. Hoffman. 4th ed. New York: Practising Law Institute, 1983.

An introduction to New York corporation law for non- specialists. Forms include shareholders' agreements, certificates of incorporation, and minutes of annual meetings. Table of cases. Appendix compares New York's Business Corporation Law with the Delaware Corporation Law and the Model Business Corporation Act.

**The New York Corporate Handbook*, prepared by the New York State Bar Association, Raymond W. Merritt, editor-in-chief. Albany, N.Y.: New York State Bar Association, 1983.

A one-volume deskbook containing 15 chapters on basic areas of corporate practice, including ethical considerations for the corporate lawyer, written by members of the New York bar.

*White, Frank

White on New York Corporations, by Isidore Kantrowitz and Sol Slutsky assisted by the Publisher's editorial staff. Harold Friedman, supervising editor. 13th ed. New York: M. Bender, 1963-

8 v. Loose-leaf supplementation.

Contents: v. 1-5, Business Corporation Law (with index at the back of vol. 5); v. 6-8, Not-for-profit Corporation Law, by Bert S. Prunty, (with index at the back of v. 8).

CRIMINAL LAW

Donnino, William C.

New York Court of Appeals on Criminal Law. Rochester, N.Y.: Lawyers Co-operative Pub. Co., 1985.

(New York Practice library)

Kept up-to-date by pocket supplements.

Groble, Patricia

Criminal Law in New York, 3rd edition by Patricia A. Groble. Wilmette, Ill.: Callaghan & Co., 1984-

2 v. Loose-leaf supplementation.

Cover title: Callaghan's Criminal Law of New York

This is the revised edition of *Criminal Law in New York* by Edward Marks and Lloyd I. Paperno.

CRIMINAL PROCEDURE

**Basic Criminal Practice*, 4th ed. Albany, N.Y.: Committee on Continuing Legal Education, New York State Bar Association, 1982. Rev. ed. of *Basic Criminal Law Practice* (1978).

Brownell, Carlton K.

Criminal Procedure in New York, 1982 rev. ed. by Carlton K. Brownell. Wilmette, Ill.: Callaghan & Co., 1982-

2 v. in 3 binders. Loose-leaf supplementation.

Contents: Part One - Practice and Forms, table of cases, table of statutes and index (in 2 v.); Part Two - Criminal Evidence, table of statutes and cases, index, sample transcript. This is the revised edition of *Criminal Procedure in New York* by Lloyd I. Paperno and Arthur Goldstein.

Criminal Trial Advocacy / Supreme Court of the State of New York, Appellate Division, First Department, Office of Projects Development, edited by Ronald E. Cohen. 6th ed. New York: Office of Projects Development, 1987.

Pitler, Robert M.
New York Criminal Practice Under the CPL, by Robert M. Pitler. B. James George, Jr., editor. New York: Practising Law Institute, 1972.
Cumulative supplements published by C. Boardman Co. until 1976.

*Rothblatt, Henry B.
Criminal Law of New York: the Criminal Procedure Law, by Henry B. Rothblatt. Rochester, N.Y.: Lawyers Co-operative Pub. Co., 1971.
Pocket part supplementation; latest is 1985.

Salisbury, Eugene W.
Manual of Procedure for Town and Village Courts of New York State by Eugene W. Salisbury. Binghamton: Gould Publications, 1976.
Loose-leaf supplementation.

*Waxner, Marvin
New York Criminal Practice, by Marvin Waxner; contributors, Marvin T. Hyman [et al.]. 1984 revision by James Zett and Naomi I. Werne. New York: M. Bender, 1973-
10 v. Looseleaf supplementation. V. 3-10 by James Zett.

Contents: v. 1-6, Criminal Procedure (text and forms), index at back of v. 6; v. 7-10, Penal Law (and miscellaneous criminal statutes, forms, also sentencing outline and tables of offenses), index at back of v. 10.

DAMAGES

Fuchsberg, Jacob D.
Damages, by Jacob D. Fuchsberg. Brooklyn, N.Y.: Edward Thompson Co., 1965-1982.
(*Encyclopedia of New York Law*, v. 9-11) Supplementation ceased in 1982).

DISCOVERY (LAW)

*Durst, John E.

Modern New York Discovery, by John E. Durst, Abraham Fuchsberg, Jack Kleiner. Rochester, N.Y.: Lawyers Co-operative Pub. Co., 1983.

(New York Practice Library) Kept up-to-date by pocket supplements.

*Kerschensteiner, Kristin M.

Examination Before Trial and Other Disclosure Devices, by Kristin M. Kerchensteiner and D. Kirk Drussel. 1984 Rev. ed. Wilmette, Ill.: Callaghan & Co., 1984-

Loose-leaf supplementation.

This is the revised edition of *Examination Before Trial and Other Disclosure Devices* by John E. Dolan (1974).

DOMESTIC RELATIONS

*Biskind, Elliott L.

Boardman's New York Family Law, with Forms, by Elliott L. Biskind. Rev. ed. New York: Clark Boardman Co.; 1964-1984.

2 v. Loose-leaf supplementation ceased in 1984.

**Family Law Practice: a Systems Manual*. Harvey I. Sladkus, editor-in-chief; editorial board members, Edward B. Alderman [et al.]. Albany, N.Y.: New York State Bar Association, 1982.

Loose-leaf supplementation.

*Foster, Henry H.

Law and the Family, by Henry H. Foster, Jr., Doris Jonas Freed and Joel R. Brandes. 2nd ed. Rochester, N.Y.: Lawyers Co-operative Pub. Co., 1986-

Kept up-to-date with cumulative supplements.

To be complete in 4 volumes. Present contents: v.1 Divorce, Separation and Annulment; v.2 Economic Aspects, Custody and Taxes; v. 3 Equitable Distribution.

See also under Family Court, Equitable Distribution and Matrimonial Actions.

DRUNK DRIVING

*Gurstenzang, Peter
Handling the DWI Case in New York, by Peter Gerstenzang. St. Paul, Minn.: West Pub. Co., 1987.

**Handling the DWI Case in New York*. Albany: New York State Bar Association, 1984.

See also under Motor Vehicles — Law and Legislation.

ELECTION LAW

Gassman, Benjamin.
Election Law; Decisions and Procedure, 2nd ed. Albany, N.Y.: Williams Press; 1962.
2 v. Kept up-to-date with pocket supplements.

EQUITABLE DISTRIBUTION

Brandes, Joel R.
Equitable Distribution Law [v. 3 of *Law and the Family*, by Henry H. Foster, Doris Jonas Freed and Joel R. Brandes] Rochester, N.Y.: Lawyers Co-operative Pub. Co., 1986.
(N.Y. Practice Library).

Foster, Henry H.
A Practical Guide to the New York Equitable Distribution Divorce Law, editor, Henry H. Foster, Jr. New York: Law & Business, 1980.

Zett, James
Equitable Distribution Actions (Chapter 60-77), by James Zett. New York: M. Bender, 1981-

Loose-leaf supplementation. This is volume 11C of *New York Civil Practice*. Index, table of statutes, and table of cases.

See also under Domestic Relations, Family Court, and Matrimonial Actions.

EXECUTORS AND ADMINISTRATORS

*Biskind, Elliott L.

Boardman's Estate Management and Accounting: law, forms, taxes, by Elliott L. Biskind. 2d ed. New York: Clark Boardman Co., 1965-1982.

2 v. Loose-leaf supplementation ceased in 1982.

Turano, Margaret Valentine

New York Estate Administration by Margaret Valentine Turano, C. Raymond Radigan. St. Paul, Minn., 1986.

(Hornbook series).

See also under Probate Law and Practice, and Wills.

EVIDENCE

Brownell, Carlton K.

Criminal Procedure in New York, 1982 rev. ed. by Carlton K. Brownell. Wilmette, Ill.: Callaghan & Co., 1982-

Part Two (in book 3) is entitled *Criminal Evidence*. It includes tables of cases and statutes, an index and a sample transcript.

Fisch, Edith L.

Fisch on New York Evidence, by Edith L. Fisch. 2nd ed. Pomona, N.Y.: Lond Publications, 1977.

Kept up-to-date with pocket supplements.

Frumer, Louis R.

Bender's New York Evidence—CPLR, by Louis R. Frumer and Elliott L. Biskind. New York: M. Bender, 1962-

7 v. Loose-leaf supplementation.

Groble, Patricia

Acme's Plaintiff's Proof of a Prima Facie Case, 1986 revision by Patricia A. Groble and Laurel Pauls Lester. Wilmette, Ill.: Callaghan & Co., 1986-

Looseleaf supplementation.

While coverage in this work is not limited to New York, many of the annotations are of New York cases. Includes an index and table of cases. This is a revision of ***Acme's Plaintiff's Proof of a Prima Facie Case*** by Stanley S. Corwin.

Kramer, Charles

Evidence in Negligence Cases, by Charles Kramer and Daniel Kramer. 8th ed. New York: Practising Law Institute, 1987.

Mottla, Gabriel V.

New York Evidence: Proof of Cases, by Gabriel V. Mottla. 2nd ed. Rochester, N.Y.: Lawyers Co-operative Pub. Co., 1966.

2 v. Kept up-to-date with pocket supplements.

Richardson On Evidence, by Jerome Prince. 10th ed. Brooklyn, N.Y.: Brooklyn Law School, 1973.

Kept up-to-date with cumulative supplements.

The 1972-1985 supplement was compiled by Jerome Prince and Richard T. Farrell.

United States [Federal Rules of Evidence].

Federal Rules of Evidence and Their New York State Parallels, [edited by] Harold Baer, Jr. New York: Practising Law Institute, 1986.

This pamphlet is organized by Federal Rules of Evidence rule numbers. The New York counterparts in the Civil Practice Law and Rules and the Criminal Procedure Law are set out for each federal rule. The author relied heavily on New York's ***Proposed Code of Evidence*** (West, 1982) in developing his annotated commentary.

FAMILY COURT

Family Court Proceedings, by James Zett [et al.]. Contributors: Stanley Alex Schwartz, David Saft, Sam Polur. New York: M. Bender, 1972-

4 v. (***New York Civil Practice*** set, v. 12, 12A, 12B, 12C)

Loose-leaf supplementation.

Contains a table of cases and statutes.

*Kerschensteiner, Kristin M.
Callaghan's Family Court Law and Practice in New York. Wilmette, Ill.: Callaghan & Co., 1981-
2 v. Loose-leaf supplementation.

Includes forms and Family Court Rules.

INSTRUCTIONS TO JURIES

Association of Justices of the Supreme Court of the State of New York. Committee on Pattern Jury Instructions.
New York Pattern Jury Instructions/Civil, 2nd ed. Rochester, N.Y.: Lawyers Co-operative Pub. Co., 1974.
2v. Kept up-to-date with pocket supplements.

Vol. 1 is in its second edition (1974); revised vol. 2 bears the date 1968. The jury instructions are accompanied by extensive case annotations. While the jury instructions were prepared by judges with the cooperation of the Judicial Conference, they are merely guides, and the trial judges need not use them.

Committee on Criminal Jury Instructions (New York)
Criminal Jury Instructions, New York, prepared by the Committee on Criminal Jury Instructions of the Office of Court Administra tion, the Supreme Court Justices Association, [and] the County Judges Association, of the State of New York. New York: The Office of Court Administration, 1979-
4 v. Looseleaf supplementation.
Contents: v. 1, Charges of general applicability (1983-); v. 2, Penal Law sec. 100.00 to 175.50 (1979-); v. 3, Penal Law 180.00 to end (1979-); Misdemeanors (1981-) [vol. not numbered]. Contains extensive statutory references.

Goodman, Budd G.
Charges to the Jury and Requests to Charge in a Criminal Case, New York. rev. ed. Wilmette, Illinois: Callaghan & Co., 1983-
2 v. Loose-leaf supplementation.

This is the revised edition of *Charges to the Jury and Requests to Charge in a Criminal Case in New York* by James L. Dowsey.

INSURANCE LAW

Weitz, Harvey

The No-fault Handbook, by Harvey Weitz and Robert Grochow. 3rd ed. New York: New York State Trial Lawyers Association, 1981-

Loose-leaf supplementation.

JURY INSTRUCTIONS

See under Instructions to Juries.

LANDLORD AND TENANT

Gallet, Jeffrey H.

New York Landlord and Tenant Handbook (Summary Proceedings). Binghamton, N.Y.: Gould Publications, 1985.

Loose-leaf supplementation.

*Rasch, Joseph

New York Landlord and Tenant, Including Summary Proceedings, by Joseph Rasch. 2nd ed. Rochester, N.Y.: Lawyers Co-operative Pub. Co., 1971.

3 v. Kept up-to-date with pocket supplements.

Table of cases and statutes; completed leases and other forms.

Rasch, Joseph

New York Landlord and Tenant: Rent Control and Rent Stabilization, by Joseph Rasch. 2nd ed. Rochester, N.Y.: Lawyers Co-operative Pub. Co., 1987.

Kept up-to-date with pocket supplements.

(New York Practice Library)

LIENS

*Bowmar, Robert

Lien Priorities in New York, by Robert H. Bowmar. Rochester: Lawyers Co-operative Pub. Co., 1987.

Kept up-to-date with pocket supplements.

(New York Practice Library).

Jensen, Carl A.
Jensen on the Mechanics' Lien Law (and Related Procedures) of the State of New York. 4th ed. Completely rewritten with new forms, by Edward Marks. New York: Clark Boardman Co.; 1963-1983.
Supplementation ceased in 1983.

LIQUOR LAWS

Liquor Control Law Reporter. (New York volume). Chicago: Ill.: Commerce Clearing House.
Loose-leaf supplementation.

MATRIMONIAL ACTIONS

*DaSilva, Willard H.
New York Matrimonial Practice, by Willard H. DaSilva. Rochester, N.Y.: Lawyers Co-operative Pub. Co., 1980-
Loose-leaf supplementation.

Part of the Lawyers' Co-op Practice Systems Library, this practical work contains forms, client interview material, and checklists.

Tippins, Timothy M.
New York Matrimonial Law and Practice. Wilmette, Illinois: Callaghan & Co., 1986-
Loose-leaf supplementation.

Zett, James
Matrimonial Actions, by James Zett, Michael E. Edmonds and Stanley Alex Schwartz. New York: M. Bender, 1971-

This is vol. 11, 11A and 11B of the ***New York Civil Practice*** set.

See also under Domestic Relations, Family Court, and Equitable Distribution.

MEDICAL MALPRACTICE

See under Physicians—Malpractice.

MORTGAGES

*Drussel, D. Kirk

Mortgages and Mortgage Foreclosure in New York, 1982 revision by D. Kirk Drussel and Mary Anne Foran; contributing editor for forms, Marvin R. Baum. Rev. ed. Wilmette, Ill.: Callaghan, 1982-
2 v. Loose-leaf supplementation.

Contains forms, tables of statutes and cases.

MOTOR VEHICLES — LAW AND LEGISLATION

Automobiles and other Motor Vehicles. Brooklyn: E. Thompson Co. 1957-1982.
(*Encyclopedia of New York Law*, v. 1-5)
Pocket part supplementation, which was published by the West Pub. Co., was discontinued in 1982.

*Rose, James M.

New York Vehicle and Traffic Law, by James M. Rose. Rochester, N.Y.: Lawyers' Co-operative Pub. Co.; 1984.
Kept up to date by pocket supplements.
(New York Practice Library)

Includes forms, charts, pleadings, and annotated client interview forms.

See also under Drunk Driving.

MOTIONS (LAW)

See under Civil Procedure.

NEGLIGENCE

Warren, Oscar LeRoy

Negligence in the New York Courts, by Oscar LeRoy Warren and Gloria C. Markuson. 3rd ed. recompiled, revised, and rewritten by Roy L. Benoit. New York: M. Bender, 1966-
Kept up-to-date by pocket supplements.

Cover title: Warren's Negligence.

See also under Summary Proceedings

PARTNERSHIP

*Merritt, Raymond W.
The Partnership Handbook, sponsored by the Committee on Continuing Legal Education of the New York State Bar Association and the New York State Society of Certified Public Accountants.
Albany: New York State Bar Association, 1986.

To be supplemented.

PATERNITY

Schatkin, Sidney B.
Disputed Paternity Proceedings by Sidney B. Schatkin. 4th ed. New York: M. Bender, 1975-?
2 v. Loose-leaf supplementation.

PHYSICIANS — MALPRACTICE

Bard, Norman
The New York Law of Medical Malpractice, 1974 to date, by Norman Bard. Rev. ed. Brooklyn, N.Y.: Winstein, Chayt & Bard (26 Court St. Brooklyn, N.Y. 11242), 1987.

This work primarily digests New York cases involving medical, dental and podiatric malpractice. It includes a table of cases, table of statutes and an index.

Kramer, Charles
Medical Malpractice, by Charles Kramer and Daniel Kramer. 5th ed. New York: Practising Law Institute, 1983.

Medical Malpractice: Strategic and Practical Principles. [Albany]: New York State Bar Association, 1986.

PROBATE LAW AND PRACTICE

Cox, Joseph A.
SPCA, [Surrogates' Court Practice Act], by Joseph A. Cox, Joseph T. Arenson, Standish F. Medina. Contributors: Lois Arnold [et. al.] New York: M. Bender, 1970-
Loose-leaf supplementation.

This is vol. 10 of the *New York Civil Practice* set.

Harris, Homer I.
Harris' New York Estates Practice Guide, by John W. Tarbox. 4th ed. Rochester, N.Y.: The Lawyers Co-operative Pub. Co., 1984.
3 v. Kept up-to-date by pocket supplements.

Rev. ed. of Harris' *Estates Practice Guide* (1968).

*Heaton, Willis Edgar
The Procedure and Law of Surrogates' Courts of the State of New York. Originally written by Willis E. Heaton, 1907. 6th ed. by Oscar Le Roy Warren, 1940. Recompiled, revised and rewritten in 1970 by Gloria C. Markuson. New York: M. Bender, 1983-
20 v. Loose-leaf supplementation.

Cover title: *Warren's Heaton on Surrogates' Courts. Warren's Heaton* is a comprehensive treatise on the powers and jurisdiction of the surrogate's court, practice under the Surrogates' Court Practice Act (SCPA), probate of wills, guardianship, and estate administration. This work includes forms, table of cases, table of statutes, and two-volume index.

New York Estates, Wills, Trusts. Chicago: Commerce Clearing House, 1967-
1 v. Loose-leaf supplementation.

New York Practice Guide: Probate and Estate Administration, by Philip B. Blank [et al.]; Joseph T. Arenson, gen. ed.; Harvey Corn, consultant; Maureen E. O'Brien, Marc Stern, contributors. New York: M. Bender; 1985-.
2 v. Loose-leaf supplementation.

Rohan, Patrick J.
EPTL [Estates, Powers and Trusts Law], by Patrick J. Rohan. New York: M. Bender, 1969-
Loose-leaf supplementation.

This is vol. 9, 9A and 9B of the *New York Civil Practice* set.

*Schlesinger, Edward S.
New York Probate, by Edward S. Schlesinger and Michael M. Mariani. Rochester, N.Y.: Lawyers Co-operative Pub. Co., 1986-
2 v. Loose-leaf supplementation.
(New York Practice Systems Library)

See also under Executors and Administrators; Wills.

PRODUCTS LIABILITY

Weinberger, Michael
Products Liability. Wilmette, Ill.: Callaghan & Co., 1982.
2 v. Loose-leaf supplementation.

REAL PROPERTY

*Biskind, Elliott L.
Law of real estate brokers; a manual for New York Lawyers, Brokers, Salesmen and Real Estate Owners and Operators; Licensing, Employment, Litigation Forms. New York, N.Y.: Clark Boardman Co., 1969-1983.
Pocket supplementation ceased in 1983.

Commercial Real Estate Leases, 1986, Milton R. Friedman, chairman. New York: Practising Law Institute, 1986.

Contesting New York State Tax Assessments, prepared by the New York State Bar Association under the auspices of its Tax Section; contributing authors, E. Parker Brown, II ... [et al.]. Albany: New York State Bar Association, 1986.

Harvey, David Charles Barrett

Harvey Law of Real Property and Title Closing, by David C. B. Harvey. Expanded and recompiled by Elliott Biskind. New York: Clark Boardman Co., 1966-1985.

3 v. Looseleaf supplementation ceased in 1985.

Lee, Harry O.

Review and Reduction of Real Property Assessments in New York, by Harry O. Lee and Wilford A. LeForestier; assisted by David R. Murphy. 2nd ed. New York: Clark Boardman Co., 1978-1983.

Supplementation ceased in 1983.

**New York Practice Guide. Real Estate*. Eugene J. Morris, general editor. New York: M. Bender, 1986-

4 v. Kept up-to-date with loose-leaf supplementation.

Contents: v. 1 Purchase and Sale by Karl B. Holtzschue; v. 2 Land Use Regulation; Landmark and Historic preservation, Environmental Regulation by Paul D. Selver; Real Estate Tax Assessments by Eugene J. Morris; v. 3 Landlord-Tenant Leasing by Louis M. Fribourg and Ralph M. Gerstein; and v. 4 Cooperatives, Condominiums and Homeowner Associations by Walter D. Goldsmith and Matthew J. Leeds.

Rasch, Joseph

The New York Law and Practice of Real Property. Mt. Kisco, N.Y.: Baker, Voorhis, 1962.

3 v. Kept up-to-date with pocket supplements published by Lawyers Co-operative Pub. Co.

**Real Estate Titles*, James M. Pedowitz, editor-in-chief; contributing authors, Norman S. Abrams [et. al.]. [Albany]: New York State Bar Association, 1984.

Kept up-to-date with pocket supplements.

Twenty-one chapters on title to real property written by members of the New York real estate bar. Includes forms and table of cases.

**Real Property Service - New York*. Rochester: Lawyers Cooperative Publishing Company, 1987-

This comprehensive service fills 14 binders and covers the following topics: titles and interests; brokers and agents; purchase and sale; financing; mortgage foreclosure; environmental land use and regulation; condominiums, cooperatives and homeowners' associations; taxation of real property; and landlord and tenant matters.

Weed, William Xenophon

Warren's Weed on the New York Law of Real Property. 4th ed., recompiled, revised and rewritten by Oscar Le Roy Warren [and others]. New York: M. Bender, 1950-

6 v. in 12. Loose-leaf supplementation.

SECURITIES

*Commerce Clearing House.

Blue Sky Law Reporter: Blue Sky Laws, Legal Investment Laws, Insurance Securities Laws, Regulations, Forms, Lists. Chicago: Commerce Clearing House, 1975-

3 v. in 4 volumes.

This looseleaf service includes New York as part of its comprehensive coverage of state securities laws.

TAXATION—LAW AND LEGISLATION

All States Tax Guide. Englewood Cliffs, N.J.: Prentice-Hall, 1960-

1 v. Weekly looseleaf supplementation.

Through the use of both tabular and textual material, this service provides brief coverage of the tax law in the 50 states, including New York, and gives contrasts with federal tax law.

Guidebook to New York Taxes. Chicago, Ill.: Commerce Clearing House. Annual.

An annual, paperbound summary of current New York tax law with cross references to the CCH *New York Tax Reporter.*

New York Tax Handbook. By Seymour F. Bernstein. Paramus, N.J.: Prentice-Hall Information Services. Annual.

A one-volume summary of current tax law with cross references to P-H *State and Local Taxes - New York*.

New York State Tax Monitor. New York: Law Planning Reports, Ltd. Vol. 1, no. 1 (Sept. issue, 1983)-

Monthly newsletter on New York taxation.

**New York Tax Reporter*. Chicago, Ill.: Commerce Clearing House, 1940-
4 v. Looseleaf supplementation.

Title was *New York Tax Service* from 1940-1947.

**New York Tax Service*, Paul R. Comeau, Robert E. Helm, Joseph H. Murphy, editorial consultants. New York: M. Bender, 1985-
6 v. Monthly looseleaf supplementation.

Volumes 1-4 of this service contain analysis of all New York state taxes; volume 5 covers New York City taxes; volume 6 contains all New York State tax forms, instructions and publications. New matter is filed behind red tabs, and the text of court decisions and administrative opinions and memoranda is filed behind blue tabs for easy reference.

New York Tax Service; State and Local, Al Taxes, All Taxables. New York, Albany, etc.: Commerce Clearing House, 1936-[1939].
3 v. Looseleaf.

Accompanied by supplement containing the full text of "leading federal and state court cases construing the New York tax law, 1903-1936."
This is the predecessor of the *New York Tax Reporter,* which is the current CCH tax service for New York.

**State and Local Taxes — New York*. Englewood Cliffs, N.J.: Prentice-Hall.
3 v. Looseleaf supplementation.

The first two volumes cover statewide taxes; they are divided by tabs into separate sections by kind of tax, e.g., franchise tax, personal income tax, and sales tax. Each section has its own "New Matter" section and index. Volume three covers New York City taxes and contains the general index to the service.

"New matter" sections contain full text of court decisions and administrative determinations. These are periodically converted to annotations in the main body of the service. The full text is not transferred to separate binders for permanent retention.

TRIAL PRACTICE

Association of Justices of the Supreme Court of the State of New York. Committee on Publications.

Bench Book for Trial Judges. Prepared by the Committees on Publications, Association of Justices of the Supreme Court of the State of New York, 1970, Bertram Harnett, Chairman. [Albany]: Judicial Conference of the State of New York, 1972.

Loose-leaf supplementation.

Broder, Aaron J.

Trial Handbook for New York Lawyers, by Aaron J. Broder. 2nd ed. Rochester, N.Y.: Lawyers Co-operative Pub. Co., 1986.

(New York Practice Library). Pocket part supplementation.

See also under Civil Procedure, Criminal Procedure, Domestic Relations Courts, Motions (Law), and Summary Proceedings.

WILLS

*Fingar, Elmer Lee

New York Wills and Trusts: Law, Forms, Taxes, by Elmer Lee Fingar, David R. Bookstaver, and John G. McQuaid. New York: Clark Boardman Co., 1961-1984.

Harris, Homer I.

Harris' New York Estates Practice Guide, by John W. Tarbox. 4th ed. Rochester, N.Y.: Lawyers Co-operative Pub. Co., 1984.

3 v. Kept up-to-date with pocket supplements.

Chapters 1 and 2 (in vol. 1) cover will drafting and execution.

*Keller, Lawrence P.
New York Wills. Rochester: Lawyers Cooperative Publishing Co., 1987.
(New York Practice Library)

*Klipstein, Harold D.
Drafting New York Wills: Law and Forms, by Harold D. Klipstein. 3rd ed. New York: M. Bender, 1983-
Loose-leaf supplementation.

*Murphy, Joseph Hawley
Murphy's Will Clauses; annotations and forms with tax effects, by Joseph Hawley Murphy, assisted by Beverly Massy, Stowell Rounds. New York: M. Bender, 1960-
4 v. Loose-leaf supplementation.

Coverage not limited to New York. Until 1978, this set had a supplementary section called "New York Notes."

See also under Executors and Administrators, and Probate Law and Practice.

WORKERS' COMPENSATION

****New York Workers' Compsensation Law Reporter.*** Fort Washington, Pa.: LRP Publications, 1987-
2 v. Loose-leaf supplementation.

The publisher projects that this new service will be a comprehensive reporter of New York workers' compensation law, including statutes, regulations, judicial decisions, and decisions rendered by the full Workers' Compensation Board (since 1984).

ZONING

*Anderson, Robert Milford
New York Zoning Law and Practice, by Robert M. Anderson. 3rd ed. Rochester, N.Y.: Lawyers Co-operative Pub. Co., 1984.
2 v. Kept up-to-date with pocket supplements.
(New York Practice Library)

*Rathkopf, Arden H.
The Law of Zoning and Planning: Analysis of the Law of Zoning, Comprehensive Citation of Cases, excerpts from Court Decisions, Essential Forms. 4th ed. New York: Clark Boardman Co., 1975-
5 v. Loose-leaf supplementation.

Coverage not limited to New York.

3. CONTINUING LEGAL EDUCATION (CLE) AND MEDIA RESOURCES

a) Printed CLE Course Materials. The New York State Bar Association and the Practising Law Institute offer many basic and advanced seminars each year that are designed for the continuing legal education of practising attorneys in New York. The course materials compiled in connection with these seminars are usually available for purchase after the date of the seminar.

In addition to course handbooks, both the New York State Bar Association and the Practising Law Institute sponsor the publication of monographic works that are not necessarily related to a particular CLE course offering. Examples of monographic works produced by the New York State Bar Association (and included in section 2 of this Chapter) are ***Real Estate Titles*** and ***The Partnership Handbook***.

Lists of currently available publications can be obtained from: CLE Department, New York State Bar Association, One Elk Street, Albany, New York 12207 and from the Practising Law Institute, 810 Seventh Avenue, New York, N. Y. 10091.

b) Non-Print CLE and Other Sources.

(1) Audiotapes. The New York State Bar Association's publications list includes many audiocassette recordings of CLE presentations. These are sold in cassette containers with accompanying program materials.

Other bar associations which produce CLE audio recordings are the Erie County Bar Association (available through the Charles B. Sears Law Library, SUNY at Buffalo), the New York State Trial Lawyers Association, the Association of the Bar of the City of New York, the Bar Association of Nassau County, the Suffolk County Bar Association, and the New York State Defenders Association.

(2) Videotapes. The New York State Library produces videotapes on New York legal research topics of general interest. These have included lectures on New York legislative history, the state budget process, the New York administrative code (*NYCRR*), and the Unified Court System. Copies of these videotapes can be obtained by sending the necessary number of blank videocassettes to Robert Allan Carter, Legislative/Governmental Services Unit, Cultural Education Center, Empire State Plaza, Albany, N.Y. 12230.

(3) Television and Radio Programs. "Capitol Connection"is WAMC Public Radio's weekly interview program with the governor. Currently hosted by Dr. Alan Chartock, a political scientist, the thirty-minute program is aired on public radio stations throughout New York State. Tapes and transcripts may be obtained for a fee from:

"The Capitol Connection"
WAMC
Box 13000
Albany, New York 12212
Tel. (518) 465-5233

WAMC projects that an index to Capitol Connection transcripts will become available in 1988.

"Inside Albany" is a weekly public affairs television program on New York State government in a "news magazine format." The program began in 1975 and is aired on public television stations throughout New York State. VHS videocassette copies of individual programs are sold for $.50 each. At this writing, there is no index to the contents of past programs. Further information is available from:

"Inside Albany"
Alfred E. Smith Building
12th Floor
Albany, New York 12225
Tel. (518) 443-5454

The New York State Commission on Cable Television operates the New York State and Community Affairs Network (NY-SCAN), which is currently available on cable television in the Albany area. NY-SCAN airs legislative and agency public hearings, important public policy addresses, news conferences, seminars, programming produced by State agencies, oral arguments before the Court of Appeals, legislative committee meetings, and other governmental proceedings (as available). The Commission is exploring possibilities for wider geographical distribution of this unique programming.

Chapter Fourteen
FORM BOOKS

This Chapter describes sets of forms tailored for the New York practitioner. Two kinds of forms are included here: substantive and procedural. Substantive forms, also called legal forms or forms of agreement, assist the attorney in preparing documents such as leases, wills, and contracts. Procedural forms, also called practice forms, assist the attorney in drafting court papers such as complaints, motion papers and orders.

The sets of forms described in this Chapter devote more space to forms than they do to practice commentary or annotations. The reverse is true for the books listed in Chapter 13 (Treatises, Practice Books, and Other Sources) and marked with an asterisk (*) to indicate that they contain forms. In those books, the forms merely supplement the text. In addition to the sources for forms listed in Chapters 13 and 14, procedural forms can also be found in ***New York Consolidated Laws Service (CLS)*** and in the ***Official Compilation of Codes, Rules and Regulations (NYCRR).***

Bender's Forms for the Civil Practice With Explanatory Notes and Cross References, by Louis R. Frumer [and] Oscar L. Warren; Joseph J. O'Connell, supervising editor. New York: M. Bender, 1963

15 v. in 32 books. Loose-leaf supplementation.

This set includes annotated forms for the CPLR, RPAPL, SCPA, EPTL, DRL and the court acts. Form numbers are keyed to the sections of the Consolidated Laws. For example CPLR Form no. 216:6 is a form for use with CPLR sec. 216. Since there is direct access into this set from the statutes, there is no subject index.

Bender's Forms for the Consolidated Laws of the State of New York Annotated. New York: M. Bender, 1941-

8 v. in 53 books. Kept up-to-date with pocket parts and replacement volumes.

This set is the most comprehensive form set for the Consolidated Laws. Since this set includes forms for the Criminal Procedure Law but not for the civil practice acts and laws, its forms complement and do not duplicate the forms found in ***Bender's Forms for the Civil Practice***. There is a two-volume index.

Bender's Forms of Pleading of the State of New York: With Suggestions for Drafting Pleadings, Explanatory Notes, Citations of Reported Cases, and Cross-References, by Oscar LeRoy Warren and Gloria C. Markuson. 1965 revision, by Rudolph Sommer [et al.] New York: M. Bender, 1965-

10 v. in 22 books. Loose-leaf supplementation.

Volume 1, pt. 2, through vol. 7 contain annotated forms for complaints in tort and negligence actions, actions on a contract, and statutory and equity complaints. Volumes 8-10 contain forms for answers and forms for special proceedings and surrogate's proceedings. Volume 1, pt. 1, gives answers to frequently asked questions about the parts of the complaint: caption, allegations, demand, and verification. The last volume of the set contains the general index and table of statutes.

Carmody-Wait 2d: Cyclopedia of New York Practice With Forms. Rochester: Lawyers Co-operative Publishing Company.

30 v. in 35 books. Kept up-to-date with pocket parts and replacement volumes.

This is a set made up of approximately one-half text and one-half annotated practice and legal forms. Coverage is civil practice with an emphasis on surrogate's and estate practice.

Medina's Bostwick Practice Manual. New York: M. Bender, 1971- Loose-leaf supplementation.

The first three volumes of this set contain basic practice forms for civil litigation, surrogate's court practice, and wills, trusts and estates. The fourth volume contains commercial, real property and matrimonial legal forms. The general index is in volume 4.

New York Forms: Practice-oriented Forms for New York Legal and Business Transactions. Rochester, N.Y.: Lawyers Co-operative Pub. Co., 1970-

7 v. Kept up-to-date with pocket supplements and revised volumes. Cover title: New York Forms, Legal and Business.

The major areas covered in this specialized form set are: leases; consumer protection, including warranties and credit reporting; estate planning; contracts; domestic relations; the U.C.C.; and forms concerning business enterprises, including professional corporations and partnerships.

State Tax Action Coordinator, Northeastern Region. New York: Research Institute of America, 1980-
1 v. Looseleaf supplementation.

This specialized form book contains complete income tax forms, individual, corporate, partnership and fiduciary, state and city, for New York and the other northeastern states (Connecticut, Maine, Massachusetts, New Hampshire, New Jersey, Rhode Island and Vermont).

Steinman, Irving I.
Steinman's Bergerman and Roth, New York Real Property Forms: Annotated. By Irving I. Steinman and Morton Roth. 2nd ed. Albany, N.Y.: M. Bender, 1948-
Loose-leaf supplementation.
Cover title: New York Real Property Forms, Annotated.

A comprehensive real property form set including both practice forms and legal forms. At this writing, the work is comprised of 4 looseleaf binders. Volume 4 contains an index and table of statutes.

State Tax Forms: New York, 1986- . Albany: State Tax Forms, 1986-

This is a two volume looseleaf service containing tax forms for City and State corporate and personal taxes.

West's McKinney's Forms. St. Paul, Minn.: West Pub. Co., [1964]-
28 v. in 43 books.
Kept up-to-date with pocket supplements and replacement volumes.

This form set is divided into sections that cover the CPLR, U.C.C., B.C.L., C.P.L., and the areas of matrimonial and family law, real property practice, estates and surrogate's pratice, local government practice, and selected other areas. Each section has an independent numbering system for the forms. Each section also has its own index and table of statutes. Since each section has an index, there is no general index covering the entire set.

Chapter Fifteen
REFERENCE BOOKS AND INDEXES

1. **BAR DIRECTORIES**
2. **GOVERNMENT HANDBOOKS AND DIRECTORIES**
3. **LEGAL ENCYCLOPEDIA**
4. **PERIODICAL AND OTHER INDEXES**

The works described in this Chapter, bar directories, government handbooks and directories, *New York Jurisprudence 2d,* and periodical and other indexes, are of general reference value. Many other specialized works, which could be categorized as reference books, are not included here because they are described in other Chapters. For example, the two handbooks on citation form, the ***Uniform System of Citation*** and the Law Reporting Bureau's ***Official Style Manual,*** are described in the Chapter on the Consolidated Laws (Chapter 4) and in Chapter 7 (Court Reports and Case Finders). The ***Abbott*** and ***West*** case digests and the *New York Law Journal Digest* - ***Annotator*** are also described in Chapter 7. The indexes to New York legislative documents and reports are described in Chapter 5 (Legislative History). The descriptions of these and other specialized works can be located through the index to this book.

1. BAR DIRECTORIES

Alphabetical Directory of Attorneys in New York State. Newark, N.J.: New York Lawyers Diary and Manual, 1982 -

This directory lists New York attorneys in one alphabet. It is based on the information contained in the bar directory section of *New York Lawyers Diary and Manual,* which lists the attorneys geographically.

Martindale-Hubbell Law Directory. Summit, N.J.: Martindale-Hubbell, Inc. 1868-

Martindale-Hubbell is an annual lawyer's directory which covers all 50 states. The New York section filled 2,334 pages in the 1987 edition. The New York section is divided into two sections. The first section, called the geographical bar roster, is arranged by city and then by each attorney's name. The biographical information given for each attorney is: date of birth, names of college and law school, date of bar admission, and either the attorney's office address or the abbreviation for the attorney's law firm.

Martindale-Hubbell saves space by using code numbers to designate colleges and law schools attended. The code numbers are identified at the front of each volume. Law firm names are also abbreviated. The following entry from the bar roster illustrates the abbreviation conventions followed:

Alice Pond...'38 '62 C.788 L.477 22 Court St.

- '38 — year of birth
- '62 — bar admission
- C.788 — college code
- L.477 — law school code
- 22 Court St. — office address

The entry for the fictitious Alice Pond indicates that she was born in 1938, was admitted to the New York bar in 1962, attended Smith College and University of Michigan Law School, and maintains an office at 22 Court Street. The city is not listed for each attorney since the geographical bar roster itself is arranged by city.

The second part of the ***Martindale-Hubbell Directory's*** New York section is called the biographical section. That section consists of descriptive law firm listings. These are paid for by the law firms. These listings provide more extensive biographical information on firm members than is found in the geographical bar roster. The listings also indicate the law firm's specialty or specialties and may provide references and "representative clients." The law firm listings are arranged alphabetically by city, then alphabetically by firm name.

New York patent and trademark attorneys are listed in a separate part of ***Martindale-Hubbell's*** New York section. Government attorneys are listed in the geographical bar roster.

New York Lawyers Diary and Manual: Bar Directory of the State of New York. Newark, N.J.: New York Lawyers Diary & Manual, 1899-

This directory is in two main parts: a directory of miscellaneous legal and law-related entities and a bar directory. Part one includes a directory of process servors by county, sources for vital statistics in all states, and directories of federal and state court officials. Part one also includes filing fees. Part two, the bar directory, is geographically arranged in two sections. The first section lists attorneys in metropolitan New York; the second section lists attorneys by city outside of metropolitan New York. This part also includes a directory of bar associations, which includes many specialized bar associations not included in Appendix C of this book.

2. GOVERNMENT HANDBOOKS AND DIRECTORIES

The Lenz & Reicker, Inc. New York State Government Reference Book. Albany: Lenz & Reicker, 1986.

Subtitled "A Practical Guide to the Legislature, Departments and Judiciary," this handbook stresses the executive departments and provides particulars of locations in Albany not found in the other handbooks that are listed in this section. For example, this work lists meeting rooms of legislative standing committees and provides foldout maps of the Empire State Plaza, the State Office Building Campus and the greater Albany area. It also includes a more comprehensive list of publications issued by governmental bodies than is found in the other handbooks.

New York (State). Dept. of State.
Manual for the Use of the Legislature of the State of New York. Albany: Dept. of State, 1840-

This handbook is usually referred to simply as the ***Legislative Manual*** or the "Bluebook." At this writing, the ***Legislative Manual*** is published biennially; from 1840-1974, it was published annually.

A partial list of contents includes: the text of the U.S. and N.Y. constitutions; lists of justices and judges of the U.S. Court of Appeals (all circuits) and for the U.S. District Courts for the districts in New York; detailed boundary descriptions of the Congressional districts in New York, a color reproduction of the state flag, biographies of the top executive officials of the twenty executive departments and the numerous divisions, boards, agencies, authorities and commissions of the executive branch; lists of current membership in the New York Assembly and Senate; lists of the legislative standing committees and their current membership; lists of judges and justices in the New York court system; a brief description of the court system; and a list of the state's court libraries. The ***Legislative Manual*** also lists proposed amendments to the New York Constitution since 1821 and the vote on them at the general election. Despite its title, ***Legislative Manual,*** it does not provide extensive information on New York's legislators; only the ***New York Red Book*** provides photographs and biographies for all of the legislators.

The predecessors of the Bluebook were:

The Constitution of the State of New York. Albany: Printed by Croswell, Barnum & Van Bentheuysen. ??-1827.

The Constitution of the United States and the State of New York. Albany: Printed by Croswell and Van Bentheuysen, 1828-1833.

Also appearing on the title pages of these two works is: "Together with the Rules and Orders, Standing Committees, and List of Members of the Senate and Assembly."

New York Red Book, Containing the Latest Information Relating to the State Government. Albany, 1892-

This handbook is usually called simply the ***Red Book.*** It is an annual publication. The ***Red Book*** contains photographs and biographies of the governor, lieutenant governor, senators, members of the Assembly, judges of the Court of Appeals, presiding justices of the Appellate Division, top officials in the state's executive departments and New York's U.S. senators and members of the House of Representatives. It also contains descriptions of the executive departments and agencies and usually provides their authorizing legislation.

New York State Directory. Bethesda, Md.: National Standards Association, Inc., 1983-

This directory provides the usual information on the three branches of government. Its real value lies in its coverage of "private sector sources," which is a listing of private individuals and private or public interest groups that are concerned with or knowledgeable about particular policy areas. For example, for "legal profession" the New

York State Bar Association's director for governmental relations is listed. This directory also lists lobbyists and political action committees (PAC's). Publication frequency is irregular.

New York Statistical Yearbook, 1967 - Albany, Office of Statistical Coordination, 1968-

This statistical handbook is now published by the Nelson A. Rockefeller Institute of Government in cooperation with the New York State Division of Budget. It originally was published by the Division of the Budget, Office of Statistical Coordination. It provides demographic, economic, educational, and fiscal information about the State. Much of the information is derived from annual reports of government agencies and federal statistical sources. Of particular interest to legal researchers are sections on social services expenditures, state budget information, real property tax equalization rates, and statistics on the court system.

3. LEGAL ENCYCLOPEDIA

New York Jurisprudence 2d. Rochester: Lawyers Co-operative Publishing Co., 1979-
Kept up-to-date with pocket parts and replacement volumes.

The expanded second edition of this legal encyclopedia covers New York civil and criminal law and procedure, statutes and administrative law. The first edition was limited to substantive civil law. Publication of the second edition is proceeding alphabetically by topic. Until publication of the second edition is complete, an interim looseleaf volume should be consulted for ***New York Jurisprudence*** titles that will be incorporated into articles appearing later in the alphabet.

New York Jurisprudence 2d (NY Jur2d) is similar in format to ***American Jurisprudence 2d (Am Jur2d),*** a legal encyclopedia that is national in scope and is also published by Lawyers Co-operative Publishing Company. Footnotes in ***NY Jur2d*** refer extensively to New York cases and statutes and to other Lawyers Co-op publications such as ***Am Jur2d, American Law Reports*** (A.L.R.), ***Carmody-Wait 2d, American Jurisprudence Trials (Am Jur Trials),*** and ***American Jurisprudence Proof of Facts (Am Jur POF).***

NY Jur2d contains a Words and Phrases volume that indicates where in ***NY Jur2d*** the listed words and phrases are explained. There is a multi-volume subject index. Due to the ongoing revision of this set, the general index must be supplemented by reference to the interim looseleaf volume mentioned in the previous paragraph.

New York Jurisprudence 2d can serve as a helpful introduction to the topics covered. As with any secondary source material, careful practice dictates that the researcher not rely solely on the text of *NY Jur2d.* The researcher must also read the cited primary authority (cases and statutes) in full and then verify their current status by Shepardizing and consulting appropriate sources for the latest developments in legislation and case law affecting the area of the law in question.

4. PERIODICAL AND OTHER INDEXES

The periodical indexes are listed chronologically by period indexed. None of these periodical indexes is limited to coverage of New York articles or issues.

Griswold, Stephen B.
Catalogue of the New York State Library; Subject Index of the Law Library, From Its Foundation to December 31, 1882. Albany: Weed, Parsons & Company, 1883-1905. 3 v.

While this work is primarily a subject access point to the book collection of the State's Law Library, it also includes references to selected articles from American, English, Irish, Scottish and Canadian law periodicals. Supplements to the 1883 volume were published in 1893 and 1903. Mr. Griswold was Law Librarian of the State Law Library. This catalog is the country's first legal periodical index.[1]

[Jones-Chipman] Index to Legal Periodical Literature.
Vol. 1 (1886) - v. 6 (1937). Boston: C.C. Soule, 1888-1939.

This index was begun under the editorship of Judge Leonard A. Jones and was continued under the direction of Frank Ellsworth Chipman. For the years 1889 to 1908, this index is the only source for comprehensive indexing to legal periodicals published in the English

[1] Leiter, ***A History of Legal Periodical Indexing*** 7 LEGAL REFERENCE SERVICES Q. 35 (Spring, 1987).

language. From 1908 to 1937, its coverage overlaps the indexing found in ***Index to Legal Periodicals*** published by thw H.W. Wilson Company.

Index To Legal Periodicals. New York: H.W. Wilson Co., 1908-

The ***Index to Legal Periodicals (ILP)*** currently indexes many legal periodicals, including the New York legal periodicals listed in Appendix A (except the legal newspapers, the ***Record*** of the Association of the Bar of the City of New York and the ***Brooklyn Barrister).*** In its main section, the index currently provides access to legal periodical articles by author and subject. The "Table of Cases" section identifies articles and case notes discussing the listed cases. The "Table of Statutes" section identifies articles and case notes that discuss particular statutes. Book reviews are indexed by the book author's name (not the reviewer's name) in the "Book Review" section of ***ILP.*** Reviewers are included as authors in the main section of the index.

The subject headings used in ***ILP*** were developed by the publisher; this is in contrast to the ***Current Law Index/Legal Resource Index*** subject headings, which were developed by the Library of Congress and are essentially the same headings that are used in most library catalogs.

ILP is updated with monthly pamphlet supplements (except for September when there is no issue published). The pamphlets are cumulated periodically. ***ILP*** is available online through WILSONLINE, which is discussed in Chapter 12 (Databases for New York Legal Research).

Current Law Index and *Legal Resource Index.* Belmont, Cal.: Information Access Corporation, 1980.

Current Law Index (CLI) and ***Legal Resource Index (LRI)*** are the product of the Information Access Corporation. In most respects, they are essentially the same index in terms of scope and indexing method, but they are issued in different formats. ***CLI*** is issued in printed format. The monthly issues are recompiled in annual volumes. ***LRI*** is issued in both microfilm and CD-ROM formats and is also available online through the DIALOG, BRS, NEXIS, LEXIS and WESTLAW services. The CD-ROM version of ***LRI*** is called Legaltrac.

CLI/LRI use Library of Congress subject headings. This means that more headings are included in ***CLI/LRI*** than are included in ***ILP.*** A difference important to New York researchers between the ***CLI*** and ***LRI*** indexes is the omission of the ***New York Law Journal*** and other major legal newspapers from the materials indexed in ***CLI.***

Like ***ILP,*** the ***LRI*** and ***CLI*** are updated monthly. However, the publication lag between issuance of an article and its inclusion in an index is shorter in ***LRI CLI*** than it is in ***ILP.*** The tedious process of consulting many cumulated volumes is eliminated when using the microfilm, CD-ROM or online versions of ***LRI*** because they are continuously cumulated.

New York Law Finder. St. Paul, Minn.: West Publishing Company, 1979-

The ***New York Law Finder*** is an annual subject index to West Publishing Company publications. It is unusual because it provides indexing to both primary sources ***(McKinney's Consolidated Laws of New York Annotated,*** the ***U.S. Code Annotated,*** and New York's rules of court) and secondary sources. Among the secondary sources indexed are: ***West's McKinney's Forms, West's New York Digest 3d, West's Federal Forms, West's Legal Forms,*** and the West handbook series.

APPENDICES

APPENDIX A

MAJOR NEW YORK LAW REVIEWS AND BAR ASSOCIATION PERIODICALS

This appendix lists major law reviews, institute publications, and periodicals published by or in cooperation with the law schools and bar associations of New York State. None of them is devoted to coverage of New York law. However, two law reviews provide periodic reviews of legal developments in the State. These are: ***Syracuse Law Review*** (substantive law) and ***St. John's Law Review*** (New York practice).

Albany Law Review
Albany Law School of Union University
80 New Scotland Ave.
Albany, NY 12208

Annual Survey of American Law
New York University School of Law
D'Agostino Hall
New York, NY 10012

Brooklyn Barrister
Brooklyn Bar Association
123 Remsen Street
Brooklyn, NY 11201

Brooklyn Journal of International Law
Brooklyn Law School
250 Joralemon St.
Brooklyn, NY 11201

Brooklyn Law Review
Brooklyn Law School
250 Joralemon St.,
Brooklyn, NY 11201

Buffalo Law Review
O'Brian Hall
SUNY/Buffalo School of Law
Buffalo, NY 14260

Cardozo Arts & Entertainment Law Journal
Benjamin N. Cardozo School of Law
Yeshiva University
55 Fifth Avenue
New York, NY 10003

Cardozo Law Review
Benjamin N. Cardozo School of Law
Yeshiva University
55 Fifth Avenue
New York, NY 10003

Catholic Lawyer
St. Thomas More Institute for Legal Research
St. John's University School of Law
Fronkes Hall
Grand Central & Utopia Parkways
Jamaica, NY 11439

Columbia Human Rights Law Review
Columbia University School of Law
Box 54, 435 W. 116th Street
New York, NY 10027

Columbia Journal of Environmental Law
Columbia University School of Law
Box B 28
435 W. 116th Street
New York, NY 10027

Columbia Journal of Law and Social Problems
Columbia University School of Law
Box 7
435 116th Street
New York, NY 10027

Columbia Journal of Transnational Law
Columbia University School of Law
Box 8
New York, NY 10027

Columbia Law Review
Columbia University School of Law
435 116th Street
New York, NY 10027

Columbia-V.L.A. Journal of Law and the Arts
Columbia University School of Law &
Volunteer Lawyers for the Arts
1285 Avenue of the Americas
New York, NY 10019

Conference on Labor Law (New York University)
Matthew Bender & Co.
235 E. 45th Street
New York, NY 10017

Cornell International Law Journal
Cornell Law School
Myron Taylor Hall
Ithaca, NY 14853

Cornell Law Forum
Cornell Law School
Myron Taylor Hall
Ithaca, NY 14853

Cornell Law Review
Cornell Law School
Myron Taylor Hall
Ithaca, NY 14853

Fordham International Law Journal
Fordham University School of Law
140 W. 62nd Street
New York, NY 10023

Fordham Law Review
Fordham University School of Law
140 W. 62nd Street
New York, NY 10023

Fordham Urban Law Journal
Fordham University School of Law
Lincoln Center
New York, NY 10023

Hofstra Labor Law Journal
Hofstra Labor Law Journal Business Manager
Hofstra University School of Law
Hempstead, NY 11550

Hofstra Law Review
Law Review, School of Law
Hofstra University
Hempstead, NY 11550

Human Rights Annual
New York Law School
57 Worth Street
New York, NY 10013

Institute On Federal Taxation (New York University)
Matthew Bender & Co.
235 E. 45th Street
New York, NY 10017

Journal of Legal Education
Business Manager, Myron Taylor Hall
Cornell Law School
Ithaca, NY 14853

Journal of the Copyright Society of the U.S.A.
New York University Law Center
40 Washington Square South
New York, NY 10012

Journal of the Suffolk Academy of Law
Suffolk Academy of Law
100 W. Main Street
East Islip, NY 11730

New York Law School Journal of International and Comparative Law
New York Law School
57 Worth Street
New York, NY 10013

New York Law School Law Review
New York Law School
57 Worth Street
New York, NY 10013

New York State Bar Journal
New York State Bar Association
One Elk Street
Albany, NY 12207

New York University Conference on Tax Planning for the Charitable Sector
Matthew Bender & Co.
235 E. 45th Street
New York, NY 10017

New York University Journal of International Law and Politics
New York University School of Law
110 W. Third Street
New York, NY 10012

New York University Law Review
New York University Law Review
110 W. Third Street
New York, NY 10012

New York University Review of Law and Social Change
New York University Review of Law
and Social Change
249 Sullivan Street
New York, NY 10012

Pace Law Review
Pace University School of Law
78 N. Broadway
White Plains, NY 10603

Record of the Association of the Bar of the City of New York
House of the Association
42 West 44th Street
New York, NY 10036

St. John's Law Review
St. John's Law Review
Fromkes Hall
Grand Central & Utopia Parkways
Jamaica, NY 11439

Syracuse Journal of International Law and Commerce
Syracuse University College of Law
E. I. White Hall
Syracuse, NY 13244-1030

Syracuse Law Review
Syracuse University College of Law
E.I. White Hall
Syracuse, NY 13244-1030

Touro Law Review
Touro College of Law
300 Nassau Road
Hungtington, NY 11743

Trial Lawyers Quarterly
New York State Trial Lawyers Association
Suite 200
132 Nassau Street
New York, NY 10038

APPENDIX B

NEW YORK LEGAL NEWSPAPERS

This list of New York legal newspapers updates and expands upon the New York portions of lists previously compiled by Carleton W. Kenyon[1] and by Anne Ashmore.[2]

Albany

New York Lawyers News. Sept. 22, 1976-Oct. 17, 1977. (w)

Buffalo

Buffalo Law Journal. Sept. 30, 1929- (semi-weekly)
Buffalo, N.Y.: Buffalo Law Journal (a division of Business First of Buffalo, Inc.).

Docket. 1928-? (d)

Legal Daily. 1921-? (d)

New York

Brooklyn Daily Bulletin. ? - ? (d)

Business Journal and General Law Review. 1975-? (w)

Court Journal and Official District Court Record. 1882-? (w)

Daily Register. 1872-1888. 37 v. (d)
(succeeded by *New York Law Journal)*
Microfilm: 1872-1888 University Microfilms International

Gerichts Zeitung. 1882-? (w)

Law Gazette. 1858. 1 v. (d)

[1] Kenyon, *Legal Newspapers in the United States* 63 LAW LIBRARY J. 241, 246 (1970).
[2] Ashmore, *Checklist of Legal Newspapers in the United States* 74 LAW LIBRARY J. 543, 550-51 (1981).

New York (cont.)

National Law Journal. Aug. 7, 1978- (w)
New York: New York Law Publishing Company
Microfilm: 1978- New York Law Publishing Company
1978- University Microfilms International *New*

New York Daily Transcript. July, 1858-1872. 28 v.
(succeeded by ***Daily Register)***

New York Law Journal. March 26, 1888- **(d. exc. Sat., Sun.)**
New York: New York Law Publ. Co.
Microfilm: 1888- University Microfilms International
1888- New York Law Publishing Company

Transcript. Jan. 5- Mar. 16, 1861. 1 v. (w)

Transcript. 1906-? (d)

Rochester

The Daily Record. May 15, 1908- (d. exc. Sat., Sun.)
Rochester, N.Y.: Daily Record Corp.

Syracuse

Register. 1938-? (d)

Troy

Upstate Legal Record. vol. 1, no. 1 (Dec. 1, 1986)- (bi-w.)
Troy: Upstate Legal Record.
Note: Editorial offices located in Albany.

White Plains

Building and Realty News and Legal Record. 1920-? (w)

Westchester Law Journal: 1932? 1936?-? (d., w.)
White Plains, N.Y.: Westchester Law Journal, Inc.
Microfilm: University Microfilm 1936?-?

APPENDIX C

BAR ASSOCIATIONS IN NEW YORK STATE

This appendix is arranged in two parts: a geographically arranged directory of general-interest bar associations, and a classified list of special-interest bar associations. Full directory information is not given for the special interest bar associations because their addresses frequently change with each election of officers. Consult the latest edition of the *New York Lawyers Diary and Manual* to locate current directory information for both the general and special bar associations in New York.

GENERAL INTEREST BAR ASSOCIATIONS IN NEW YORK STATE

Albany

New York State Bar Association
One Elk Street
Albany, NY 12207
(518) 463-3200

Albany County Bar Association
Albany County Court House
Albany, NY 12207
(518) 445-7691

Auburn

Cayuga County Bar Association
Hon. Peter E. Corning, President
Court House
Auburn, NY 13021
(315) 253-1306

Bath

Bath Bar Association
Wendy Lee Gould, President
3 Robie Street
Bath, NY 14810
(607) 776-4164

Binghamton

Broome County Bar Association
The Bache Building
71 State Street
Binghamton, NY 13901
(607) 723-6331

Bronx

Bronx County Bar Association
851 Grand Concourse
Bronx, NY 10451
(212) 293-5600

Brooklyn

Bay Ridge Lawyers Association
Lawrence D. Moringiel, President
8910 Third Avenue
Brooklyn, NY 11209
(718) 238-5445

Brooklyn Bar Association
123 Remsen Street
Brooklyn, NY 11201
(718) 624-0675

Buffalo

Bar Association of Erie County
1360 Statler Towers
Buffalo, NY 14202
(716) 852-8687

Carmel

Putnam County Bar Association
P.O. Box 44
Carmel, NY 10512
(914) 225-4904

Commack

Suffolk County Bar Association
340 Veterans' Memorial
Commack, NY 11725
(716) 728- 5230

Corning

Corning Bar Association
Jacob Welch, President
17-19 E. Market Street
Corning, NY 14830
(607) 962-4641

Coxsackie

Greene County Bar Association
Thomas Fori, President
41 Reed Street
Coxsackie, NY 12051
(518) 731-6118

Eastchester

Eastchester Bar Association
Domenick Porco, President
155 Fisher Avenue
Eastchester, NY 10709
(914) 779-1648

Elmira

Chemung County Bar Association
Everett Weiermiller, President
303 William Street
Elmira, NY 14901
(607) 733-8866

Fort Plain

Montgomery County Bar Association
Allen H. Samuels, President
7 Canal Street
Fort Plain, NY 13339
(518) 993-2313

Fredonia

Bar Association of Northern Chautauqua, Inc.
Lydia Romer, President
2 West Main Street
Fredonia, NY 14063-0109
(716) 673-1361

Geneseo

Livingston County Bar Association
Court House
Geneseo, NY 14454
(716) 243-2500

Goshen

Orange County Bar Association
P.O. Box 88
Goshen, NY 10924
(914) 294-8222

Harrison

Mamaroneck Harrison Larchmont Bar Association
Jack Geoghan, President
550 Mamaroneck Avenue
Harrison, NY 10528
(914) 381-4300

Herkimer

Herkimer County Bar Association
George F. Aney, President
401 Prospect Street
Herkimer, NY 13350
(315) 866-6600

Holley

Orleans County Bar Association
Jeffrey R. Martin, President
P.O. Box 200, 66 Village Square
Holley, NY 14470
(716) 638-6331

Homer

Cortland County Bar Association
Phillip R. Rumsey, President
25 S. Main Street
Homer, NY 13077
(607) 749-7296

Hudson

Columbia County Bar Association
Charles Inman, President
12 S. Fourth Street,
Hudson, NY 12534
(518) 828-3365

Ithaca

Tompkins County Bar Association
David Gersh, President
404 North Cayuga Street
Ithaca, NY 14850
(607) 277-3300

Jamaica

Queens County Bar Association
90-35 148th Street
Jamaica, NY 11435
(718) 291-4500

Jamestown

Jamestown Bar Association
Wilson C. Price, III, President
P.O. Box 1219
Jamestown, NY 14702
(716) 664-7414

Johnstown

Fulton County Bar Association
Carmel K. Greco, President
8 S. William Street
Johnstown, NY 12095
(518) 762-3103

Kingston

Ulster County Bar Association
U.P.O. Box 3515
9 Main Street
Kingston, NY 12401
(914) 331-4977

Lake George

Warren County Bar Association, Inc.
Warren County Municipal Center
Lake George, NY 12845
(518) 792-9239

Lake Placid

Essex County Bar Association
James Brooks, President
Olympic Drive
Lake Placid, NY 12946
(518) 523-1555

Liberty

Federation of Bar Associations of the 3rd Judicial District
Harold Sussman, President
73 Dwyer Avenue
Liberty, NY 12754
(914) 292-6110

Sullivan County Bar Association
Steven Katz, President
3 Maple Street
Liberty, NY 12754
(914) 292-2000

Lockport

Lockport City Bar Association
Wally Moxham, President
280 East Avenue
Lockport, NY 14094
(716) 433-1344

Long Beach

Long Beach Lawyers Association
Samuel Ungar, President
326 W. Park Avenue
Long Beach, NY 11561
(516) 431-1000

Long Island City

Long Island City Lawyers Club
Charles N. Forchelli, President
32-02 30th Avenue
Long Island City, NY 11102
(718) 278-6117

Lowville

Lewis County Bar Association
Joseph Mcguire, President
7557 State Street
Lowville, NY 13367
(315) 376-6546

Middletown

Middletown Bar Association
Burt J. Blustein, President
135 North Street
Middletown, NY 10940
(914) 343-0681

Mineola

Bar Association of Nassau County
15th and West Streets
Mineola, NY 11501
(516) 7474070

Nassau Lawyers' Association of Long Island
Arnold Cohen, President
114 Old Country Road
Mineola, NY 11501
(516) 741-7771

Middletown

Middletown Bar Association
Burt J. Blustein, President
135 North Street
Middletown, NY 10940
(914) 343-0681

Mineola

Bar Association of Nassau County
15th and West Streets
Mineola, NY 11501
(516) 747-4070

Nassau Lawyers' Association of Long Island
Arnold Cohen, President
114 Old Country Road
Mineola, NY 11501
(516) 741-7771

Mt. Vernon

Mount Vernon Bar Association
Richard Ross, President
22 W. First Street
Mt. Vernon, NY 10550
(914) 664-5869

New Berlin

Chenango County Bar Association
Kevin Dowd, President
13 S. Main Street
New Berlin, NY 13411
(607) 847-8151

New City

Rockland County Bar Association
60 S. Main Street
New City, NY 10956
(914) 634-2149

New Rochelle

New Rochelle Bar Association
John A. Vasile, President
249 Huguenot Street
New Rochelle, NY 10802
(914) 632-9300

New York

Association of the Bar of the City of New York
42 West 44th St.
New York, NY 10036
(212) 382-6600

New York County Lawyer's Association
14 Vesey Street
New York, NY 10007
(212) 267-6646

Newark

Wayne County Bar Association
James J. Kaufman, President
165 E. Union Street
Newark, NY 14513
(315) 331-7171

Newburgh

Newburgh Bar Association
Thomas J. Murphy, President
717 Broadway
Newburgh, NY 12550
(914) 562-1515

Niagara Falls

Bar Association of the City of Niagara Falls
Earl Bridges, President
800 Main Street
Niagara Falls, NY 14302
(716) 285-5152

North Tonawanda

Bar Association of the Tonawandas
Michael Anthony Rossi, President
150 Payne Avenue
North Tonawanda, NY 14120
(716) 694-1712

Oakfield

Genesee County Bar Association
Raymond F. Cianfrini, President
87 N. Main Street
Oakfield, NY 14125
(716) 343-0464

Ogdensburg

St. Lawrence County Bar Association
John E. Mellon, President
414 Jay Street
Ogdensburg, NY 13669
(315) 393-1630

Olean

Cattaraugus County Bar Association
Daniel R. Palumbo, President
410 Exchange National Bank Bldg.
Olean, NY 14760
(716) 373-2175

Oneonta

Otsego County Bar Association
Robert P. Nydan, President
48 Dietz Street, Suite E
Oneonta, NY 13820
(607) 432-7521

Oswego

Oswego County Bar Association
Doren Norfleet, President
214 West First Street
Oswego, NY 13126
(315) 343-4016

Owego

Federation of the Bar of the 6th Judicial District
Thomas R. Emnett, President
20 Court Street
Owego, NY 13827
(607) 687-1776

Peekskill

Peekskill Bar Association
P.O. Box 2114
Peekskill, NY 10566
(914) 737-3515

Penn Yan

Yates County Bar Association
Donald Schneider, President
307 Liberty Street
Penn Yan, NY 14527
(315) 536-2100

Plattsburgh

Clinton County Bar Association
Norman Dame, President
62 Brinkerhoff Street
Plattsburgh, NY 12901
(518) 561-2130

Port Chester

Port Chester-Rye Bar Association
Michael Keesee, President
312 Westchester Avenue
Port Chester, NY 10573
(914) 937-3880

Port Jervis

Port Jervis Bar Association
P.O. Box 1114
Port Jervis, NY 12771
(914) 856-5178

Portville

Allegany County Bar Association
Raymond Bulson, President
6 S. Main Street
Portville, NY 14770
(716) 933-8792

Poughkeepsie

Dutchess County Bar Association
P.O. Box 4865
Poughkeepsie, NY 12602
(914) 473-2488

Rochester

Monroe County Bar Association
Suite 400
39 State Street
Rochester, NY 14614
(716) 546-1817

Saratoga Springs

Saratoga County Bar Association
Kate Ferrara, President
P.O. Box 156
Saratoga Springs, NY 12866
(518) 584-3900

Schenectady

Schenectady County Bar Association
612 State Street
Schenectady, NY 12305
(518) 355-0587

Schoharie

Schoharie County Bar Association
James Bryant, President
254 Main Street
Schoharie, NY 12157
(518) 295-7500

Seneca Falls

Seneca County Bar Association
Nicholas Midey, Jr., President
P.O. Box 199
Seneca Falls, NY 13148
(315) 568-5861

Shortsville

Ontario County Bar Association
Robert Zimmerman, President
39 West Main Street
Shortsville, NY 14548
(716) 289-4040

Sidney

Delaware County Bar Association
Paul F. Eaton, Jr., President
P.O. Box 270
Sidney, NY 13838-0270
(607) 563-3565

Staten Island

Richmond County Bar Association
P.O. Box 593
Staten Island, NY 10314
(718) 442-4500

Syracuse

Onondaga County Bar Association
505 State Tower Building
Syracuse, NY 13202
(315) 471-2667

Troy

Cohoes Bar Association
Michele A. Santucci, President
22 - 1st Street
Troy, NY 12180
(518) 272-7500

Rensselaer County Bar Association
Richard Hanft, President
P.O. Box 1054
Troy, NY 12181
(518) 274-1700

Tupper Lake

Franklin County Bar Association
Jeremiah Hayes, President
64 Park Street
Tupper Lake, NY 12986
(518) 359-3241

Utica

Oneida County Bar Association
239 Genesee Street
Suite 303
Utica, NY 13501
(315) 724-4901

Wampsville

Madison County Bar Association
Biagio J. Distefano, President
Madison County Family Court, P.O. Box 607
Wampsville, NY 13163
(315) 366-2241

Warsaw

Wyoming County Bar Association
Mark Haynes, President
Court House
Warsaw, NY 14569
(716) 786-3148

Watertown

Jefferson County Bar Association
Wilfreda Stone, President
120 Washington Street
Watertown, NY 13601
(315) 782-6810

Watkins Glen

Schulyer County Bar Association
Stewart E. McDivitt, President
Franklin & Fourth Streets
Watkins Glen, NY 14891
(607) 535-7694

Waverly

Tioga County Bar Association
Gerald Keene, President
443 Fulton Street
Waverly, NY 14892
(607) 565-8283

Wayland

Steuben County Bar Association
John F. Leyden, President
13 North Main Street
Wayland, NY 14572
(716) 728-5230

White Plains

Northern Westchester Bar Association
Bill Macreedy, President
175 Main Street
White Plains, NY 10601
(914) 946-3700

Ossining Bar Association
Frank Arcuri, President
222 Mamaroneck Avenue
White Plains, NY 10605
(914) 328-1500

Westchester County Bar Assciation
Suite 400
300 Hamilton Avenue
White Plains, NY 10601
(914) 761-3707

White Plains Bar Association
Michael Nordell, President
235 Main Street
White Plains, NY 10601
(914) 946-8800

Yorktown Bar Association
Diane Selker, President
111 Grove Street
White Plains, NY 10601
(914) 285-2000

Whitehall

Washington County Bar Association
Frank H. Kingsley, Jr.
167 Broadway
Whitehall, NY 12887
(518) 499-0270

SPECIAL INTEREST BAR ASSOCIATIONS IN NEW YORK STATE

Bankruptcy
Bankruptcy Lawyers Bar Association (New York City)

Civil Service
Association of New York State Civil Service Attorneys, Inc. (New York City)

Commercial
Commercial Lawyers Conference, Inc. (Valley Stream)

Customs and International Trade
Customs and International Trade Bar Association (New York City)

Federal
The Federal Bar Association, Empire State Chapter (New York City)

Federal Bar Council (New York City)

Human Rights
Bar Association For Human Rights of Greater New York (New York City)

Immigration
American Immigration Lawyers Association, New York Chapter (New York City)

Federal Immigration Bar Association (New York City)

Matrimonial
American Academy of Matrimonial Lawyers, New York Chapter (Buffalo)

Minority
Association of Black Lawyers of Westchester County (White Plains)

Association of Black Women Lawyers, Inc. (New York City)

Minority *(cont.)*

Black Bar Association of Bronx County (Bronx)

Macon B. Allen Black Bar Association (Queens)
(St. Albans)

Metropolitan Black Bar Association (New York City)

Minority Lawyers of Western New York (Buffalo)

National Lawyers Guild (New York City Chapter)

Nationality

Columbian Lawyers Association - First Judicial Department
(New York City)

Columbian Lawyers Association of Brooklyn (Brooklyn)

French-American Bar Association, Inc. (New York City)

Puerto Rican Bar Association of New York (New York City)

Public Defender

New York State Defenders Association, Inc. (Albany)

Religious Affiliation

Guild of Catholic Lawyers, Inc. (Scarsdale)

Jewish Lawyers Guild, Inc. (New York City)

Protestant Lawyers Association of New York, Inc.
(Brooklyn Heights)

Trial

Association of Assigned Counsel of New York
County Family Court (New York City)

Association of Trial Lawyers of the City of New York
(New York City)

Trial *(cont.)*

Brooklyn-Manhattan Trial Counsel Association, Inc. (Brooklyn)

Kings County Criminal Bar Association (Brooklyn)

Nassau-Suffolk Trial Lawyers Association (Farmingdale)

New York Criminal and Civil Courts Bar Association (New York City)

New York State Trial Lawyers Association (New York City)

Western New York Trial Lawyers Association (Buffalo)

Women

Association of Black Women Lawyers, Inc. (New York City)

Bronx Council of Women Lawyers (Bronx)

Brooklyn Women's Bar Association, Inc. (Brooklyn)

Central New York Women's Bar Association (Syracuse)

Metropolitan Women's Bar Association (New York City)

Mid-Hudson Women's Bar Association (Poughkeepsie)

Nassau County Women's Bar Association (Mineola)

New York Women's Bar Association (New York City)

Queens County Women's Bar Association (Boro Hall Station)

Women *(cont.)*

Rockland County Women's Bar Association
(New York City)

Staten Island Women's Bar Association
(Staten Island)

Westchester Women's Bar Association
(White Plains)

Women Lawyers of Western New York (Buffalo)

Women's Bar Association of Orange & Sullivan
Counties (Newburgh)

Women's Bar Association of the State of New York
(New York City)

Workers' Compensation

New York State Workers' Compensation Bar Association
(New York City)

APPENDIX D

PUBLISHERS OF NEW YORK LEGAL MATERIALS

American Association of Law Libraries
53 West Jackson Blvd.
Chicago, IL 60604
(312) 939-4764

Association of the Bar of the City of New York
42 West 44th Street
New York, NY 10036
(212) 382-6650

Attorneys Aid Publications
Box 283
Kew Gardens, NY 11415

Bender, See Matthew Bender

Buffalo Law Journal
361 Delaware Avenue
Suite 200
Buffalo, NY 14202
(716) 852-6221

Capitol Microfilm Service
Rotterdam Industrial Park
Schenectady, NY 12306
(800) 635-3635

Callaghan & Company
3201 Old Glenview Road
Wilmette, IL 60091
(312) 256-7000

Clark Boardman Company, Ltd.
435 Hudson Street
New York, NY 10014
(212) 929-7500

Columbia University Press
562 W. 113th St.
New York, NY 10025
(212) 316-7100

send orders to:
136 S. Broadway
Irvington-on-Hudson, NY 10533
(914) 591-9111

Commerce Clearing House
4025 W. Peterson Avenue
Chicago, Illinois 60646
(312) 583-8500

Cornell University Press
124 Roberts Place
P.O. Box 250
Ithaca, NY 14851
(607) 257-7000

send orders to:
714 Cascadilla St.
Ithaca, NY 14851

Daily Record Corporation
11 Centre Park
P.O. Box 6
Rochester, NY 14601
(716) 232-6920

Doran Publications, Inc.
1 Northway 10 Executive Park
P.O. Box 391
Clifton Park, NY 12065
(518) 877-7492

Empire State Report
545 Eighth Avenue
New York, NY 10018
(212) 239-9797

Foundation Press, Inc.
170 Old Country Road
Mineola, New York 11501
(516) 248-5580

Fred B. Rothman & Co.
10368 West Centennial Road
Littleton, CO 80127
(800) 457-1986

Garland Publishing, Inc.
136 Madison Avenue
New York, NY 10016
(212) 686-7492

General Code Publishers, Inc.
72 Hinchey Road
Rochester, NY 14624
(716) 328-1810

Government Research Service
701 Jackson
Topeka, Kansas 66603
(913) 232-7720

Gould Publications
199/300 State Street
Binghamton, NY 13901
(607) 724-3000

Hamilton Printing Co.
P.O. Box 232
Rensselaer, NY 12144
(518) 477-9345

Hein, see Willaim S. Hein & Co.

Infosources Publishing
118 West 79th Street
New York, NY 10024
(212) 595-3161

Jury Verdict Research
5325B Naiman Parkway
Solon, Ohio 44139
(800) 321-6910

Jury Verdict Review
24 Commerce St.
Suite 1722
Newark, NJ 07102
(201) 624-1665

LRP Publications
P.O. Box 579
Fort Washington, PA 19034-2801
(215) 628-3113

Law & Business, Inc.
Prentice-Hall
855 Valley Road
Clifton, NJ 07013
(201) 472-7400

Law Journal Seminars-Press
111 Eighth Avenue
Suite 900
New York, NY 10011
(800) 221-8195 or (212) 741-8300

Lawyer's Co-operative Publishing Co.
1 Graves Street
Rochester, NY 14694
(800) 572-0430 or (716) 546-5530

Leader Publications
111 Eighth Avenue
Suite 900
New York, NY 10114-0410

Lenz & Riecker, Inc.
One Columbia Place
Albany, NY 12207
(518) 436-8647

Little, Brown & Company
Law Division
34 Beacon Street
(P.O. Box 2158)
Boston, MA 02108
(800) 343-9204

send orders to:
200 West St.
Waltham, MA 02254

Lond Publications
Call Hollow Road
Pomona, NY 109770
(914) 354-3521

Martindale-Hubbell, Inc.
P.O. Box 1001
Summit, NJ 07901
(201) 464-6800

Matthew Bender & Co., Inc.
235 E. 45th St.
New York, NY 10017
(212) 661-5050 or 1 (800) 821-2232

Michie Co.
P.O. Box 7587
Charlottesville, VA 22906
(804) 972-7600 or 1 (800) 446-3410

Microform, Inc.
Frankford Arsenal, Bldg. 28
Philadelphia, PA 19137-0907
(215) 289-5700

National Attorneys' Publications, Inc.
P.O. Box 150
East Setauket, NY 11733-0150

New York Jury Verdict Reporter, Inc.
577 Main Street
P.O. Box 310
Islip, NY 11751
(516) 581-1930

New York Land Institute
P.O. Box 365
Albany, NY 12201
(518) 465-7412

New York Law Publishing Company
111 Eighth Avenue
New York, NY 10011
(212) 741-8300

New York Lawyers Diary and Manual
240 Mulberry St.
P.O. Box 1226
Newark, NY 07101-1226
(800) 526-9246

New York Legislative Service, Inc.
299 Broadway
New York, NY 10007
(212) 962-2826

New York Planning Federation
301 South Allen Street
Albany, NY 12208
(518) 489-8116

New York State Bar Association
One Elk Street
Albany, NY 12207
(518) 463-3200

New York State Directory
National Standards Assoc., Inc.
5161 River Road
Bethesda, MD 20816
(800) 638-8094 or (301) 951-1389

Oceana Publications, Inc.
75 Main Street
Dobbs Ferry, NY 10522
(914) 693-1733

Oxford University Press, Inc.
200 Madison Avenue
New York, NY 10016
(212) 679-7300

Panel Publishers
14 Plaza Road
Greenvale, NY 11548
(516) 484-0006

Plenum Publishing Corp.
233 Spring St.
New York, NY 10013
(800) 221-9369 or (212) 620-8000

Practising Law Institute
810 Seventh Avenue
New York, NY 10019
(212) 765-5700

Prentice-Hall, Inc.
Route 9W
Englewood Cliffs, NJ 07632
(201) 592-2000

send orders to:
200 Old Tappan Rd.
Old Tappan, NJ 07675

Research Institute of America
589 Fifth Avenue
New York, NY 10017
(212) 755-8900

Rothman, See Fred B. Rothman & Co.

Shepard's McGraw-Hill
402 N. Cascade Ave.
Colorado Springs, CO 80901
(800) 525-2474 or (303) 5521

send orders to:
P.O. Box 1235
Colorado Springs, CO 80901

University Microfilms International
300 N. Zeeb Road
Ann Arbor, MI 48106
(800) 521-0600 or (313) 761-4700

University Publications of America, Inc.
44 North Market Street
Frederick, MD 21701
(800) 692-6300 or (301) 694-0100

Upstate Legal Record
P.O. Box 433
Troy, NY 12181
(518) 273-1521

Warren, Gorham & Lamont, Inc.
210 South Street
Boston, MA 02111
(800) 922-0066

West Publishing Company
P.O. Box 64526
50 W. Kellogg Blvd.
St. Paul, MN 55102-1611
(800) 328-9352 or (612) 228-2500

William S. Hein & Co., Inc.
1285 Main Street
Buffalo, NY 14209
(716) 882-2600

Williams Press, Inc.
P.O. Box 4025 Patroon Station
Albany, NY 12204-0024
(518) 434-1141

APPENDIX E

PUBLISHERS OF CHARTERS, CODES AND ORDINANCES

The New York municipalities listed in this Appendix have contracted with commercial publishers for the publication of their current charters, codes or ordinances. In some cases, only the latest material is produced by the publisher listed here, while earlier material, which is still in effect, is found in another source. That earlier material may have been produced by a different publisher, or it may have been published by the municipality itself. The researcher should be aware of the possibility that the search for local authority can require the use of several sources.

Hundreds of municipalities are not listed here. The Clerk of an unlisted municipality can advise the researcher on how to access the charter, code or ordinances of that municipality.

In this listing, the Municipal Code Corporation is abbreviated "MCP," the General Code Publishers Corporation is abbreviated "GCP," and Lenz & Riecker is abbreviated "L & R." When the name of a municipality is followed by an asterisk (*), the municipality had contracted with the General Code Corporation but publication was still pending as of October, 1987.

Municipality	**Type**	**County**	**Publisher**
Albany	City	Albany	GCP
Albion	Village	Orleans	GCP
Albion*	Town	Orleans	GCP
Alden	Town	Erie	GCP
Alden	Village	Erie	GCP
Amenia*	Town	Dutchess	GCP
Amherst	Town	Erie	GCP
Amityville	Village	Suffolk	GCP
Amsterdam	City	Montgomery	GCP
Ardsley	Village	Westchester	GCP
Athens	Village	Greene	GCP
Attica	Village	Wyoming	GCP
Auburn	City	Cayuga	MCP
Aurora*	Town	Erie	GCP
Avon*	Town	Livingston	GCP

Babylon	Town	Suffolk	GCP
Babylon	Village	Suffolk	GCP
Baldwinsville	Village	Onondaga	GCP
Bath	Town	Steuben	GCP
Bath	Village	Steuben	GCP
Bayville	Village	Nassau	GCP
Beacon	City	Dutchess	GCP
Bedford	Town	Westchester	GCP
Bellerose	Village	Nassau	GCP
Bellport	Village	Suffolk	GCP
Bethel	Town	Sullivan	GCP
Bethlehem	Town	Albany	GCP
Binghamton (Traffic)	City	Broome	GCP
Binghamton	City	Broome	MCP
Binghamton	Town	Broome	GCP
Black River	Village	Jefferson	GCP
Blasdell	Village	Erie	GCP
Boonville	Village	Oneida	GCP
Boston*	Town	Erie	GCP
Brighton	Town	Monroe	GCP
Brightwaters	Village	Suffolk	GCP
Broadalbin	Village	Fulton	GCP
Brockport	Village	Monroe	GCP
Brookhaven	Town	Suffolk	GCP
Brownville	Town	Jefferson	GCP
Brownville	Village	Jefferson	GCP
Brunswick*	Town	Rensselaer	GCP
Buchanan	Village	Westchester	GCP
Buffalo	City	Erie	MCP
Caledonia	Village	Livingston	GCP
Camillus	Village	Onondaga	GCP
Canajoharie	Village	Montgomery	GCP
Canandaigua	Town	Ontario	GCP
Canisteo	Village	Steuben	GCP
Canton	Town	St. Lawrence	GCP
Canton	Village	St. Lawrence	GCP
Carmel*	Town	Putnam	GCP
Carthage	Village	Jefferson	GCP

Cedarhurst	Village	Nassau	MCP
Champlain	Town	Clinton	GCP
Champlain	Village	Clinton	GCP
Chatham	Village	Columbia	GCP
Chaumont	Village	Jefferson	GCP
Cheektowaga	Town	Erie	GCP
Chenango	Town	Broome	GCP
Chester	Town	Orange	GCP
Chester	Village	Orange	GCP
Chili	Town	Monroe	GCP
Chittenango	Village	Madison	GCP
Churchville	Village	Monroe	GCP
Clarence	Town	Erie	GCP
Clarkson*	Town	Monroe	GCP
Clarkstown	Town	Rockland	GCP
Clayton	Village	Jefferson	GCP
Clayton	Village	Jefferson	GCP
Clifton Park	Town	Saratoga	GCP
Clifton Springs	Village	Ontario	GCP
Clinton	Village	Oneida	GCP
Cobleskill	Village	Schoharie	GCP
Coeymans*	Town	Albany	GCP
Cohocton	Village	Steuben	MCP
Cold Springs	Village	Putnam	GCP
Colden	Town	Erie	GCP
Colonie	Town	Albany	GCP
Colonie	Village	Albany	GCP
Columbia	County	Columbia	GCP
Corinth	Village	Saratoga	GCP
Cornwall*	Town	Orange	GCP
Cornwall-On-Hudson	Village	Orange	GCP
Cortland	City	Cortland	GCP
Cortlandt	Town	Westchester	GCP
Coxsackie	Village	Greene	GCP
Crawford	Town	Orange	GCP
Croton-On-Hudson	Village	Westchester	GCP
Cuba	Village	Allegany	GCP
Dannemora	Village	Clinton	GCP

Deruyter	Village	Madison	GCP
Dewitt	Town	Onondaga	GCP
Delhi	Village	Delaware	GCP
Deposit	Village	Broome & Delaware	GCP
Dexter	Village	Jefferson	GCP
Dickinson	Town	Broome	GCP
Dobbs Ferry	Village	Westchester	GCP
Dolgeville	Village	Fulton & Herkimer	MCP
Dunkirk	City	Chautauqua	GCP
Dutchess	County	Dutchess	GCP
East Aurora	Village	Erie	GCP
East Fishkill	Town	Dutchess	GCP
East Greenbus	Town	Rensselaer	GCP
East Hampton	Town	Suffolk	GCP
East Hampton	Village	Suffolk	GCP
East Hills	Village	Nassau	GCP
East Rochester	Village	Monroe	GCP
East Rockaway	Village	Nassau	GCP
Eden	Town	Erie	GCP
Elbridge	Village	Onondaga	GCP
Ellenville	Village	Ulster	GCP
Ellery	Town	Chautauqua	GCP
Ellicott	Town	Chautauqua	GCP
Elma	Town	Erie	GCP
Elmira	City	Chemung	MCP
Elmsford	Village	Westchester	GCP
Endicott	Village	Broome	GCP
Esopus	Town	Ulster	GCP
Evans	Town	Erie	GCP
Fair Haven	Village	Cayuga	GCP
Fairport	Village	Monroe	GCP
Farmingdale	Village	Nassau	GCP
Farmington	Town	Ontario	GCP
Fayettville	Village	Onondaga	GCP
Fishkill	Town	Dutchess	GCP
Fishkill	Village	Dutchess	GCP

Floral Park	Village	Nassau	GCP
Florida	Village	Orange	GCP
Flower Hill	Village	Nassau	GCP
Forestburg	Town	Sullivan	GCP
Fort Edward*	Town	Washington	GCP
Fort Edward	Village	Washington	GCP
Fort Plain	Village	Montgomery	MCP
Frankfort	Town	Herkimer	GCP
Frankfort	Village	Herkimer	GCP
Freeport	Village	Nassau	GCP
Fulton	City	Oswego	GCP
Garden City	Village	Nassau	GCP
Gates	Town	Monroe	GCP
Geddes	Town	Onondaga	GCP
Geneseo*	Town	Livingston	GCP
Geneseo	Village	Livingston	GCP
Glens Falls	City	Warren	GCP
Glenville	Town	Schenectady	GCP
Gloversville	City	Fulton	GCP
Goshen	Town	Orange	GCP
Goshen	Village	Orange	MCP
Grand Island	Town	Erie	GCP
Great Neck	Village	Nassau	GCP
Great Neck Estates	Village	Nassau	GCP
Great Neck Plaza	Village	Nassau	GCP
Greece	Town	Monroe	GCP
Greenburgh*	Town	Westchester	GCP
Greene	County	Greene	GCP
Greenport	Town	Columbia	GCP
Greenport	Village	Suffolk	GCP
Greenwood Lake	Village	Orange	GCP
Guilderland	Town	Albany	MCP
Hamburg	Town	Erie	GCP
Hamburg	Village	Erie	MCP
Hamlin	Town	Monroe	GCP
Hammondsport	Village	Steuben	GCP
Hamptonburgh	Town	Orange	GCP
Hancock	Village	Delaware	GCP

Harriman	Village	Orange	GCP
Harrison	Town	Westchester	GCP
Hartland	Town	Niagara	GCP
Hastings-On-Hudson	Village	Westchester	GCP
Haverstraw	Town	Rockland	GCP
Haverstraw	Village	Rockland	GCP
Hempstead	Town	Nassau	GCP
Hempstead	Village	Nassau	GCP
Henrietta	Town	Monroe	GCP
Hewlett Harbor	Village	Nassau	GCP
Highland Falls	Village	Orange	GCP
Hilburn	Village	Rockland	GCP
Hilton	Village	Monroe	GCP
Holland*	Town	Erie	GCP
Homer	Village	Cortland	MCP
Honeoye Falls	Village	Monroe	GCP
Hornell	City	Steuben	MCP
Hudson	City	Columbia	GCP
Hudson Falls	Village	Washington	GCP
Hunter	Town	Greene	GCP
Huntington	Town	Suffolk	GCP
Huntington Bay	Village	Suffolk	GCP
Hyde Park	Town	Dutchess	GCP
Irvington	Village	Westchester	GCP
Island Park	Village	Nassau	GCP
Islandia	Village	Suffolk	GCP
Islip	Town	Suffolk	GCP
Johnson City	Village	Broome	MCP
Johnstown	City	Fulton	MCP
Johnstown	Town	Fulton	GCP
Kenmore	Village	Erie	MCP
Kent	Town	Putnam	GCP
Kinderhook	Town	Columbia	GCP
Kinderhook	Village	Columbia	GCP
Kings Point	Village	Nassau	GCP
Kingston	City	Ulster	GCP
Kingsbury	Town	Washington	GCP
Kirkland	Town	Oneida	GCP

LaGrange	Town	Dutchess	GCP
Lake George	Village	Warren	GCP
Lake Grove	Village	Suffolk	GCP
Lake Success	Village	Nassau	GCP
Lakewood	Village	Chautauqua	GCP
Lancaster	Town	Erie	GCP
Lancaster	Village	Erie	GCP
Larchmont	Village	Westchester	GCP
Laurel Hollow	Village	Nassau	GCP
Lawrence	Village	Nassau	GCP
Le Roy*	Town	Genesee	GCP
Lewiston	Town	Niagara	GCP
Lewiston	Village	Niagara	MCP
Liberty	Town	Sullivan	GCP
Liberty	Village	Sullivan	GCP
Lindenhurst	Village	Suffolk	GCP
Little Falls	City	Herkimer	GCP
Liverpool	Village	Onondaga	GCP
Livonia	Town	Livingston	GCP
Lloyd	Town	Ulster	GCP
Lockport	City	Niagara	GCP
Long Beach	City	Nassau	MCP
Lynbrook	Village	Nassau	GCP
Lysander*	Town	Onondaga	GCP
Malone	Town	Franklin	GCP
Malone	Village	Franklin	GCP
Malverne	Village	Nassau	GCP
Mamaroneck	Town	Westchester	GCP
Mamaroneck	Village	Westchester	GCP
Manchester*	Town	Ontario	GCP
Manchester	Village	Ontario	GCP
Manilus	Village	Onondaga	GCP
Manorhaven	Village	Nassau	GCP
Marcellus	Village	Onondaga	MCP
Marlborough	Town	Ulster	GCP
Massapequa Park	Village	Nassau	GCP
Massena	Town	St. Lawrence	GCP
Massena	Village	St. Lawrence	GCP

Mechanicville	City	Saratoga	GCP
Menands	Village	Albany	GCP
Mendon	Town	Monroe	GCP
Middletown	City	Orange	GCP
Mill Neck	Village	Nassau	GCP
Millerton	Village	Dutchess	GCP
Mineola	Village	Nassau	GCP
Mohawk	Village	Herkimer	GCP
Monroe	County	Monroe	GCP
Monroe	Town	Orange	GCP
Monroe	Village	Orange	GCP
Montgomery*	Town	Orange	GCP
Montgomery	Village	Orange	GCP
Monticello	Village	Sullivan	GCP
Moreau	Town	Saratoga	GCP
Mount Kisco	Village	Westchester	GCP
Mount Morris*	Town	Livingston	GCP
Mount Morris	Village	Livingston	GCP
Mount Pleasant*	Town	Westchester	GCP
Mount Vernon	City	Westchester	GCP
Nassau	Village	Rensselaer	GCP
Neversink	Town	Sullivan	GCP
New Baltimore	Town	Greene	GCP
New Berlin	Village	Chenango	GCP
New Castle	Town	Westchester	GCP
New Hartford	Town	Oneida	GCP
New Hyde Park	Village	Nassau	GCP
New Paltz*	Town	Ulster	GCP
New Rochelle	City	Westchester	GCP
New York	City		L & R
New York	City		Williams
New Windsor	Town	Orange	GCP
Newark	Village	Wayne	GCP
Newburgh	City	Orange	GCP
Newfane	Town	Niagara	GCP
Niskayuna*	Town	Schenectady	GCP
Nissequogue*	Village	Suffolk	GCP
North Castle	Town	Westchester	GCP

North Collins	Village	Erie	GCP
North East	Town	Dutchess	GCP
North Greenbush	Town	Rensselaer	GCP
North Haven	Village	Suffolk	GCP
North Hempstead	Town	Nassau	GCP
North Hills	Village	Nassau	GCP
North Hornell	Village	Steuben	GCP
North Tarrytown	Village	Westchester	GCP
North Tonawanda	City	Niagara	GCP
Northport	Village	Suffolk	GCP
Northville	Village	Fulton	GCP
Nyack	Village	Rockland	GCP
Ocean Beach	Village	Suffolk	GCP
Ogden	Town	Monroe	GCP
Old Field	Village	Suffolk	GCP
Old Westbury	Village	Nassau	GCP
Olean	City	Cattaraugus	MCP
Oneida	City	Madison	MCP
Oneonta	Town	Otsego	GCP
Onondaga	Town	Onondaga	GCP
Ontario*	Town	Wayne	GCP
Orangetown	Town	Rockland	GCP
Orchard Park	Town	Erie	GCP
Ossining	Town	Westchester	GCP
Ossining	Village	Westchester	MCP
Oswego	City	Oswego	GCP
Owasco*	Town	Cayuga	GCP
Owego	Town	Tioga	GCP
Owego	Village	Tioga	MCP
Oyster Bay	Town	Nassau	MCP
Palmyra	Village	Wayne	GCP
Parma	Town	Monroe	GCP
Patchogue	Village	Suffolk	GCP
Patterson	Town	Putnam	GCP
Pawling	Town	Dutchess	GCP
Pawling	Village	Dutchess	GCP
Peekskill	City	Westchester	GCP
Pelham	Village	Westchester	GCP

Penn Yan	Village	Yates	GCP
Perinton	Town	Monroe	GCP
Phoenix	Village	Oswego	GCP
Piermont	Village	Rocklan)d	GCP
Pittsford	Town	Monroe	MCP
Pittsford	Village	Monroe	MCP
Plandome	Village	Nassau	GCP
Plattekill	Town	Ulster	GCP
Plattsburgh	City	Clinton	GCP
Pleasant Valley	Town	Dutchess	GCP
Poestenkill	Town	Rennsselaer	GCP
Pomona	Village	Rockland	GCP
Port Chester	Village	Westchester	GCP
Port Dickinson	Village	Broome	GCP
Port Jefferson	Village	Suffolk	GCP
Port Jervis	City	Orange	GCP
Potsdam	Town	St. Lawrence	GCP
Potsdam	Village	St. Lawrence	GCP
Poughkeepsie	City	Dutchess	MCP
Poughkeepsie	Town	Dutchess	MCP
Pound Ridge	Town	Westchester	GCP
Putnam	Town	Putnam	GCP
Quoque	Village	Suffolk	GCP
Ramapo	Town	Rockland	GCP
Red Hood	Town	Dutchess	GCP
Rensselaer	City	Rensselaer	GCP
Rhinebeck	Village	Dutchess	GCP
Rhinebeck*	Town	Dutchess	GCP
Richfield Springs	Village	Otsego	GCP
Riga	Town	Monroe	GCP
Riverhead	Town	Suffolk	GCP
Rochester	City	Monroe	GCP
Rockland	County	County	GCP
Rockville Center	Village	Nassau	GCP
Rome	City	Oneida	MCP
Root*	Town	Montgomery	GCP
Rosendale	Town	Ulster	GCP
Roslyn	Village	Nassau	MCP

Roslyn Harbor	Village	Nassau	GCP
Rotterdam	Town	Schenectady	GCP
Rouses Point	Village	Clinton	GCP
Russell Gardens	Village	Nassau	GCP
Rye	City	Westchester	GCP
Rye	Town	Westchester	GCP
Saddle Rock	Village	Nassau	GCP
Sag Harbor	Village	Suffolk	GCP
Salina	Town	Onondaga	GCP
Saltaire	Village	Suffolk	GCP
Sands Point	Village	Nassau	GCP
Saranac Lake	Vilage	Franklin	GCP
Saratoga Springs	City	Saratoga	GCP
Saugerties	Village	Ulster	GCP
Scarsdale	Village	Westchester	GCP
Schenectady	City	Schenectady	GCP
Schoharie	Village	Schoharie	GCP
Schroeppel*	Town	Oswego	GCP
Scotia*	Village	Schenectady	MCP
Scottsville	Village	Monroe	MCP
Sea Cliff	Village	Nassau	GCP
Seneca Falls	Village	Seneca	GCP
Shandaken*	Town	Ulster	GCP
Shawangunk	Town	Ulster	GCP
Shelter Island	Town	Suffolk	GCP
Shortsville	Village	Ontario	GCP
Skaneateles	Town	Onondaga	GCP
Skaneateles	Village	Onondaga	MCP
Sloan	Village	Erie	GCP
Smithtown	Town	Suffolk	GCP
Sodus	Town	Wayne	GCP
Sodus	Village	Wayne	GCP
Solvay	Village	Onondaga	GCP
Solvay	Village	Onondaga	MCP
Somers	Town	Westchester	GCP
South Floral Park	Village	Nassau	GCP
South Glens Falls	Village	Saratoga	GCP
South Nyack	Village	Rockland	GCP

Southampton	Town	Suffolk	GCP
Southampton	Village	Suffolk	GCP
Southeast*	Town	Putnam	GCP
Southold	Town	Suffolk	GCP
Spencerport	Village	Monroe	GCP
Spring Valley	Village	Rockland	MCP
Springville	Village	Erie	GCP
Stanford	Town	Dutchess	GCP
Stoney Point	Town	Rockland	GCP
Suffern	Village	Rockland	GCP
Suffolk	County	Suffolk	GCP
Sweden	Town	Monroe	GCP
Sylvan Beach	Village	Oneida	GCP
Syracuse	City	Onondaga	MCP
Thomaston	Village	Nassau	GCP
Thompson	Town	Sullivan	GCP
Tonawanda	City	Erie	GCP
Tonawanda	Town	Erie	GCP
Trenton*	Town	Oneida	GCP
Troy	City	Rensselaer	MCP
Tuckahoe	Village	Suffolk	MCP
Tupper Lake	Village	Franklin	GCP
Tuxedo	Town	Orange	GCP
Tuxedo Park	Village	Orange	GCP
Unadilla	Village	Otsego	GCP
Union	Town	Broome	GCP
Union Vale	Town	Dutchess	GCP
Utica	City	Oneida	MCP
Valatie	Village	Columbia	GCP
Valley Stream	Village	Nassau	GCP
Vestal	Town	Broome	MCP
Victor	Town	Ontario	GCP
Victor	Village	Ontario	GCP
Village of the Branc	Village	Suffolk	GCP
Walden	Village	Orange	GCP
Walkill	Town	Orange	GCP
Walton	Village	Delaware	GCP
Wappinger	Town	Dutchess	GCP

Wappinger Falls	Village	Dutchess	GCP
Warsaw	Village	Wyoming	GCP
Warwick*	Town	Orange	GCP
Warwick	Village	Orange	GCP
Waterford	Town	Saratoga	GCP
Watertown	City	Jefferson	GCP
Watervliet	City	Albany	MCP
Waverly	Village	Tioga	GCP
Wawarsing	Town	Ulster	GCP
Webster*	Town	Monroe	GCP
Webster	Village	Monroe	GCP
West Carthage	Village	Jefferson	GCP
West Haverstraw	Village	Rockland	MCP
West Seneca	Town	Erie	GCP
Westbury	Village	Nassau	GCP
Westchester	County	Westchester	GCP
Westfield	Village	Chautauqua	GCP
Westhampton Beach	Village	Suffolk	GCP
Wheatland	Town	Monroe	GCP
White Plains	City	Westchester	MCP
Whitesboro	Village	Oneida	GCP
Williamson	Town	Wayne	GCP
Williamsville	Village	Erie	GCP
Wilson	Town	Niagara	GCP
Wilson	Village	Niagara	GCP
Windsor	Town	Broome	GCP
Windsor	Village	Broome	GCP
Wolcott	Village	Wayne	GCP
Woodbury	Town	Orange	GCP
Yonkers	City	Westchester	GCP

APPENDIX F.

NEW YORK LAW LIBRARIES

Scope. This list includes academic, court, and association law libraries and the Law and Social Sciences division of the State Library; it excludes law firm libraries. General collections are not listed, but it is appropriate to mention that the collections of the New York State Archives, New York Historical Society, and the New York Public Library include invaluable resources, especially for legal historians.

Arrangement. This list of law libraries in New York State is arranged geographically. The two major sections divide the libraries into Upstate New York Law Libraries and Greater Metropolitan New York Law Libraries. Those sections in turn are arranged by municipality in alphabetical order.

Access. Almost all law libraries have a specialized service mission. The primary clientele of an academic law library is the faculty and students of its law school and university. The primary clientele of a bar association library is the association's membership. The primary clientele of a court library is the judges or justices and the court staff. Usually, service to attorneys is also included in the service mission of court libraries.

Especially in Metropolitan New York, where law library resources and seating space are at a premium, many law libraries allow access only to their primary clientele. In some libraries, non-primary clientele can use collections on a fee-basis. In most upstate communities, court libraries are open to the public. The availability of reference service varies considerably among law libraries.

The researcher is advised to write or call in advance of a visit to a law library to determine the library's access and service policies.

GREATER METROPOLITAN NEW YORK LAW LIBRARIES

Brooklyn

Appellate Division Library (2nd Dept.)
45 Monroe Place
Brooklyn, NY 11201
(718) 875-1300

Brooklyn *(cont.)*

Brooklyn Bar Assn. Library
123 Remsen St.
Brooklyn, NY 11201
(718) 624-0675

Brooklyn Law School Library
250 Joralemon St.
Brooklyn, NY 11201
(718) 780-7974

Judges Library-Criminal Court
120 Schermerhorn St.
Brooklyn, NY 11201
(212) 643-4065

Kings Co. District Attorney's Office
210 Joralemon St.
Brooklyn, NY 11201
(718) 802-2174

New York City Transit Authority Law Library
Rm. 1333
370 Jay St.
Brooklyn, NY 11202
(718) 802-2174

Supreme Court Library, Brooklyn
Rm. 349
Supreme Court Bldg.
Brooklyn, NY 11201
(718) 643-8080

U.S. District Court for the Eastern District of N.Y.
225 Cadman Plaza E.
Brooklyn, NY 11201
(718) 330-7483

Flushing

CUNY Law School at Queens College
65-21 Main St.
Flushing, NY 11367
(718) 575-4240

Hempstead

Hofstra University
School of Law Library
Hempstead, NY 11550
(516) 560-5898

Huntington

Touro College
School of Law Library
300 Nassau Rd.
Huntington, NY 11743
(516) 421-2320

Jamaica

St. John's Univ. School of Law Library
Grand Central and Utopia Parkways
Jamaica, NY 11439
(212) 990-6161

Supreme Court Library, Queens Co.
General Court House
88-11 Sutphin Blvd.
Jamaica, NY 11435
(212) 520-3140

Mineola

Nassau Co. Supreme Ct. Law Library
100 Supreme Court Dr.
Mineola, NY 11501
(516) 535-3883

New York (Manhattan)

Association of the Bar of the City of New York Library
42 W. 44th St.
New York, NY 10036
(212) 381-6741

Bronx Supreme Ct. Library
851 Grand Concourse
New York, NY 10451
(212) 590-3678

Civil Court of the City of New York Library
111 Centre
New York, NY 10013
(212) 344-0600

Columbia Univ. Law Library
435 W. 116th St.
New York, NY 10027
(212) 280-3737

District Attorney's Office Library, New York Co.
One Hogan Pl.
New York, NY 10013
(212) 553-9344

Fordham Univ. Law Library
Lincoln Sq.
140 W. 62nd St.
New York, NY 10023
(212) 841-5223

Institute of Judicial Administration Library
One Washington Square Village
New York, NY 10012
(212) 598-7721

New York (Manhattan) *(cont.)*

New York City Law Dept.
Corp. Counsel's Library
Rm. 6 B1, 100 Church St.
New York, NY 10013
(212) 566-4418

New York Co. Lawyers' Ass'n. Library
14 Vesey St.
New York, NY 10007
(212) 267-6646

New York Law Institute Library
120 Broadway
New York, NY 10271
(212) 732-8720

New York Law School Library
57 Worth St.
New York, NY 10013
(212) 431-2333

New York State Dept. of Law Library
2 World Trade Center
Rm. 4749
New York, NY 10047
(212) 488-7445

New York State Office of the Special State Prosecutor
2 Rector St.
New York, NY 10006
(212) 406-9645

New York State Supreme Ct. 1st Jud. Dist. (Crim.)
100 Centre St.
17th Floor
New York, NY 10013
(212) 374-5598

New York (Manhattan) *(cont.)*

New York Supreme Ct. Law Library, 1st Jud. Dist. (Civil)
60 Centre St.
New York, NY 10007
(212) 374-8384

New York University Law Library
40 Washington Sq., S.
New York, NY 10012
(212) 598-3071

Appellate Division Library (1st Dept.)
27 Madison Ave.
New York, NY 10010
(212) 532-1000

Surrogate's Ct. Law Library
New York County
Hall of Records, 31 Chambers St.
New York, NY 10007
(212) 374-8275

Yeshiva University
Benjamin N. Cardozo School of Law Library
55 Fifth Ave.
New York, NY 10003
(212) 790-0222

Riverhead

Supreme Ct. Law Library, 10th District, Riverhead
Rm. 210, Suffolk Co. Court House
Griffing Ave.
Riverhead, NY 11901
(516) 548-3766

Staten Island

Supreme Ct. Library
Richmond Co. Court House
Staten Island, NY 10301
(718) 390-5291

White Plains

Pace University School of Law Library
78 N. Broadway
White Plains, NY 10603
(914) 681-4273

White Plains

Supreme Ct. Library, 9th Jud. Dist.
Westchester Co. Court House
White Plains, NY 10601
(914) 285-3900

UPSTATE NEW YORK LAW LIBRARIES

Albany

Albany Law School Library
Union University
80 New Scotland Avenue
Albany, NY 12208
(518) 445-2340

Appellate Division Library (3rd Dept.)
Justice Building
Empire State Plaza
Albany, NY 12223
(518) 474-3632

New York Court of Appeals Library
Eagle Street
Albany, NY 12207
(518) 455-7770

Albany *(cont.)*

New York State Dept. of Law Library
The Capitol
Albany, NY 12224
(518) 474-3840

New York State Dept. of Social Services Legal Affairs Library
40 N. Pearl Street
Albany, NY 12243
(518) 474-9506

New York State Div. of Criminal Justice Services
Executive Park Tower
Stuyvesant Plaza
Albany, NY 12203
(518) 453-6930

New York State Legislative and Government Services Library
Empire State Plaza
Albany, NY 12230
(518) 474-7495

New York State Legislative Library
Room 337
State Capitol
Albany, NY 12224
(518) 455-4000

New York State Library
Law/Social Science Unit
Cultural Education Center
Empire State Plaza
Albany, NY 12230
(518) 474-5943

New York State Office of Court Administration
Empire State Plaza
Agency Bldg. 4, 10th Floor
Albany, NY 12223
(518) 445-2340

Auburn

Supreme Court Law Library
Cayuga Co. Court House
Auburn, NY 13021
(315) 253-1279

Binghamton

Supreme Court Library
Rm. 107
Broome Co. Court House
Binghamton, NY 13901
(607) 772-2119

Buffalo

Charles B. Sears Law Library
State Univ. of New York at Buffalo
John Lord O'Brian Hall, Amherst Campus
Buffalo, NY 14260
(716) 636-2041

Supreme Court Library
92 Franklin Street
Buffalo, NY 14202
(716) 852-0712

Catskill

Chase Memorial Library
Greene County Courthouse
P.O. Box 691
Catskill, NY 12414
(518) 943-3130

Delhi

Delaware Supreme Court Library
Court House
Delhi, NY 13753
(607) 746-2603

Elmira

Supreme Court Library
Hazlett Building
203-205 Lake St.
Elmira, NY 14901
(607) 737-2983

Herkimer

Herkimer Co. Law Library
Court House
Main Street
Herkimer, NY 13350
(315) 867-1172

Ithaca

Cornell University Law Library
Myron Taylor Hall
Ithaca, NY 14853
(607) 255-7236

Kingston

Supreme Ct. Law Library, 3rd Jud. Dist.
Court House
Kingston, NY 12401
(914) 339-5680

Lake George

Supreme Ct. Library
Warren Co. Municipal Center
Lake George, NY 12845
(518) 761-6443

Newburgh

9th Judicial Dist. Law Library
104 Second St.
Newburgh, NY 12550

Poughkeepsie

State of New York Supreme Ct. Library
Joseph F. Barnard Memorial Law Library Assn.
County Court House
10 Market St.
Poughkeepsie, NY 12601
(914) 431-1815

Rochester

Appellate Division Law Library (4th Dept.)
525 Hall of Justice
Rochester, NY 14614
(716) 428-5480

Saratoga Springs

Supreme Ct. Library
Two City Hall
474 Broadway
Saratoga Springs, NY 12866
(518) 584-4862

Schenectady

Joseph F. Egan Memorial, Supreme Ct. Library
Schenectady Co. Judicial Bldg.
Schenectady, NY 12307
(518) 382-3310

Syracuse

Supreme Court Library
500 Court House
Syracuse, NY 13202
(315) 425-2063

H. Douglas Barclay Law Library
Syracuse Univ. College of Law
E. I. White Hall
Syracuse, NY 13210
(315) 423-2527

Troy

Supreme Ct. Library
Court House
2nd St. Annex
Troy, NY 12180
(518) 270-3717

Utica

Supreme Ct. Law Library, 5th Jud. Dist.
Oneida Co. Ct. House
Utica, NY 13501
(315) 798-5703

Watertown

Supreme Ct. Law Library
Court House
Watertown, NY 13601
(315) 785-3064

Wampsville

Madison Co. Law Library
Court House
Wampsville, NY 13163

APPENDIX G

NEW YORK LEGAL ABBREVIATIONS

The legal abbreviations listed in this appendix are arranged in letter-by-letter, alphabetical order.

A

A.	Assembly (bill)
Aband. Prop.	Abandoned Property Law
Abb. Ap. Dec.	Abbott's Court of Appeals Decisions
Abb. Ct. App.	Abbott's Court of Appeals Decisions
Abb. Ct. of App. Dec.	Abbott's Court of Appeals Decisions
Abb. Dec.	Abbott's Court of Appeals Decisions
Abb. Dig.	Abbott's Digest
Abb. N.C.	Abbott's New Cases
Abb. N. Cas.	Abbott's New Cases
Abb. New Cas.	Abbott s New Cases
Abb. N.S.	Abbott's Practice Reports, new series
Abb. N.Y. App.	Abbott's Court of Appeals Decisions
Abb. N.Y. Dig.	Abbott's New York Digest
Abb. N.Y. Dig. 2d	Abbott's New York Digest 2nd
Abb. N.Y. Digest	Abbott New York Digest
Abbott P.R.	Abbott's Practice Reports
Abbott Pract. Cas.	Abbott's Practice Reports
Abbott Pr. Rep.	Abbott's Practice Reports
Abbott's N.C.	Abbott's New Cases
Abb. Pl.	Abbott's Pleadings Under the Code
Abb. Pr.	Abbott's Practice Reports
Abb. Pr. (n.s.)	Abbott's Practice Reports, new series
Abb. Prac	Abbott's Practice Reports
Abb. Prac [NS]	Abbott's Practice Reports, new series
Abb. Pr. Rep.	Abbott's Practice Reports
A.B.C.L.	Alcoholic Beverage Control Law
A.B.C.N.Y.	Association of the Bar of the City of N.Y.
A.C.A.L.	Agriculture Conservation & Adjustment Law
A.C.G.L.	Alternative County Govt. Law
A.C.L.J.	American Civil Law Journal
A.D.	Appellate Division Reports, 1st series

AD2d or A.D. 2d	Appellate Division Reports, 2d series
Agric. & M.	Agriculture and Markets Law
Agric. Conserv. & Adj.	Agricultural Conservation and Adjustment Law
Agric. & Mkts.	Agriculture and Markets Law
Alb. Law J.	Albany Law Journal
Alb. L.J.	Albany Law Journal
Alb. L. Rev.	Albany Law Review
Alb. L.S. Jour.	Albany Law School Journal
Alco. Bev. Co.	Alcoholic Beverage Control Law
Alco. Bev. Cont.	Alcoholic Beverage Control Law
Alt. Co. Gov.	Alternative County Government Law
Alt. County Gov't.	Alternative County Government Law
A.M.L.	Agrigulture and Markets Law
Anth.	Anthon's New York Nisi Prius Reports
Anth. N.P.	Anthon's Nisi Prius Cases
Anth. N.P.R.	Anthon's Nisi Prius Reports, 1st series
Anthon's Rep.	Anthon's Nisi Prius Reports
Ap.	N.Y. Supreme Court Appellate Division Reports
Ap. 2d	N.Y. Supreme Court App. Div. Rpts., 2nd series
A.P.A.	State Administrative Procedure Act
A.P.L.	Abandoned Property Law
App. Div.	Appellate Division Reports, first series
App. Div. 2d	Appellate Division Reports, second series
App. Div. N.Y. Sup. Ct.	N.Y. Supreme Ct., Appellate Division
App. T.	Supreme Court, Appellate Term
Arms. Con. El.	Armstrong's Contested Election Cases
Arms. Con. Elec.	Armstrong's Contested Election Cases
Arms. Elect. Cas.	Armstrong's Contested Election Cases
Arts & CA.	Arts and Cultural Affairs Law
Arts & Cult. Aff.	Arts and Cultural Affairs Law
Atty. Gen. [Inf Opns]	Opns. of the N.Y. Attorney-General/Informal
Atty. Gen. Op. N.Y.	Opns. of the N.Y. Attorney General/Informal

B

B.	Barbour's New York Reports
B.	Senate concurrent resolution
B.A.N.	Bond anticipation note
Bank.	Banking Law
Banking	Banking Law
Barb.	Barbour's Supreme Court Reports
Barb.Abs.	Barbour's Abstracts of Chancellor's Opinions
Barb.App. Dig.	Barbour's Digest
Barb.Ch.	Barbour's Chancery Reports
Barb.Ch.Pr.	Barbour's Chancery Practice
Barb.Ch.Rep.	Barbour's Chancery Reports
Barb.Cr.Law	Barbour's Criminal Law
Barb.Cr.P.	Barbour's Criminal Pleadings
Barb.Cr.P.	Barbour's Criminal Practice
Barbour	Barbour's Supreme Court Reports
Barbour's Ch. R.	Barbour's Chancery Reports
Barb.R.	Barbour's Supreme Court Reports
Barb. S.C.R.	Barbour's Supreme Court Reports
Barb.Sup. Ct.	Barbour's Supreme Court Reports
Baxt. Elect. Cas.	Baxter's Contested Election Cases
B.C.L.	Business Corporation Law
Ben. Ord.	Benevolent Orders Law
B.L.	Banking Law
Blake Ch. Pr.	Blake's Chancery Practice
Bl.Chy.Pr.	Blake's Chancery Practice
Bliss N.Y. Co.	Bliss's New York Code
B.O.L.	Benevolent Orders Law
Bos.	Bosworth's Superior Court Reports
Bosw.	Bosworth's Superior Court Reports
Brad.	Bradford's Surrogate Reports
Bradb.	Bradbury's Pleading and Practice Reports
Bradf.	Bradford's Surrogate Reports
Bradford's Sur.R.	Bradford's Surrogate Reports
Bradf.Rep.	Bradford's Surrogate Reports
Bradf.Sur.	Bradford's Surrogate Reports
Bradf.Sur.R.	Bradford's Surrogate Reports
Bradf.Surr.	Bradford's Surrogate Reports
Brad.R.	Bradford's Surrogate Reports

Brad.Sur.	Bradford's Surrogate Reports
Brightly Dig.	Brightly's Digest
Br.L.R.	Brooklyn Law Review
Brookl.Bar.	Brooklyn Bar Association
Brookl.J.Int.L.	Brooklyn Journal of International Law
Brookl.L.Rev.	Brooklyn Law Review
Brookl.Rec.	Brooklyn Daily Record
Brooklyn Bar.	Brooklyn Barrister
Brooklyn L. Rev.	Brooklyn Law Review
Browne	Browne's Civil Procedure Reports
Buffalo L. Rev.	Buffalo Law Review
Buff.L.Rev.	Buffalo Law Review
Buff.Super.Ct.	Buffalo Superior Court
Bu.L.R.	Buffalo Law Review
Burr.Pr.	Burrill's New York Practice
Bus. Corp.	Business Corporation Law

C

C	City
C.	Assembly concurrent resolution
C.	Cowen's New York Reports
Cai.	Caines' Cases in Error
Cai.	Caines' Reports
Cai.	Caines' Term Reports
Cai. Cas.	Caines' Cases in Error
Cai.Cas.Err.	Caines' Cases in Error
Cain.	Caines' Cases in Error
Cain.	Caines' Reports
Cain.	Caines' Term Reports
Cain.Cas.in Error	Caines' Cases in Error
Cain.C.E.	Caines' Cases in Error
Cain.E.	Caines' Cases in Error
Caines	Caines' Reports
Caines' Cas.	Caines' Cases
Caines' R.	Caines' Reports
Cain R.	Caines' Reports
Cains.R.	Caines' Reports
Cai.Pr.	Caines' Practice

Cai. R.	Caines' Reports
Cai.T.R.	Caines' Term Reports
CAJR	N.Y. State Commission on Admin. of Justice
Can. L.	Canal Law
Canal	Canal Law
Cardozo L.Rev.	Cardozo Law Review
Carmody-Wait	Carmody-Wait Cyclopedia of N.Y. Practice
Cb.L.R.	Columbia Law Review
C.C.A.	Civil Court Act
C.C.E.	Caines' Cases in Error
C.C.L.	Cooperative Corporations Law
C.C.P.	Code of Criminal Procedure
C.C.P.	Code of Civil Procedure (Throop Code)
C.C.Supp.	City Court Reports, Supplement
C.G.C.M.	Court Martial Reports, Coast Guard Cases
Ch.	Chancery
Child. Ct.	Children's Court
C.H.Rec.	City Hall Recorder
C.H.Rep.	City Hall Reporter
Ch.Sent.	Chancery Sentinel
Cir. Ct.	Circuit Court
City Civ. Ct. Act	New York City Civil Court Act
City Crim. Ct. Act	New York City Criminal Court Act
City Ct. R.	City Court Reports
City H. Rec.	City Hall Recorder
City H. Rep.	City Hall Reporter
Civ.Pro.	Civil Procedure Reports
Civ.Proc.	Civil Procedure Reports
Civ.Proc.N.S.	Civil Procedure Reports, new series
Civ.Pr.Rep.	Civil Procedure Reports
Civ. R.	Civil Rights Law
Civ. Rights	Civil Rights Law
Civ. S.	Civil Service Law
Civ. Serv.	Civil Service Law
C.J.I.	Criminal Jury Instructions
C.L.	County Law
Clarke	Clarke's Chancery Reports

Clarke Ch.	Clarke's Chancery Reports
Clarke C.R.	Clarke's Chancery Reports
Clarke's Chy.	Clarke's Chancery Reports
Cl. Ch.	Clarke's Chancery Reports
C.L.R.	Columbia Law Review
C.L.R.	Clarke's Chancery Reports
Co.	County
Co. Ct.	County Court
Code Crim. Proc.	Code of Criminal Procedure
Code R.	Code Reporter
Code Rep.	Code Reporter; N.Y. Code Reporter
Code Rep.[NS]	Code of Procedure Reports, new series
Code R.N.S.	Code Reporter, new series
Col. & Cai.	Coleman and Caines' Cases
Col. & Cai. Cas.	Coleman and Caines' Cases
Cole Cas.	Coleman's Cases
Cole.Cas.Pr.	Coleman's Cases
Coleman	Coleman's Cases
Colem. & C.Cas.	Coleman & Caines' Cases
Colem. Cas.	Coleman's Cases
Col.J.Environ.L.	Columbia Journal of Environmental Law
Colum Hum. Rts. L. Rev.	Columbia Human Rights Law Review
Colum. J.L. & Arts	Columbia Journal of Law and the Arts
Colum.J.L. & Soc. Probs.	Columbia Journal of Law and Social Problems
Colum. J. Transnat'l L.	Columbia Journal of Transnational Law
Colum. L. Rev.	Columbia Law Review
Com.	Commerce Law
Com. L.	Commerce Law
Comm'n. App.	Commission of Appeals
Com. Pl.	Common Pleas
Comst.	Comstock's Reports
Con.	Connoly's Reports
Cond. L.	Condemnation Law
Conf. on Char. Found.	Conference on Charitable Proceedings, NYU Proceedings
Connoly	Connoly's Surrogate Reports

Conn.Surr.	Connoly's Surrogate Reports
Conn.Surr.Rep.	Connoly's Surrogate Reports
Const.	Constitution
Con.Sur.	Connoly's Surrogate Reports
Coop. Corp.	Cooperative Corporations Law
Cor.	Cornell Law Review
Co.Rep.	Code Reporter
Cor. L.	Correction Law
Cornell Int'l L. Forum	Cornell International Law Forum
Cornell Int'l L. J.	Cornell International Law Journal
Cornell L. Q.	Cornell Law Quarterly
Cornell L. Rev.	Cornell Law Review
Co.R.N.S.	Code Reporter, new series
Corr.	Correction Law
Correct.	Correction Law
Counsellor	Counsellor (New York City)
County	County Law
Cow.	Cowen's Reports
Cow.Cr.Dig.	Cowen's Criminal Digest
Cow.Crim.	Cowen's Criminal Reports
Cow. Cr. Rep.	Cowen's Criminal Reports
Cow.N.Y.	Cowen's Reports
C.P.	Code of Procedure (Field Code)
C.P.	Civil Procedure Reports
C.P.A.	Civil Practice Act
C.P.L.	Criminal Procedure Law
C.P.L.R.	Civil Practice Law and Rules
C.P.R.(N.S.)	Civil Procedure Reports, new series
Crim. Proc.	Criminal Procedure Law
C.R.L.	Civil Rights Law
C.S.L.	Civil Service Law
Ct. Cl. Act	Court of Claims Act
Cy.	Connoly's Surrogate Reports

D

D.	Denio's Reports
Daily Trans.	N.Y. Daily Transcript. old and new series
Dai.Reg.	New York Daily Register

Dal.	Daly's Reports
Daly	Daly's Common Pleas Reports
Daly's R.	Daly's Common Pleas Reports
D.C.L.	Debtor and Creditor Law
Debt. & Cred.	Debtor and Creditor Law
D.E.C.	Department of Environmental Conservation
Def. Em. A.	Defense Emergency Act
Delehanty	N.Y Miscellaneous Reports
Dem.	Demarest's Surrogates' Reports
Demarest	Demarest's Surrogate Reports
Dem. Sur.	Demarest's Surrogate's Reports
Dem.Surr.	Demarest's Surrogate's Reports
Den.	Denio's Reports
Denio	Denio's Reports
Denio(NS)	Denio's Reports
Denio R.	Denio's Reports
Dep.	State Department Reports
D.O.L.	Department of Labor
Dom. Rel.	Domestic Relations Law
D.O.T.	Department of Transportation
Dr. & Cr.	Debtor and Creditor Law
D.R.L.	Domestic Relations Law
Duer	Duer's Superior Court Reports

E

E.	Assembly resolution
E.C.B.A.	Erie County Bar Association
E.C.L.	Environmental Conservation Law
Ed.Ch.	Edwards' Chancery Reports
Ed.Ch.R.	Edwards' Chancery Reports
Ed.C.R.	Edwards' Chancery Reports
Ed. Dept. Rep.	New York State Dept. of Education Reports
Ed. L.	Education Law
Edmonds' St. at Large	Edmond's Statutes at Large
Edm. Sel. Ca.	Edmond's Select Cases
Edm. Sel. Cas.	Edmond's Select Cases
E.D.N.Y.	U.S. District Court for the Eastern Dist. of New York

E.D.P.L.	Eminent Domain Procedure Law
E.D.R.	Education Department Reports
E.D.S.	E.D. Smith's Common Pleas Reports
E.D. Smith	E.D. Smith's Common Pleas Reports
E.D. Smith R.	E.D. Smith's Common Pleas Reports
Educ.	Education Law
Edw.	Edwards' Chancery Reports
Edwards' Ch. R.	Edwards' Chancery Reports
Edw. Ch.	Edwards' Chancery Reports
Edw. Rep.	Edwards' Chancery Reports
El.Cas.	Armstrong' N.Y. Election Cases
Elec.	Election Law
Elect.	Election Law
Elect.Cas.N.Y.	Armstrong's N.Y. Election Cases
E.L.L.	Employers' Liability Law
El. L.	Election Law
Em. Dom. Proc.	Eminent Domain Procedure Law
Emp. Liab.	Employers' Liability Law
Empl'rs Liab.	Employers' Liability Law
Encyc of Forms	Encyclopedia of Forms and Precedents
Encyc P & P	Encyclopedia of Pleading and Practice
Energy	Energy Law
En. L.	Energy Law
Envtl. Conserv.	Environmental Conservation Law
E.P.T.L.	Estates, Powers and Trusts Law
Est. Powers & Trusts	Estates, Powers and Trusts Law
Ex. L.	Executive Law
Exec.	Executive Law

F

Fam. Ct. Act	Family Court Act
F. Ct. A.	Family Court Act
FOIL	Freedom of Information Law
Fordham Int'l L.F.	Fordham International Law Forum
Fordham Int'l L.J.	Fordham International Law Journal
Fordham L. Rev.	Fordham Law Review
Fordham Urban L.J.	Fordham Urban Law Journal

G

G.A.L.	General Associations Law
Gard. N.Y. Rep.	Gardenier's New York Reporter
Gard. N.Y. Rept.	Gardenier's New York Reporter
G.B.L.	General Business Law
G. City L.	General City Law
G. Con. L.	General Construction Law
Gen. Assn.	General Associations Law
Gen. Bus.	General Business Law
Gen. City	General City Law
Gen. Cons.	General Construction Law
Gen. Mun.	General Municipal Law
Gen. Obl.	General Obligations Law
Gen. Oblig.	General Obligations Law
Gen. Rule	General Rules of Practice
Gen. Tr.	General Term
Gib.	Gibbons' Surrogate Reports
Gibbons	Gibbons' Surrogate Reports
Gibb. Sur.	Gibbons' Surrogate Reports
Gib. Sur.	Gibbons' Surrogate Reports
G.M.L.	General Municipal Law
G.O.L.	General Obligation Law
Green, Cr.L.Rep.	Green's Criminal Law Reports (N.Y.)
Greene	Greene's Reports (7 N.Y. Ann. Cases)
Guild Law.	Guild Lawyer (N.Y. Chapter, National Lawyers' Guild)

H

H.	Hill's Reports
Hall	Hall's Superior Court Reports
H. & D.	Lalor's Supplement to Hill & Denio's Reports
H.F.C.	Held for further consideration (bills)
High.	Highway Law
Hill	Hill's Reports
Hill & Den. or Hill & Denio	Lalor's Supplement to Hill & Denio's Reports

Hill & Denio	Lalor's Supplement to Hill & Denio's Reports
Hill & Den. Supp.	Lalor's Supplement to Hill & Denio's Reports
Hill & D. Supp.	Lalor's Supplement to Hill & Denio's Reports
Hill N.Y.	Hill's Reports
Hilt.	Hilton's Common Pleas Reports
H.L.	Highway Law
Hoff.	Hoffman's Chancery Reports
Hoff. Ch.	Hoffman's Chancery Reports
Hoff. C.R.	Hoffman's Chancery Reports
Hoffm.Ch.	Hoffman's Chancery Reports
Hoff.N.Y.	Hoffman's Chancery Reports
Hofstra L. Rev.	Hofstra Law Review
Hop.	Hopkins' Chancery Reports
Hopk.	Hopkins Chancery Reports
Hopk.C.C.	Hopkins' Chancery Reports
Hopk. Ch.	Hopkins' Chancery Reports
Hopk. Chanc.Rep.	Hopkins' Chancery Reports
Hopk. Rep.	Hopkins' Chancery Reports
Hough	Hough's Vice-Admiralty Reports
Hough V.-Adm.	Hough's Vice-Admiralty Reports
How.	Howard's New York Practice Reports
How A.Cas.	Howard's Appeal Cases
How App.	Howard's Appeal Cases
How. App. Cas.	Howard's Court of Appeals Cases
Howard Pr.	Howard's Practice Reports
Howard's Spec. Term Rep.	Howard's Practice Reports
How.Cas.	Howard's Court of Appeals Cases
How. Ct. App. Cas.	Howard's Court of Appeals Cases
How N.S.	Howard's Practice Reports, new series
How P.R.	Howard's Practice Reports
How. Prac.	Howard's Practice Reports
How. Prac. N.S.	Howard's Practice Reports, new series
How. Prac. N.S.	Howard's Practice Reports, new series
How. Pr.Rep.	Howard's Practice Reports
How. Pr. Sup.C.	Howard's Practice Reports

H.P.R.	Howard's Practice Reports
H.Pr.	Howard's Practice Reports
Huff.Ch.	Huffman's Chancery Reports
Hun	Hun's Supreme Court Reports

I

I.L.	Insurance Law
Ind. L.	Indian Law
Indian	Indian Law
Inf. Op. N.Y. Att'y Gen.	Informal Opinion of the Attorney General
Ins.	Insurance Law

J

J.	Johnson's Reports
J.	Senate joint resolution
J. & V.	Jones & Varick (statutory revision of 1789)
J.C.	Johnson's Cases
J.C.	Johnson's Reports
J.Ch.	Johnson's Chancery Reports
J.C.R.	Johnson's Chancery Reports
J.L.	Judiciary Law
Jo.Ch.	Johnson's Chancery Reports
Joh.Ch. Rep.	Johnson's Chancery Reports
John.	Johnson's Reports
John.Cas.	Johnson's Cases
John.Chan.	Johnson's Chancery Reports
John.Ch.Rep.	Johnson's Chancery Reports
Johns.	Johnson's Reports
Johns.C.	Johnson's Cases
Johns. Cas.	Johnson's Cases
Johns. Ch.	Johnson's Chancery Reports
Johns. Ch. Cas.	Johnson's Chancery Reports
Johnson	Johnson's Reports
Johnson N.Y.R.	Johnson's Reports
Johnson R.	Johnson's Reports
Johnson's Cases in Error	Johnson's Cases
Johnson's Rep.	Johnson's Reports

Johns.R.	Johnson's Reports
Jones & Sp.	Jones and Spencer's Superior Court Reports
Jones & Spen.	Jones and Spencer's Superior Court Reports
Jones & V. Laws	Jones and Varick's Laws
J.R.	Johnson's Reports
J. Rep.	Johnson's Reports
J.S.	Jones and Spencer' Superior Court Reports
Jud.	Judiciary Law
Jud.Coun.N.Y.	N.Y. Judicial Council Annual Report
Judic.	Judiciary Law
Judic. -Ct. of Claims	Court of Claims Act
Judic. -Family Ct. Act	Family Court Act
Judic. -N.Y. City C.C.A.	New York City Civil Court Act
Judic. -N.Y. City Crim. Ct. Act.	New York City Criminal Court Act
Judic. -U.C.C.A.	Uniform City Court Act
Judic. -U.D.C.A.	Uniform District Court Act
Judic. -U.J.C.A.	Uniform Justice Court Act
Jur.	Jurist (Law & Equity Reporter)
Jur.N.Y.	Jurist (Law & Equity Reporter)

K

K.	Keye's Reports
K.	Legislative resolution
K. & R.	Kent & Radcliff's Revised Acts of 1801
Kent & R.St.	Kent & Radcliff's Revised Acts of 1801
Kern.	Kernan's Reports
Kerr	Kerr's Reports
Key.	Keyes' Reports
Keyes	Keyes' Reports
K.I.R.S.	Key item [budget] reporting system

L

L.	Assembly joint resolution
L.	Lansing's Select Cases in Chancery
L.	Lansing, Supreme Court Reports
L.	Laws of New York

L.	Legislative resolution
Lab.	Labor Law
Lab. L.	Labor Law
Labor	Labor Law
Lalor	Lalor's Supplement to Hill & Denio's Reports
Lalor's Supp.	Lalor's Supplement to Hill & Denio's Reports
Lans.	Lansing's Reports
Lans. Ch.	Lansing's Select Cases in Chancery
Lansg.	Lansing's Supreme Court Reports
Lans. Sel. Cas.	Lansing's Select Cases in Chancery
Law & Eq. Rep.	Law & Equity Reporter
Law N.	Law Notes (Northport, N.Y.)
Law Notes	Law Notes (Northport, N.Y.)
Law Rev. Comm.	Law Revision Commission
Lawyers Co-op	Lawyers Co-operative Publishing Company
L.B.D.C.	Legislative Bill Drafting Commission
Legis.	Legislative Law
Leg. L.	Legislative Law
Leg.N.	Legal Notes on Local Government
Lien	Lien Law
Liv.	Livingston's Judicial Opinions
Liv. Cas.	Livingston's Cases in Error
Liv. Judic. Op.	Livingston's Judicial Opinions
Liv. Jud. Op.	Livingston's Judicial Opinions
Liv. L. Mag.	Livingston's Law Magazine
Liv. L. Reg.	Livingston's Law Register
L.L.	Lien Law
L.N.	Law Notes (Northport, N.Y.)
L.Notes	Law Notes (Northport, N.Y.
Local Fin.	Local Finance Law
Loc. Fin. L.	Local Finance Law
Lock. Rev. Ca.	Lockwood's Reversed Cases
Lock. Rev. Cas.	Lockwood's Reversed Cases
Lock. Rev'd. Cas.	Lockwood's Reversed Cases
Loc.Laws	Local laws
Lom.C.H.Rep.	Lomas's City Hall Reporter
L.R.B.	Labor Relations Board

L.Sup.H. & D.	Lalor's Supplement to Hill & Denio's Reports

M

M.	New York Miscellaneous Reports
M2d	New York Miscellaneous Reports, 2nd series
Mag. Ct.	Magistrates' Courts
Mar. Ct.	Marine Court
McCart.	McCarty's N.Y. Civil Procedure Reports
McCartney	McCartney's Civil Procedure
M.D.L.	Multiple Dwellings Law
Med.Leg.N.	Medico-Legal News
Med.L.J.	Medico-Legal Journal
Med.L.P.	Medico-Legal Papers
Menken	Menken's Reports
Mental Hyg.	Mental Hygiene Law
Ment. Hy.	Mental Hygiene Law
M.H.L.	Mental Hygiene Law
M.H.R.L.	Municipal Home Rule Law
Mil.	Military Law
Mil.	Mills' Surrogate Court Reports
Mills	Mills' Surrogate Court Reports
Mills Sur.	Mills' Surrogate Court Reports
Mills Surr. Ct.	Mills' Surrogate Court Reports
Misc.	Miscellaneous Reports, 1st Series
Misc.2d	Miscellaneous Reports, 2d Series
Miscel.	Miscellaneous Reports
Misc. Rep.	Miscellaneous Reports
M.L.	Military Law
Month.Law Bul.	Monthly Law Bulletin
Month.L.Bull.	Monthly Law Bulletin
Monthly L.Bul.	Monthly Law Bulletin
Monthly Leg.Ex.	Monthly Legal Examiner
Moult.Ch.	Moulton's Chancery Practice
Moult.Ch.P.	Moulton's Chancery Practice
M.R.L.	Multiple Residence Law
Msc.	Miscellaneous Reports
Msc.2d	Miscellaneous Reports, 2d series

Mult. Dwell.	Multiple Dwelling Law
Mult. Res.	Multiple Residence Law
Mult. Resid.	Multiple Residence Law
Mun. Ct.	Municipal Courts
Mun. Home Rule	Municipal Home Rule Law

N

Nav.	Navigation Law; Naval Law
NCCUSL	National Conference of Commissioners on Uniform State Laws
NCr.	New York Criminal Reports
N.D.N.Y.	U.S. District Court for the Northern District of New York
N.E.	North Eastern Reporter, first series
N.E.2d	North Eastern Reporter, second series
New York R.	New York Reports
New York Supp.	New York Supplement
Nichols-Cahill	Nichols-Cahill Annotated N.Y. Civil Practice Acts
Noble	Noble's Current Court Decisions
No.East.Rep.	North Eastern Reporter
Not-For-Profit Corp.	Not-for Profit Corporation Law
N-P.C.L.	Not-for-Profit Corporation Law
N.P.C.L.	Not-For-Profit Corporation Law
N.Y.	New York Reports, first series
N.Y.2d	New York Reports, second series
N.Y. Admin. Code	Official Compilation of Codes, Rules & Regulations of the State of New York
N.Y. Ann. Ca.	New York Annotated Cases
N.Y. Ann. Cas.	New York Annotated Cases
N.Y. Anno. Cas.	New York Annotated Cases
N.Y. Anno. Dig.	New York Annotated Digest
N.Y. Annot. Dig.	New York Annotated Digest
N.Y. App. Dec.	N.Y. Court of Appeals Decisions
N.Y. App. Div.	N.Y. Appellate Division Reports
N.Y. Bank. Law	N.Y. Banking Law
N.Y. Bflo. Super. Ct. Gen. Tr.	Superior Court of Buffalo, General Term

N.Y. Buffalo Super. Ct.	Superior Court of Buffalo
N.Y.C.A.	N.Y. Court of Appeals Reports
N.Y.C. Adm.C	New York City Administrative Code
N.Y. Cas. Err.	Caines' N.Y. Cases in Error
N.Y. Cas. in Error	Caines' N.Y. Cases in Error
N.Y.C.B.A.	Association of the Bar of the City of N.Y.
N.Y.C.B.A. Bull.	Bulletin of the Assoc. of the Bar of the City of N.Y.
N.Y.C.B.T.L.	N.Y. City Business Tax Law
N.Y.C.C.D.	N.Y. Current Court Decisions
N.Y.C.C.H.	CCH N.Y. Advance Digest Service
N.Y.C.Char.	N.Y. City Charter
N.Y.C. City Ct.	City Court of the City of New York
N.Y.C. City Ct. Gen. T.	City Court of the City of New York, General Term
N.Y.C. City Ct. Rep.	N.Y. City Court Reports
N.Y.C. City Ct. Supp.	N.Y. City Court Reports Supplement
N.Y.C.C.P.	Court of Common Pleas For the City and County of New York
N.Y.C.C.P. Gen. T.	Court of Common Pleas For the City and County of New York, General Term
N.Y.C. Dom. Rel. Ct.	Domestic Relations Court of the City of New York
N.Y.C. Gen. Sess.	Court of General Sessions of the Peace In and For the City & County of New York
N.Y.Ch.	N.Y. Chancery Sentinel
N.Y. Ch.	Court of Chancery (N.Y.)
N.Y. Ch.	New York Chancery Courts
N.Y. Child. Ct.	N.Y. Children's Courts
N.Y.C. H. Rec.	New York City Hall Recorder
N.Y. Ch. Sent.	New York Chancery Sentinel
N.Y. City Civ. Ct.	New York City Civil Court
N.Y. City Civ. Proc. R.	New York Civil Procedure Reports
N.Y. City Cr. Ct.	New York City Criminal Court
N.Y. City Ct. R.	New York City Court Reports
N.Y. City Ct. Rep.	City Court Reports; New York City Court Reports
N.Y. City Ct. Supp.	N.Y. City Court Reports Supplement

N.Y. City H. Rec.	City Hall Reporter; New York City Hall Recorder; Roger's New York City Hall Recorder
N.Y. Civ. Prac. L. & R.	Civil Practice Law and Rules
N.Y. Civ. Pro. Rep.	Civil Procedure Reports
N.Y. Civ. Pro. Rep.	New York Civil Procedure Reports
N.Y. Civ. Pro. Rep. (n.s.)	New York Civil Procedure Reports, new series
2 N.Y. Civ. Pro. Rep. [MCarty]	McCarty's Civil Procedure Reports; Civil Procedure Reports (McCarty's); New York Civil Procedure Reports (McCarty's)
N.Y. Civ. Proc. Rep.	N.Y. Civil Procedure Reports
N.Y. Civ. Proc. R. (n.s.)	New York Civil Procedure Reports, new series
N.Y.C.J.I.	New York Criminal Jury Instructions
N.Y.C.L.L.	N.Y. City Local Laws
N.Y.C. Magis. Ct.	City Magistrates' Court of the City of New York
N.Y.C. Mar. Ct.	Marine Court of the City of New York
N.Y.C. Mar. Ct. Gen. T.	Marine Court of the City of New York, General Term
N.Y.C. Mun. Ct.	Municipal Court of the City of New York
N.Y. Cn.	N.Y. University Conference on Labor
N.Y. Co. Ct.	N.Y. County Courts
N.Y. Code R.	New York Code Reporter
N.Y. Code R. (n.s.)	New York Code Reporter (New Series)
N.Y. Code Rep.	New York Code Reporter
N.Y. Code Rep. (n.s.)	New York Code Reporter (New Series)
N.Y.Code Rptr.	New York Code Reporter
N.Y.Code Rptr. (n.s.)	New York Code Reporter (New Series)
N.Y.Code R.N.S.	New York Code Reports (New Series)
N.Y. Com. Pl.	N.Y. Common Pleas
N.Y. Comp. Codes R. & Regs.	Official Compilation of Codes, Rules & Regulations of the State of New York
N.Y. Cond.	New York Condensed Reports
N.Y. Cond. Rep.	Condensed Reports; N.Y. Condensed Reports
N.Y. Const.	New York Constitution
N.Y.Cont.L.Ed.	N.Y. Continuing Legal Education

N.Y.Cont.Leg.Ed.	N.Y. Continuing Legal Education
N.Y. County B. Bull.	N.Y. County Lawyers Association Bar Bulletin
N.Y. County Law Ass'n B. Bull.	N.Y. County Lawyers Association Bar Bulletin
N.Y.C.P.	New York Civil Procedure Reports
N.Y.Cr.	New York Criminal Reports
NY Crim. Rep.	New York Criminal Reports
N.Y.C.R.R.	Official Compilation of Codes, Rules and Regulations of the State of New York
N.Y. Cr. R.	New York Criminal Reports
N.Y. Cr. Rep.	New York Criminal Reports
N.Y.C. Spec. Sess.	Court of Special Sessions of the City of New York
N.Y.C. Super. Ct.	Superior Court of the City of New York
N.Y.C. Super. Ct. Gen. T.	Superior Court of the City of New York, General Term
N.Y. Ct. Adm.	Court of Admiralty
N.Y.Ct.App.	New York Court of Appeals
N.Y. Ct. Cl.	New York Court of Claims Reports
N.Y. Ct. Cl.	Court of Claims Reports; N.Y. State Court of Claims Reports
N.Y. Ct. Jud.	N.Y. Court of the Judiciary
N.Y. Ct. Tr. Imp.	N.Y. Court for the Trial of Impeachments
N.Y. Daily L. Gaz.	N.Y. Daily Law Gazette
N.Y. Daily L. Reg.	N.Y. Daily Law Register
N.Y. Daily Reg.	N.Y. Daily Register
N.Y. Daily Tr.	N.Y. Daily Transcript
N.Y. Dep't. Ed. R.	New York State Department of Education Reports
N.Y. Dep't. R.	New York State Department Reports
N.Y. Dist. Ct.	N.Y. District Courts
N.Y.D.L.W.C.Dec.	N.Y. Dept. of Labor Workmen's Comp. Decisions
N.Y. Dom. Rel. Ct.	N.Y. Domestic Relations Courts
N.Y.D.R.	N.Y. Department Reports
N.Y.El.Cas.	N.Y. Election Cases
N.Y. Elec.Cas.	N.Y. Election Cases

N.Y. Elect.Cas.	N.Y. Election Cases
N.Y.E.T.R.	N.Y. Estate Tax Reports (Prentice-Hall)
N.Y.F.	N.Y. Law Forum
N.Y. Fam. Ct.	N.Y. Family Court
N.Y. Gen. Sess.	N.Y. Courts of General Sessions
N.Y. Gen. Tr.	N.Y. General Term (Supreme Court)
N.Y.J.Int'l & Comp. L	N.Y. Law School J. of Int'l. and Comp. Law
N.Y.Jud.Rep.	N.Y. Judicial Repository
N.Y. Jur.	New York Jurisprudence
N.Y. Jur. 2d	New York Jurisprudence 2d Series
N.Y. Just. Ct.	N.Y. Justice Courts
N.Y.L.	New York University Law Review
N.Y.Law Bul.	N.Y. Monthly Law Bulletin
N.Y.Law (Consol.)	N.Y.Consolidated Laws Service
N.Y. Law Forum	New York Forum
N.Y.Law Gaz.	New York Law Gazette
N.Y.Law J.	New York Law Journal
N.Y.Law (McKinney)	McKinney's Consolidated Laws of New York Annotated
N.Y.Law Rev.	New York Law Review
N.Y. Laws	Laws of New York
N.Y.L.C.Ann.	N.Y. Leading Cases Annotated
N.Y.L.C. Anno.	New York Leading Cases Annotated
N.Y.L.Cas.	N.Y. Leading Cases
N.Y.Legal Obs.	New York Legal Observor
N.Y.Leg.N.	New York Legal News
N.Y.Leg.Obs.	New York Legal Observor
N.Y.Leg.Reg.	New York Legal Register
N.Y.L.F.	N.Y. Law Forum
N.Y.L.Gaz.	New York Legal Gazette
N.Y.L.J.	New York Law Journal
N.Y.L.O.	New York Legal Observor
N.Y.L.R.B.	New York State Labor Relations Board
N.Y.L.R.B.Dec.	New York State Labor Relations Board Decisions and Orders
N.Y.L.Rec.	New York Law Record
N.Y.L.Rev.	New York Law Review
N.Y.L. Sch. L. Rev.	New York Law School Law Review

N.Y. Mag. Ct.	New York Magistrate's Courts
N.Y. Mayor	New York Mayor's Courts
N.Y.Misc.	New York Miscellaneous Reports
N.Y.Misc. 2d	New York Miscellaneous Reports (2nd series)
N.Y.Mo.Law Bul.	New York Monthly Law Bulletin
N.Y.Mo.L.Bul.	New York Monthly Law Bulletin
N.Y.Mo.L.R.	New York Monthly Law Reports
N.Y.Mo.L.Rec.	New York Monthly Law Record
N.Y.Month.L.Bul.	New York Monthly Law Bulletin
N.Y.Month.L.R.	New York Monthly Law Reports
N.Y.Month.L.Rep.	New York Monthly Law Reports
N.Y. Mun. Ct.	N.Y. Municipal Courts
N.Y.Mun.Gaz.	N.Y. Municipal Gazette
N.Y.Off.Dept.R.	New York Official Department Reports
N.Y.Op.Att.Gen.	Opinions of the Attorney-General of New York
N.Y.Ops.Atty.Gen.	Opinions of the Attorney-General of New York
N.Y. Oyer & T.	Court of Oyer and Terminer
N.Y. Police Ct.	N.Y. Police Courts
N.Y.P.R.	New York Practice Reports
N.Y.Pr.	New York Practice Reports
N.Y.Pr.Rep.	New York Practice Reports
N.Y.P.S.C.(1st D.)	New York Public Service Commission, 1st Dist.
N.Y.P.S.C.(2nd D.)	New York Public Service Commission, 2nd Dist.
N.Y. Pub. Emp. Rel. Bd.	N.Y. State Public Employment Relations Board Decisions
N.Y. Pub. Serv. Comm'n. Dec.	New York State Public Service Commission Dec.
N.Y.R.	New York Court of Appeals Reports
N.Y.R.C.	New York Railroad Commission Reports
N.Y.Rec.	New York Record
N.Y. Recorders Ct.	New York Recorders Court
N.Y.Reg.	New York Daily Register (1872-1889)
N.Y. Rep.	New York Court of Appeals Reports
N.Y.R.L.	New York Revised Laws
N.Y.R.S.	New York Revised Statutes

N.Y.S.	New York Supplement, 1st Series
N.Y.S.2d	New York Supplement, 2d Series
N.Y.S.B.A.	New York State Bar Association
N.Y.S.Ct.	New York Superior Court Reports
N.Y.S.D.R.	New York State Department Reports
N.Y. Sea Grant L. & Policy J.	N.Y. Sea Grant Law and Policy Journal
N.Y.Sen.J.	New York Senate Journal
N.Y.S.L.R.B.	New York State Labor Relations Board
N.Y.Spec.Term.Rep.	Howard's Practice Reports
N.Y. Sp. Sess.	N.Y. Courts of Special Sessions
N.Y.S.R.	New York State Reporter
N.Y.St.	New York State Reporter
N.Y.State R.	New York State Reporter
N.Y.St.Ba.A.	New York State Bar Association Bulletin
N.Y.St. B.A. Antitrust L. Symp.	New York State Bar Association Antitrust Law Symposium
N.Y.St.B.J.	New York State Bar Journal
N.Y. St. Dept. Rep.	New York State Department Reports
N.Y.St.R.	New York State Reporter
N.Y. St. Reg.	New York State Register
N.Y. St. Rep.	New York State Reporter
N.Y. Sup.	N.Y. Supreme Court
N.Y. Sup. Ct.	Supreme Court Reports (N.Y.)
N.Y.Sup.Ct.Rep.	Thompson & Cook's N.Y. Supreme Ct. Reports
N.Y.Sup.Ct.(T. & C.)	Thompson & Cook's N.Y. Supreme Ct. Reports
N.Y.Super	N.Y. Superior Court Reports
N.Y.Super.Ct.	N.Y. Superior Court Reports
N.Y.Super.Ct.Rep.	N.Y. Superior Court Reports
N.Y.Supl.	New York Supplement, first series
N.Y.Supp.	New York Supplement, second series
N.Y.Supp.2d	New York Supplement, second series
N.Y.Supr.	New York Superior Court Reports
N.Y.Supr.Ct.R.	New York Superior Court Reports
N.Y.Supr.Ct.Repts. (T.&C.)	Thompson & Cook's N.Y. Supreme Ct. Reports

N.Y.Suprm.Ct.	New York Supreme Court Reports
N.Y. Sur.	N.Y. Surrogate's Courts
N.Y.Tax Cas.	N.Y. Cases (CCH)
N.Y. Town Ct.	N.Y. Town Courts
N.Y.T.R.	New York Term Reports (Caines')
N.Y.Trans.	New York Transcript
N.Y.Trans.App.	New York Transcript Appeal
N.Y.Trans.N.S.	New York Transcript, new series
N.Y.Trans.Rep.	New York Transcript Reports
N.Y.T.Rep.	Caines' Reports
N.Y.U.Conf.Charitable	New York University Conference on Charitable Foundations Proceedings
N.Y.U.Conf.Lab.	New York University Conference on Labor
N.Y.U.Inst.Fed.Tax.	New York University Institute on Federal Taxation
N.Y.U.Intra.L.Rev.	New York University Intramural Law Review
N.Y.U.J.Int'l. Law & Pol.	New York University Journal of Law and Politics
N.Y.U.L.Center Bull.	New York University Center Bulletin
N.Y.U.L.Q.Rev.	New York University Law Quarterly Review
N.Y.U.L.R.	New York University Law Review
N.Y.U. L. Rev.	New York University Law Review
N.Y.U.L.T.	New York University School of Continuing Education in Law and Taxation
N.Y.Unconsol.Laws	New York Unconsolidated Laws
N.Y.U.Rev.L. & Soc. Change	New York University Review of Law and Social Change
N.Y.U.T.I.	New York University Tax Institute
N.Y. Vill. Ct.	N.Y. Village Courts
N.Y. Week.Dig.	New York Weekly Digest
N.Y.Wkly.Dig.	New York Weekly Digest

O

OA	Advisory Opinion
OML	Open Meetings Law
Opns.Atty.Gen.	Opinions of the Attorney-General of New York/Formal Opinions

Opns.Counsel SBEA No.	Opinions of Counsel of State Board of Equalization and Assessment
Opns.St.Comp.	Opinions of the State Comptroller
Op. N.Y. Att'y.Gen.	Opinions of the Attorney General (Formal)
Op. N.Y. Comp.	Opinions of the Comptroller
Opt. County Gov't.	Optional County Government Law

P

Pace L. Rev.	Pace Law Review
Pai.	Paige's Chancery Reports
Pai.Ch.	Paige's Chancery Reports
Paige	Paige's Chancery Reports
Paige Ch.	Paige's Chancery Reports
Paige Ch. Rep.	Paige's Chancery Reports
P.A.L.	Public Authorities Law
Panel	The Panel, Assoc. of Grand Jurors of New York County Bar
Park.	Parker's Criminal Cases
Park.C.R.	Parker's Criminal Reports
Park.Cr.Cas.	Parker's Criminal Cases
Park.Crim.L.	Parker's Criminal Reports
Park.Crim.Rep.	Parker's Criminal Reports
Park. Cr. R. (or Rep.)	Parker's Criminal Reports
Park.Cr. Rep.	Parker's Criminal Reports
Parker	Parker's Criminal Reports
Parks Rec. & Hist. Preserv.	Parks, Recreation and Historic Presentation Law
Partners or Partnership	Partnership Law
P.B.L.	Public Buildings Law
P.Cl.R.	Parker's Criminal Reports
Penal	Penal Law
Pen. L.	Penal Law
P.E.R.B.	New York State Public Employment Relations Board
PERB	Public Employment Relations Board Reports
Pers. Prop.	Personal Property Law
P.H.F.L.	Public Housing Finance Law

P.H.L.	Public Housing Law
P.H.N.Y.E.T.R.	Prentice-Hall N.Y. Estate Tax Reports
PJI	New York Pattern Jury Instructions-Civil
P.L.	Partnership Law
P.L.L.	Public Land Law
P.O.L.	Public Officers Law
Power	Power's Surrogate Court Reports
Powers	Power's Surrogate Court Reports
Power's Sur.	Power's Surrogate Court Reports
Power Sur.	Power's Surrogate Court Reports
Pow.Surr.	Power's Surrogate Court Reports
P.P.L.	Personal Property Law
PPPL	Personal Privacy Protection Law
P.R.H.P.L.	Parks, Recreation and Historic Presentation Law
Priv. Hous. Fin.	Private Housing Finance Law
P.R.L.	Parks and Recreation Law
PSC	New York State Public Service Commission
PSC	Public Service Commission Reports
PSCR [1st Dist.NY]	Public Service Commission of New York, First District, Proceedings
PSCR [2d Dist,NY)	Public Service Commission of New York, Second District, Reports of Decisions
P.S.L.	Public Service Law
Pub. Auth.	Public Authorities Law
Pub. Bldg. (or Bldgs.)	Public Buildings Law
Pub. H.	Public Health Law
Pub. Health	Public Health Law
Pub. Hous.	Public Housing Law
Pub. L.	Public Lands Law
Pub. Lands	Public Lands Law
Pub. Off.	Public Officers Law
Pub. Serv.	Public Service Law
PUR	Public Utilities Reports
PUR (n.s.)	Public Utilities Reports, New Series
PUR3d	Public Utilities Reports, Third Series
P.W.L.	Public Works Law

Q

Queens B.Bull.	Queens County Bar Association Bulletin
Queens C.B.A.Bull.	Queens County Bar Association Bulletin

R

R.	Senate resolution
R.A.	Revised Acts
Rac. Pari-Mut. Wag. & Breed.	Racing, Pari-Mutuel Wagering and Breeding Law
Rapid Trans.	Rapid Transit Law
R.C.L.	Ruling Case Law
R.C.L.	Religious Corporation Law
R.C.P.	Rules of Civil Procedure
Real Est. Rec.	Real Estate Record
Real Property	Real Property Law
Real Prop. A. & P.L.	Real Property Actions & Proceedings Law
Real Prop. Acts.	Real Property Actions and Proceedings
Real Prop. Tax	Real Property Tax Law
Rec.Ass'n.Bar City of N.Y.	Record of the Association of the Bar of the City of New York
Rec. Ct.	Recorder's Courts
R.E.C.L.	Rural Electric Cooperative Law
Record	Record of the Association of the Bar of the City of New York
Record of N.Y.C.B.A.	Record of the Association of the Bar of the City of New York
Redf.	Redfield's Surrogate Court Reports
Redf. Sur.	Redfield's Surrogate Court Reports
Reg.	Daily Register (New York)
Rel. Corp.	Religious Corporations Law
Relig. Corp.	Religious Corporations Law
Ret. & Soc. Sec.	Retirement and Social Security Law
Retire & Soc. Sec.	Retirement and Social Security Law
R.L.	Railroad Law
Rob.	Robertson's Superior Court Reports
Robertson	Robertson (N.Y. Superior Court Reports)
Rob.Mar.	Robertson & Jacob's N.Y. Marine Court Reports

Rob.Sr.Ct.	Robertson's Superior Court Reports
Rob.Super.Ct.	Robertson's Superior Court Reports
Robt.	Robertson's Superior Court Reports
Rog.C.H.R.	Rogers' City Hall Recorder
Rog.Rec.	Rogers' City Hall Recorder
R.P.A.P.L.	Real Property Actions and Proceedings Law
R.P.L.	Real Property Law
R.P.T.L.	Real Property Tax Law
R.R.	Railroad Law
R.S.S.L.	Retirement and Social Security Law
R.T.L.	Rapid Transit Law
Rural Elec. Coop.	Rural Electric Cooperative Law
R.W. & B.L.	Racing, Pari-Mutuel Wagering and Breeding Law

S

S.	New York Supplement
S.2d	New York Supplement, second series
S.	Senate (bill)
S.	Session (of legislature)
San.Ch.	Sandford's Chancery Reports
Sand.	Sandford's Superior Court Reports (N.Y.C.)
Sand. Ch.	Sandord's Chancery Reports
Sand. Ch. R.	Sandford's Chancery Reports
Sand. Chy.	Sandford's Chancery Reports
Sandf.	Sandford's Superior Court Reports
Sandf. Ch.	Sandford's Chancery Reports
Sandford R.	Sandford's Superior Court Reports
Sandford's S.C.R.	Sandford's Superior Court Reports (N.Y.C.)
Sandford's Sup.Ct.R.	Sandford's Superior Court Reports (N.Y.C.)
Sand.R.	Sandford's Superior Court Reports (N.Y.C.)
Sand. S.C.	Sandford's Superior Court Reports (N.Y.C.)
Sands.Ch.	Sandford's Chancery Reports
Sand. S.C.R.	Sandford's Superior Court Reports (N.Y.C.)
S.A.P.A.	State Administrative Procedure Act
Sarat. Ch. Sent.	Saratoga Chancery Sentinel
S.B.	Special Bulletin, N.Y. Dept. of Labor

SBEA	New York State Board of Equalization and Assessment
S.C.C.L.	Second Class Cities Law
Scott	Scott's Reports
S.C.P.A.	Surrogate's Court Procedure Act
S.C.(T. & C.)	Thompson & Cook's Supreme Court Reports
S.D.N.Y.	U.S. District Court for the Southern District of New York
SDR	State Department Reports
Sec. C.C.	Second Class Cities Law
Second Class Cities	Second Class Cities Law
Sel. Cas. Mayor's Ct. N.Y.C.	Select Cases of the Mayor's Court New York City
Seld.	Selden's Reports
Selden	Selden's Reports
Selden Notes	Selden's Notes of Cases
Seld. Notes	Selden's Notes of Cases
Seld.R.	Selden's Reports
S.F.L.	State Finance Law
Sheld.	Sheldon's Reports, Superior Court of Buffalo
Sick.	Sickel's Reports
Sick. Op.	Sickel's Opinions of the N.Y. Attorneys General
Sil.	Silvernail's Reports (Court of Appeals)
Silv.	Silvernail's Reports (Court of Appeals)
Silv.	Silvernail's Reports (N.Y. Criminal Reports)
Silv.	Silvernail's Supreme Court Reports
Silv. App.	Silvernail's Supreme Court Reports
Silv.Cit.	Silvernail's New York Citations
Silvernail	Silvernail's Supreme Court Reports
Silvernail Ct. App.	Silvernail's Reports (Court of Appeals)
Silv. Sup.	Silvernail's Supreme Court Reports
Silv. Unrep.	Silvernail's Unreported Cases
S.L.	State Law
S.L.G.	Statute of Local Governments
S.L.S.	St. Lawrence Seaway Development Corporation

Sm.E.D.	E.D. Smith's Common Pleas Reports
Smith	E.D. Smith's Common Pleas Reports
Smith	E.H. Smith's Reports (Court of Appeals)
Smith	E.P. Smith's Reports (Court of Appeals)
Smith C.P.	E.D. Smith's Common Pleas Reports
Smith Ct. App.	E.P. Smith's Reports (Court of Appeals)
Smith E.H.	E.H. Smith's Reports (Court of Appeals)
Smith E.P.	E.P. Smith's Reports (Court of Appeals)
Soc. Serv.	Social Services Law
Soil & Water Conser. Dist.	Soil and Water Conservation Districts Law
Soil & Water Conserv. Dist.	Soil and Water Conservation Districts Law
S.P.P.D.L.	State Printing and Public Documents Law
S.R.	New York State Reporter
S.S.	Silvernail's Supreme Court Reports
S.S.C.	Sandford's Superior Court Reports (N.Y.C.)
S.Ser. L.	Social Services Law
S.S.L.	Salt Springs Law
State	State Law
State Fin.	State Finance Law
State Print. & Pub. Docs.	State Printing and Public Documents Law
State R.	New York State Reporter
State Rep.	New York State Reporter
Stat. Local Gov'ts.	Statute of Local Governments
Stat. of Loc. Gov.	State of Local Governments Law
S.T.C.	State Tax Commission
St. Fin.	State Finance Law
St. John's L. Rev.	St. John's Law Review
St. Print. & Pub. Doc.	State Printing and Public Documents Law
Sup. Ct.	Supreme Court
Sup. Ct. Gen. T.	Supreme Court, General Term
Sup.Ct.R.(N.Y.)	N.Y. Supreme Court Reports
Supp.	New York Supplement
Surr. Ct. Proc. Act	Surrogate's Court Procedure Act
S.W.C.D.L.	Soil & Water Conservation Districts Law
Sween.	Sweeny's Superior Court Reports
Sweeny	Sweeny's Superior Court Reports

Swen.	Sweeny's Superior Court Reports
Sy.J.Int.L.	Syracuse Journal of International Law
Sy.L.R.	Syracuse Law Review
Syracuse J.Int'l L.	Syracuse Journal of International Law
Syracuse J.Int'l L. & Com.	Syracuse Journal of International Law and Commerce
Syracuse L. Rev.	Syracuse Law Review
SYRUCL	Syracuse University College of Law

T

T	Town
T & C	Thompson and Cook's Supreme Court Reports
Tax	Tax Law
T.C.L.	Transportation Corporations Law
Th. & C.	Thompson and Cook's Supreme Court Reports
Themis	American Themis
Thomp. & C.	Thompson and Cook's Supreme Court Reports
Tiff.	Tiffany's Reports
Tiffany	Tiffany's Reports
Til. & Sh.Pr.	Tillinghast & Shearman on N.Y. Practice
T.L.	Tax Law
Touro L. Rev.	Touro Law Review
Town	Town Law
Town L.	Town Law
T.R.A.N.	Tax & revenue anticipation note
Trans.Ap.	N.Y. Transcript Appeals Reports
Transc. App.	N.Y. Transcript Appeals Reports
Transp.	Transportation Law
Transp. Corp.	Transportation Corporations Law
Tr.App.	N.Y. Transcript Appeals Reports
Tr. L.	Transportation Law
Tr. (N.Y.)	Caines' Term Reports
Tuck.	Tucker's Supreme Court Reports
Tuck.	Tucker's Surrogate Court Reports
Tuck. Sur.	Tucker's Surrogate's Court Reports

U

U.C.C.	Uniform Commercial Code
U.C.C.A.	Uniform City Court Act
U.D.C.A.	Uniform District Court Act
U.J.C.A.	Uniform Justice Court Act
U.L.	Unconsolidated Laws
U.L.A.	Uniform Laws Annotated
Unconsol.	Unconsolidated Laws
Uniform City Ct. Act	Uniform City Court Act
Uniform Dist. Ct. Act	Uniform District Court Act
Uniform Just. Ct. Act	Uniform Justice Court Act

V

V.	Village
V. & T.L.	Vehicle and Traffic Law
Veh. & Traf.	Vehicle and Traffic Law
Vehicle & T.	Vehicle and Traffic Law
V.F.B.L.	Volunteer Firemen's Benefit Law
Vill.	Village Law
Village	Village Law
V.L.	Village Law
Vol. Fire Ben.	Volunteer Firefighter's Benefit Law

W

Wait Co.	Wait's Annotated Code
Wait Dig.	Wait's Digest
Wait Pr.	Wait's New York Practice
Wait Tab. Ca.	Wait's New York Table of Cases
W.C.L.	Workers' Compensation Law
W.D.N.Y.	U.S. District Court for the Western District of New York
Week.Dig.	N.Y. Weekly Digest (1876-88)
Week.Trans. Rep.	N.Y. Weekly Transcript Reports
Wen.	Wendell's Reports
Wend.	Wendell's Reports
Wendell	Wendell's Reports
Wend.Rep.	Wendell's Reports
West's N.Y. Dig.	West's N.Y. Digest 3d

Wh.	Wheeler's Criminal Cases
Wheel. Cr. Cas.	Wheeler's Criminal Cases
Wheel.Cr.Rec.	Wheeler's Criminal Recorder
Wheeler C.C.	Wheeler's Criminal Cases
Wheeler Cr.Cas.	Wheeler's Criminal Cases
Win.	Winer's Unreported Opinions (N.Y. Supreme Court, Erie County)
Wkly.Dig.	New York Weekly Digest
Wms.Ann.Reg.	Williams' Annual Register
Work. Comp.	Workers' Compensation Law
W.T.R.	Weekly Transcript Reports

Y

Yates Sel. Cas.	Yates' Select Cases

APPENDIX H

INTERSTATE COMPACTS, AGREEMENTS, AND AGENCIES OF WHICH NEW YORK IS A PARTY OR MEMBER

Agreement on Qualifications of Educational Personnel — Education Law § 3030

Atlantic States Marine Fisheries Compact — Environmental Conservation Law § 13-0371

Buffalo and Fort Erie Bridge Compact — Public Authorities Law §§ 1299(e),(f)

Bus Taxation Proration and Reciprocity Agreement — Vehicle and Traffic Law § 406-409

Civil Defense and Disaster Compact — 1951 Laws of New York, ch. 674; 1975 Laws of New York, ch. 112

Compact for Education — Education Law § 107

Compact on Mental Health — Mental Hygiene Law § 67.07

Delaware River Basin Compact — Environmental Conservation Law §§ 21-0701 through 21-0723

Driver License Compact - Vehicle and Traffic Law §§ 516, 501a, 516b

Great Lakes Basin Compact — Environmental Conservation Law §§ 21-0901 through 21-0915

Great Lakes Fishery Commission — Great Lakes Fishery Act of 1956, as codified in 16 U.S.C. § 931 et seq.

International Joint Commission — Treaty of January 11, 1909 between the United States and Great Britain, 238 U.N.T.S. 97.

Interpleader Compact — CPLR § 1006

Interstate Agreement on Detainers — Criminal Procedure Law § 580.20

Interstate Compact for the Supervision of Parolees and Probationers — Executive Law § 259m

Interstate Compact on Juveniles — 1955 Laws of New York, ch. 155; McKinney's Unconsolided Laws § 1801-1806; CLS Unconsolidated Laws, Chap. 74.

Interstate Compact on the Placement of Children — Social Service Law § 374a

Interstate Corrections Compact — Corrections Law §§ 100-109

Interstate Library Compact — Education Law §§ 293-297

Interstate Oil and Gas Compact — Environmental Conservation Law § 23-2101

Interstate Bridge Commission — Transportation Law §§ 25-27

Lake Champlain Bridge Compact — 1927 New York Laws, ch. 321; 1982 New York Laws, ch. 598

Mid-Atlantic Regional Fishery Management Council — Fishery Conservation and Management Act of 1976 as codified at 16 U.S.C. § 1801 et. seq.

Mutual Military Aid in an Emergency Compact — Military Law § 22-a

New England Interstate Water Pollution Control Compact — Environmental Conservation Law §§ 21-0101 through 21-0117

New York/Canada International Bridge Compact — 1869 New York Laws, ch. 550

New York/Connecticut Boundary — State Law § 2

New York/Massachusetts Boundary — State Law § 3

New York/New Jersey Boundary — State Law § 3

New York/Pennsylvania Boundary — State Law § 6

New York/Rhode Island Boundary — 1941 New York Laws, ch. 757; 1942 New York Laws, ch. 171; 1942 New York Laws, ch. 739; 1943 New York Laws, ch. 365

New York/Vermont Boundary — State Law § 4

Niagara Falls Bridge Commission — H.R.J. Res. 688, 75th Cong., 2d Sess. (1938), 52 Stat. 767.

Non-Resident Violator Compact — Vehicle & Traffic Law § 517

Northeastern Forest Fire Protection Compact — Environmental Conservation Law § 9-1123

Ogdensburg Bridge Compact and Port Authority — Public Authorities Law §§ 700-717; §§ 725-734

Ohio River Valley Sanitation Compact — Environmental Conservation Law §§ 21-0301 through 21-0317

Palisades Interstate Park Compact — Parks and Recreation Law §§ 9.01-9.09

Port Authority of New York and New Jersey — 1921 New York Laws, ch. 154; McKinney's Unconsolidated Laws §§ 6401-6423; CLS Unconsolidated Laws Ch. 151

Railroad Passenger Transportation Compact (New York/Connecticut) - 1968 Laws of New York, ch. 824

Susquehanna River Basin Compact — Environmental Conservation Law §§ 21-1301 through 21-1321

Thousand Islands Bridge Authority — Public Authorities Law §§ 575-592

Tri-State Sanitation Compact — Environmental Conservation Law §§ 21-0501 through 21-0525

Uniform State Laws Commission — Executive Law § 165

Waterfront and Airport Compact — 1953 New York Laws, ch. 882; McKinney's Unconsolidated Laws § 9801-9873; CLS Unconsolidated Laws Ch. 307.

NAME INDEX

SUBJECT INDEX